MW00668962

HOME!

HOME!

THE
Evonne Goolagong
STORY

Evonne Goolagong Cawley & Phil Jarratt

SIMON & SCHUSTER
AUSTRALIA

A sincere note of thanks to my co-author Phil Jarratt and his wife Jackie. Under sometimes difficult circumstances, their expertise, friendship and love have helped to make the writing of this book one of the truly rewarding experiences of my life.

Evonne Goolagong Cawley

This book is dedicated to Roger, Kelly and Morgan, my family, without whose love I could not complete life's journey …

and, to my two Mums, Linda Goolagong and Eva Edwards, who showed me the way.

HOME! THE EVONNE GOOLAGONG STORY

First published in Australasia in 1993 by
Simon & Schuster Australia
20 Barcoo Street, East Roseville NSW 2069

A Paramount Communications Company
Sydney New York London Toronto Tokyo Singapore

Copyright © Goolagong Productions Pty Ltd 1993

All rights reserved. No part of this publication may be reproduced, stored in a retrieval system, or transmitted, in any form or by any means, electronic, mechanical, photocopying, recording or otherwise, without the prior permission of the publisher in writing.

National Library of Australia
Cataloguing in Publication data

Cawley, Evonne, 1951–   .
Home! : the Evonne Goolagong story.

Includes index.
ISBN 0 7318 0381 7.

1. Cawley, Evonne, 1951–   . 2. Tennis players — Australia — Biogaphy. 3. Women tennis players — Australia — Biography. I. Jarratt, Phil, 1951–   . II. Title.

796.342092

Designed by Deborah Brash/Brash Design
Maps and family tree prepared by Greg Campbell/Design to Print
Typeset in Australia by Asset Typesetting Pty Ltd
Printed in Hong Kong by South China Printing Co. (1988) Ltd

Title page: Exploring the Jowalbinna rock art galleries, Cape York Peninsula, 1992

Double page spread: At Brewarrina fish traps, 1993. A special place in my heart.

Contents

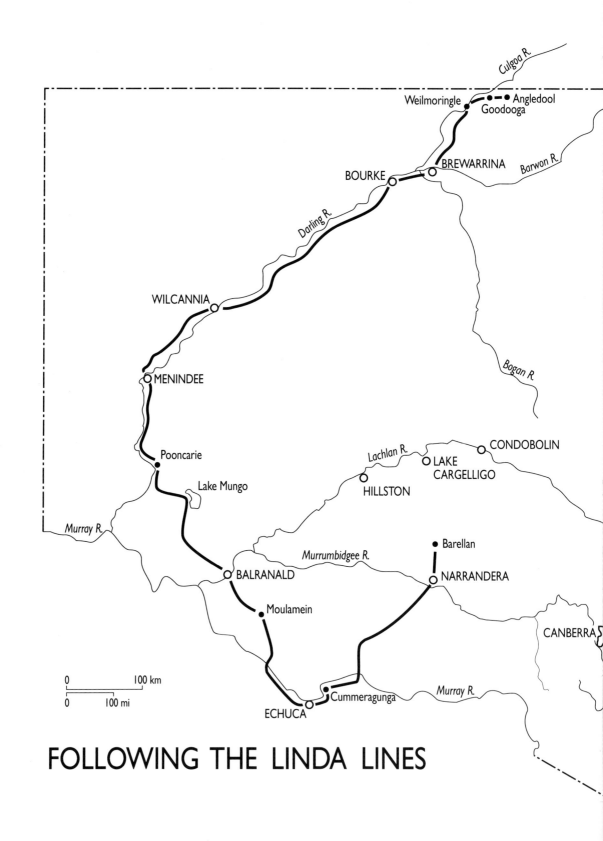

FOLLOWING THE LINDA LINES

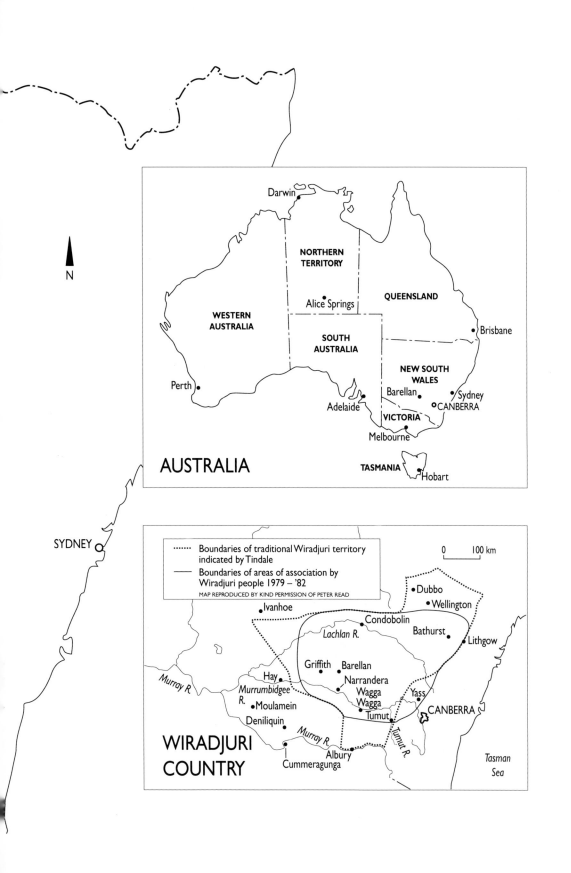

N

AUSTRALIA

Darwin

NORTHERN
TERRITORY

QUEENSLAND

Alice Springs

WESTERN
AUSTRALIA

SOUTH
AUSTRALIA

Brisbane

NEW SOUTH
WALES

Perth

Barellan

Sydney

CANBERRA

Adelaide

VICTORIA

Melbourne

TASMANIA

Hobart

SYDNEY

WIRADJURI
COUNTRY

Boundaries of traditional Wiradjuri territory
indicated by Tindale

Boundaries of areas of association by
Wiradjuri people 1979 – '82

MAP REPRODUCED BY KIND PERMISSION OF PETER READ

0   100 km

Dubbo

Wellington

Ivanhoe

Condobolin

Lachlan R.

Bathurst

Lithgow

Griffith

Barellan

Hay

Narrandera

Yass

Murray R.

Murrumbidgee
R.

Wagga
Wagga

Moulamein

Tumut

CANBERRA

Deniliquin

Murray R.

Tumut R.

Albury

Tasman
Sea

Cummeragunga

On the road to Wilcannia, 1993

Introduction

Aboriginal law never change.
Old people tell us ...
'You gotta keep it'.
It always stay.
Never change.

But learning can be different.
So now I've got to teach my children with book.
They forget how to learn Aboriginal way.
That why I write this book ...
To bring my children back.

Big Bill Neidjie (from Kakadu Man)

Linda Goolagong in 1949

WHEN MY MOTHER DIED in March 1991, my husband Roger Cawley and I were at home in Naples, Florida, with our children, Kelly and Morgan.

In the shock and sadness of the moment there was absolutely no confusion about what we had to do. The trauma of a sudden trip was too much for the children, but Roger and I were on a flight out of Naples/Fort Myers within hours; the beginning of a long and exhausting journey halfway across the world to the tiny Australian wheat-belt town of Barellan.

This was a journey we had made many times before, and not always for pleasure. But for me this trip was cloaked in incomparable sadness. I closed my eyes in the night sky over the Pacific and felt my spirit set adrift. The stars we used to watch and name as kids were nowhere to be seen. The universe was not the same. Melinda Violet Goolagong was dead at 61.

Mum's was the biggest funeral Barellan has ever seen. The council put a special water-truck on early duty to spray the 2-kilometre (1¼-mile) dirt track to the cemetery, but the traffic raised a dust storm anyway. When we had laid Mum to rest next to my father, Kenny, I looked through my tears at the extraordinary collection of people who had come from everywhere to share in the sadness that eight Goolagong children felt. Mum had come to know people from all walks of life, and wherever she was known she was loved and respected, but when I looked out over that sea of grieving faces what astonished me was that I knew so few of them.

Perhaps there were strangers who had been drawn by the fame of the Goolagong name, but the vast majority were Mum's friends and family, and hundreds of them were our people — the Wiradjuri. The Goolagongs, the Hamiltons, the Ingrams, the Briggs, the Sloanes, the Carrs, the Coes, the Wightons, the Nadens, the Dargens, the Gilberts and the Cooneys. I didn't know it at the time but the history of my own family was part of the history of the Wiradjuri people, that strong clan of Aborigines who have survived so many forms of white persecution and still roam that part of central New South Wales bounded by the three great rivers, the Lachlan, the Murrumbidgee and the Murray.

As I spoke to the mourners that day my mind kept racing back across the years to those carefree days swimming in the irrigation canal at the 'Three Ways', the Aboriginal mission outside Griffith, or in a billabong by the Lachlan at 'The Murie', the camp favoured by the Condobolin Wiradjuri clans. I heard again words that I had thought were made up to amuse us as children, like 'bubul' which meant bum, or 'gwangy' which meant 'mad', or 'buray' which meant 'fart'. I remembered stories and signs, like the appearance of the little bird, the willy-wagtail, which meant someone had died; and the bogey man, who was not a figment of our imaginations but a real fear of our parents, sent from the Welfare to take Aboriginal children away from their families.

I had always been proud of my Aboriginal heritage but not until Mum died did I realise how little I knew about it, and how little I knew about my own family, my own parents. Mum had taught me how to behave, how to live in a way which would make her proud, but what did I really know about *her*? About her early life, the things she did, the places she travelled, the sports she played, the way she felt? These were not things that were discussed in our house when I was growing up, and yet I have come to realise that there was a transmission of feelings, a spirituality that linked us that was very Aboriginal.

From 1953 my family lived in a white town, and from 1966 I lived in a white society, but the former didn't make us white, and the latter never made me anything other than what I am — a proud Aboriginal woman, a Wiradjuri Koori. Throughout my tennis career I now realise I stayed close to my Aboriginal roots: from my early days in Sydney when I would seek refuge from the arduous routine at the Victor A. Edwards Tennis School amongst friends at the Aboriginal Foundation, through the occasions when I just could not go on with the tennis tour until I had once again sat with my people by the three rivers and felt the cooling breeze of their commonsense, and on to more recent times when I have taken great delight in introducing my son Morgan to his heritage by reading to him the legends of the Quinkans, those 'good blokes' and 'bad blokes' who rule the spirit world of Cape York Peninsula.

From very early days the media determined that my Aboriginality would not be forgotten, and in the paternalistic (and sometimes racist, frequently sexist) tones of the time I was dubbed a 'picaninny', 'the champ with the soft brown eyes', 'dusky', 'tawny' and a whole range of descriptions I have managed to forget. None of this offended or even annoyed me at the time, and I find it difficult to look over the scrapbooks of my career now with anything other than wry amusement.

My tennis spoke for itself; my race made me different and therefore newsworthy. And I was different, am different. I think it showed in my approach to tennis. I thought and felt like an Aborigine. I would wonder why people got so upset when they lost. Surely it didn't matter that much? Why couldn't I get mad with my opponents, the way my coach, Vic Edwards, wanted me to? As my playing career went on I became more and more determined not to change, not to allow tennis to alter my perception of who I was.

Certainly I wanted to win. Certainly I developed the determination of a champion, and perhaps I always had it. But I believe the way I played the game reflected a calmness, a serenity of spirit which I now equate with being Aboriginal. In fairness to my coach Mr Edwards, to whom I owe so much and with whom I had so many differences, I must say that he never once tried to change who I was, to make me 'less Aboriginal'. He completely rejected the racist assertion that the will to succeeed was lacking in the Aboriginal make-up and, despite the business college, the elocution lessons and the other trappings of white society with which he surrounded me in those early years, he recognised my needs and feelings as an Aborigine and tried to accommodate them. No one could have been a more congenial host to the Aboriginal friends I brought to his home in Roseville.

Roger and I flew home to Florida after Mum's funeral and tried to get on with a life which, to me, seemed increasingly aimless. Our children, both born in Beaufort, South Carolina, were typical young Americans, growing further and further apart from my heritage, despite the Quinkan stories and the trips home. I suppose they had grown apart from Roger's British heritage too, although both Kelly and Morgan played soccer, which gladdened their father's expatriate heart.

Roger and I had our company directorships and a varied portfolio of business interests, we had a lovely home, good friends and, most important, a boat we could take out fishing. Was it a symptom of an impending mid-life crisis that I was so restless, so completely detached from our life in America? I thought not. It went deeper than that.

We discussed my problems as a family group and resolved to spend the American summer on a long touring holiday in Australia, driving the back roads in a way I hadn't experienced since those long-ago days when I was driven through the night from one bush tournament to the next.

Our holiday was wonderful. I celebrated my fortieth birthday with a big party in the sports ground at Barellan, then we motored slowly along the east coast, spending time in small towns and fishing villages — and indulging ourselves with a magnificent week of sports fishing.

At the airport in Cairns Roger said he looked at our faces — the children's as well as mine — and realised that the time had come. I was coming home, as I always knew I would.

In the three or four months that passed while we packed up our house, sold cars and extricated ourselves from our American life, my mind was never far from the expectation of what I would do in Australia. We knew there would be all kinds of offers to be associated with tennis centres, resort complexes and the like, but I knew that if I was to look backwards in Australia it would be a lot further back than over two decades of an exciting tennis career. I wanted to go back 40,000 years, to begin to understand something about my people, about who I was. And I wanted to picture that crowd at Mum's funeral and be able to place every face in the grand scheme of my life, in the greater family known as the Wiradjuri.

With these thoughts in mind we dragged out the paperwork on two projects which had long been stalled through our involvement in other things, or just a feeling that the timing wasn't right.

Not long after my second Wimbledon crown in 1980 we had been approached about making a movie of my life, a Cinderella story about the little Aboriginal girl from the backblocks who conquered the tennis world. Considerable research had been done and, in the heady financial climate of the mid-1980s, there had been no shortage of backers. But I had always felt there was something wrong. In the various scripts and treatments I seemed to undergo a miraculous metamorphosis at about the age of 13, from Aborigine to tennis star, and it was game, set and match from there on.

In Sydney in 1985 we had discussed another project, a television documentary about Aboriginal culture, with producer David Hill and writer Phil Jarratt.

The following summer the Jarratts stayed with us at our home on Hilton Head Island, South Carolina, while we further explored the idea.

Somehow the years slipped by while Roger carried around the ideas in a manilla folder and I became far more interested in Aboriginal culture than I was in my memories of tennis. In the American autumn of 1991 the manilla folder was on our table most nights while we pored over those ideas again.

On our return to Australia in December 1991 I found Phil Jarratt's phone number in Noosa Heads, Queensland, and dialled it. I said, 'Gong here. Can we talk?'

We decided to settle in Noosa ourselves, and during the summer we fished and discussed a new approach to the project. Phil had travelled widely in the Australian bush in recent years and knew a lot about Aboriginal life. I felt he had an understanding and appreciation of my own feelings about Aboriginality that stemmed from personal experience, rather than from a distant academic base. Together we kept coming back to the same starting point: my life story and my preoccupation with my Aboriginal ancestry were one and the same. Some people had said I was the most famous Aborigine in the world,

Left: Morgan and Steve Trezise study 'The Bad Spirit' in the Quinkan Galleries, 1992 *Right:* Under a river red gum tree, Wilcannia, 1993

but conversely, would I have achieved the same degree of success if I had been born white? It seemed to me that being an Aborigine and being a champion were simply two sides of the same coin.

As Big Bill Neidjie puts it in his book *Kakadu Man*:

Skin can be different,
but blood same.
Blood and bone …
all same.
Man can't split himself.

And so the seeds of this book were sown.

In my tennis career I was most often fortunate to have a supportive — sometimes adoring — press. But there were also occasions when my own people used the media to attack me for failing to be the kind of Aborigine they believed I should be. This was particularly so when I went to South Africa in 1971. I make no excuses now for what I did then, or at any other stage of my life. But I will say to my critics now, as I did then, that they should perhaps consider the sacrifices you have to make to be the best in the world at anything. You have to shut off your mind from everything to achieve your goal.

If I shut out certain things that others thought were obvious, then perhaps it was because in my life, tennis, in retrospect, was only a part. If I hadn't become a champion who would listen to me now?

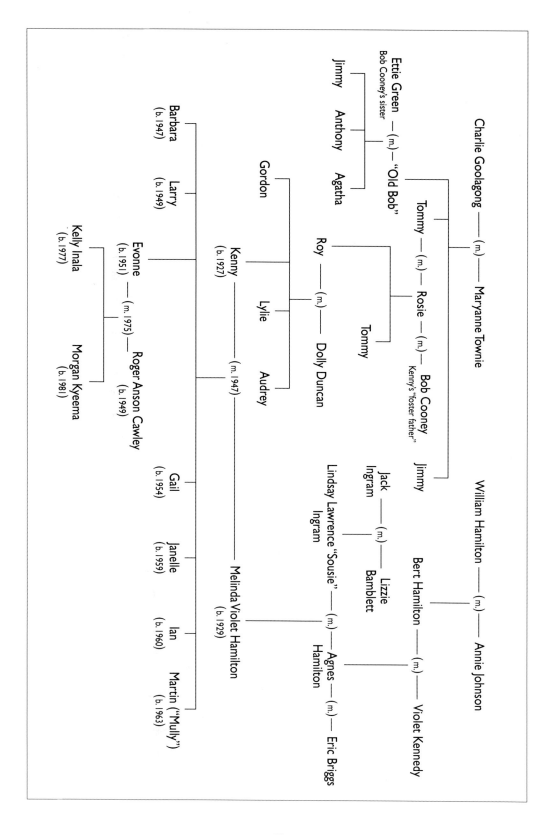

PART 1

The Barellan Leader

The Barellan Goolagongs

Chapter 1

*T*WO HUNDRED YEARS AGO Europeans had yet to venture across the Great Dividing Range which runs the length of the Australian east coast, separating the lush coastal strip from the harsh and sometimes arid interior. The rough, unforgiving and beautiful country beyond the Range, to the west and south-west of what is now Sydney, was the province of the Wiradjuri, one of the hundreds of tribal groups of nomadic Aborigines who then roamed the continent as they had done for at least 40,000 years.

Each of these 'tribes', or language groups, was composed of several clans, which were extended family groups based on either the father's or the mother's line of descent. Clan members could not marry one another and, depending on whether the clan followed the paternal or maternal line, children became members of either the father's or mother's clan. Through the rites of the clan its members were irrevocably associated with particular tracts of land and with totems from the Dreaming, the spiritual belief system that underpinned Aboriginal life and placed constant emphasis on the idea that all living things were an extension of their environment.

But Aboriginal society was neither strict nor inflexible, despite a moral code which was built around the religion of the Dreaming. In fact life was based around loose groupings of people of different clans who shared the same language and the same interests in hunting or fishing or food gathering. Customs, beliefs and lifestyles varied from one language group to the next and across a wide variety of environments. The Wiradjuri people of central New South Wales were fortunate in inhabiting an area bounded by three great rivers, a region where food was plentiful. In the summer the men might stand naked in their dugout canoes spearing fish; in the winter they might stalk possums along the river banks at night, keeping warm with flying fox skins draped over their shoulders.

The first contact between the European invaders and the Aborigines in the year after 1788 was basically friendly, but as the tentacles of white settlement spread in the early 1800s, so did resistance to enforced changes of lifestyle. The concept of property ownership, so clear to the squatter, had no meaning

to the nomads of the western plains, and they did not unde.........
man's anger when they attempted to 'trespass'. The Wi...
Windradyne was one of the first to organise resistance to the s....
1820s, but it was an impossible battle, and as the pockets of resist....
up, so the invaders became more intent on wiping out what remain....
culture which far predated their own.

The colony — and later state — of New South Wales was the front....
in the battle for Aboriginal survival, the place where Aborigines were firs....
dispossessed of their land, and thus their spiritual and cultural centre. The
Wiradjuri, like many other language groups, fell prey to white diseases and
— the worst disease of all — despair.

The white man approached the black man in Australia with feelings which
ranged from loathing to pity, and with everything from bullet to Bible, but
there was always a constant theme: the necessity to 'civilise the savages'. This
fundamentally megalomaniacal mission was quite open in the early years of
settlement, but in later times it became an insidious campaign of slow genocide
masquerading as 'welfare'. In broad terms Aboriginal welfare meant keeping
the Aborigine where he could do the least harm to white society while his
race withered and died. From about 1840 the colonial governments began to
establish 'reserves' in places that suited their own deployment of overseers.
Thus began the tragic enforced removal of Aborigines from their traditional
lands, but government enthusiasm soon waned when the administration realised
the costs of confinement.

The church became involved in Aboriginal 'welfare' in the early 1820s,
but it was not until the various denominations noticed the atrocities of physical
and mental abuse being sanctioned on government reserves and by the dreaded
Native Police in the 1870s that they became involved in establishing missions.
These missions offered Aborigines a way of life that was somewhere between
the traditional mode and that of the west, whereas the earlier government
reserves had essentially been prisons. One of the earliest of these was
Warangesda, established in 1879 on the Murrumbidgee River near Darlington
Point in the traditional lands of the Wiradjuri. (Half a century later my mother
was born in a mud-walled shepherd's hut close to the mission.)

It didn't take the government long to realise that mission confinement was
such an effective way of controlling the 'Aboriginal problem' that it could not
be left in the hands of the churchmen. In 1883 the Aborigines Protection Board
was established to administer the lives of the estimated 9000 'full-blood' and
'half-caste' Aborigines in New South Wales, and by the turn of the century
more than 100 'reserves' had been set up along the lines of Warangesda. The

Protection Act of 1909 gave government the
of the towns and into the reserves at will, and
which prevented them buying alcohol or associ-
amendment gave the Board the power to take
raining' and to remove 'half-castes' from the
costs of running the reserves, assimilation
half white) became the Board's economic
bers in this way, the remaining Aborigines
as the land was leased back to farmers.
was modified and given different names over
aim — to obliterate the identity of Australia's traditional
and their connection to traditional lands — remained the same until
a referendum in 1967 finally granted Aborigines full citizenship. In 1972, the
year after I won my first Wimbledon, the Commonwealth Government of
Australia proclaimed for the first time a policy of 'self-determination' for
Aborigines and supported the concept of Aboriginal land rights. A further 20
years would pass, however, before the government of Australia would
acknowledge that there were prior claims on this land — our land.

In the years immediately after World War I the Murrumbidgee Irrigation
Scheme was expanding fast and changing the dust bowl towns of south-western
New South Wales into fertile and cash-rich communities. The speculator's game
was to pick which towns would prosper and to move in and establish business
there before the change.

This was why the newspaper proprietor John Arthur Bradley in 1924 began
publication of a modest weekly to service Barellan, a dry and dusty town
of about 800 sheep and wheat farmers situated between Binya and
Moombooldool. He called the newspaper the *Barellan Leader*.

Bradley purchased a secondhand Double Royal printing press from the editor
of the *Cootamundra Herald* and arranged for it to be transported by truck to
Barellan, but the rough roads between the two towns proved too much. The
press fell off and was irreparably damaged.

It was stored in a room of a house on Bendee Street, which served as
the editor's quarters and the editorial and advertising office of the *Leader*, but
the new paper ended up being printed 100 kilometres (60 miles) away in Temora.
This fact did nothing to stem the delight of the 800 folk who called Barellan
home. On publication day a local wit was said to have charged into the bar
of the Commercial Hotel and declared: 'Naked Nellie ['Bare-Ellen' was the
nick-name of the town] has a rag at last.'

But the irrigation scheme didn't come as far as Barellan and Naked Nellie's 'rag' was doomed from the start. It struggled on until World War II when J. A. Bradley was forced to amalgamate the paper with others in the region and close the Bendee Street office. There being no market for a shopfront house in a fading town, the *Barellan Leader* office was offered for rent to itinerant farmhands and shearers, but more often than not it stood musty, dusty and disused, the Double Royal printing press still standing in the back room.

This was the way it was in 1953 when Frank Gladman towed my parents' blue Chevrolet utility into town, laden with the bits and pieces that they had accumulated in the six years they had been married. I was just two and too young to recall the journey, but according to Mr Gladman, a shearing contractor who was my father's employer, we were a motley lot, our goods and chattels piled high in hessian bags in the back, five of us pressed into the cabin around Dad at the wheel.

Although the family was growing so fast it was difficult for anyone to keep track, in 1953 we Goolagongs consisted of my father Kenny, my mother Linda, Barbara, 6, Larry, 4, me, 2, and baby Kevin, just a couple of months old. Since my parents had met and fallen in love at a fruit-pickers' camp on the banks of the Murrumbidgee River just after the war, they had moved from camp to camp, from tumbledown shack to earthen floor hut, always on the fringes of white settlement at places like Griffith, Tarbogan and, most recently, Binya. As children we didn't appreciate it at the time, but the move into the heart of Barellan was an important one for our parents. It gave our family some kind of permanence and, I suppose, some kind of respectability in white eyes. It also made us the only black family in a white town.

According to the townsfolk of Barellan there had never been an Aboriginal family before us, nor has there been one since. It seems strange to me now that in a region where seasonal work, such as shearing and fruit picking, was the mainstay of the economy, and in a town which lay in a direct line between well-used Wiradjuri camps, no Aboriginal families had settled. I began to see why when I went through the back files of the *Barellan Leader* at the museum in Temora. In the edition of 31 May 1928 I found the following item:

KEEPING ABOS AWAY FROM THE PICTURES

As the result of a new regulation in Darwin prohibiting aborigines from entering a town at night, 150 were ejected from a local picture show on Thursday.

When we arrived in Barellen in 1953 there was no picture show and no overt indication of racial discrimination, although my brother Larry remembers being given a hard time in his first years of school. Certainly at the time of our arrival there were still many laws in place which effectively made Aborigines second-class citizens. My distant relative Ernest 'Gundy' Wighton of Condobolin has shown me, with a mixture of amusement, resentment and pride, his 'Certificate Of Exemption' issued by the NSW Government under the Aborigines Protection Act in 1952. This 'dog tag' certified that Gundy, a 'light Aborigine aged 29 years ... is a person who in the opinion of the Aboriginal Welfare Board, ought no longer be subject to the provisions of the Aborigines Protection Act'. In other words, Gundy had shown himself responsible enough to be considered an honorary 'white feller' and could drink legally in the pub. Some 1200 of these bizarre certificates were issued between 1943 and 1964, while thousands of Aborigines were refused them on the grounds of employment, morality or the cut of their clothing.

I wonder now if my father had such a certificate. Certainly he was no stranger to the bar of the Commercial Hotel in Barellan, although, according to his old shearing mate John Emerson, they were both barred from the War Memorial Club more often than they were admitted.

Frank Gladman, who had taken up shearing contracting in Barellan in 1950, saw my father shearing in Griffith and was impressed enough to offer him permanent employment and a house to live in, but in fact Kenny Goolagong had very little shearing experience at that time. A quiet, reserved man who only revealed his impish humour to those he knew and trusted, Kenny had worked at the usual run of jobs open to an unskilled Aborigine: loading wheat, cleaning silos, picking fruit and tinkering with cars whenever he got the opportunity. (This passion for spending all day under the hood of a car was inherited by my brother Larry.)

My father was born in Condobolin, NSW, in 1927, around the time that 'Condo' was considered a safe camp for Wiradjuri people, who were being hounded from their homelands by government agencies in the pursuit of the doctrine of assimilation. Historian Peter Read has documented the flow of families into Condobolin in the 1920s as camps in places like Cowra, Hillston, and Euabalong were closed down, and it seems likely that branches of the Goolagong family moved into the Condobolin mission at that time. However, the Goolagong line can be traced back a long time before that in the Condobolin region, even though there is virtually no documentation of our existence!

In piecing together the fragments of my family history I have relied heavily on regional and Aboriginal historians who have shared what they have learned unselfishly, but in the final analysis much of it gets down to educated guesswork, and this is what I have employed.

My father's forebears probably took, or were given, the Goolagong name from the Wiradjuri word 'gulagallang' which means a lot, or a big mob, which is what they would have formed at the campsite which is now the town of Gooloogong, on the Lachlan River between Forbes and Cowra.

This seems more likely to me now than the lyrical translation I was given during my tennis career — tall trees, still waters — which became my corporate logo and adorned many of the products manufactured under my name.

Robert Ellis, a farmer and shearer by trade and a historian by inclination, helped me establish some of the early movements of my line of Goolagongs. Mr Ellis, who has published history books about the Wiradjuri homelands, wrote to me in 1992: 'My special interest is the Wiradjuri people, including your ancestors, whose territory once took up about a fifth of what is now New South Wales ... The story about Eugowra is one an old white lady, 96, told me nearly 30 years ago.'

Mr Ellis enclosed a page of his book detailing the 'Eugowra Incident', which is said to have taken place at a camp on the opposite bank of the Lachlan, about 20 kilometres (12½ miles) from Gooloogong, in 1896.

> The natives of this area were experiencing a complete tribal breakdown, a breakdown of the kind which inevitably followed white settlement. The people here were displaced from their hunting grounds and their sacred areas, they were desperately short of food and fearful of reprisals if caught stealing. In addition, many of the women had become involved with white trappers, fencers or shepherds, etc. This created much inner tribal conflict and added to the growing resentment, the misunderstandings and the general feeling of hopelessness which had begun to overshadow the individual and tribal life of all.
>
> One day the evident despair and distrust finally came to a head and the Aboriginal men, women and children of this group began fighting amongst themselves. The fighting became fierce and vicious.
>
> When the awesome battle came to an end almost every man, woman and child was either dead or dying.

As horrific as this episode appears to have been, I know now that it was not an isolated incident as despair took hold of my people. In Condobolin I was told of a more recent occurrence when during a corroboree (an Aboriginal gathering) a brawl broke out between Wiradjuri from different camps with similarly lethal results.

In his letter, Mr Ellis told me he understood there were about 11 survivors of Eugowra who eventually found their way to the Condobolin Aboriginal mission. He wrote, 'One of these people was a young boy [who] I understand was your grandfather on your Dad's side. About 30 years ago — I can't recall

The Condobolin Boomerangs football team, circa 1945

exactly — he was an old man at the football in Eugowra when the Condobolin team played there. There were several of your cousins or descendants playing and I had a bit of a chat to him. Although he was reluctant to talk about it, he acknowledged that such a massacre did once occur. The year seems a little in doubt.'

Mr Ellis had it almost right. My research has revealed that in fact he spoke to Old Bob Goolagong, a brother of my great-grandfather Tommy. (The town of Goolagong is said to be named after their youngest brother, Jimmy.)

I am not a detective; I have sought out the evidence and tried to place it in the most plausible order, which, given the vagaries of Aboriginal history and the absolute uncertainty of our genealogy, is all that can be done. But imagine my excitement when, in Condobolin in the spring of 1992, an old man named Tony Rose described the very football match of Robert Ellis's recollection, and told me not only of the extraordinary performance of my grand-uncle Jimmy Goolagong (who was a natural at rugby league and celebrated every try he scored by somersaulting backwards to the centreline) but of the regular presence at Aboriginal football matches of Old Bob Goolagong.

Great-grandfather Tommy Goolagong was one of several sons of Charlie Goolagong and Maryann Townie. He was probably born in about 1880 and he may also have been a survivor of the Eugowra massacre.

Tommy and his wife Rosie had two sons, Tommy and my grandfather Roy.

Left: Kenny Goolagong aged 12, 1939 *Right:* Agatha Goolagong, singer and pianist, in the 1930s

His brother Bob married Ettie Green and had three children — two boys, Jimmy and Anthony, and a daughter, Agatha. Roy took up with Dolly Duncan, whose father, Godfrey 'Gundy' Ritchie was the head stockman on Booberoi Station.

Dolly, whose funeral I attended in Condobolin in 1989, was in those days a fine hockey player and, along with her six sisters, formed the backbone of the premiership-winning Condobolin women's hockey team of the 1930s. Now only Dolly's sister Rose, my Auntie Rosie, survives of the Old People (those who still know and respect Aboriginal language and lore), but the memories of the sisterhood that took Condobolin to the top of the hockey premiership table all those years ago, still linger on in 'Condo'.

Likewise the memories of Grandfather Roy and his generation are strong. I'll never forget Tony Rose, 81-years-young, looking me in the eye on the verandah of the Condobolin Hospital and telling me, 'The name of Jimmy Goolagong will never die.' But Jimmy wasn't the only famous one in the family. His sister Agatha, a statuesque and attractive girl, judging from the one faded photograph I have found, played hockey and sang and played the piano. In fact, according to Tony Rose, there was nothing she couldn't do.

'I tell you what,' Tony told me, 'she could ride a pushbike. She'd hitch up her dress and tuck it into her bloomers and away she'd go. In a race she'd beat the blokes by yards.'

According to Tony — and other guardians of local legend in Condo —

Agatha Goolagong might have become the first member of the family to receive international acclaim. 'This American singer bloke come to town and his pianist got sick, so Agatha filled in for her. Well, the bloke heard her sing and that was that. He wanted to take her back to America with him and make her famous. But she wouldn't go, Aggie, she stayed in Condo.'

The Condobolin Mission was on the river bank at a place called Willow Bend, but many of the Goolagongs and other members of their clan chose to set up camp on a nearby floodplain called The Murie, where other Wiradjuri who had been thrown off the reserves had gathered. My earliest memories of Condo are of this camp, of sitting up at night listening to the adults playing guitars and singing by the campfire, and of days spent playing on the muddy bank of the creek.

But long before I was even born, the Goolagongs were at The Murie, and Jimmy was evidently the life of the party. Everyone who knew The Murie in those days has a Jimmy Goolagong story, but I particularly like the one told by Auntie Junie Mason, a distant relative and an older sister of the poet Kevin Gilbert. 'There was a bull-riding contest in Condo and Jimmy rode his steer to a standstill. You wouldn't believe it, they gave the prize to the mayor's son. Jimmy could see I was angry so he came up to me and said, "No matter, my gel, next year I'll paint myself white and then maybe I'll win." '

My distant relative Gundy Wighton (he of the exemption certificate) remembers Jimmy having a few too many in the Railway Hotel one Saturday afternoon and stripping off and riding his horse down the main street. He got as far as the Condobolin Hotel (about half a dozen blocks) before he was stopped by the police. In fact Jimmy seems to have spent quite a bit of time in the clutches of the law. To 'square off' with the constabulary he took a second job (he worked as a station hand) tending horses for the mounted police. One day in court on a public nuisance charge, he was asked by the magistrate which station he worked on. He replied, 'I work for two stations, Your Honour. Brambles Station and the police station.'

Not so many stories are told of Jimmy's cousin Roy, a quiet, dignified man like my father. Roy was as good a horseman as Jimmy, but not as flashy. He was a jockey who rode trackwork and did the circuit of picnic race meetings up and down the Lachlan. He was returning from trackwork one morning, riding one horse and leading another, when a dog bit his horse on the foreleg, causing it to rear up and throw him. Roy suffered head injuries and had to have a steel plate inserted.

Roy and Dolly had three sons — Gordon, my father Kenny, and Lylie — and a daughter, Audrey. Then something happened in their relationship that is not discussed in the Goolagong family, whether out of propriety or simple ignorance of the facts I know not. I do know that Dolly left Roy and took up with Jimmy, and together they had Kathleen (known as 'Chookie'), Joey, Neville (known as 'Wee Wee'), Eric, Charlie, and Ivan. (Ivan had a twin brother, Arnold, who died tragically in infancy.)

There was no wedge driven through the family over the potentially hurtful matter of Dolly's change of husbands. That is not the Aboriginal way. As a little girl visiting The Murie I can remember both Jimmy and Roy as old men, but it was Jimmy I saw with my grandmother, and naturally it was him I took to be my grandfather.

Aboriginal custom was — and is — the free movement of children between different branches of the family. When I was very small my older sister Barbara was frequently away across the Murray River in Swan Hill, Victoria, staying with a branch of my mother's family. Likewise, my younger sister Janelle and brother Ian lived for a time in Melbourne with my mother's half-brother, Fred Briggs. Anyone who has any difficulty understanding how my mother could send me off at the age of 11 to live with a white family in Sydney to further my tennis career, should consider the pattern of the lives of so many Aboriginal children. Not that Aboriginal tradition made my going any easier for Mum. I often wonder now how I would feel if my son Morgan, aged 11, was asked to leave us to further his sporting aspirations.

Gundy Wighton recently described quite beautifully the circumstances surrounding my father Kenny's departure from his natural family in Condobolin at an early age. 'See, what happens is the Old People will take a shine to a young feller. They'll want to buy him some lollies, and then the next thing he's coming out to stay at their camp, and soon it's as much a home to him as his real home. He's got two homes! And the Old People rear him up as if he was their h'own.' (Gundy adds an aitch here and there in that delightful bush manner I hadn't heard for so long.)

In Kenny's case the Old People were Bob Cooney and his wife Rosie, Kenny's grandmother. (Rosie had married Bob Cooney after Tommy's death.) Bob worked on a station near Peak Hill, which was where Kenny spent much of his boyhood. So in Condobolin Kenny was perhaps the least known of the Goolagongs, a quiet lad who slipped in and out of The Murie to see the family but spent most of his time on the station with Bob Cooney, learning the ways of the bush. Bob Cooney is, of course, long dead, and no one can shed much light on Kenny's formative years, but I believe he went to school for a time, possibly in Peak Hill. He could read and write, skills my mother never acquired. After the war Kenny drifted around from job to job, from one branch of the family to the next. Auntie Junie Mason had been fostered out to Agnes Briggs, my mother's mother, and she remembers the family camping on the Murrumbidgee River in the 1940s during the peach-picking season. Junie, who has been very ill in recent years, has become drawn and terribly fragile. But I have seen pictures of her back then and she was a very attractive woman. No more so, apparently, than my mother. Imagine Kenny Goolagong's delight, then, when he happened upon the Briggs camp one night in 1946 and found himself in the company of two pretty young women!

Mum never told me the circumstances of this meeting, but Junie Mason recalls to this day Kenny walking into the camp, quiet, compact, reserved, shy, handsome. 'And he was fun to be around,' she says. 'We all liked Kenny. Linda seemed to like him a real lot.'

Melinda Violet Goolagong was born in 1929 in a mud-walled shepherd's hut just outside the Warangesda Mission at Darlington Point. She was brought up as Linda Briggs under the care of Eric Briggs, whose fascinating lineage has often been held to be my own, but in fact she was the daughter of Agnes Hamilton and Lindsay Lawrence Ingram (usually known as 'Sousie' but sometimes as 'Tich'). Linda was the only child of that union before her mother took up with Eric Briggs and Sousie started another family of four children.

I know very little about the Ingram line, other than that the family is one of the most important of the Wiradjuris, and can be traced back to the establishment of both Warangesda and Maloga Missions.

The Ingram family were spread out around all the Wiradjuri camps at that time — at Euabalong James Ingram had married into the Goolagong side of the family already, through one of Gundy Ritchie's daughters — and it is difficult to know when and where Sousie took up with Agnes. At the time of my mother's birth in 1929, however, they were living in the mud hut at Warangesda. In recent years I have walked around in what remains of that tiny hut with my sister Barbara, both of us marvelling at how Gran could have coped in that primitive space.

I know nothing about the circumstances of Agnes' departure from Ingram or her marriage to Eric Briggs, although the Briggs genealogy, researched meticulously over 30 years by members of that family, reveals that Eric Briggs married Agnes Hamilton (no date) and they had one girl (adopted). Auntie Junie Mason, who was taken in as a foster child by Eric and Agnes when she and Mum were both in their early teens, remembers Mum as this only child.

Although I know so little about my grandfather Sousie's family, I know

Clockwise from top left: My mother's father, Lindsay Lawrence Ingram (right), with his cousin Joe Sloan in the 1940s; Dolly and Jimmy Goolagong with some of their children, 1940s

Baby Linda held by her mother Agnes, 1930

quite a bit about the Briggs, who are not blood relations. Eric Briggs was a descendant of George Briggs, a Bass Strait sealer who came out from England as a free man in 1806. Briggs abducted a Tasmanian Aboriginal woman by whom he had several children, including a son, John — Eric Briggs' grandfather. In 1844 John Briggs married Louise Esmae Strugnell, said to be a daughter of Truganini, often mistakenly referred to as the 'last full-blood Tasmanian Aborigine'.

In the 1850s the Briggs family moved to Victoria, eventually settling at Coranderrk, near Healesville, where members married into the strong clans of the Kulin tribe. Some time later the Briggs moved to Cummeragunga, a government Aboriginal station on the Murray River, established in 1882. Cummeragunga was to produce some of the leading Aboriginal citizens of the twentieth century, including Pastor Sir Douglas Nicholls, who became governor of South Australia, and the Stawell Gift winner and 1929 world sprint champion Lynch Cooper. But it was also one of the most controversial of the government-run 'missions', where cruelty was commonplace. In 1939, the brutality of officials there led to a mass walk-off, and the Aboriginal population crossed the Murray and refused to accept New South Wales Government administration. Cummeragunga was also the place where Eric Briggs fell in love with Agnes Hamilton after her relationship with Sousie Ingram had soured.

As a small child I can remember Granny Briggs coming to stay with us at Barellan from time to time. She was a very old lady and she used to smoke a lot, which I think is what caused her death in the end. Mum used to take us all to the town rubbish tip and fossick around looking for odds and ends that she could recycle. Gran would come along, bringing up the rear, and from time to time she'd stop, bend down and pick up a piece of dirt and eat it. It was all we could do to stop from giggling, but I found out many years later that many of the Wiradjuri women used a special kind of clay as a remedy for stomach upsets. The faded, torn photograph I have of Agnes at the time of her marriage to Eric Briggs does not tally with my memory of this dirt-chewing old lady. She was an attractive woman, her hair neatly fashioned in the style of the 1930s, her hem-line revealing a pair of shapely legs.

Agnes was a daughter of Bertie Hamilton, whose parents were Annie and Willie Hamilton. A photo taken by The Aborigines Protection Board last century and now in the Museum of Victoria shows Annie and Willie as a strikingly handsome couple, posed formally in the Victorian style with four of the 10 children they eventually had. The youngest of Annie and Willie's children, Agnes, married William Cooper, one of the most prominent of early

Left: Grandma Agnes with dashing Eric Briggs in the early 1930s *Right:* Mum as a little girl, with her mother Agnes and stepfather Eric Briggs

Aboriginal rights activists. In 1933 William, along with Pastor Doug Nicholls and others formed the Aborigines Advancement League and began lobbying government for better conditions for Aborigines living on reserves like Cummeragunga. In October 1937 William presented the government with a petition of 1814 signatures of Aborigines from all over the country demanding these rights. When the petition was ignored the residents of Cummeragunga took direct action and went on strike, signalling the beginning of the end of black acceptance of an inferior position in Australian society.

While I am proud of my family link with William Cooper, I am no less proud to be associated with his son, Lynch Cooper, a fine runner who won the 1928 Stawell Gift (still Australia's leading sprint race) and went on to win the world sprint championships the following year.

(Eric Briggs' father William was also a sportsman of note, playing cricket in several representative Aboriginal teams. Briggs family legend has it that he was selected to tour England with the Aboriginal team of 1868 and got as far as the dock before he backed out, fearful that his wife Maggie might not survive his absence. As it turned out, his assessment of Maggie's condition was sadly correct. She died a matter of weeks later.)

I'm not sure when Agnes and Eric left Cummeragunga but it was most likely in the early 1920s, a time of great movement amongst the clans as the Aborigines Welfare Board had begun enforcing its declared policy of separating Aboriginal children from their families. The 1921 report of the Aborigines Welfare Board declared that 'the continuation of this policy of dissociating the children from camp life must eventually solve the Aboriginal problem'. This was the period when in Aboriginal society the term 'welfare man' became indelibly linked with the horror of enforced separation, a stigma which still existed throughout my formative years a generation or more later.

When I was growing up in Barellan I didn't understand the disgraceful nature of this situation. The Welfare 'bogey man' was an abstraction to me, although the threat became real when there was a loud knock on the door! 'Run and hide. It's the Welfare man come to take you away,' my mother would sometimes say. And I would run and hide, and I never spoke to strangers who came to the house.

I have frequently been confused while researching my family's history. With every layer I unravel, more questions than answers are revealed. But I think I know now the kind of world both my parents had come from when they met in that camp on the 'Bidgee nearly half a century ago. And I think I know what kind of people they must have been — young and full of hope, despite their impoverished circumstances, and the fact that they were Wiradjuri Kooris in a time when the conventional wisdom was that theirs was a dying race.

I have never seen a wedding photo and none of Linda or Kenny's living relatives could confirm whether my parents actually married, although years later when I was about to be married Mum insisted in the press that she had had a church wedding. It would have been most uncharacteristic for Mum to lie about that — or anything for that matter — but where were the pictures? Why could no one remember the event? Mum may have been 17 and pregnant with Barbara, but in Aboriginal society there would have been no stigma about that. I started hunting out birth certificates. My sister Barbara's revealed that Linda and Kenny were married at Moulamein on 4 July 1947. This certificate, issued only a few months after that date, seemed likely to be correct. But the birth certificates of my younger sisters Gail and Janelle, born years later, gave the wedding date as 23 July 1947. Still puzzled, I began to search for court records. Eventually the marriage details were found in the records not of the Moulamein court but of Balranald. And they revealed that my parents were married at St Martin's Church of England hall, Moulamein on 23 July 1947, my mother aged 17, my father 21. But the mystery was still not completely solved because I believe Kenny was 20 at the time of his marriage, not 21. Why had he put his age up?

I thus have a somewhat uncertain image of Kenny and Linda starting out in life together, knowing only that to improve their lot in life they would have to live in the white man's world, and play by his rules.

Kenny and Linda Goolagong, shortly after
their wedding in 1947

Chapter 2

*M*ELINDA VIOLET HAMILTON (as she was known on her wedding certificate) became Linda Goolagong, and she and Kenny set up the first of many homes in a settlement of family and friends at Moulamein, on the Edward River not far from Swan Hill.

Several of the Briggs clan had moved there from Darlington Point, and after my sister Barbara was born in the Swan Hill Hospital in 1947, she was handed around the camp at Moulamein as if it were a game of pass-the-parcel. There was no question of neglect or lack of interest on my mother's part — quite the opposite — but she and Kenny were young and trying to make their way in the world. It was the Aboriginal way that care of the first-born child should fall to the Old People: in this case Agnes and Eric Briggs.

According to family lore, baby Barbara spent so much time with Grandma Agnes that she took to sucking her breasts, a practice which caused Grandpa Briggs to scold her laughingly, 'Get away, gel. They mine!'

Work was scarce at Moulamein and Kenny ventured further afield looking for jobs fruit-picking up around Griffith, or for station work in a wide arc of the Wiradjuri country, taking in the bush towns of Condobolin, Lake Cargelligo, Hillston and Hay. After a time the elder members of the Briggs family moved across the Murray River to Swan Hill, taking Barbara with them while Kenny and Linda roamed from camp to camp around the south-west plains.

If this sounds irresponsible on the part of my parents, please understand it was not. Not only was the nomadic lifestyle part of our heritage, in those years it was also essential for economic survival, particularly for those who wished to rid themselves forever of the psychological chains of mission handouts.

With Linda pregnant with a second child, however, Kenny sought temporary refuge at the mission at the Three Ways, just outside Griffith. Here there were members of the Goolagong, Briggs, Charles, Naden and many more of the Wiradjuri families. Here Kenny could leave his young wife, who was getting fatter with child by the day, while he picked fruit in the season or worked the stations, or — a new string to his bow — he could get casual days of work in the shearing sheds.

Shearing was a skill Kenny had picked up while working as a station hand on Glenroy Station, under the tutelage of Clancy Charles Sr, a distant relation. Dad was no 'gun' shearer in those days, but he cared about the quality of all his work, however menial its nature, and in shearing there was a sense of creativity he had otherwise experienced only under the hood of one of his old 'bomb' cars.

It didn't take long for Kenny Goolagong to scrape together enough money to buy the elementary building materials needed to knock up a corrugated iron shack which would represent a kind of independence for his growing family. He built the earthen-floor home in an Aboriginal camp at Tarbogan, just outside Griffith, and by the time Larry was born at Griffith Base Hospital in 1949, the Goolagongs had their first real home.

I have no memory of the shack at Tarbogan, but it remained the Goolagong family's principal place of residence for several years. When Mum had everything just so, Kenny drove her and Larry down to the Victorian border at Swan Hill and wrested Barbara from the care of the Old People. But it was not a matter of thanking them very much and plucking my sister from their midst. Aboriginal families are not like that. Barbara was as much loved

Left: Linda with her first-born, Barbara, in 1948 *Right:* Kenny (left) with Clancy Charles at our Tarbogan home in 1952

by her grandparents as she was by our mother and father, and as much a part of the Briggs family as she was a Goolagong; thus her life for many years would be divided between the two generations of the family.

Barbara recalls the shack at Tarbogan as basic and small, but turned into a home by our mother's deft touch as a decorator. Throughout her life, Linda, starting from basically nothing but her ingenuity, created around her a living environment that was as inventive as it was clean. When she wasn't scrubbing, sweeping or polishing, she was busy making decorative nick-nacks to place on the makeshift table, or sewing colourful patches on a chaff bag to cover a hole in a wall.

The shack at Tarbogan was my first home, and it was almost my last. I was born in the Griffith Hospital on 31 July 1951, in the middle of a bitterly cold winter in the Riverina. My mother came up with the names in our family, and for me she chose Evonne. It has often been suggested that my name resulted from Linda's misspelling of 'Yvonne' on the birth certificate — my mother could not read or write — but until the day she died, Mum always insisted that she had given me the name she intended.

Barbara was back in Swan Hill at the time of my birth, possibly to alleviate the pressure on Mum as she approached the arrival of her third child. She returned to live with us in Tarbogan before I had my second birthday, because she distinctly remembers two things about me as a baby — the fact that I couldn't or wouldn't walk, and the fact that one day I almost died.

Of my tardiness in standing up on my own two feet, says Barbara: 'You was unbelievable! Here you were, almost two years old and crawling around like a little baby. Mum was terrified there was something wrong with you and eventually took you to see a doctor. He said you were just lazy.'

Of the day I nearly died there are several accounts, but as Barbara remembers it, I had taken a real shine to Kenny, and liked to crawl around his feet while he worked in the yard or on one of his cars. One day I watched him siphon petrol by sucking the air out of a hose. Later, when he had disappeared inside the house to get something, I evidently picked up the hose and mimicked his actions. No one knows how much petrol I drank, but it was enough to make me turn blue and start to choke.

Mum raced out and found me and started screaming at Dad to do something, but the car was in pieces. He looked stunned for a moment. She didn't wait around to debate the issue. She picked me up in her arms and ran, barefoot, to the highway where she hailed down a car and got me to the Griffith Hospital, where they immediately pumped out my stomach.

There is one other thing Barbara recalls about our life in Tarbogan: the tennis balls. 'You were crawling around inside the car while Dad worked on it, and somewhere under the back seat you found this rotten, greasy old tennis ball, a memento of the previous owner, I suppose, because Mum and Dad didn't play tennis. You wouldn't let it out of your sight. Any time we'd go somewhere in the car you'd sit in the back, holding this ball like some kind of security blanket, giving it a little squeeze from time to time. Mum had to keep buying you another one when you lost it.'

Sometime early in 1953 we left the shack at Tarbogan and moved, briefly, to Hillston, presumably because Dad had regular work there. When we returned to Tarbogan, for some reason we couldn't move back into our shack immediately. Perhaps Kenny had loaned it to a needy friend. We set up camp in a settlement further out of town with Clancy and Ethel Charles and their kids. (Clancy was the son of the man who had taught Dad to shear.) Again, we were in the bosom of the extended family, and that shared camp must have been a happy one for me because it led to a lifelong friendship with the Charles family. (Auntie Ethel was up near the top of my postcard list when I later travelled the world on the tennis tour.)

We moved back into our own shack, but only long enough for Mum to get everything in its place, then pack it all up in the fruit boxes and chaff bags again. How frustrating this must have been for Linda, with three children at her skirt and another on the way. But there was nothing she could do,

Barbara (second from right) with some of the Hillston relations

other than to kiss her husband goodbye for months at a time. And Dad was not itinerant by choice. He followed the work wherever it took him because there burned in Kenny Goolagong a quiet but nonetheless strong ambition to be respected as a hard worker and a good provider.

Just after Kevin was born (like me, at Griffith Hospital) we moved into an old farmhouse at Binya, about 6 kilometres (4 miles) out of the little town of Barellan on the Griffith road. The tumbledown old house was luxury to us, but the isolation made it hard on Mum.

The reason for the move was so that Dad would be central to the shearing work he had started to get regularly from Frank Gladman, a new contractor in the area. Mr Gladman had bought a shearing run of 1800 sheep in 1950, and by 1953 had built it up to more than 45,000 sheep. At certain times of the year he had a team of six shearers working with him, but most of the time he could make do with just two helpers. But they had to be good men. His brother-in-law had the makings of a good shearer and wasn't afraid of hard work, and for his other permanent helper Mr Gladman chose Kenny Goolagong.

When I asked Mr Gladman nearly 40 years later what it was about my father that appealed to him, he said, 'Well, he was a good shearer, but more than that, you could rely on him. I liked his style. He was a feller who got on top of himself, if you know what I mean.'

We moved from the farmhouse at Binya into a house just outside Barellan, and we had already moved five times in a year when Mr Gladman bought the *Barellan Leader* house for 500 pounds and offered it to my father as part of his wage. Mr Gladman is a bit hazy on the actual financial arrangements but, according to his wife Jean Gladman, the bank manager suggested a nominal rent of a shilling a week, which was less than Kenny earned from the shearing of one sheep.

It was a good deal. It was permanent, and it was right in the middle of a town with shops and a school. When Frank Gladman towed our sick car into town that day and unloaded us at the house in Bendee Street, Mum carried the last of the pillowcases full of clothes and nick-nacks into the house and took my father by the arm. 'No more moving now, Kenny,' she said softly. 'This is our home.'

I lived in Barellan for just 12 years, and for the last three of them I divided my time between there and Sydney. That's five years fewer than I spent living in America. The Wiradjuri had no connections with Barellan — indeed, we were the first Aboriginal family to live there — and the Goolagongs had no ties to the town through family or friends. Frank Gladman simply gave Dad a job and a house, and they happened to be in Barellan. Yet Barellan will always be the place I consider my real home, the place where I learnt life's first lessons and discovered the passion that would completely rule the first half of my life, and which, in the curious way of these things, put Barellan on the world map in a manner that wheat and irrigation never could.

The little wheat town was — and still is — dominated by the huge grain silos beside the railway tracks. Apart from when I won Wimbledon in 1971, the proudest day in Barellan history was 2 January 1932, when 116 teams of horses delivered 13,000 bags of wheat to the silos in a day, creating a new Australian record. There is still a photograph of this momentous event in pride of place at the War Memorial Club, and in the bar of the Commercial Hotel you can still buy an argument that the wheat carting record will always be Barellan's proudest moment.

But there were dark moments in Barellan's history too. Like so many Australian bush towns constructed primarily of timber, fire was a constant danger, particularly when the hot summer northerlies blew across the plains. The worst of Barellan's many fires was in February 1928, when a blaze wiped out several of the commercial buildings in Yapunyah Street, including the then offices of the *Barellan Leader*. (This prompted the move to the building in Bendee Street, which was to become our home a quarter of a century later.)

Another fire shortly after World War II again gutted parts of Yapunyah Street, this time destroying the town's second hotel. The Commercial Hotel was untouched but, in the interests of free trading, the rival publican secured a special licence to operate a 'temporary bar' in an empty shop on the main street. The 'Temp'ry Bar' was still operating as a saloon when my family arrived in town, and for many years after.

Since my first memories of any town were of Barellan, I find it difficult to compare it to anywhere else. I have been back with family and friends many, many times in later years, of course, and the people I take home are always intrigued to see this piece of 'the real Australia'. And I suppose that is what Barellan is — a piece of living history. But it is not the town I knew in the 1950s. The tyranny of not enough distance (the big centre of Griffith is only half an hour away) has killed its commercial heart, the trains no longer run, and the tourists drive straight past Evonne Goolagong Park, unless a call of nature beckons them to the little brick dunny (toilet block) which forms the centrepiece of my Barellan monument.

Barellan won't die — in fact its newer residents claim it is entering a new period of prosperity — but its reason for existence has changed. It is

Yapunyah Street, Barellan, in 1992

now a simple dormitory for the bigger country centres around it. And it is highly unlikely that the juke box in Tony's Vienna Cafe will ever play another Strauss waltz or a Bill Haley rocker.

But 1953 Griffith was a long, bumpy drive away, or nearly an hour on the train. Consequently Yapunyah Street's commercial side — the other side is the railway and the silos — groaned under the weight of big business. There were two grocery stores, three garages, two banks, a police station and a tiny hospital, two hardware stores and Mrs Morrison's frock shop. The town's cafe society was well catered for by Tony's mildly exotic Vienna Cafe and the more sedate Barellan Cafe, which once badly misread the market when it advertised 'afternoon teas for men on the move'. Barellan's menfolk were more inclined to move fairly quickly from the workplace to the 'six o'clock swill', an hour of feverish beer drinking before the absurd licensing laws of the period forced the pubs to close and working men to stagger home drunk to take out their frustrations on wives and families.

Our house on Bendee Street was one door up from the War Memorial Club, one block back from the shops and the pub, and one block the other way from Barellan Central School, where Barbara belatedly began her schooling. She remembers: 'I was nearly seven when I started school, but we'd moved around so much it just wasn't worth starting anywhere else. Even at Barellan it was tough for me, being the eldest. By the time I was eight I was responsible for Larry, you and Kevin, and Gail was on the way. If there was trouble with the other kids, or Mum had to go to Griffith to do the shopping, I just didn't get to school.'

Perhaps it was the time she spent in the company of her grandparents, or perhaps it was just her nature, but Barbara took on the responsibility of looking after her younger brothers and sisters with patience and love. She later became a nurse, which was understandable, given the training she got caring for us.

Larry started school the year after Barbara and he was trouble from day one. According to Barbara he'd scream his head off from the moment he woke and realised it was a school day until he was pushed through the gates at the corner of Mulga Street and Boree Street. Then, however, he would adopt a mask of composure which would see him through the day.

Larry needed to be composed because he was the first of the Goolagong children to encounter racism. He is now a big, gentle man whose mission in life is to minister to the welfare of his people, the Wiradjuri. Back then, however, he was a stocky little kid with a short fuse. You called him a 'boong' or a 'coon' at your peril, as several children at the Barellan Central School found out.

Larry, I later discovered, became the family 'enforcer'. Do the wrong thing by any of the Goolagongs and you answered to him. He must have been a good one, because I don't recall ever hearing a racist slur at school, and I never once felt that my colour set me apart from the other children. On reflection, I suspect that the Goolagong family was placed by many of the white folk of Barellan in a class apart from the mission Aborigines they saw in Griffith. Indeed, a family friend Clarrie Irvin has since told me, 'Everyone thought a lot of the Goolagongs, and they were never regarded as Aborigines, just citizens of the town.'

My parents never felt that they had made any kind of transition, of course, and returned to the family camps at Griffith and Condobolin as often as they could. They simply had their sights on a better life for their children, and living like white folk in a white town was the way to attain it.

According to Larry, the schoolyard taunts diminished as we proved ourselves to be good at sport and lessons, Dad showed through hard work and camaraderie that he was at heart a 'white man', and Mum showed with the scrubbing brush and the wood-fired copper that no one was cleaner than a Goolagong. It amuses me when, even today, people who knew us back then prefix their remarks with phrases like 'neat as a pin' or 'always immaculate' or 'spotlessly clean', as if it was some kind of miracle that an Aboriginal family could be at all interested in personal hygiene.

The *Barellan Leader* house had no front yard. It abutted Bendee Street in quite an ugly manner and must have been a source of considerable annoyance to house-proud Mr Gerald Dunlop next door. The house itself had three bedrooms and a boarded-up room in which the printing press was stored, seemingly awaiting the day when Naked Nellie would again cry out for her own rag. Linda created another bedroom by hanging a curtain across a corner of the lounge room and squeezing a bed behind it.

The lounge room had a fireplace which spread its heat through most of the rooms, although I can recall some bitter winter nights. Fortunately our family grew much faster than our budget for bedding, so we slept top-to-toe. For a time there were four of us girls sharing a double bed, which was cosy except for the bedwetter. If your memory is long you may understand when I say that this was initially a pleasant sensation on a cold night, although, as the liquid cooled and we each fully woke, filled with either guilt or anger, it became decidedly less so. The culprit — yes, sometimes it was me — was duly beaten with a pillow and we would strip the sheets and return to our mattress draped in overcoats, chaff bags and whatever we could find to keep out the chill. Sometimes we'd be lucky enough to find one of Mum's 'waggas'. These were chaff or sugar bags sewn together to make a blanket, and sometimes adorned with patches of warm or colourful fabric that Mum had rescued from the rubbish tip.

The kitchen had a wood stove where we'd boil the kettle for our hot water. There was no bathroom as such, but we had a big tub, which served as a bath. Between the kitchen and the rest of the house there was a verandah-cum-washroom, which is where we'd put the tub for privacy, once we'd filled

A rare photo of the *Barellan Leader* house, seen from the rear, near the tennis courts

it with hot water from the kettle. Unfortunately this was also the main entrance to the house, so we had to be careful about when we bathed.

We also had an outside chip heater, or copper, which Mum used for washing. When I was small I used to love to sit in the warm water in the basin on top of the heater, especially when it was raining. The warmth coming from below and the cold drops on my face — it's one of those sensations that stays etched forever in my memory.

Then there was the outside toilet, down in the corner of the backyard. The long trip at night was filled with terror for a small child — especially if we'd been listening to the serial 'The Squeaky Door' on the wireless — and, of course, we never had a torch.

Finally there was the printing press room, our own private jungle for rainy days. Mum didn't seem to mind us playing in there, despite the dust and grease that inevitably found its way on to our clothes and caused even more hard labour over the copper. I was fascinated by the little blocks of metal type, which I regarded as treasures and stored in special places, regardless of the fact that the boarded-up room was full of them.

We were so short of space in that house I often wonder why Dad didn't organise to have the press removed so we could open up the room. Perhaps, like the imposing sign on the façade of the building, it represented authority of some kind, for, regardless of their acceptance in Barellan, neither of my parents ever overcame totally a basic fear and distrust of those who could exercise power over them.

In my mother's case this fear of authority manifested itself in the Welfare bogey man of which I have already spoken: a terror of the knock on the door, which she managed to pass on to me at a very early age. For me I suppose it was a kind of game, albeit one that I knew verged on reality from the urgency of Mum's instruction to 'run and hide'. When Linda was growing up it was commonplace for Aboriginal children to be taken from their families and for the girls to be put 'into service', or if too young for that, to be kept in a holding pen such as Cootamundra Girls' Home.

Historian Peter Read has estimated that almost 6000 children were taken from their families between 1883 and 1969, either under the Aborigines Protection Act or under Child Welfare legislation. The effect on Aboriginal families was, of course, quite devastating. An organisation called Link-Up — which has been most helpful to me in my family search — was established in 1981 and has resurrected many family associations, but for every child who finds his or her family, 10 more will go through life not knowing what their heritage is, some not even knowing they are Aboriginal.

So my mother's fears were understandable, if a little illogical. Although assimilation was alive and well when I was growing up, the Goolagongs were unlikely candidates to be torn apart in the name of welfare. Also, it has to be remembered, my mother could neither read nor write, and although she was intelligent and perceptive, her fears were often exacerbated because of this terrible disadvantage in the white man's world.

My father's fears are more difficult to explain. He never spoke of his feelings, and only ever vented them after his Friday night celebration of the end of the working week in the bar of the Commercial Hotel. But I suspect he feared a loss of identity, a gradual erosion of his Aboriginal soul as he submitted to the will of his own ambition. In a way it was a double-bind. The Koori in Kenny told him that nothing was more important than family; the 'gubba' (Wiradjuri for white man) in him told him that for his family's sake he had to live like a white man. And underlying this conflict within himself, was the unconscious fear of his generation — that whatever he tried to accomplish, the white man would take away.

During those early days in Barellan Dad took us away whenever he could, to places where he could be himself. When the car was in working order and he had a free weekend, before he left for work on Friday morning he would order Mum to pack a few things and Barbara to supervise the preparation of the fishing kit.

There was a good, moist drain in the backyard and no shortage of earth-worms. After school Barbara and Larry would fill a Sunshine Powdered Milk tin with worms while I fashioned sinkers from lead Mum had liberated from the tip. Kenny would forego his session at the Commercial, come home early for a brief wash and we would load up the car and get away with the long southern dusk ahead of us.

On these fishing expeditions we would always go to the same place, a lovely sandy bend of the Murrumbidgee near Darlington Point, just a couple of kilometres from where Mum was born. By now there were five children, but Linda somehow managed to find a bed for us all inside the long-suffering family vehicle — babies on the floor, bigger kids top-to-toe on the seats. On warm nights Kenny would string a tarpaulin from the side of the car to a couple of sapling gums, and provide a cool sleeping shelter for Mum. He never slept at night on these excursions. His practice was to get us set up in our camp, then to head off down to the river to fish all night, usually returning at first light with a bag of Murray cod or yellowbelly which we would cook whole in the ashes and devour around the campfire.

As we got older we became more interested in fishing, but our main interest

Left: With baby Gail at our Darlington Point fishing camp, 1956 *Right:* Swimming in the irrigation canal at Three Ways, near Griffith

at the river was swimming and, while Dad rested from his labour of the night, we would push each other into the river and dive-bomb the unsuspecting as Mum watched from a shady spot high on the bank, always preoccupied with whatever craftwork she had in her hands.

I remember on one such occasion Larry and I were dangling our feet in the water, doing nothing in particular, while the smaller kids played further upriver. I felt something touch my leg and let out an involuntary scream. 'What is it?' Larry asked. Barbara appeared from behind us and pulled baby Gail from the water, shaking her noisily back into the land of the living.

'What's goin' on down there?' Linda called from the trees.

'Nothin', Mum,' Barbara lied. 'Gail's just got a tickle in her throat.'

On other weekends we would drive to the mission at Three Ways, near Griffith, where we could be with our people. It was in the irrigation canal at Three Ways that I learnt to swim, a fact that I recently found difficult to comprehend when I drove over the three-way bridge and looked down at the dark and mysterious water. Perhaps it looked more inviting all those years ago.

Three Ways mission in 1950

A couple of times a year we would make the longer trip to Condobolin, camping at The Murie with all the Goolagongs. I used to love these trips, partly because there was always music and excitement by the campfire, and partly because of the reunions with the tribe of kids I so seldom saw. Chief among these was my best friend in Condo, Nanny Goolagong. Nanny was my age and had the use of a horse, which she used to ride bareback along the riverbank. I've known her for almost 40 years but I didn't know until I sought out Nanny while researching this book that her real name was Lorraine.

We usually only made the pilgrimage to Condo for special occasions, like birthdays or Christmas. In fact we were on our way to The Murie the year I discovered there was no Santa Claus. Maybe that's a sad Christmas for many people, but my memories of it are filled with joy.

We'd left for Condo on the afternoon of Christmas Eve, the poor Chevrolet laden with gifts and Goolagongs. Dad's aim was to reach The Murie by nightfall, but the car started playing up and we had to make several stops. We were a long way short of Condo at dusk when the axle broke. There was no prospect of getting any repair work done that night and, in any case, we were on a back road and Dad was faced with a long walk. We had no alternative but to make our Christmas Eve camp by the side of the road.

Dad went to the boot to get out our camping gear and, still his ever-present shadow, I followed him. When he opened the trunk and shuffled the luggage I saw our stockings filled with gifts from Santa. I said nothing but immediately registered another of life's cruel realities.

Mum and Dad helped us tear paper into strips and we decorated a little scrubby tree. Then we sat around it on our tarpaulin and sang Christmas carols. 'Silent Night' was Mum's favourite so we sang that twice. I can't have been very old but I have a clear memory of drifting into sleep that night, my head in my father's lap, and catching a glimpse of both my parents, silhouetted in the moonlight.

They were a good-looking couple and they loved us. We might have been stuck on a backroad in western New South Wales on Christmas Eve, but we were the luckiest kids in the world.

Chapter 3

KENNY GOOLAGONG was my first and most enduring hero. I idolised him from the moment I first became aware of his presence, probably at the tea table in our little shack at Tarbogan.

As soon as I could crawl, I crawled after him wherever he went. And when finally I walked, much to the relief of my mother and my sister Barbara, I attached myself to Kenny's leg and walked wherever he walked.

My first recollections of my father are, I suppose, of a man in his mid-twenties; a fine-featured man of medium height and athlete's physique, who dressed immaculately and hid his thinning dark hair beneath a 'town' hat. Kenny loved to come home from work, scrub up and don the clothes he enjoyed wearing, the clothes that set him apart from the other men — classic black lace-up shoes, sports slacks, and a white shirt, open-necked and sleeves rolled to just above the elbow. If he was going to the pub, he would add the fedora and pop his packet of Log Cabin tobacco and Tally Ho papers into the shirt pocket. The tobacco and papers were an integral part of my father. As a small child I would sit with him while he taught me the fine art of rolling a smoke, laughing if I messed up.

If ever I need reminding of what Dad looked like — and now, almost 20 years since his death, just occasionally I do — I conjure up a recent picture of his younger brother Lylie, promenading along Bathurst Street, Condobolin, on his way to the TAB (the government-run betting agency). Lylie, now in his sixties, lost an arm breaking through a window to escape a house fire many years ago, but in every other way he is the image of Dad: the same jaunty air, roguish smile, quiet dignity and snappy sense of style. Around Condo, Lylie is known as 'Tappy', after a well-known race-caller, John Tapp, who affects a similar style of 'race day' dress.

If Kenny were alive today and promenading around Barellan, he would probably be known for his smart dress style as 'Beau Brummel' or something similar. When he arrived in the town in 1953, however, he was known simply as 'that blackfeller Frank Gladman's hired'.

No one who knew my father has a bad word to say about him. When

Left: Kenny Goolagong in 1953 *Right:* Lylie Goolagong in 1992

I have asked about him the same descriptions keep recurring: 'hard-working', 'honest', 'beautiful manners', a 'quiet, decent bloke', and yes, 'exceptionally clean'. The resulting picture seems a little bland, which my father wasn't. For there was another side to Kenny, which was both his making and his undoing, and even though I am a big girl now, people like to protect me from what they see as the unfortunate truth.

Kenny Goolagong had a larrikin (mischievous) streak about a metre wide. Dad liked a drink. Well, on occasion he liked a few drinks.

'He was a legend,' says his old shearing mate John Emerson. 'By Christ I've been kicked out of some good bars with Kenny.'

'He'd take a drink at the weekends,' tells family friend Clarrie Irvin, 'and sometimes he wouldn't be at his best first thing Monday, but in that he was no different from most of the workers in town.'

'He could be led astray by a few of the blokes around the town,' recalls Frank Gladman, his former boss. 'He was all right on the beer, but when they got him onto the plonk he'd go off. If we were away working and he got onto it, we'd come home the next day knocked up from having to listen to his nonsense all night. Kenny wouldn't be affected at all!'

Dad's agreement with Frank Gladman didn't exactly put us on easy street but it did improve our financial position and give us a degree of permanence Mum had never had. The Gladman team of three shearers regularly got through 500 head a day, and the going rate of one shilling and sixpence per sheep shorn should have resulted in Kenny taking home a wage considerably better than that of a farm labourer. But while the arrangement guaranteed Dad first call when there was shearing to be done, it didn't guarantee year-round work. And there were other factors.

According to Frank Gladman, the Goolagongs arrived in Barellan with a trail of debts stretching right around the Riverina. Although major loans to Aborigines (the very few that were made) had to be approved by the Aborigines Welfare Board, Kenny's neat and tidy appearance and natural charm had enabled him unwittingly to chalk up small slates throughout the district. Soon after our arrival in Barellan he asked Frank Gladman for a loan to get the creditors off his back.

'How much?' Mr Gladman asked.

'Not sure, boss.' Kenny produced a bulging envelope of unpaid bills. Gladman totted up the score and found that Dad owed more than 2000 pounds, more than a year's wages back in those days.

Frank Gladman rocked back in his chair on the other side of the desk in his contractor's office in a corner of the house. Eventually he said: 'I'll help you, Ken, but we have to do it my way. I'll loan you the money and take out of your wages what you can afford until you're squared up. But from here on in, I'll look after all the money for you.'

Without Frank Gladman's help my father may have ended up in gaol, the family may have become destitute and we children may have been taken away. Such scenarios were commonplace in the Aboriginal community at that time. Instead, Dad paid off his debts and worked for Mr Gladman for 15 years, at the end of which time he owned his own house. Sometimes we did it tough, but there was almost always food on the table and we never saw ourselves as poor people.

All of this I weigh up against the criticism of Frank Gladman I have heard, that his approach was too paternalistic, that my father was little better than his slave. I know that Frank Gladman came to love and respect my father, and, with his wife Jean, came to know and love all of the Goolagongs. And while I have reservations now about others taking too much control of the personal affairs of Aboriginal families, in our case there was probably no

Kenny at work, shearing for Frank Gladman

alternative, other than the horrific one I have mentioned.

Frank Gladman kept a book on Kenny's earnings and told him that all he had to do was ask how much he had. According to Mr Gladman, Dad asked one time and was told he had almost 100 pounds, aside from his living allowance and his repayments. 'He withdrew the lot and it was gone,' Frank Gladman recalls. 'I never volunteered his financial situation again.'

The Gladman shearing team worked the stations within about a 100-kilometre (60-mile) radius of Barellan. Mostly Frank Gladman picked his team up at first light and dropped them home each night, but when they worked the stations further out they often camped overnight.

On such occasions, station owner Clarrie Irvin points out, 'Kenny's conduct was exemplary. He would sit down to his meal and never say much, but he was known for never leaving the dinner table without thanking the station owner's wife. That was pretty rare in a shearer.'

Frank Gladman recalls a visit to one of these stations. 'We'd worked a long, hard day without a break, except for smoko (a tea-break). Our normal practice was to wash up in the homestead and then eat our tea down at the huts, but this evening the station owner came up to me as we knocked off and asked me to help fix up a wash basin at the huts. He said his wife would not have a dark bloke in the house. That was the only time I ever struck that kind of thing. I fixed up a basin and washed up with Ken down at the huts.'

Frank Gladman and Ken Goolagong became mates — good mates — but in the employer/employee relationship there was an invisible line that could not be crossed. Kenny crossed it once, and lived to regret it.

Leading up to the big shearers' strike of 1956 there was an increasing number of union agitators around the sheds, extolling the virtues of collective bargaining and grass-roots organisation to protect the rights of the working man. (Imagine what they would have thought had they discovered the full extent of Dad's 'contract' with Mr Gladman!) According to him, they got in Kenny's ear and when a group on a neighbouring station claimed the sheep were 'wet' and declared a 'cut-out' (a strike), Dad refused to shear.

Frank Gladman remembers: 'It had nothing to do with our situation but Ken had it through his head that he wasn't going to shear. I told him we were, and if he wasn't he could pack it in then and there. The whole lot! Ken stood his ground so that was it for me. I got the truck and backed it up to the *Barellan Leader* house and started loading the furniture. I told Linda I was taking them back to Tarbogan. She was upset but she calmed down and helped me load up.'

The loading was almost finished by the time word spread that the Goolagongs were being run out of town. One of our neighbours, Mrs Beryl Trembath, made haste down Bendee Street and gave Frank Gladman a verbal blast that echoed all the way from the Commercial Hotel to the school and back up the lane to the War Memorial Club. Mr Gladman did his best to ignore the abuse and went back into the house for another load. Beryl Trembath followed him inside and delivered a vicious uppercut to his jaw.

It was all too much for Linda. She cried, 'Oh my goodness! I wish I could jump up in the air and forget to come down.'

Left: Frank Gladman (left) with Kenny *Right:* Frank and Jean Gladman at home in Jimboomba, Queensland, in 1992

Protests notwithstanding, the Goolagongs and all their belongings went back to Tarbogan, setting up camp in the old shack as though the last few years had never happened. Mum wasn't speaking to Dad, and Dad wasn't speaking to anyone. It lasted about a week. Kenny phoned the Gladmans and Frank Gladman came out and helped us load up the truck again.

Strangely, Larry is the only one of us who remembers anything about this traumatic incident, which has become etched in Barellan folklore. I know it happened because I have heard three separate (and similar) accounts of it, but perhaps as smaller children we saw it as an adventure, rather like a holiday trip to The Murie. Barbara must have been with Grandma Agnes in Swan Hill, because she can remember nothing about it.

When he wasn't shearing Kenny took whatever work he could find. Sometimes there was none and we scratched by until child endowment allowance day. I can remember feeling so sorry for Dad one night. He came home and we had eaten the last of the food. He sat down at our linoleum-topped table and drank a mug of Vegemite and hot water. I can still see his expression now, not sad but slightly quizzical, as if there had to have been some dreadful mistake and a fresh pantry-load of food was on its way.

During these periods we lived more off the land than was our normal

season, and Larry and
would make delicious
 be paid for his labour
comings we loved, the
emoving the tripe and

got fill-in work in the
 mainly as a sweeper.
ped a routine by which
 40 winks in the course
as quick and thorough.
Wheat Board inspector
ed, but only until the
hey demanded Kenny's
tion to Kenny that he

old work mate at the
ny didn't file much —
th, it made me realise
how well liked he was wherever he went in the workplace. It read: 'Do you remember Bill Ellis, engine driver and operator of the machinery at Garoolgan Silos about 1955 when you were also on the job? Well, that's me, and I still have happy memories of our association. You would never let me carry a kerosene tin of water. Reckoned I was too old, I suppose, but you will be pleased to know that at 85 years I could still carry one.'

In the mid-1950s Kenny found another way to supplement his income — grave-digging. John Emerson, one of his mates from the pub and later a shearing companion, put him up to it. Mr Emerson, a big, loud, effervescent fellow, rolled into the Commercial Hotel one afternoon and found Kenny at the bar. 'Goolie, can you use a shovel? Charlie Olsen's being buried and there's no one to dig the hole.' Dad apparently began to protest but Emerson explained that Olsen was a Lutheran and that section of the cemetery had sandy soil, and besides, there was 20 pounds to be split.

They drove to the cemetery at the edge of town, where both Ken and Linda now rest, and quickly dug the hole. In the pub they waited out the funeral service, then returned and filled the grave in. John Emerson declared it wasn't the easiest 10 pounds he'd ever made, but it was a long way short of the hardest too. The two shearers became Barellan's unofficial grave-diggers.

John Emerson, who now lives in Canberra and is as loud and as affable as I remembered him in Barellan, was a great soulmate for my father and, as we grew up alongside the Emersons' six children, our two families became very close.

Mr Emerson's mother had been 'reared up by an ol' black gin'. He too had grown up alongside Aborigines at the Cow Shed Hill settlement outside Leeton, among them a branch of my mother's family, the Ingrams. He felt he understood Aborigines better than most white men, and in a way he identified more with them. 'I was a free thinker when I arrived in Barellan and the town was split down the middle between the Masons and the Tykes [Roman Catholics]. I didn't fit in too well at first.'

He and Kenny, however, got on like a house on fire. They were both periodically barred from the Commercial Hotel for bad behaviour and in 1955 John Emerson was banned for life from the War Memorial Club. How this happened illustrates the raucous nature of the shearing life. Mr Emerson remembers that: 'The manager of the club hated Kenny and me equally, so I was off to a bad start. Anyway, a shearing contractor named Digger Olsen walked past me in the club one day with a bottle of beer tucked under his arm. I tapped the bottle and told him I'd give him a hand to drink it. Well, Olsen turned on me and said he'd see me in the saleyard. That meant a blue [a fight]. I dropped the kids at home and my old dad heard about it and wanted a piece of the action, so I took him as my second. When we got to the yard Olsen had his father-in-law and another bloke, so it was three against two, but it didn't take long. Olsen was out like a light and I had to pull Dad off the old bloke before he killed him. The manager of the club reckoned I'd picked a fight and barred me.'

My father wasn't involved in this scrap and I would find it hard to believe he ever behaved like that, except for those few occasions when I saw him turn, in drink, into a person I neither knew nor liked. I always rationalised that it was the alcohol speaking, not my father, but at those times I felt only sorrow for him.

Ever since they introduced us to it 200 years ago, European Australians have claimed that Aborigines are physiologically unable to cope with alcohol. They might be right; certainly there is evidence throughout Aboriginal Australia that the two don't make a great mix. But I am inclined to believe that the problem is a cultural one. For too long the white man used alcohol as a tool of oppression, and now he is paying the price of the problems caused by Aboriginal alcohol abuse, problems that particularly in country towns can affect the whole community.

However there is also another side to this, one that I have noted particularly while travelling through the backblocks of Australia to research this book. It is that white men in the bush drink just as much as black men, but for one it is a time-honoured tradition, while for the other it is a social problem of great magnitude.

My father's drinking made him socially acceptable to the working men of Barellan, not the reverse, and when he stuck to beer he enjoyed the bonhomie of the bar, and was fine. On Friday nights Mum would prepare our supper and get a little tense as the evening wore on. Sometimes, when she could stand it no more, she would send Barbara up the road to drag him out of the pub. I would tag along, holding my big sister's hand as we marched through the still evening air, taking in the smells of everyone else's dinner.

The Commercial Hotel now seems to me one of the more ordinary examples of the old-style Australian pub, but back then it seemed an exciting, forbidden place. We would stand at the bat-wing doors waiting to be noticed, sniffing the pungent aroma of hops and watching the men of the town observing their secret rites — rites so bizarre that grown women, unless they were barmaids, were only allowed to glimpse the proceedings as they came up to the servery in the Ladies Lounge to order their lemon squashes or sherries.

'Bullshit, Kenny,' Mr Emerson might be saying, 'I'll lay you a fiver to a hidin' you'll never shear 200 of the bastards in a day.'

'My oath, I will,' Kenny would respond, raising himself up on his toes a little unsteadily to confront the bigger man. 'My bloody oath I will and I'll have your fiver framed on me wall!'

'Mum says you have to come home and have your supper.' Barbara would be able to contain herself no longer. The bar would fall silent momentarily as the other drinkers would recollect that they had families too, and Dad would collect his hat and bid the publican goodnight. Often the night air would have an intoxicating effect on him — or perhaps he just didn't seem so drunk in the company of other drunks — and he would weave along Boree Street, holding on to us for support. Then he would break into his signature tune: 'I got the bull by the tail and a downhill pull, and everything's gonna be fiiiine!'

Barbara and I would laugh at his silly song — we still do — and hold him upright while he attended to a call of nature. Kenny was a good man who worked hard to support his family, and if he hadn't earned the right to let his hair down a little on a Friday night, then who had?

Larry was also frequently called into service to rescue Dad from the pub. He remembers Kenny and John Emerson making him guide them home the long way and stopping in the back lane to drink more bottles of beer. He says now: 'I think they'd do it just to get me going. They'd pass me the bottle and then sit there giggling and smoking while I drank from it.'

As Larry got older and bigger his rescue missions to the pub became more dangerous, although he didn't know it at the time. 'I suppose I realised I'd become a man when I found out Dad would get into arguments in the pub when he was full and threaten fellers that he'd get his son on to them! It was a crazy, drunken threat, because I was gentle as a lamb until the grog got a hold of me, too.'

As Larry got older he and Kenny would leave us behind sometimes and head off to our Darlington Point camp for a 'boys' weekend'. Alcohol usually figured prominently, but Larry was always the responsible one, the one who carried Kenny up the riverbank to sleep it off under the tarpaulin. 'He was a dead weight too,' Larry says.

Barbara, Larry and I laugh now when we remember our father like that, but there are other memories, too, of nights when we would huddle in bed and hold hands while he thundered and ranted about the house in a drunken rage, blaming Linda for all his woes. Mum would give as good as she got and it sometimes seemed inevitable that the argument would become physical. Once or twice I can recall seeing Dad in this state raise his fist to hit Mum, and then hesitate, as though he were hoping someone would intervene, and Larry or Barbara would stand between them and we would all end up crying.

Sometimes Mum called the local policeman who would come and lock Dad up for the night to sleep it off. It was all forgotten the next day when he returned, although I suspect he felt sheepish and remorseful. But sometimes we would be woken up in the middle of the night with Mum's instruction to grab a blanket and run, Dad was on the rampage again.

I'm sure Linda didn't believe he meant us any harm, but she hated us to see Kenny like that, and she didn't want us to be frightened by the noise. So we would steal down the back lane and over to our hiding place at the football oval, there to wait out Cyclone Kenny.

If this paints my father as some kind of alcoholic monster, that's not how it was at all. John Emerson remembers only the good times with Kenny, the camaraderie of grog. 'When they chucked us out of the pub me and Kenny would share a bottle of twopenny dark in the gutter, and he'd tell me I was the whitest blackfeller he'd ever known. Then the next day we'd be working together, side by side at work and play. That was your father.'

I remember the other side as well, and it would be doing Kenny Goolagong an injustice in death to remember only part of the way he was in life. Besides, heroes are human too.

Before we leave the subject of alcohol, I have to admit that I sometimes wonder if grog played a role in Kenny's burning, the night in 1961 that my father became a 'human torch'. Alcohol has never been mentioned in conjunction with this near-tragic accident, but it always seemed to me to be too silly a thing to do sober!

Kenny had been shearing all weekend on a property out of town, and when he started to drive home around midnight he realised he was almost out of petrol. Fortunately he ran out not far from a property owned by Sam Taylor, a man he knew. Dad woke up the Taylors and Sam poured some fuel into an open drum for him. Kenny hoisted the drum onto his shoulder the way the garbage men used to, and set off down the driveway. By the time he got to the car he had sloshed petrol all over his shirt, but he was too tired to care. He poured the fuel into the tank — then rolled a cigarette for the walk back up to Taylor's shed. He struck a match and whoof!

SHEARER BECAME A HUMAN TORCH AT SANDY CREEK was the headline in the Griffith newspaper, and for once it was pretty apt. Sam Taylor heard Dad's cries and raced to help him tear his burning clothes off. Then he rushed him to the little hospital at Barellan. Kenny was in a bad way, suffering from third degree burns all over his neck and under his arms, and he was taken by ambulance to Griffith Hospital where he was admitted in a critical condition.

I remember going to see him very soon after it happened. I had been fretting for him and Mum decided, against her better judgment, that I would have to see that he was alive. I saw he was alive, but the smell of his burnt flesh was just dreadful.

Dad had been very lucky, but he was badly scarred nonetheless. He couldn't lift his arms above his head for more than a year afterwards and he took to wearing a tie to cover up the scars around his neck. Worse, from the point of view of our immediate future, was the fact that he couldn't work for three months. Mum had no alternative but to take Barbara out of school immediately — she was just finishing her second year of high school — and send her to work to support the family.

That was the beginning and the end of many things for Barbara — it may have even been the beginning of the end of a promising career in tennis, a sport we had only just taken up. I don't know what Dad made of the whole thing because he rarely spoke of his night of terror. He didn't smoke any less either, but he was more selective about where he lit up.

Chapter 4

*I*T IS DIFFICULT TO IMAGINE my mother marrying a man more different in character to herself. Kenny was quiet, reserved, diligent, and given to binge drinking. Melinda Goolagong was cheerful, bubbly, noisy, energetic, resourceful and sober in her habits. (Mum never smoked and the only drink I ever knew her to have was a pina colada we tricked her into during her trip to Europe after our daughter's birth in 1977. She got quite giggly.)

I suppose they shared the 'problem' of being Aboriginal in the time of assimilation, but the marriage was built upon a much more solid foundation than just that. Linda was still 17 and Kenny 20 when Barbara was born, and childbirth dominated her life for the next 15 years as she had eight children and two miscarriages. With a baby at the breast and at least one tugging at her skirts, Linda watched her youth slip away all too soon. Her slim, girlish figure became matronly, her breasts sagged under the weight of our hungry lips and her health disintegrated. She developed high blood pressure and became arthritic. But she never lost her wonderful spirit, nor her gorgeous mane of jet-black hair.

I can picture her now in a floral-printed cotton dress and thongs (flip-flops) (you could hear her coming from a mile away, which was sometimes useful for us), wetting her forefinger on her tongue and wiping a smudge from my face before sending me off to school. Her face didn't seem to age. It was unlined and she had beautiful bushy eyebrows which she plucked in a rare concession to vanity. She wore no make-up except a little rouge and lipstick for special occasions, such as church.

Linda was brought up by the Briggs family as a Christian, but I don't think they were fussy about what brand of Christianity it was, and nor was Mum. She used to say, 'There's only one God, so what does it matter which church you go to?' She sent us to the Church of England Sunday School but she shared herself liberally around all of the town's church services, even the Catholic mass, generally choosing the religion by the quality of the singing.

Every so often we'd all head off to church on a Sunday morning. Dad would be up early, polishing our shoes, and we would all put on our 'Sunday best' and walk down the street together, greeting the neighbours as we went. When I picture scenes like that I'm put in mind of those American situation comedies of the 1950s — shows like 'Father Knows Best' — where everyone and everything is painfully 'nice'. Well, that's the way it was in Barellan. Maybe as soon as we turned the corner our neighbours would curse us, but if they did I was never aware of it, and if my mother ever felt that she didn't belong in a white town, then her pride never let her show it.

Linda's life in Barellan was not easy but it was very simple. She had babies, cleaned the house and put the meals on the table for us. There was room for little else, although as Barbara got older she helped look after the babies. But the babies kept coming!

Mum had Barbara in 1947, Larry in 1949, me in 1951, Kevin in 1953, Gail in 1954, Janelle in 1959, then Ian in 1960 and Martin in 1963. The two youngest were just babies when I left home permanently at 14, but in those early years in Barellan the family was big enough to constitute a problem fitting into a car or around a dining table, not to mention the awesome financial responsibility our sheer numbers must have placed upon my father.

Dad was away a lot during the week, so the household chores fell to us as soon as we were old enough to handle them. Being the eldest, Barbara worked the hardest and probably suffered the most. If anything went wrong Barbara was the one 'old enough to be responsible'. But we had time for fun, too.

Mum played the guitar and sometimes she'd pull it out and strum while she sang the old country favourites or her beloved hymns. On hot summer nights she'd soak a towel in cold water and lie across the end of our bed and sing 'You Are My Sunshine' while she fanned a cooling breeze over us.

When our family finances allowed it we sometimes had a treat after tea. Kenny would dig into his pocket for a few shillings and a couple of us would be sent up to Tony's Vienna Cafe for ice-creams. I can remember on those warm summer evenings running all the way home to get there before the ice-cream started to melt, then sitting in the lounge room, dripping ice-cream on the couch while we listened to the serials on the wireless. When television started in Australia in 1956, Tony's was the first place in Barellan to have one, and after tea we'd wander up the road for our ice-creams, and eat them while we sat and gazed in awe at 'The Cisco Kid' or 'I Love Lucy'.

Of course it wasn't too long before we had our own television. I don't know how Dad worked the finances with Mr Gladman — maybe by the late 1950s we had paid off all our debts — but I can recall him proudly announcing that a set was about to be delivered. I can also remember us scrabbling about on the floor trying to tune it in. Initially we all watched almost every hour of transmission, but in time normal life resumed. Dad liked to watch the limited sporting coverage at the weekends, but Mum never became a couch potato. She had too little leisure time as it was, and what she could steal she applied to her creative pursuits.

I have mentioned our trips to the rubbish tip at the edge of town, and often when I talk about this, people laugh a little too eagerly. I suppose to many people it is kind of amusing, this Aboriginal woman trailing a vast tribe of kids across a landscape of broken bottles and rubble. To me it is one of the most cherished memories I have of my mother, because it speaks so vividly of her inventiveness, of her indomitable spirit. Linda was a recycler all her life. She travelled the world and mixed with people of all walks of life, but if she were alive and you visited her in Barellan today, she would probably take you on an expedition to the tip. I get quite emotional these days when I go back to her house, where my sister Janelle now lives, and look at the mobiles and wall-hangings, made from other people's rubbish, that hang amongst the family memorabilia. I can almost hear Linda saying: 'What do you want chuck that out for? We can use that!'

When we had money Mum liked to catch the train into Griffith on a Saturday and do 'a real shop'. A real shop meant buying all the delicacies you couldn't get at our fairly basic stores in Barellan. It also meant chatting for hours with all our family and friends from the Three Ways (we all called it 'Freeways') mission. We'd get up early and catch the old steam train to town, then spend all morning wandering up and down the shopping centre. Sometimes we'd run into Aborigines from the mission who'd been drinking, and they'd ask Linda for 'two bob' (about 20 cents). Mum was never judgmental about this, although it was behaviour far removed from her own. She would just laugh and say, 'Oh get away, you don't need my two bob, bud.'

We would be left for hours playing in the park that ran (and still runs) along the middle of the main street. When it was time to catch the train home Mum would come to fetch us and, if no one was looking, pull up a few plants by the roots and pop them into her bag for replanting at home.

As in most country towns, the biggest event of the year in Barellan was the 'show', a cross between an agricultural exposition and a country fair, with a bit of carnival thrown in. We girls always had a special dress for the occasion and we would go along with the rest of the town to marvel at the Scottish dancing, the wood chopping and the cake display, and to make ourselves sick on fairy floss and toffee apples.

There were many competitions run in conjunction with the show, and one

Me (left) with Larry and Barbara in the Griffith park while Mum does the shopping

year Mum entered Gail in the baby show. I can remember going along to the final judging in the town hall. All the mothers stood in a line on the stage, holding their pride and joy. The judges conferred and then announced that Gail Goolagong was the winner. The head judge approached Mum to present a cup. Linda was overcome with a volatile mixture of emotions — perhaps fear was one. She started to bawl and fled from the stage with Gail while the judges looked quizzically after her.

But Gail wasn't the only one to grace the stage of the town hall at an early age. In 1956 Mrs Lucy Smith, who ran the general store in Barellan with her husband Stan, organised a children's fashion parade to raise funds for the hospital. She wanted me to model one of the outfits from her shop. Mrs Smith, who came to Barellan in 1910 at the age of one, still lives in the same house across the other side of the tennis courts, and she still has vivid memories of the fashion parade. 'You were a timid little thing, but I knew you'd look lovely in the frock I had in mind so I asked your mother if she'd mind. I think Mrs Goolagong was secretly thrilled, but she said that you didn't have any white socks to wear. I told her I thought we could fix that. You made a lovely little model and we raised 110 pounds for the hospital.'

In her neat cottage in Barellan in the spring of 1992, Mrs Smith rummaged around for a few minutes and came out with the program for the parade, the yellowing paper folded neatly inside a novel. It read: 'Yvonne Gooligong.

Small girl frock of polished piqué made from a Kostoris fashion fabric. Finished with lace trimmed bib front and little black bow. Of special interest to mothers because it keeps its fresh look and requires no starching.'

Mum was always taking in animals, despite the fact that we had no room and barely enough money to feed ourselves. But she was a sucker for a lame dog, or a bird with a damaged wing, or a rabbit that had been caught in a trap. She told us: 'It doesn't matter. If you see an animal that needs help, you bring it home.' So in addition to our permanent dog, Spider, and our pet cockatoo, the *Barellan Leader* house was usually home to a dozen or so itinerant dogs and cats, rabbits, goats and sheep.

Spider was around for most of my childhood — when I came home from Sydney one time I found that he'd been buried in the backyard — and we had the same cockatoo for many years. This cockie used to wake us up by mimicking Mum's calls, and then would follow us to school regularly.

We were all kids with independent spirits, but we were close enough in age to stick together, to look after each other and to play together. We even performed community service together, taking a picnic lunch across the fields to the cemetery, where we would first clean up the untended grave sites before sitting down on the tombstones to eat.

Our playing often involved bringing home the evening meal. We were great shots with a 'bundi', the root of a mallee tree used as a club. We would take Spider and our stray dogs out into the fields to sniff out rabbits. When we got close enough we would let fly with our bundis. We usually went home with a rabbit for Mum's stew.

We sometimes chased goannas up trees and fetched witchetty grubs to vary our bush tucker diet, but our favourite delight was the yabbie. The dams and creeks around Barellan seemed to be full of these freshwater crustaceans. Our method of catching them was to tie a piece of meat to a length of cotton, throw it into the water and slowly pull it towards the bank. When the yabbie appeared we would flick it onto the grass, then into a kerosene tin filled with water to keep them alive until suppertime.

We would wander for kilometre after kilometre across the plains and wheat fields, looking for mischief. Once we were a long way from home picking mushrooms. On the way home Larry got bored and started flicking lit matches into the tinderbox-dry wheat fields as we walked. He flicked one match too many and a gust of wind took hold of the flame and set a fire raging across the field. We girls panicked and started screaming. Larry, being of a more practical, if foolhardy bent, took off his pullover and started beating out the flames with it, finishing off the job by rolling around in the embers.

Larry, his mates and his slug gun. Early 1950s

Larry singed his hair and eyebrows and ruined his clothes, and had a lot of explaining to do. But, he assures me, it was not the calamity I had registered it to be. In my memory we had almost wiped out the entire Barellan wheat crop. 'Nah,' Larry says, 'about half a tennis court.'

On another of our wanderings Larry took along his newly-acquired slug gun (air-rifle) to shoot birds. According to Larry: 'Barbara was acting up and wouldn't carry the dead birds, so I shot her in the back of the neck.' In Larry's defence, I will say that this is not as diabolical as it sounds. Barbara had hurried on ahead in a huff. Larry and I were a long way behind and Larry didn't think the slug would carry. But it did. It deposited itself in Barbara's neck and she ran screaming across the fields towards home. Frightened of the consequences — from Mum, not Dad, who seldom raised the strap — Larry 'went bush' and hid. He returned to our house, contrite and ready to face his belting, many hours later.

By far the grandest adventure Barellan had to offer us was the exploration of the internal labyrinth of the wheat silos. This was what we did when we wanted to be really bad: we sneaked in through the trapdoor of the 30-metre-high (100-foot) silo and dodged the rats and the puddles all the way to the end of the tunnel, then climbed the ladders to the very top of the vast, sky-lit bin. There we would plank-walk 7 or 8 metres (23 or 26 feet) across the tops of the bins, yahooing and trying to catch the pigeons trapped beneath the skylights. When you crossed an empty bin, the idea was never to look down into the 30-metre (100-foot) abyss. Larry tells me now that sometimes he would have to find an iron bar in the railyards and break the padlock on the trapdoor to get in. I must say I don't remember that, but if it is true it is perhaps an indication of the dangers that lurked within. Larry also recalls that one day the grim shadow of the caretaker blocked the light as we made our way back to the trapdoor. We ran back into the silo and made a lot of noise. When the caretaker moved around the outside of the building to check, we made our escape. Of course he knew who we were, but it was far better to face the music another day when tempers had cooled.

Barbara loved school but only went when Mum didn't need her help. Larry hated it and bawled and howled but was sent every day. Kevin put up with it, as long as he could come home at lunchtime to suck on a baby's bottle. I was the lucky one. I liked school and I went every day. But in the beginning I was scared, which is not terribly surprising, because I was scared of just about everything to do with people. ('Run and hide! It's the Welfare man.')

Years later, when I was playing tennis in Sydney a man came up to me after a match and introduced himself as Mr Hurst, a teacher I'd had in my first years at school in Barellan. He said, 'I can't believe this is the same person. I used to have to come up behind you in class because if you saw me coming towards you, you'd start to tremble.'

Barellan Central School was quite small — perhaps 150 students — but it was a neat, cared-for little school. Once I settled into the routine I enjoyed it. Getting there was the problem. When I started school in 1956 there were five of us under 10 years old. Our house was pandemonium every morning. Barbara did her best to help — and was always late as a result — but we would often have to ask permission to come home (about 300 metres or 327 yards) for things we had forgotten.

One day I realised I'd forgotten something but there was no way I was going to put my hand up and ask the teacher if I could go and get them. At recess, however, Mum stood at the school gates waving my knickers in the air. 'Evonne, you forgot these!' I had never been as embarrassed as I was, walking across the school yard to take public receipt of my underclothes.

Almost from the moment I could walk I had shown an athletic inclination, but at school for the first time my abilities were directed, although not to where they would eventually shine. In the yard at lunch time I was the champion rope jumper, and at my first athletics carnival I won the long jump, hop, step and jump and the 100-yard (91-metre) dash to take out the individual championship. I suppose that was my first taste of winning. I can remember being very impressed with the pennant.

But by this time athleticism was nothing more than was expected of a Goolagong. Both Barbara and Larry had already started to excel at whatever sports they played. Larry loved rugby league, and at the Riverina schoolboys carnival he was judged to be the player to watch in the four-stone-seven (28 kilogram) division. The newspaper report, which Linda clipped and pasted into her book of baby names, noted, 'Larry Goolagong, a coloured midget from Barellan, was tipped by good judges as a rugby league star of the future.'

I became a shocking tomboy and spent all my time outside the classroom trying to prove that I could beat the boys at any game they chose. Unfortunately for their developing male egos, I could. I could do better cartwheels, longer handstands and — shades of Jimmy Goolagong — more dramatic somersaults. I was small but strong, and my size must have been deceptive because they kept letting me play in the apparent belief that I was just on a lucky streak.

Playing softball I pitched unplayable curve balls and broke a bat once, such was the power of my hitting. At cricket the boys could never get me out and I would have to be talked into retiring so someone else could have a turn. I must have been unbearable, because it never occurred to me that I had a gift for any of this, that maybe I should ease up for the sake of the game. Running, jumping, belting balls … these were simply the things I loved to do. Perhaps the boys got their own back in the classroom, watching me tremble as the teacher approached, hoping against hope that no one would ask me to say or do anything.

I was not silly. I was actually quite good at my lessons, once I overcame my fear of that authoritarian figure, the teacher. But it would not have taken an Einstein to work out that perhaps my future lay in athletic pursuits. Nevertheless, in those early years of school none of my teachers actively encouraged me to concentrate on a single sport, and I certainly wasn't going to choose one game over another, for that was all they were — games.

In 1956, my first year of schooling — when I was whipping the boys by day and wetting the bed by night — Australia was hosting its first Olympiad, the Melbourne Games. Australia was sports mad, and crazy for its Olympic heroes Dawn Fraser and Betty Cuthbert.

Our family, too, was swept up in the excitement of this momentous sporting event taking place, as the television commentators kept telling us, in our own backyard. So swept up were the Goolagongs, in fact, that for a time we didn't notice the momentous event that had begun to take place just beyond our outside toilet. Across the laneway the men of the town were pegging out an area that looked big enough to hold … well, a tennis court.

$\mathcal{C} \, h \, a \, p$

$\mathcal{G}$ RAZIER BILL KURTZMAN had played some te
the game with a passion. It was more than a
training ground for life itself. Master the disciplines of st
and you have mastered the knack of putting order and
life. And, more so than in other sports, the environment s
was constructive to good citizenship, a quality he valued — a
of his generation did — higher than most.

This was why he was very interested in the proposal to resurface
courts at the North Barellan Tennis Club, an active little club a few
out of the main town, which suffered from the quality of its three cou
In Barellan itself there were courts at the Catholic school but they too wer
in disrepair. Yet there were good players in the district, like Jack Wade and
Stan Smith, who had played at White City. Bill Kurtzman talked the matter
over with his close friend Reuben Irvin and the two men, both graziers, decided
to help bankroll the project if it had the support of the tennis club committee.

Bill Kurtzman then went to Melbourne to investigate the costs of various
types of surfacing. The financial news was good, but when he got back to
Barellan he found that there was a distinct apathy within the committee of
the North Barellan club. Maybe they thought the fund-raising would be too
much like hard work? Bill Kurtzman, who despised apathy as much as he
revered citizenship, pocketed his cheque book and moved on.

But he had never been a quitter, and now that he had time on his hands
he decided to mount a campaign. He had just turned 60 but he had put in
long, hard years building up his farm and he looked considerably older. His
face was gnarled like the roots of an old tree and he walked with a limp,
the result of a farming accident. Childless, he and his wife Priscilla had recently
put on a share farmer to lessen their workload, and they had taken a little
place in town. So it was to downtown Barellan, the bustling hub of the CBD,
that Bill Kurtzman looked next for his tennis court project.

The War Memorial Club in Bendee Street had some land adjoining the
access lane behind it, and Bill Kurtzman figured that at the rate at which

ave no problem
club under its
machines were
Vales. Once he
was interested,
rt a committee
War Memorial

— a remote
isted entirely
'posh' accent
estruction of
(the White
years, during
ip to believe
n Canberra

ttle part of
stations for
to become
half-castes'

...ow this was determined by people
...ately no knowledge of our complex family tree is beyond me, but
they did, and I suppose we were meant to take it as a compliment. And maybe
we did.

The relative isolation of country towns in those days made it possible to
turn a blind eye to almost everything that occurred beyond our small sphere
of influence ... except sport, of course, which was of paramount importance.
In that Australia was entering a golden age, not just in tennis but in cricket,
athletics, swimming, you name it. And the Melbourne Olympic Games was
just around the corner. Australia was sports mad, so was it any wonder that
Mr Kurtzman was deluged with offers of help to make the War Memorial
Tennis Club a reality? Between Bill Kurtzman, Reuben Irvin, the licensed club
and the donations of the townsfolk, there was enough money to build four
red loam courts, provided that the labour was volunteered. Reuben Irvin's son
Clarrie, one of the best players from the North Barellan club, remembers
being involved in bringing the dirt for the base of the courts from the edge
of town. 'I was on the scoop, loading the trucks. But everyone helped in
whatever way they could. It was a real community effort and it was a great

credit to Bill Kurtzman, because he organised it.'

When the courts and the modest little clubhouse were completed in 1956 the entire town turned out for the opening ceremony and the tournament that followed. (Except possibly me. If I was there I don't remember a thing about it.) Mrs Lucy Smith from the general store was there with her husband Stan, and she remembers it as 'a really marvellous turnout. You see, if you don't go to everything in a country town, you don't do anything. And I souvenired a couple of the balls used in the tournament.'

If I registered anything about the construction of the War Memorial Tennis Courts it was that there was a red-brick wall going up so close to our backyard that I could count the bricks in it, and it looked ideal for my obsession. For by then I had moved on from squeezing tennis balls for security as we drove along in the family car, and had become an obsessive wall hitter.

Barbara says Larry started it, back at the shack in Tarbogan. He took one of my balls from the back of the car and started hitting it against a wall with a stick. Barbara soon joined in the fun and Kenny, seeing them amused, fashioned a racquet from the side of a fruit crate, carving a rough handle out of the box wood. It might just as easily have been a cricket bat, but it was a tennis racquet.

Barbara recalls: 'You watched us the first couple of times, bouncing the ball off the wall and hitting it back, and you were fascinated. I think it opened up a whole new world of possibilities to you. Not only could you squeeze it, you could whack it! You were only tiny but you gave it a go. After that we could never get the racket away from you. Later, when we moved to Barellan, you would take off by yourself with the racquet and hit the ball against the chimney. If you couldn't find the racket you'd use a broomstick.'

From the chimney I progressed to the wall of the old butcher shop two blocks away, and finally to the practice wall the club built on the other side of the courts. Before the completion of the Barellan tennis courts I had never actually seen tennis played, unless it was a glimpse of one of our Davis Cup triumphs on the Cinesound Newsreel at the cinema. The game I played was of my own invention and paid scant attention to the rules of lawn tennis.

But all that was about to change. In the early part of 1956 — well before my fifth birthday — Mum bought me a little wooden racquet at the toy shop in Griffith. I remember this distinctly because it was so unlike Linda to single out a child for special attention, other than for a birthday. She was always scrupulously fair with special treats. But she had seen me hitting balls against the wall for long enough to know that this was more than a passing phase. If I knew nothing about tennis, she and Kenny knew even less, but I suppose they figured it kept me amused.

Soon after I got that racquet I competed in an athletics carnival where there were cash prizes! (I hope the amateur athletics people can't prosecute retrospectively.) Sixpence for this race, threepence for that jump, and so on. I competed in everything and won ten bob (about a dollar), which was a fortune to me. I must have been exhausted but I ran all the way home in excitement and then calmed myself down by hitting balls against the wall for several hours.

The toy racquet didn't last long. I can't remember if I wore holes in it or if it succumbed from too much use as a weapon, but it didn't matter because the courts were operating now, and racquets were coming out of attics and trunks all over town.

Mr Kurtzman was elected president of the War Memorial Tennis Club and he hired an old fellow, Ned Emerson, as caretaker. Old Ned's son, John Emerson, was that good friend of Kenny's, and *his* son Jack was in our gang, so when no one was playing we pretty much had the run of the courts. I used to love to walk behind Old Ned when he sprayed the line markings. He did such a perfect job, so precise. Mum admired his work, too, and in return Old Ned gave her supplies to white-wash the walls of our house. Mum didn't know much about tennis, but white was something she revered.

Barbara and Larry, by this time getting quite grown up, were the first to actually borrow the net from the War Memorial Club lock-up and attempt a real game of tennis. Soon the three of us were borrowing racquets from the neighbours — Mr Dunlop next door was particularly generous with his — and even baby Kevin would try to join in. We must have been hopelessly inept but it was great fun, and I loved everything about tennis: the grit of the court beneath my bare feet (but not in the scorching midday sun), the swing of the racquet, the thwack of rubber on gut, the thrill of hitting a ball perfectly — or what I thought was perfectly!

On summer nights with the townsfolk playing their social mixed doubles under lights, I would dawdle back from the toilet, taking in the rituals of the game: the giggles of the wives as they muffed their shots, the thundering calls of 'Mine!' as their husbands dashed across court chasing down a lob that was easy work for their partner, and the softer call of 'Dash it!' when the return ploughed into the net. I'm sure many people who discover they are destined to be athletes before they know what kind, go through a period of revelation, not necessarily sudden, when they realise instinctively that this is their game, that this could become their way of life. I think I realised that those first couple of summers in Barellan when the War Memorial Tennis Club became my playground.

Barbara joined the club in 1957 when she was 10, and Larry the following year, and they started playing in club tournaments. It was more than I could bear to watch them head off across the lane in their pressed whites. Sometimes I would watch them play — wanting them to win, but at the same time wanting one of them to fall down lame so that I would be called upon to rescue the Goolagong honour — but more often I would turn my back on the courts and hit against the practice wall the entire day. Forehand, backhand, thwack, thwack. I would count how many times I could hit the ball on the first bounce and etch the number deep in the red dirt with a stick, determined to better it the next day. This was my own little tournament, my own little world. On hot days my bare feet would burn in the red dirt and I would have to take time out to run across to the tap on the tennis club lawn to soak them — and sometimes not just my feet but all of me!

I had no idea at the time, but my wall-hitting was being watched by a number of interested townsfolk who had seen that I was developing the ability to hit the ball cleanly every time, and place it exactly where I wanted it. One of these observers was Stan Smith from the general store, whose house was directly opposite the practice wall. Mr Smith's playing days were behind him, but he had been the best men's singles player in Barellan until the war, and before that he had been the best junior player in Grenfell, a town to the north. He had even gone to White City to represent the district.

Mr Smith prided himself in his knowledge of the game and was regarded as a good judge of a player. He quietly pulled a garden chair into a corner of his yard where he could watch me unobtrusively. 'He used to sit there for hours upon hours,' Mrs Lucy Smith told me recently. 'He was interested in your development as a player, of course, but mostly he just loved to watch grace in tennis, and he believed you had it.'

Word must have filtered back to my parents that I was developing some talent, because one day as Barbara and Larry went off to play, Linda said, 'Take Evonne with you.'

'No Mum, she's too little.'

'Take her anyway, let her have a go.'

'She's too little. They won't let her play.'

Mum smiled. 'I reckon they might.'

Barbara and I played doubles together and won convincingly. Aged only seven, I was given special dispensation to join the club — sort of like a Certificate of Exemption, but for age rather than colour.

Having established the War Memorial Tennis Club, Bill Kurtzman started to look for a coaching program to induct new blood into the club. Senior players like Jack and Albert Wade and Clarrie Irvin ensured that Barellan was well represented in district competion, but youngsters like the Goolagongs and Pam Jackson (who later beat me in the final of the first tournament I played in Barellan) needed the encouragement of a concerted coaching effort, he felt. The little Barellan club could not hope to employ a full-time coach, but in those days country towns were often serviced by visiting coaches who conducted clinics during school holidays.

Mr Kurtzman contacted Bill Williams, a successful coach from Wagga who at the time had a young protégé from Tarcutta, near Wagga Wagga, named Tony Roche, who looked promising. Williams agreed to conduct Barellan's first coaching clinic during the August school holidays in 1960. There were a limited number of vacancies and I was considered too young, but Barbara enrolled and apparently impressed Williams with her range of strokeplay and powerful hitting.

The following year, however, Bill Kurtzman decided to take the coaching clinic a step further. He made an approach to the Victor A. Edwards Tennis School (VAETS) based in the northern Sydney suburb of Roseville, and acknowledged as the finest coaching school in Australia at the time and one with a special interest in bush clinics.

Victor Edwards' father, Herbert, had been a tennis coach in London (where Victor had been born in 1909) and later in the Netherlands. Herbert Edwards had also worked from time to time as a consultant engineer on the construction of tennis courts and playing fields, and it was in this capacity that he had come to Australia in the early 1920s. He had won a commission to design the White City courts in Sydney, but somehow the job went to someone else and Herbert had found himself coaching tennis in Sydney. He had done well as there were no other professional coaches in the city, and in 1925 the Edwards family had bought a large home in Roseville and established a tennis coaching school there. After the death of old Mr Edwards, this became VAETS, an almost military-like establishment devoted to the method of mass instruction, known as 'The Drill', pioneered by Herbert and perfected by Victor.

Although it had many critics, the VAETS mass instruction technique, based on highly-disciplined and endless repetition of footwork and strokeplay, was a major breakthrough in Australian tennis, teaching the rudiments of the game to thousands of children, while at the same time giving would-be champions a solid foundation of correct play on which they could build. Until you had mastered The Drill, you didn't even get to hit balls! VAETS also broke new

A young Mr Edwards leads the Drill at VAETS, early 1950s

ground in the way Victor Edwards, who as a young man had worked in the bush as a jackaroo, was prepared to take his techniques to the country centres.

From the early 1950s VAETS established a network through country towns in New South Wales to which Mr Edwards would send coaches to conduct clinics in the May and August school holidays. The requirement of the local organisers was that they sign up no fewer than 80 students for the week-long course. At one such clinic in Grenfell Vic Edwards discovered a talented youngster called Jan Lehane. Seeing her potential, he put to her parents the proposition that Jan be allowed to go to Sydney for intensive training while living with the Edwards family in Roseville. Jan did just that, growing up with the Edwards girls and attending school with them; by 1960 she had become the number one female player in Australia.

So when Bill Kurtzman phoned VAETS in early 1961 and suggested that Barellan be considered for a clinic, he got a sympathetic hearing from Vic Edwards, who agreed to detour through the town on his next bush trip and talk to Mr Kurtzman. Apparently he was as good as his word, and in a matter of weeks met Bill Kurtzman at the War Memorial Club, where Vic Edwards told him he would need to enrol a minimum of 80 students at four pounds (eight dollars) a head. Kurtzman said he was sure he would have no trouble getting that many starters from the surrounding district, and the two men agreed to stage the first VAETS clinic in August 1961.

Bill Kurtzman took an instant liking to Vic Edwards: the military bearing, the no-nonsense man-to-man talk, the rather dashing figure he cut with his clipped moustache and ever-present cigarette. For his part, Vic Edwards was impressed with our little town. He liked the War Memorial tennis courts, the tidy streets with their neat, well-tended houses, and he liked Bill Kurtzman's honest country manner. But when he drove off towards Sydney I doubt that Vic Edwards gave Barellan another thought until he read about me in his instructors' report more than six months later.

Throughout the early part of 1961 I tagged along to the tennis club with Barbara and Larry, playing with a borrowed racquet whenever I could, sometimes just watching. Most of the time there was no shortage of racquets. Mr Dunlop next door frequently loaned me his, or Mr Smith would offer me his, and finally Mrs Jean Gladman, the wife of my father's boss, loaned me hers more or less permanently. Well, I don't know that it was a permanent loan but it became so.

My sister Janelle was just a baby and she picked up Mrs Gladman's racquet when I left it on the lounge after a game one day. Mum found her prodding the fire with it, the head blackened and the smell of burning gut heavy in the air. I bawled my eyes out when I came home from school and discovered what had happened, for it had become my favourite racquet. Mum was usually the disciplinarian in our house, but in this instance I felt Kenny's wrath. The cost of the racket would come out of his wages, he assured me, and I believed it for more than 30 years, until Frank Gladman told me otherwise.

It was also in 1961 that our family received its first media attention, and the misspelling of my name — something which still persists and annoys me just a little — was established. The local paper in Narrandera recorded in 'Town Tennis Club Notes', by 'Unorthodox' that we had played in a tournament. 'Without doubt,' wrote Unorthodox, 'the most crowd-pleasing players were the Goolagong children, Barbara, Yvonne and Lance (tiny tots) playing with the skill of adults and getting all the fun in the world from their tennis.'

I don't know how Larry felt about becoming 'Lance', but I'm sure I was prepared to overlook becoming 'Yvonne', given the enormity of this first brush with fame. Certainly these minor inaccuracies were of no concern to my mother. After Barbara read the column to her she carefully pasted the clipping into a scrapbook.

Just before the August school holidays that year Bill Kurtzman came to our house one evening and told my parents that the tennis club wanted all three of the tennis-playing Goolagong children to attend the VAETS coaching clinic. The club would pay our fees. I was absolutely thrilled, not just for the opportunity to take some real lessons, but because the club had bent the rules and allowed a 10-year-old (and only just 10 at that!) to participate.

Mum gave our tennis whites an extra turn in the copper and had us looking spick and span for the big day, when we shyly crossed the lane to join the 80 or so other kids from around the district. At precisely 8 a.m. the coaching clinic began and we formed a parade in front of the VAETS instructors, Faith Martin and Colin Swan.

Faith Martin was probably about 30 then, but she had an ageless, timeless look that could have placed her in any age group, in any era. Colin Swan, a few years younger, was a stocky fellow with black hair going prematurely grey, and with a real sparkle in his eye. I can't remember my exact feelings on being introduced to our coaches but, given my fear of anyone in authority, I imagine I was scared stiff. The day's proceedings began with an inspection of our tennis whites — part of Vic Edwards' military approach — and heaven help any child with scuffed shoes or dirty shorts. We passed muster by a fairly safe margin, thanks to Linda's diligence over the copper.

As much as I'm sure I would have been intimidated by the prospect of being corrected in front of 80 of my peers for having scuffed shoes, or being sent to run around the courts 10 times for not paying attention during The Drill, I actually cared enough about the game at that tender age to welcome

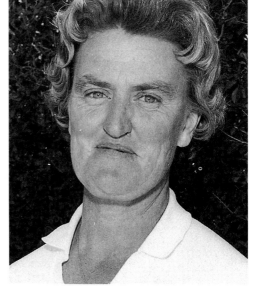

Colin Swan and Faith Martin, circa 1962

any kind of instruction. For the first time in my life I wanted to learn, and Faith and Colin must have responded to that because they seemed to like me.

Faith Martin now recalls: 'You meant business. You wanted to be a tennis player and you concentrated very hard on doing everything right, doing it the way you were shown. You took it all very seriously. And your movement across the court — you were like a gazelle. One of the things I first noticed about you — and I noticed it, I suppose, because I used to do it myself — was that even before the coaching school started for the day you'd be out there hitting the ball against the practice wall, over and over again. Of course that first year we saw you, Barbara was a much better player. Barbara had a beautiful style. But there was something about you, something very special. You were doing extraordinary things for a kid of that age.'

A few days into the week-long clinic Faith Martin and Colin Swan conferred over the progress of their 80 Barellan students. The VAETS method relied heavily on systematic reports from the field, documenting both the prospects of individuals and of the town as a future host for coaching clinics. While the primary function of the country clinics was to teach the rudiments of the sport to rural kids who might otherwise miss out on first-class coaching, Vic Edwards was not averse to using them also as talent scouting opportunities. I have already mentioned his discovery of Jan Lehane in this manner, and it was also through VAETS classes that he first spotted John Newcombe and Kim Warwick.

But neither Faith nor Colin had so far 'spotted a star', and they were loathe to blow it first time around. They agreed I was promising, but, in the way of many well-meaning white people of the time, were concerned about the effect of perhaps only brief sporting fame on someone of my background — on an Aborigine. After all, I was a perfectly happy little Aboriginal girl living in a nice little town at the end of the road, so why spoil things for me?

If Faith and Colin had initial misgivings about making too much of their discovery of me, I don't believe they stemmed from anything other than a desire to protect me from a sometimes-cruel world. Australia had yet to emerge from its long slumber of the 1950s and social justice was a term for the future. Aborigines had no vote and virtually no rights, and whenever one of our race had 'made it' in the eyes of white men, he turned around and threw it all away. Or so it seemed to many whites. Just a few months earlier Australia had witnessed the final tragedy of Albert Namatjira, the Aboriginal painter whose Red Centre landscapes had become internationally renowned, but who drank himself to a premature grave after being gaoled for supplying alcohol to a relative. (Namatjira was the first famous Aborigine I ever heard of, and I was so impressed that I began childish imitations of gum trees in his style.)

No doubt these were some of the thoughts running through their heads as they pondered the 'Evonne problem'. Would they really be doing me a favour? Would I have what it takes to make it in the white world? And tennis in Australia in 1961 was truly the whitest of worlds.

There was also another line of thinking at work, and Colin Swan was the first to voice it. 'For a 10-year-old she's amazing, but it could be a flash in the pan. Tennis this week, netball the next. Who knows if she'll stick at it?'

Both Colin and Faith knew in their hearts that I would stick with it, but they had already negotiated with Bill Kurtzman to make the Barellan coaching clinic an annual event, so they decided to wait and see how I had progressed over the following 12 months before jumping up and down on the spot and proclaiming me a future champion. In their report to Mr Edwards they noted the potential of the three Goolagongs and suggested that the tennis club be given every encouragement to continue its support of us.

Before she left Barellan Faith Martin had a final word with Bill Kurtzman. 'Bill, you've got a good one here. I really think Evonne could go all the way, so look after her.'

In the year that followed Mr Kurtzman certainly did that, driving me around the bush tournaments and consoling me when I lost, which I did from time to time, playing in age groups three and four years my senior. But losing meant more to him than it did to me. My obsession with tennis was about mastering the game, not winning it, although I can remember in those early days fantasising about winning Wimbledon long before I knew what it was.

I was not exactly a voracious reader but I would sometimes pick up girls' magazines at the Smiths' general store. In one called *Princess* I read a fairy tale story about a young tennis player who came from nowhere to win fame and fortune at a place called Wimbledon. She lived happily ever after. That was what I wanted too, so Wimbledon became my Holy Grail.

By my birthday in 1962 my tennis had matured considerably. Barbara and Larry hit the ball harder but I placed it where I wanted it to go. Hour after hour on the practice wall was beginning to pay off, and not only could I feel the improvement in my strokes, I had Stan Smith nodding his approval from his front garden vantage point. I played as much tennis as I could, and it was never enough. Age group singles tournaments, doubles with Barbara, mixed doubles with the adults … wherever I could get a game. Sometimes after school the headmaster, Mr Robinson, would ask me to play doubles with his group, which included Mr Hammond, the local policeman. Once I would have run a mile to avoid eye contact with such a figure of authority, but tennis had made me fearless, and I loved those matches, returning the serves as hard as they came at me, matching the men of our town stroke for stroke.

During that year I played against Barbara in a club tournament for the first time. She beat me, but not by much. The next time we met on the court Mum came to watch. I remember this because watching tennis was not high in her priorities. There was always too much cleaning and washing to be done to allow Linda the luxury of an hour sitting on her behind watching a white ball being belted from one end of the court to the other. But here she was, sitting on the bench, looking as interested as Mum could be expected to look, given that she didn't know the rules of the game. (Linda saw me play very few times throughout my career, and never really grasped the rules. Once, during the Australian Open, when I was a set and 5–0 up in the second, she asked my husband Roger if I was winning.)

I beat Barbara that day, again not by much, but by enough and I never lost to her again. Years later she told me that Mum had asked her to lose to me. Mum had said: 'You can't beat your little sister again, let her win

With Barbara after a match in Barellan

Linda watches me play in Barellan, Mully on her knee and Ian playing beside her

this time. Do it for me.' This may have been the first (and possibly the last) fixed match in the history of the Barellan War Memorial Tennis Club, although Barbara maintains that she did not throw it, that I won fair and square anyway.

Soon after that Kenny had his terrible accident with the can of petrol, and while he recovered in hospital Barbara had to leave school and find work to support the family. She continued to play tennis but it was never again as much a part of her life as it was mine.

I could hardly wait for Colin Swan and Faith Martin to arrive in town. As it turned out, they were as anxious to see me as I was to see them. Faith recalls: 'Colin and I were terribly excited to see you again. You'd grown a little but your tennis had grown a lot. The flashes of brilliance we'd seen the year before had been patched together into a very strong game. And, of course, you were beautiful to watch.'

Before the clinic in August 1962, Mr Kurtzman presented me with a Dunlop-Slazenger racquet for showing the most improvement over the year since the last clinic. It was a beautiful racquet and remained my favourite, even when I had several.

The clinic had its amusing moments. Late one afternoon a delicious cooking smell wafted across the courts from our house. Someone asked me if we were having a family barbecue. Auntie Ethel had caught a goanna and she was roasting it whole in the backyard, but there was no way I was going to tell anyone that. I just nodded and giggled to myself.

Several days into the clinic Colin and Faith again conferred with Bill Kurtzman and decided to phone Vic Edwards about me. Faith remembers: 'It wasn't something we did lightly, I can tell you. You didn't disturb the boss man unless it was important, but we believed you were. Colin got on to him first, then he asked me to confirm what Colin had told him. I did and, somewhat reluctantly I thought, he agreed to drive down from Sydney. His last words to me were, "She'd better be bloody good." '

Chapter

*D*URING THE COACHING CLINIC one afternoon Fa Swan ordered all of us to form a drill assembly o of the tennis club. Moments later a car pulled up and a tall looking man in a V-necked white sweater and long creams got out like he might have been the captain of the England cricket team, bu in fact the boss of the Victor A. Edwards Tennis School.

We didn't quite salute him, but it almost seemed the thing to do. He smil slightly as Colin Swan introduced him to us, then spoke briefly, but I don't think any of us listened to what he said. We were too busy staring at the alien. When he came to Barellan that winter of 1962, Vic Edwards was 52 years old and like no one I had ever seen in my life. He was tall, broad-shouldered and upright, like the storybook flying ace, Biggles. He was, I suppose, almost a caricature of himself, except that Vic Edwards demanded to be taken seriously, and generally was. He had worked as a jackeroo and an overseer in the western division — the badlands of New South Wales — before the war and had picked up the swagger of the horseman. He had risen to the rank of major in the Australian Army during World War II, where he used his Britishness as a battering ram on his colonial subordinates, and the legacy of this was his brusque manner, foul mouth (in private) and clipped moustache. In short, he was a man's man with a commanding presence.

Around the tennis club he always wore the uniform of the pre-war tennis bum, the debonair Jack Crawford look: cable-knit sweater over cream shirt and long cream slacks, loosely cuffed and wide of waistband.

He was everything I imagined an English gentleman to be, through my studious reading of *Princess* magazine. I don't want to paint too romantic a picture, but the word 'immaculate' seemed to fit. People turned to look at him in the street, especially in Barellan, where Kenny Goolagong would have topped the best-dressed list most days. In fact, if I am to be totally honest, I saw in Vic Edwards some of the qualities my father — my first and only father — aspired to. Kenny loved to dress with dash too, but in personality he was much more down-to-earth. In 1962, however — the year that Kennedy

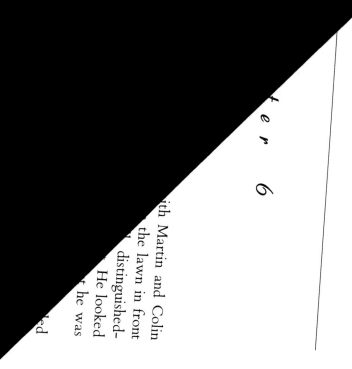

he Native Welfare

allow Aborigines

' — there can be

creams.

found out he was

as very gentle with

from him. Indeed

to Barellan to see

ept the real purpose

at knowledge might

ential embarrassment

standards.

and Bill Kurtzman

n tennis writer Bud

me in the early 1970s

nd only read for the

to be extracts from

ones me from Barellan

… Long trip, had to fly, just — [in fact I'd just turned 11] … but Col and Faith Martin are good judges of talent, can't dampen their interest by disregarding their call, like to see what gets them that excited … the girl is named Evonne Goolagong, Aboriginal, and I'd say the trip was worth it, in a way … She has athletic ability, no doubt of that, moves beautifully, fast … Bill Kurtzman's a good man and apparently she's his protégée, like to help him and her, but how? Strokes aren't much, but ability's there … No such thing as a natural tennis player because of the racquet work involved, but this girl's a natural athlete and ability can be developed … Her father's a wanderer, a shearer, knew plenty like him when I worked in the scrub … no money, no idea what it would take for their daughter to get on in tennis … probably don't care … big family, can't centre attention on her just because she's a fair tennis player. Aboriginal aspect might not sit well in tennis circles … but a challenge … interesting to see how far first Aboriginal could go in tennis if properly handled … maybe an inspiration to her people … I'll talk more to Kurtzman … must talk to Eva too, maybe we could bring the girl to Sydney for holidays, see what she's like, if she'd fit in … maybe by then her family will have moved on and that's that … interesting challenge to think about …

Edwards told the British magazine *Woman* in 1970: 'What impressed me about her then, and what is impressing everyone now, is her easy and gracious stance on the court, her awareness of the bounce of the ball and the way she can move to it, her timing and the natural way in which she holds the racquet and the way it seems to swing and move naturally with her body.'

Faith Martin remembers the outcome of that week and Mr Edwards' immediate impressions of me a little differently.

> I'm sure he didn't fly down because he drove me back to Sydney in his car. I'll never forget that trip because for the first time in our association I threatened the boss man! I told him that if he didn't do something about you, then I would, and I meant it. Victor Edwards turned to look at me as we drove along, and he said: 'If you white bitches can't get on together, imagine what they'd do to her!' This was the way he talked in private, never in public, of course. I think he was genuinely concerned about you and didn't want you to be hurt, but I was very involved by this stage, so I retorted, 'You always say a champion is a champion no matter what. I've never gone over your head before but by God I will if you don't do something about this little girl.'
>
> Vic asked me if I really meant that and I said I did. Then he talked for a while about having Jan Lehane living with his family and I got the impression that he really wasn't keen on doing that again. So we got back to Sydney and I talked to my mother, who lived next-door to me, about making my old bedroom available for you if I was to bring you down. She agreed to that so then we just had to wait and see what the boss decided. I arranged for an equipment sponsorship from Dunlop and sent you a little note of encouragement.
>
> A couple of weeks went by before Mr Edwards called me into his office. He said: 'I've decided to bring Evonne up for the NSW LTA [Lawn Tennis Association] age championships next year. We'll see how it goes from there.' That was it, that was all he said.

My mother was the first to break the news to me that I would be going to Sydney 'one of these days'. No specific date was ever mentioned, but both Linda and Kenny would from time to time say something about 'when you go to Sydney' or 'when you go off to become a tennis champion'. I suspect the repetition of this information was as much to convince themselves that it was the right thing to do, as it was to prepare me for it. I am certain the trip was never put to me as an option; I just accepted that this was what had been decided for my future.

During that second coaching clinic in 1962 Faith Martin had come over to our house and had a long chat with Mum about my tennis, explaining that I had the potential to become a champion but that I would need to face the stronger competition offered in Sydney. She also encouraged Linda to become involved with the tennis club and to share in my success. Mum did make an effort to come along and mix with the other mothers, but she was so shy it was excruciating for her.

It was Kenny rather than Linda who encouraged me to prepare myself for a life as a tennis player. While I think he found it difficult at first to come to terms with the idea that a game like tennis could become a job, 'getting ahead' was a concept he applauded. Frank Gladman had helped Kenny get ahead, and now Bill Kurtzman and Mr Edwards were doing the same thing for me. Mum found it more difficult to understand. As far as she was concerned it was just like the Welfare men coming to take your babies. On the other hand, everyone was so excited about it that some good must come of it. But Sydney … Linda had never been there but she'd seen it on television and knew there were more buildings and more cars than you saw in Griffith on a busy Saturday morning.

Barbara, who was away nannying in the bush during part of this time, was fantastic when she was around. She had never been to Sydney either, but she had a clearer world view than either of my parents, and the prospect of me playing in the big tournaments was perhaps even more exciting for her than it was for me. In fact Barb, who might have been a great tennis player herself, never offered me anything but love and support. There was no envy, no jealousy. It was only years later, when her first marriage failed and she moved to Sydney and struggled to make ends meet, that she began to feel cheated, perhaps even a little resentful. But this was something she worked through by herself and never even discussed with me until she started helping me with the research for this book.

'Evonne's going to have a great time in the Big Smoke, aren't you, Mooch?' I'd nod enthusiastically. 'Don't you worry, Mum, as long as she looks both ways before she crosses the road and minds her manners, she'll be right,' Barbara would say as we cleaned up the table and stacked the dishes.

The Goolagongs had a long time to prepare themselves for my departure. Mr Edwards made his offer just after the August school holidays in 1962 and, although no one had told me, I wasn't to go to Sydney until the May holidays the following year. Furthermore, the offer was contingent upon my continued good form in local events, so that summer Mr Kurtzman and I covered a lot of road driving to tournaments in towns an hour or two apart, like Leeton, Narrandera, Ganmain, Temora, even as far afield as Cowra and Young, three to four hours away. Sometimes Barbara would come with us and partner me in the doubles, and sometimes Pam Jackson, who was beginning to show a lot of promise, would come too. What I remember most about those trips is driving home at night in fear of Mr Kurtzman losing control of the car on the narrow country roads. He was always an enthusiastic talker while he drove — especially after I'd won — and sometimes found it difficult to keep to the bitumen.

The support from the townsfolk was fantastic. The stalwarts of the tennis club were right behind me, of course. Clarrie Irvin remembers driving me to tournaments to relieve Mr Kurtzman. He told the older man, 'Bill, don't do it all yourself. We're here to help. All you have to do is say the word.' There were many other similar offers.

Even people who had little to do with the club helped. Cecil Dicker, who ran the Shell petrol station, donated petrol for my travels; others chipped in with money to cover meals and other expenses. And as the local press began to devote more space to me, the support grew. Barellan was proud of me, but when I look back on their generosity, I think the townsfolk should have been just as proud of themselves. Clarrie Irvin says now that: 'There wasn't a lot of money around, but people don't mind giving to a good cause. And there's no doubt that Barellan was richly rewarded for every penny it gave.'

I fared well in the district tournaments that summer, winning a string of titles, and my appointment with destiny in Sydney was confirmed. As the

Left: Mr and Mrs Kurtzman, ready to take me to a tournament *Right:* Before the second VAETS coaching clinic in Barellan, in a tennis dress made out of a sheet, and holding the racquet presented to me by Mr Kurtzman

departure date drew nearer, the townsfolk rallied around. Dressmaker Mrs Jessie Douglas was charged with the responsibility of making me a tennis frock to replace the threadbare one that Linda had made without a pattern and from a bedsheet. The tennis club bought me a suitcase and Mrs Jean Gladman was told to fill it with clothes.

Someone gave her a gorgeous red overcoat that fitted me perfectly, but for the rest she had to go to Griffith. For my 'going away' wardrobe, Mrs Gladman selected a simple white blouse and sweater, white accessories and a pleated tartan skirt. When I look now at pictures of me standing beside the rain puddles at Narrandera Airport that chilly morning, I can see a frightened little girl putting on a very brave face, clutching my Dunlop-Slazenger racquet to my heart like a security blanket.

My whole family went over to the airport by car, everyone dressed in their finest, Mum heavy with child again. The Kurtzmans and the Gladmans were there, along with several others. Barbara remembers that Mum was determined not to cry — I was only going for two weeks — but she was terribly worried about me flying. The plane seemed to take forever to load

Left: The young champion: trophies on display in the backyard *Right:* Off to Sydney for the first time

88

and prepare for take-off, but finally I was called to board. There were hugs and kisses, but no tears, and I turned my back on my family and friends and quickly walked across the tarmac towards the Airlines of New South Wales 'Fokker Friendship'.

'Evonne, turn around for a picture.' It was Mrs Gladman. I turned and posed for her, and saw Mum and Barbara bawling their eyes out. I bit my lip and hurried onto the plane.

Faith Martin drove to the airport in Sydney to pick me up, presumably because she was the only one who would recognise me, although the airport terminal wasn't exactly overflowing with 11-year-old Aboriginal girls holding tennis racquets. She brought with her Mrs Eva Edwards and her two younger daughters, Jenifer and Patricia. They spotted me immediately, still starry-eyed after my first plane ride, and whisked me off to the car. There were some awkward moments — the girls seemed to me a little stand-offish — but I probably was preoccupied with my first sight of a city. I well remember seeing the magnificent harbour and the bridge for the first time. When Faith explained that the man in the little booth was collecting a toll I was astonished. 'We don't have to pay any money to cross our bridge at Barellan,' I said. Everyone laughed. I was doing well. I had made my first joke.

Jenifer Edwards was a year older than me, Patricia a year younger. Patricia was the budding tennis player and the one whose room I would share and later partner in doubles, but Jenifer, who didn't play tennis, was the one I warmed to more readily. She was easygoing and full of fun and I knew, almost immediately, that we would be friends.

It took me longer to appreciate Mrs Edwards, the woman who would become my second Mum. Eva Prentice Edwards was a country girl from north-western New South Wales. Her grazier father sent her to a Sydney convent for her schooling and she became a schoolgirl tennis champion. So we had plenty in common and I was to come to love her dearly, but there was still an initial distance between us, which wasn't helped that first night when I came downstairs after having showered and she chastised me for not having dried my hair. She looked up from reading her newspaper and regarded me from the top half of her bifocals. She said, 'Go and dry your hair. You'll catch your death of cold.'

I had never seen a hair dryer, much less used one, but I think it was Jenifer who showed me how to operate it. The big, comfortable two-storey house at Roseville Chase exuded the warmth of a happy home, but there was no happiness in it for me that night. After supper I excused myself and went to my room — two white and gold Queen Anne-style beds with white quilted bedcovers and a window with a view over the garden and the tennis court — and sobbed quietly into my pillow.

The Edwards home in Warrane Road, Roseville Chase, was just around the corner from the Victor A. Edwards Tennis School in Duntroon Avenue, which consisted of the original house that Herbert Edwards had bought in the 1920s, and five tennis courts. The house was now command headquarters for VAETS, but a section of it was retained for Gran Edwards, Vic's mother May, a truly remarkable old lady with whom I was to become very friendly. The VAETS courts were primarily used for mass instruction, the bread and butter of the school. The loam court at the Edwards' home was for private use, or for one-to-one coaching of star pupils. Fred Stolle, Jan Lehane, Martin Mulligan and Bob Hewitt had all been tutored at the private court, but in my first days in Sydney I was put into the mass instruction classes, along with hundreds of children who would never play anything more taxing than a round of social doubles. This cast no slur on me. As Faith Martin later explained, the idea was to make me feel relaxed about the routine of the school. It must have worked because I soon came to like the routine, the camaraderie.

The individual coaching, or just Patricia and me with Mr Edwards on the home court, was much tougher. He would stand at the net pounding balls at us for hours on end. Forehand, backhand, forehand, backhand … the same

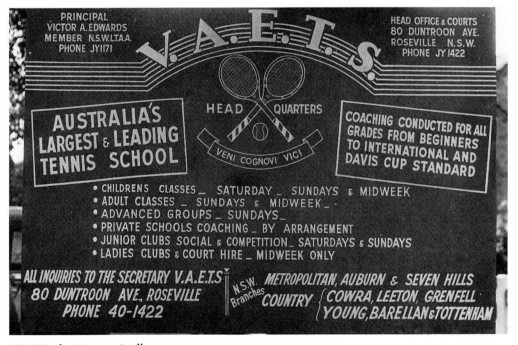

VAETS: the sign says it all

spot requiring the same stroke, time after time. At the end of each session he would run us ragged from one corner of the court to another combining all the strokes we had practised. I quite enjoyed the hard workouts, for their variety and because I liked to push myself.

If we ever let up, Mr Edwards would boom, 'What's the matter? Do you want a chair?' This never bothered me, but Patricia would get quite emotional about it. Before practice I'd tell her to pretend she didn't hear a word, but that didn't always work. There would be harsh words and often she would leave the court in tears. I guess having a father as your coach didn't make it easy for her. Sometimes I thought that perhaps I was taking away the attention she should have been getting, as if I was intruding in the relationship between father and daughter.

I didn't know what to think about all this emotion — bedtime was my crying time — so I just focused my attention on the tennis, on improving my game as quickly as I could.

In the second week of the holidays I competed in my first big tournament at White City, the tennis complex on the eastern fringe of the city of Sydney which Herbert Edwards might have built, but hadn't. I have rarely suffered from nerves in my tennis career but my first appearance at White City in the Under-13 Grass Court Championships was almost as frightening as my first match at Wimbledon. The preliminary matches on the outer courts in front of half a dozen interested parties weren't too bad, but by the time I met Janine Murdock in the semi-final on centre-court, I was a bundle of nerves.

Janine was a kind of 'moonball' player, who could really throw your rhythm out with these great, looping shots. I started to play a little shakily, double-faulting and making unforced errors. In the end the scoreline for the single set was 6–4, and I had been beaten by the girl who would go on to win the championship. Naturally, I was a little disappointed, but Mr Edwards actually seemed pleased.

'Nerves,' he said. 'Must learn to control them. You were beaten by a lesser player because of them, and that won't happen again. But you did well, Evonne. Making the semi-finals in your first big tournament is a fine effort.'

Later, when I thought about the match — not that I was much given to reflection on any of my matches — I felt a lot better, too. I knew I had played below my best and I'd only been beaten by one service break. That wouldn't happen again — at least not against Janine Murdock.

Mr Kurtzman and Mum were at the airport to pick me up at the end what seemed like the longest two weeks my life. It was so good to be home, and I had so much to tell them, about the Harbour Bridge and my own chest of drawers and the ocean beach at Dee Why and all sitting down together at dinner ... oh, and finishing in the top four in the championships.

As we drove into Barellan and turned off Old Narrandera Road towards our house a strange sensation came over me. I was home, and very glad to be, but somehow I knew that everything had changed. While Kenny and Linda Goolagong's humble house in Bendee Street, Barellan would always be home, I had the distinct — and slightly frightening — feeling that I would not be spending much more time in it.

PART 2

Growing Up White

Serving tea for the family in Barellan

Chapter 7

At the end of that first trip to Sydney in May, 1963, I came home to Barellan, my bags weighed down with treats for the family. I had a bag of brussel sprouts — a new vegetable I had tried for the first time at the Edwards' table and loved — and several jars of creamed honey.

The honey was a gift from Mrs Edwards for Linda — 'from your number two mum to your number one mum', as she put it when she hugged me goodbye at the airport. Although I had only spent two weeks with her, I knew already that I would come to love Mrs Edwards, that she would indeed become my number two mum. And that realisation left me confused, and perhaps a little frightened of my own feelings. After all, I had no need of a second family; my first family was perfectly adequate, thank you very much, and I loved my parents, my brothers and sisters, our crowded house in Bendee Street and our noisy, chaotic existence.

However, when Mr Edwards took me aside after Patricia and I had our last lesson together for the holidays, he had said, 'We're going to be seeing a lot more of you, of course. Would you like that?' And I had grinned and nodded my enthusiastic reply. Would I like it? I would love it. I was going to be a tennis champion and go to Wimbledon, like the girl in *Princess* magazine.

Now, here I was back in Barellan, little Evonne, Vonnie, little Mooch … barefoot and running across the frosty grass in the early morning to keep my toes from going numb. 'G'day, champ. How was the big smoke?' It was one of the funny Tubb brothers, opening up the butcher shop for the day. 'Good,' I said, running on to buy a loaf of bread for Mum. Good. Good. Good. No matter how many times I was asked that question over the next week, I never tired of smiling and giving my monosyllabic response. It was so good to be home.

At home and school my life resumed its normal pattern. Lessons, chores, hitting against the wall. Midweek matches with the men, weekend age competitions. Tennis, tennis and more tennis. But during that long winter of 1963 there were subtle changes to my perceptions, and to other people's perceptions of me. Even my schoolfriends noticed small things. When I winced at the pain of burrs in my bare feet, they would tease me, 'What's the matter? The big city made you go soft?'

In researching this book, it was refreshing to hear people I had known since I was a small child, like Lucy Smith and Jean Gladman, say of me then: 'She never changed. She was just Evonne.' And to that core of family, friends and supporters in Barellan, I remained 'just Evonne' throughout my career. But in small ways things were different after that first trip to Sydney. For one thing, I was becoming a minor celebrity. Over the next 30 years I would develop methods of dealing with the mixed blessing of fame, but back then it was an exciting new game. Barbara, Larry and I had had our names in the local newspapers frequently since we began playing competition tennis, but after my win in the under-16 girls singles at West Wyalong in the Easter tournament just before I left for Sydney, the local papers started to write bigger and bigger articles about me. At West Wyalong it helped that I thrashed the local junior champion Denise Block in the final. 'An 11-year-old Barellan girl astounded players in the big Easter tournament,' the *Barellan Leader* enthused from its base in distant Temora, probably unaware that the Goolagongs were the occupants of the old newspaper office, and that the original *Leader* printing press was my rainy day playground. Bill Williams, the professional coach from Wagga, who had conducted the first coaching clinic in Barellan, was at the West Wyalong tournament, and he told the *Wagga Daily Advertiser* that I had 'all the attributes of a champion player of the future'.

Just before my twelfth birthday in July Mr Kurtzman and Dad drove all of the Goolagongs to a tournament in Narrandera. When we arrived we discovered that there had been a breakdown in communication. It was an open tournament for adults. There were no age divisions. We looked at each other and shrugged, then Bill Kurtzman watched proudly while Barbara, Larry and I won the open singles, doubles and mixed doubles. Linda was thrilled when we collected our 'prize money' — a collection of household goods like sheets, kitchen appliances and crockery. Looking back on that outing, I wonder if the 'communication breakdown' was actually between Mr Kurtzman and us, if he had actually planned the surprise to test my mettle against the adults. If so, it was a clever tactical move, because word of our achievement spread around Barellan and the fund Mr Kurtzman had set up to pay for my next trip to Sydney received a healthy injection of cash.

Mr Kurtzman fell ill that winter and had to go to hospital in Sydney for several weeks, but that didn't stop the tennis caravan. Clarrie and Dot Irvin drove me to tournaments and, when our car was up to the task, Kenny even drove me to some.

As Barbara's work commitments forced her to pass up more and more tournaments, I began to play doubles with a promising junior from a property near Gundagai. Frances Luff was a handy singles player, but a much better doubles player, and she dragged me across the line to win several tournaments around the south-west that year. When I went back to Sydney for another two weeks in August, Frances came, too, to play her first city tournaments.

Frances was with us, in fact, when the Edwards family and I travelled to Newcastle in September for the Mattara Age Championships. This was a grand adventure for me. My tournament travel in the Riverina usually involved a long drive across flat wheat country, followed by a night billeted in the spare bedroom of someone's house. Not only was our drive to Newcastle along a coastal route which took in the Hawkesbury River, Lake Macquarie and several ocean beaches in between, but when we arrived we would be checking into a motel — a new invention from America in which you could drive your car right up to the door of your room!

Frances and I and Mr and Mrs Edwards shared adjoining rooms, and in the mornings we took to getting together in the Edwards' room to have cups of tea and await our room service breakfasts. We girls took turns making the tea in an alcove off the bedroom. When it came to my turn I disappeared into the alcove and was still busy when Mrs Edwards started to get impatient. 'Come on, Vonnie. What's keeping you?'

I called back, 'It's coming. It takes a while to get the tea out of these silly little bags.'

Mrs Edwards shook her head then laughed until she cried. 'Oh dear,' she said, 'we've got a bit to learn yet, haven't we?'

Indeed I had much to learn about tea bags, and life in general. But I was getting a pretty good handle on tennis. I won the under-13 singles at Newcastle and the doubles with Patricia Edwards in our first tournament as a team. Before I turned 13 I had won more than 80 singles and doubles age titles, and had the trophies, beauty cases and brush-and-comb sets to prove it.

That spring I travelled to Bathurst for a country championship. Dad drove Barbara and me from Barellan in our old jalopy, labouring up the hills with great difficulty. We checked into a hotel near the tennis courts, rather than sleep in the car, because Kenny was determined that we should get a good night's sleep. We didn't. The revellers downstairs in the bar kept us up until late. Unfortunately Kenny was one of them. He was suffering the next morning but he rallied in time to watch me beat Janine Murdock in the under-13 final, answering her moonballs with smashes directed at her weak backhand.

But I couldn't wait to get back to Barellan after that October long weekend,

In Newcastle for the Mattara Age Championships

and my excitement had nothing to do with tennis. We had a new baby. Martin Goolagong was Mum's eighth and, as it turned out, her last child. He was gorgeous, brown-eyed and chubby-cheeked, and with Barbara away working as a nanny, I was chief nurser and pram-pusher.

We all loved him but we hated that name, which Mum had taken from the 'Baby's Days' scrapbook in which she kept our newspaper clippings. She had prevailed upon Kenny to read through the list of boys' names and their meanings and, when he reached Martin (which meant 'unyielding') she cried, 'Stop! That's the one.' But we didn't think so. Martin was a good name for a bank teller or a policeman, not so good for a little Aboriginal baby, squirming all over the floor.

When Martin was only a couple of months old, the Barellan War Memorial Tennis Club hosted its first major exhibition tournament. Vic Edwards organised the players from his own coaching stable, and the event featured some of Australia's better players of the time. Fred Stolle had just lost in the first of his three Wimbledon finals, while Martin Mulligan, who lost the Wimbledon final to Rod Laver in 1962, had just successfully defended his Italian championship. Jan Lehane was the Vic Edwards protégée who would have been Australia's best female player, had it not been for Margaret Smith (later Court) who beat her in four successive Australian Championships. The fourth member of the troupe was Madonna Schacht, who was to take out the Queensland singles title the following year.

Barellan had never seen such a galaxy of stars, and the townsfolk turned out in force to watch them play. The wooden benches at our little tennis club were packed with spectators and behind them people stood five deep. Pam Jackson — Barellan's other junior prospect — and I were the ballgirls and the entire Goolagong clan came over from the house to watch. Pam and I were allowed to warm up with the players and I felt a little guilty that I might have put Jan Lehane off her game when I aced her. She looked somewhat stunned, but took it in good heart.

Afterwards the players came over and met my family and talked and joked for a while. We liked Martin Mulligan a lot, and he seemed to take a shine to his little namesake, who was wrapped in a shawl on Linda's knee.

Mum said, 'He's got the same name as you.'

Martin replied: 'What's that? Mulligan? Better call him Mully.'

And he was Mully ever after.

I finished primary school in December 1963 and, after a quiet Christmas at home, headed back to my other home in Sydney. On the last day of the year Mr Edwards pushed me hard all the way through a lesson on the home

court, running me all over the place in the humidity of a Sydney summer.
When we finished he sat down beside me and handed me a towel to wipe
away the sweat. He said, 'You've done well, pet. You've come a long, long
way and next year you can go a long way further. But it's going to be hard
work. Are you prepared to put everything into it?' I nodded. 'Good,' he said.
'Now go and wash up for lunch.'

I wasn't aware of it, but already Vic Edwards and Bill Kurtzman had
had long discussions about my future, a matter they had also taken up with
Linda and Kenny. Mr Edwards had explained that if I was going to make
tennis my career, sooner or later I would have to live permanently in Sydney,
where I could devote myself to a training program and compete against the
best players available. Mr Kurtzman agreed, and offered, if my parents were
willing, to expand his fund-raising activities on my behalf to help cover the
considerable costs of my moving to Roseville to live with the Edwards family.

Kenny, who believed that 'getting ahead' was second only to being happy
in life's priorities, felt that I should go when the time was right, and he helped
convince Mum. So, without my knowledge or consent, it was decided at the
beginning of 1964 that if I continued on my winning way, I would move to
Sydney under the guardianship of Mr and Mrs Edwards in two years' time.
I can't remember when I was officially informed of the plan; it just seeped
into my consciousness gradually over the first few months of 1964. In April
it became official when Mr Edwards told the *Australian Women's Weekly*. 'Yvonne
will live permanently with the Edwards when she is 14, finishing off her
schooling in Sydney,' the *Weekly* announced. 'She would like to pass her Leaving
Certificate, but at present has no ambition other than becoming a champion
tennis player.'

The year 1964 was to be the best so far of my brief career, and it began
as it was to continue — in a flurry of activity. In the first week of January
I won the under-14 singles of the Manly Hard Court Age Tournament, competed
in the under-16 singles and reached the semifinals of the doubles with Patricia.
More importantly, I won the first prize that really meant anything to me since
the pennant I won at athletics day in Barellan — a red transistor radio. I
dubbed it the 'Red Terror', and over the next few years it seldom left my
side. The Beatles were all the rage and their songs dominated the airwaves.
Within a few weeks I knew all the words to 'Please Please Me', 'She Loves
You' and 'I Wanna Hold Your Hand'. But I must have suffered from Beatles
overkill, because later on I became more interested in black soul music, B. B.
King and Jimi Hendrix, and Jenifer Edwards' constant and loud playing of
Beatles records down the hall used to drive me batty.

The following week Mr Edwards drove us to the other side of Sydney for the NSW Hard Court Age Tournament at Canterbury, where in the under-13 singles final I met 'Moonballer' Murdock again. Having beaten her in Bathurst a few months earlier, I was quietly confident of despatching her again. But I also felt that it didn't really matter. I would certainly play my best tennis, but I'd won a transistor last week, maybe this week it would be someone else's turn. And then I saw the gallery.

The stands were packed with people who had come to see me play. I had no vanity about attracting the biggest crowd of the tournament, and only years later realised that it was my colour as much as my tennis that had brought in the crowd. (I was 'that little Aboriginal girl' they'd heard about.) I did, however, feel a certain responsibility to produce my best for them. I got off to a good start against Janine and felt my confidence grow with every winner. In the end she only took one game from me.

When I look now at the yellowing newspaper cuttings I am so glad that I never read match reports then, and that Mr Edwards wisely refrained from showing them to me. Had I seen the *Sun-Herald*'s report I doubt I would have fitted my head through the doorway to the bedroom I shared with Patricia.

'Brilliant 12-year-old aboriginal (sic) girl tennis prospect Yvonne (sic) Goologong (sic) from Barellan could give women's tennis a big lift in a few years,' the paper said. 'She is easily the best player in NSW and probably in Australia at her age.' Of my final against Janine, the paper said: 'She showed amazing accuracy and the ability to hit the lines with lusty forehand drives. Her service is accurate, her return of service splendid and her backhand good, but not as strong as her forehand.'

At the end of the article I also detected the deft hand of Victor Allan Edwards, who was a master at using the media to further his own ends. The Sydney Sunday papers were (and still are) widely read throughout New South Wales, particularly in the country areas, including Barellan. No doubt all the people intimately concerned with determining my future would have read in the final paragraph: 'Already she is at a big disadvantage because there is no competition in the country fitting to test her ability at anywhere near her own age. It can only be found in Sydney or interstate competition.'

From Canterbury we went straight to White City, Sydney's tennis headquarters, for the Country Championships. This annual event attracted country players of all ages from all over New South Wales, in 1964 more than 800 of them. It was also a considerable challenge for me because the youngest age division was under-15, meaning that I would be playing girls almost three years my senior.

I dropped the first set in the semifinal and gave myself a scare, but then took out the final in straight sets from Newcastle girl Anne Thursby. Frances Luff and I made it to the semis in the under-15 doubles, too. Then I went back to Roseville and slept for a couple of days. I had won three tournaments in as many weeks and the Goolagong name was on everyone's lips in Sydney tennis circles. Back home in the Riverina the *Wagga Daily Advertiser* named me as its first 'Sportsman of the Week' for the year. I won a basket full of Heinz soups, which went down very well with the Goolagong family.

Mr Edwards eased up on the training schedule for what was left of the holidays and allowed me some time to get to know my Sydney sisters better. The Edwards had five daughters, but the three older ones had left home. Although Patricia — or Trisha, as most of her friends called her — was my room-mate, I continued to find I had more in common with Jenifer, who was an affable, easygoing type who had a refreshing lack of interest in tennis. Trisha, on the other hand, could be quite intense. I sometimes felt that there was an element of resentment in our relationship, that I had perhaps come between Mr Edwards and her, but she never suggested that, not even when we argued.

Trisha and I did share a prepubescent fascination with boys. We would talk and giggle into the night about boys we had seen at tennis tournaments. One we regarded as rather special was John Alexander, who lived not far away. John had won the under-13 boys singles at Canterbury and was widely regarded as a hot prospect for the future. In our bedroom at Roseville he was widely regarded as 'very cute'. A couple of times we plucked up the courage to phone him, but the moment there was an answer we would hang up and collapse in a fit of giggles.

At the end of that extraordinary January I flew home and started my secondary education at Barellan Central School. Because primary and secondary schools were both housed in the same place, there was not the same distinction between the two schools as existed in larger towns. Nevertheless, a clear line was drawn between the juvenile approach of one and the assumption of the other that we had miraculously transformed during the holidays into responsible teenagers.

First formers were expected to conduct themselves with maturity and, for the first time, to do homework. Having already experienced the world — well, Sydney and Newcastle — I believed I was well down the road to responsible behaviour, but homework I had a problem with. For one thing, there was no time. When I had finished hitting on the practice wall I had to help Mum get the kids' supper. Then there were Mully and Ian to look after, dishes to wash, the list of chores was endless. For another thing, there was no space. Barely a moment of the day went by when our linoleum-topped kitchen table was not in use for vegetable peeling, sewing, nappy-changing, sorting of washing, you name it.

No time and no table space doesn't sound like much of an excuse, but it must have worked because I can't remember ever getting into much trouble over my failure to do homework.

Sometime during the early part of 1964 we were visited by a newspaper photographer from the city, who took a series of photographs which have come to represent to the world the Goolagong family lifestyle in Barellan. We were the Aborigines who were okay, the neat, clean, respectable ones. I have no complaints about the image we presented. We were neat, clean and respectable, but so were a great many Aboriginal families. Of course it was my tennis that brought the cameras into our house, and the images that went out were entirely positive and hopefully did some good for the image of Aborigines generally. But when I look at those photographs now, I can't help but wonder why they were an exception — why the only other photos of Aboriginal life you ever saw were of squalor.

The photographer took pictures of me playing tennis, standing courtside with my Dunlop-Slazenger racquet and my best tennis frock, playing with my kid brothers and sisters and doing chores around the house. The picture

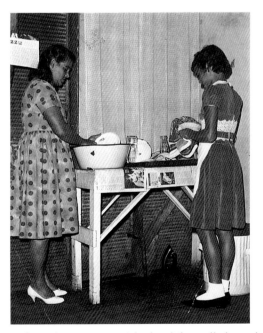 

Left: Helping Mum with the dishes, all dressed up for the photographer *Right:* Reading to the kids, Gail, Janelle and Kevin

I like best shows me pouring tea (real tea, no tea bags) for the family from Mum's best teapot. The Goolagongs are sitting upright around the kitchen table, Kenny in the white shirt and tie he had taken to wearing since his 'human torch' accident, Mum in her favourite floral print dress. I am wearing a pretty blue dress that I got for my second trip to Sydney, and in which I felt almost regal, like a character out of *Princess* magazine. I look at that photo now through the mists of time, and I can still feel the luxury of that dress, and know that I would never, ever have been allowed to wear it around the house while I poured the tea!

That Easter, Albury Tennis Club was celebrating its fiftieth anniversary with a big tournament featuring some of the current stars of Australian tennis as well as all the top country players. Mr Kurtzman told me I had been invited to play. To me it was just another tournament and the more good players the better, but to Bill Kurtzman this was something special. He said, 'Margaret Smith will be playing. Albury's her home town.'

This may sound ingenuous, but in 1964 the name Margaret Smith meant nothing to me. She was the Australian singles champion and had been since 1960. She was also the reigning Wimbledon champion. Nothing. I'm sure I'd heard of her, but it was not exactly a name you could never forget. I don't know how many times I've read that this trip to Albury was a pilgrimage to meet my idol — and it is true that by the time I met her in the Wimbledon final, Margaret was the player I most admired — but it simply wasn't true when I was 12 years old.

The truth was that I just didn't know much about tennis beyond my own experience of it. I fancied John Alexander, but that had nothing to with tennis. I admired Jan Lehane, because I'd seen her play on my home court. But I was far more interested in playing tennis than I was in watching it, and that remained the case throughout my career. And I certainly never read about tennis!

Nevertheless, Mr Kurtzman was very excited about this opportunity to meet the queen of Australian tennis, so I was too. Clarrie and Dot Irvin drove me to Albury, the big country centre on the Victorian border, and stayed with me until Mr Kurtzman arrived at the end of the first day of the tournament. On the second day I met Margaret Smith. The Wimbledon champion, then 22, was tall, imposing, but just a little bit shy. We did not have a long and animated discussion, but she was very nice and wished me well with my tennis. According to the papers, which published a photo of me gazing in awe at Margaret, I asked her, 'Gee, how does it feel to be a Wimbledon champion?' I don't remember that, but if it was in the papers then it must be true.

Meeting Margaret Smith (now Court) in Albury, 1964

At the start of the May holidays I once again followed the now-familiar ritual of packing my bags and racquets for Sydney. It had been a year since my first visit, but leaving Barellan didn't get any easier. In the last day or two before my departure I would become very quiet, very subdued. Normally that would be the sign for Larry to joke me out of my mood, or for Mum to say, 'What's the matter with you, Mooch? Seen a willy wagtail?' (The appearance of this small bird was an Aboriginal sign that something sad had happened, like a death in the family.)

But no one would say anything when I was about to leave for Sydney. They all knew what I was going through, and they were feeling the sadness, too.

In Sydney any contact I had with my real family was a bonus, so I was delighted one night when Barbara dropped in at the Edwards home with some friends from Tranby Aboriginal College. She'd been sponsored by the Rotary Club of Griffith to do a secretarial course in Sydney and to undertake some Aboriginal studies at Tranby. The business school was at Dee Why on the northern beaches and she was billeted nearby at Collaroy, so the Edwards place was on her way home. Barbara stayed about an hour that night, then went straight home to Collaroy and Mrs Turner.

As Barbara recalls it, Mrs Turner confronted her. 'You're late.'

'I'm sorry, I should have called. I just dropped in to see Evonne.'

Mrs Turner bristled. 'You have no right to do that without my permission, no right at all. As for this tennis ballyhoo, a lot of fuss about nothing. Who does Evonne think she is, the Queen?'

Barbara was almost 17 and had a mind of her own. She didn't last long with Mrs Turner or the secretarial course. But Mrs Turner, who believed that she was performing a community service for a needy Aboriginal family, had an attitude which was shared by a surprising number of people who, through church or charity organisations, became involved in Aboriginal welfare. The attitude was that it was wrong to create heroes out of Aboriginal achievers because it gave Aborigines false hopes, unrealistic expectations. Better to quietly teach the young ones the skills of the white man while our blackness was being crossbred into extinction.

My first engagement back in Sydney in May was the 1964 NSW Lawn Championships and the under-13 title I had missed out on the previous year. When I arrived at White City on the first day of the tournament I was ushered into the clubhouse and introduced to a Mr Shirley, who handed me a trophy while the photographers took pictures. I had apparently been honoured by the American magazine *Sports Illustrated* with their Award of Merit. Since this was

Receiving the *Sports Illustrated* award, 1964

the first international recognition of my tennis ability, I suppose the award should figure in my memory as some kind of landmark. But to be honest, I didn't understand what it was for at the time, and immediately put it out of my mind. Until recently, when I started to pore over old scrapbooks, had someone told me I had won a *Sports Illustrated* award, I would have denied it.

I beat my arch rival Janine Murdock to take out the NSW under-13 singles title, then Trisha and I took the doubles crown. As seems inevitable in sport, the media started to refer to me as the 'next Margaret Smith', and even 'better than Margaret Smith at the same age' — comparisons which can so often be the kiss of death. But by this time I was safely back in Barellan with more important things to worry about, like pushing Mully's pram and thinking up new excuses for not doing my homework.

Chapter 8

'*I* SAW YESTERDAY A SIGHT that will stay in my mind forever — a slim brown aboriginal girl from the bush, playing tennis on a posh North Shore court, her face alive with delight.'

Journalist Frank Margan wrote these words in the Sydney *Daily Telegraph* on 12 January 1965. He continued:

'In four years that girl will be playing at Wimbledon in the All-England Tennis Championships. She will be our first aborigine tennis star. A year or two after her first appearance at the holy of holies, she may well become the first aborigine to become champion of the world in any sport.'

No prizes for guessing who Mr Margan had been talking to, but had his research gone beyond listening to Mr Edwards sing my praises, he would have known that there had already been an Aboriginal world champion — my distant relative Lynch Cooper from Cummeragunga, who in 1929 added the world sprint championship to his Stawell Gift trophy. Of course, Frank Margan could not have foreseen that another Aborigine, Lionel Rose, would win the world bantamweight boxing title while I was still at school.

For all this, the article was one of the best that had been written about me, because it portrayed my relationship with Vic Edwards the way it really was then — him pushing, prodding, cajoling me to try harder; me grinning and bearing it because I knew it was working. Whenever I came to Sydney, but particularly for the long summer holidays, I could feel my tennis improve in leaps and bounds. At the beginning of 1965 I had just won my sixth New South Wales title, meaning that I held every title that was available to me in that State. It was becoming obvious, even to me, that Mr Edwards knew what he was doing. And I was beginning to understand the necessity, as well as the inevitability, of my move to Sydney.

Back home in Barellan Bill Kurtzman was already hard at work raising the funds for the move which, it had been decided, would take place after I had completed my second year at high school. This was not the first time that a small community had rallied behind a potential champion, but I doubt that too many bush towns had taken up the cause of an individual as willingly

My last year at Barellan Central School. Spot the Aborigine!

or as decisively. According to Clarrie Irvin, once Bill Kurtzman had explained the goal — to make me a champion — and what was required, there was very little dissent.

When I had dinner with Clarrie and Dot at their home in Barellan not so long ago, Clarrie told me, 'Mr Kurtzman [he was Mr Kurtzman, not Bill, to all of us] had a notebook and he wrote down every promise of every penny, and he was around to collect on payday too. We mainly had street collections. No one minded chipping in, and I tell you what, the people of Barellan have been richly rewarded for every cent they gave.'

As well as the street collections, Mr Kurtzman organised exhibition matches throughout south-west New South Wales. In Gundagai, that lovely old town on the Murrumbidgee River, my friend Frances Luff and I played an exhibition singles match in front of a capacity crowd, then teamed to play her sister and a friend in a fairly lopsided doubles match that nevertheless gave the spectators a few laughs. I sometimes wonder whether Bill Kurtzman collected much money on those nights, after deducting the price of getting there and a couple of hamburgers for supper.

But then the cost of sending me to Sydney was not huge. Mr Kurtzman and Mr Edwards had worked out that VAETS needed a subsidy of three pounds a week as long as I was at school, on top of the travel and equipment allowance that Dunlop had agreed to provide. This was the equivalent of six dollars at a time when most of the men in Barellan would have been earning somewhere between $20 and $50. Not a huge request to a community of 900 people, but why should they have given me anything? Clarrie Irvin says it was a mixture of civic pride and a genuine affection for the Goolagong family. Not everyone, mind you, had a warm inner glow about the Goolagongs all the time. There were people in Barellan who regarded Kenny Goolagong as a damned nuisance when he had had a few drinks, and Larry when he was on the grog was regarded as a bit of a tearaway too. The police would knock on the *Barellan Leader* door first if there had been a disturbance or a theft, and Larry was the prime suspect. Larry shakes his head and laughs about it today, but there were times when the police came to him first, not because he was the town's most exuberant youth, but because he was black.

For the most part, though, the townsfolk of Barellan saw us, I think, as a family doing the best we could, for our community as well as for ourselves. And if a few coins in Bill Kurtzman's money jar could help a young kid on her way, then why not?

Until 1965 the closest I had been to romance was *Princess* magazine and waiting up for Barbara to come home from her dates. The characters in *Princess* seemed to me to be from another planet. I could relate better to the boys Barbara went out with. I loved it when I managed to stay awake until I heard her come in.

'Barb, what happened? Was he nice? Did he kiss you goodnight?'

'He was a dag, Mooch. Tell you all about it in the morning.'

I would insist on an immediate blow-by-blow description, and Barbara would humour me. We'd end up rolling around the bed giggling, until Gail woke up whingeing about the noise. Barbara was pretty and outgoing and had lots of boyfriends, but it never occurred to me that I, too, might one day be dating boys. I just wasn't that type. I was confident enough to beat them up on the tennis court, but there was no way I could walk up to a boy in the schoolyard and start talking to him. No way!

Then along came Colin Bandy. He was in my class and he was good at sport and kind of cute. I can't remember if I was more thrilled or scared when he asked me to go to the pictures with him. Since our arrival in Barellan a picture show had been established at the School of Arts. In Barellan it was the place to go for your date, unless you wanted to be sent home to your parents for smooching in a booth at Tony's Vienna Cafe.

Dad was less than delighted, but at 14 I was allowed to go out on my first date.

'Don't be late,' Kenny warned as I left to meet Colin outside the show. There was no chance of that. I was horrified that he might try to hold my hand. Or worse, kiss me. We got through the newsreel and the cartoon, but soon after the feature started he slid his hand into mine and squeezed it. I closed my eyes and imagined the practice wall, and the ball hitting the same spot time after time after time …

The year whizzed by. Colin and I didn't become an item, and in September I went back to Sydney, then on to Brisbane for my first interstate tournament, playing for NSW Combined High Schools against Queensland. Then home one more time, basically to pack my bags and kiss the folks goodbye. Despite the best intentions of Mr Edwards and Mr Kurtzman, my schooling had been shot to pieces that year, largely as a result of the amount of commuting I was doing between the city and the bush. Obviously the solution was to make my home where the tennis was, but as the time drew nearer for me to make my permanent move to Sydney, there was talk about Mr Edwards being made my legal guardian and I could see that Kenny, for all his initial enthusiasm, was having second thoughts.

According to his shearing and drinking mate John Emerson, Kenny was deeply concerned that I would be lost forever to the family. He recalls: 'It had started to get beyond his [Kenny's] control, what with Edwards and Kurtzman and Ron Matthews from the War Memorial Club all pushing for Evonne to move away permanently. Kenny had encouraged it at first, but I think he suddenly saw what could happen, and he didn't much like it. It drove a wedge into that marriage, too.'

I don't recall the matter of my leaving causing any major fights at home, but if Dad really did express such a view, he needn't have worried on that score. But I, too, was having misgivings. Having prepared for this day for so long without even considering that I had options, I suddenly needed to talk it through with someone who could assess it objectively. One day I sought out the headmaster, Mr Robinson, after everyone else had gone home.

Mr Robinson was not my tennis partner on this occasion. He had on the hat of the scholar. I told him the plan for me to go to Sydney. He scratched what was left of his hair. 'I had heard that,' he said. There was a very long pause, during which he searched the small office with his eyes, as if he was trying to locate an annoying blowfly. Eventually, when his eyes settled back on me, I knew he was about to tell me something I didn't want to hear.

'You'd probably have to repeat second form, then when the tennis thing blows over, you'll be a year behind your friends.'

'But it's not going to blow over, sir. I want to be a tennis player.'

Mr Robinson looked anguished. He was a handy player himself; he probably would have loved to call it a career. But he said, 'I can't recommend the move, Evonne. I think you should finish your schooling here and have something to fall back on. Then try your luck with tennis.'

I thanked him and excused myself. At the moment of their giving, those thanks may well have been laced with irony, but in a way I do owe Mr Robinson much for his advice. If I had gone into his office a confused little girl, I came out a determined young lady who knew exactly what she was going to do with her life, headmaster's permission granted or not.

As I was preparing to move to Sydney that spring, a group of Aboriginal activists and students was preparing to move out on a journey which would turn out to be far more significant than mine. For the previous two American summers, civil rights activists had launched 'Freedom Rides' across the Deep South, putting state colour laws to the test and exposing the racism and paternalism that prevailed at almost every level of southern American society. In Sydney, a prominent young soccer star and Aboriginal leader named Charles Perkins was impressed by the media coverage the Freedom Rides got, and the way in which they focused world attention on the inequalities in America.

Could not an Australian Freedom Ride achieve the same goal? Despite some watering down of their assimilation policies in the early 1960s, the state governments in Australia had not really come to grips with the issue of equality. While some, like the New South Wales Government, paid lip-service to equal rights, the reality was tragically flawed, particularly in the country towns. But the times they were a changin' all over the world. Better-educated young Aborigines were not about to accept the lives endured by their parents, and Perkins had no trouble recruiting a busload for the ride through north-western New South Wales.

At Walgett they picketed the Returned Servicemen's League (RSL) Club, which allowed Aboriginal servicemen in on Anzac Day but at no other time. At Moree they picketed the swimming pool, which allowed Aboriginal children in half a day a week but no blacks for the rest of the week. There was a confrontation with police and some arrests, but the local council backed down and allowed them in. It was a small victory in a long battle, but the Freedom Riders showed many Aborigines for the first time that they could stand up and fight for their rights. The publicity the ride generated also shamed many white Australians, and was perhaps a contributing factor in the masssive vote in favour of Aboriginal rights at the 1967 referendum.

I knew nothing about Charles Perkins or the Freedom Ride at the time, but, in the strange way of these things, Perkins, some of his Freedom Riders and the rights they fought for, were all about to figure in my new life in white, middle-class, suburban Sydney.

I said tearful goodbyes to my friends at Barellan Central School. Then Mr Kurtzman took me to Wagga to receive the local newspaper's 'Sportsman of the Year' award. I don't remember anything about the presentation, but I do remember Bill Kurtzman driving me home that night with tears in his eyes as we talked about my new life in Sydney. I thought at the time that he was just proud that I'd won the award, but in hindsight I'm sure it went deeper than that. Perhaps he was only then beginning to realise that I was no longer Barellan's property, that the machine he had set in motion was moving into high gear and that he would no longer be able to drive it.

I flew to Sydney straight after Christmas and moved back into my room with Trisha, just like any other holiday. That was what I told myself whenever I let my mind wander onto the permanence of this separation from my family — it was just another holiday.

Luckily I didn't have a lot of time to dwell on it. I had been selected, along with other members of my North Shore tennis club, as an usherette at White City for the Davis Cup rubber against Spain. The Spanish team was accompanied by about 400 noisy supporters, whose expenses were funded by public subscription back home. They had plenty of reasons to be cheerful and they turned the courts at White City into a bull-ring as they hoisted their goatskins of wine, banged drums and sang in the stands.

I thought it was wonderful, watching their antics as I escorted dignitaries to their seats, but the tennis establishment thought otherwise. The central umpire eventually had to call for order before the Spanish hero, Manuel Santana, began his match with Fred Stolle. Then, whenever Santana stole a point, the fans would errupt again. 'Olè Manola!' But it didn't help. Fred won easily.

Throughout that hot January in Sydney Mr Edwards worked Trisha and me on the backyard court, sending us over to VAETS to get in some match play or even hit against the wall, whenever he had other obligations. Frances Luff came to Sydney from Gundagai and the training intensified. Suddenly it was almost February and I hadn't even thought about going back to school. But Mr and Mrs Edwards had.

Although both Trisha and Jenifer went to the Catholic college Monte Sant'

Angelo in North Sydney, I was enrolled at the state-run Willoughby Girls High. Ostensibly this was because I was not a Catholic, but it may also have been because I was repeating second form. This put me in the same year at school as Trisha, and Mr Edwards may have surmised that it would have been a bit much for us to share a bedroom, a tennis coach and a classroom simultaneously. If so, it was an astute judgment, for although Trisha and I were room-mates and doubles partners, even good friends for half-a-dozen years or more, we were never as close as sisters, despite the media's insistence that we were. We both needed time and space of our own, particularly as we grew older.

Willoughby Girls High was like three or four Barellan Schools rolled into one, and I found it quite daunting on my first day. The physical education teacher called me out in front of the class and proceeded to test my temperament. She said, 'I suppose you can run, Evonne?'

I said I could.

'Then you'll be on the running team. Swim? Good, you're on the swimming team.'

She kept on with it and the girls in the class thought it was a huge joke. I laughed, too, and it became the ice-breaker. I suppose it was rather like

School days at Willoughby

going to an American college on a sports scholarship. There was an expectation of prowess that I had never felt in Barellan.

I hated the regimentation of my new school, and the strict enforcement of the wearing of school uniform. I had never had to wear stockings, hat and gloves in my life and they made me feel claustrophobic and homesick for the wheatfields of home. Trisha said I looked wonderful in my new uniform and insisted on taking a photo of me standing on the front steps at the Edwards house. I sent the picture home to Barellan after having written on the back, 'See the beer bottles [by the steps]. I was wondering why Patricia wanted me to stand there. She wanted to get the beer bottles in. Mr Edwards said you'll probably think they drink all the time.'

Fortunately I soon made a friend at school in Helen Conwell, a girl from the country who was as much a tomboy as I was. She couldn't stand to see inactivity during recess and lunch. 'Look at those girls over there,' she'd say. 'How can they sit there for an hour and do nothing?'

I became the complete sporting all-rounder at Willoughby, the sports teacher's pet, junior house captain, member of the sprint relay team, and individual sprint and broad jump champion. And in the summer I swam for the school, too. But no tennis, except when the commerce master, Mr Hensley, pulled me out of one of his teacher's classes to play with him on the school court. 'Come on,' he'd say. 'You need the practice.' This didn't go over well with my teacher.

Generally, tennis was for every other waking moment, and in that first year of living with the Edwards family, I realised how determined Vic Edwards was to see I reached the top.

As a coach Mr Edwards certainly had the runs on the board, to borrow a metaphor from another sport beloved of Australians. He had nurtured Fred Stolle, Martin Mulligan and John Newcombe, to name just a few, and I had no quarrel with his abrasive technique on the court. I knew that his gruff manner, no matter how hurtful it may have been at the time, was a device to make me fight for every point, run every ball down. But his psychological tactics off the court were a constant mystery to me. He worked very hard on the Goolagong legend, for example, telling every reporter who'd accept a drink that I would win Wimbledon. Not one day. I would win in 1969, then 1970, then revised again to 1974. I was greater than Margaret Smith at the same age, and so on. Why did he do this? Did he think that the pressure of people's expectations would make me work harder? If he did, then there was a part of me he never quite understood, for I did what I did in tennis to fulfill my own expectations and no one else's.

One afternoon a week I would change bus queues and go to North Sydney instead of Roseville, to Monte Sant'Angelo school where Patricia, Jenifer and I had elocution lessons. This was another part of Mr Edwards' preparation for stardom, and one I found quite embarrassing. The name Goolagong was an elocution teacher's delight. 'Repeat after me,' Madam Hagney would say, 'GOOL-ARR-GONG'. And two dozen girls in plaits and pigtails would recite Wiradjuri in their very best North Shore enunciation. The Goolies along the Lachlan would never have recognised their name.

From Mrs Edwards I learnt deportment, etiquette and grooming, although not in any formal way. Eva Edwards was at heart still the girl from Angledool, and she had no time for false airs or pomposity. Nevertheless, she had an old-fashioned and heartfelt belief in the essential components of 'being a lady', and she ensured that I got a grounding in all departments.

I have been painted many times in the media as an Eliza Doolittle, an Aboriginal urchin who was saved from the savages and taught civilised ways by the Edwards family. It wasn't like that, and I was delighted — for Linda Goolagong's sake, particularly — when Mrs Edwards set the record straight in a newspaper interview in 1980: 'When Evonne came to me she was already a perfect little lady,' Mrs Edwards said. 'Mrs Goolagong is a fine woman with more commonsense than most of us, and many deep down thoughts. She'd trained her daughter well.'

As time went by I played doubles less with Frances Luff and more with Trisha. We became the 'tennis twins'. We wore matching dresses and off we'd go together to the tournaments. I'd win the singles and Trisha and I would win the doubles. Then we'd come home together, put our trophies on the sideboard and start training for the next one. That was the pattern of our lives.

We would also ogle boys together. Our fascination with John Alexander continued, but I also had a crush on Roger Taylor, a big, tall, good-looking tennis player from Sheffield in England. I remember the first time I saw him at White City, this gorgeous guy moving about the court with such power. I was transfixed. I don't know how long I stood there watching him play but it must have become obvious because he turned around and winked at me. I fled in embarrassment.

Roger Taylor, a working class lad who hadn't gone to the right school or learnt his tennis at the right club, was Britain's best player at that time. He was a fitness fanatic who worked out in the gym every day and built his tennis around his agility and power. Along with John Newcombe, Tony Roche and Cliff Drysdale, he was one of the original members of the 'Handsome

Tricia Edwards (left) and me after winning a doubles match at White City, 1964

Eight', a touring troupe in the early days of open tennis. Almost a decade after I fell madly in love with him at White City, I played tennis with him in Stockholm. By this time I had my own Roger — in fact we'd just been married in Barellan a month earlier — and I felt able to tell him what that wink did to me all those years ago. This time it was Roger Taylor's turn to be embarrassed.

During most school holidays I'd try to get home to Barellan unless I was playing in a tournament, but sometimes — during the long summer break or on long weekends — I'd go with the Edwards family to their holiday cottage at Wamberal on the New South Wales Central Coast. On these occasions, away from the tennis court, I naturally gravitated more towards Jenifer. We'd hang out on the beach together or get up very early and go fishing. I'd have to bait Jenifer's hook; she refused to touch worms.

I loved those beach holidays because we became a real family away from that consuming passion, tennis, which ruled our lives. I wasn't a champion in the making at Wamberal, just a teenager with a red transistor radio. The only orders Mr Edwards barked at us there were to sweep the sand out of the house or get up on the roof and clean the leaves out of the gutters. The evenings were reserved for cards games and Scrabble, in which words like 'game', 'set', 'match' and 'serve' were banned.

Towards the end of my first year at Willoughby Girls High something happened that makes me realise — with the wonderful benefit of hindsight — just how much of myself I had blocked out, or at least put into storage. During a history period we were asked to write an essay about a day in the life of an early settler. I took on the assignment with gusto, for this was a subject on which I was well versed, having been brought up on the 'frontier'. I wrote feelingly about the hard life of the pioneers, getting up before dawn to plough the fields and working all day with their animals. And, as if life wasn't tough enough, they had to contend with marauding Aborigines! My settler knew what to do when the blacks came in to steal his sheep. He reached for his gun and shot them.

That was what I wrote in 1966.

Chapter 9

I HAD MORE THAN A DOZEN age titles to my credit when Vic Edwards decided in November 1966 that it was time for me to have a crack at the 'big time'.

Admittedly the big time wasn't all that big — the NSW Open and Junior Grass Court Championship at White City — but it was to be my first tussle with the best players in the country. Mr Edwards told reporters that he'd 'brought Evonne along quietly but I think now is the time for her to have some stiffer competition. I don't think many of the juniors playing at the moment will be able to beat her. There could be only one — Lesley Hunt of Western Australia.'

Lesley Hunt was a blonde firecracker who, at 16, was a year older than me, and who had been mistaken for a boy when she first attracted attention at Kooyong in Melbourne at the age of 14. She had had short, spiky hair and a boyish figure, and she had hit the ball with the power of a grown man. Since then she had grown her hair and developed a figure, but she still hit the ball like a man. When she started beating players like Karen Krantzcke, then the New South Wales number one woman player, and Kerry Melville, the Victorian under-19 champion, there were the inevitable comparisons with Margaret Smith. The prospect of meeting Lesley in the NSW championships didn't concern me in the least. In fact I was looking forward to the encounter, but it was not to be.

Hoping against hope that I was on my way to my first open final, I despatched Holland's Lidy Venneboer in straight sets, then Evelyn Terras of France — the number four seed — went down without taking a game. Next up was Australia's number five, Gail Sherriff, a girl with a forehand that could drill holes in you. We met on a windy outside court in front of a large crowd. *The Sydney Morning Herald* tennis reporter Alan Clarkson wrote in a long account of this relatively minor encounter:

> Of the 64 matches played yesterday none gave more pleasure, nor provided a better and more exciting contest, than the clash between 15-year-old Aboriginal girl Evonne Goolagong and Gail Sherriff in the women's singles.

Miss Sherriff, fifth seeded for the singles event, won 6–2, 6–3, but not until she had summoned all her experience and skill.

The scores did not give a true indication of the tenseness and closeness of the match. Miss Sherriff, who has a forehand as if she was cracking her worst enemy, unleashed her power-laden shots in an effort to knock her younger opponent off the court. But on many of these occasions, the smooth-stroking Miss Goolagong relished the pace and put the ball back with equal ferocity ... and often out of the older girl's reach.

In the under-19 championships I reached the quarter-finals before being knocked out by Queensland's Lexie Kenny, so Mr Edwards was happy enough. 'You did well, honey,' he said. 'Now next year we'll really show 'em.'

With school and tennis finished for the year I went home to Barellan. But not home to the *Barellan Leader* house on Bendee Street. Kenny and Linda had rented a run-down but spacious weatherboard house around the corner in Yarran Street. It had been the residence and surgery of Dr Polner, the local GP, and quite a stylish home in its day. There was even a run-down tennis court in the backyard, on which a cow grazed contentedly.

Sure, the place needed work, but it was so much more comfortable than the *Leader* office. I think Mr Edwards had talked to my parents about finding a new house during the year when I insisted on sending the small amount of money I had down to them to help finance the construction of a new septic system toilet to take the place of the backyard toilet. He'd said to me, 'You could pour a small fortune into that dump and never see the benefit. Better to get them into something else.'

It seemed so long since I'd seen everyone. Mum looked a little plumper, maybe a little older; Kenny was a little balder, and Larry, who was working in the wheat silos over at Hillston and playing guitar in a band called the 'Red Velvets' ... well, Larry had, ah, filled out. 'It's the good life, Mooch,' he explained. 'Hard work and hard drinkin'.'

Kevin had a Beatles haircut, Gail, Ian and Janelle had shot up in height, and Mully! My cute little bundle of baby was a young man, and a tearaway at that! He didn't much like being picked up and squeezed by his big sisters, but Barbara and I couldn't leave him alone.

After several years of nannying, Barbara had finally started to train as a nurse that year at Narrandera Hospital, where she had taken up with a fellow named Bill Bevan.

'He's asked me to marry him,' she told me when we had a moment to ourselves.

'And what did you say?'

The family at our new Yarran Street home in 1966. From left, back: Gail, Kevin, me, Larry and Barbara; front, Janelle, Ian and Mully

Barbara giggled. 'I told him I'd think about it in my own sweet time. That put him in his place. He must have thought I'd go down on hands and knees and thank him for asking me. But he's pretty nice.'

It took some time for me to digest all of this — Barbara almost married, Larry a country rock star, Mully all grown up ... It seemed like the world had kept turning without me, and for the first time in a year I felt that perhaps I had made a huge mistake, that I belonged in Barellan, not with the Edwards family in Roseville. The feeling stayed with me over Christmas and occasionally it gnawed at me like a hunger pain or a stitch in my side, but there was little time to dwell on it.

On Boxing Day the War Memorial Tennis Club put on a social evening in my honour. Everyone in town seemed to be there to watch me play a few sets with Clarrie Irvin and some of the better players. Then the juniors presented me with a beach towel and Bill Kurtzman got up and made a very emotional speech about how proud of me he was. I could feel the tears gathering in the corner of my eyes as he presented me with a writing case from all the club members, but I focused on Gail Sherriff's forehand and how I would deal with it next time, and got through my little thank you speech without a sob. I told them the gift would inspire me to write regular letters home, not that I needed much inspiration. I was a prolific letter writer in those early days, as much as anything to combat my homesickness.

The next day I flew back to Sydney to get ready for the first of the January tournaments, and was soon so immersed in my preparation for that busy month that any thoughts about returning to Barellan had to be put on hold. I played in the Manly Seaside Tournament and reached the quarter finals of both the open and under-19 events. In the women's I went down to Holland's Betty Stove, but not before stretching her to 7–5 in the first set. I was finding it a little difficult to get used to losing so often, but Mr Edwards kept reassuring me. 'Honey, these girls are stronger, smarter, more experienced,' he'd say. 'Learn from them, and only let them beat you once.'

This may have been sound advice, but my defeat the following week at Canterbury did nothing to halt my growing self-doubts. In the semi-final of the under-17 event, my old rival Janine Murdock trapped me on the baseline and moonballed me to death in a match which lasted more than two hours. The more moonballs she popped up to me, the more opportunities I gave her to dictate the play, and Janine won in three sets — my first age title defeat in three years. Mr Edwards was bitterly disappointed, but he tried to keep his feelings from me and concentrated on pouring praise on Trisha for her win in the under-15s, which was a tremendous breakthrough for her in singles competition. Perhaps he sensed that I was going through a homesickness crisis, and thought it best to see if I bounced back without any prompting.

And, of course I did bounce back. In fact 1967 was destined to be the year in which the Goolagong hype-machine really cranked into high gear. The reason for this had only a little to do with me. This was the very height of Australia's golden age of tennis. Rosewall, Laver, Newcombe and Roche carried the flag for the men; Margaret Smith carried it for the women. Oh, there were other good women players, but Margaret so dominated women's tennis in the mid-1960s that the others were just sparring partners for her. But in 1967 Margaret Smith had traded the tennis court for Barry Court, a son of the former premier of Western Australia, Sir Charles Court. She had decided there was another side of life beyond tennis, and she had opted to discover its joys.

Margaret's retirement left a large open space at the top of the pyramid of Australian women's tennis. Jack Kramer wrote in his Sydney *Daily Telegraph* column: 'Women's tennis in Australia has struck a relatively bad patch in recent

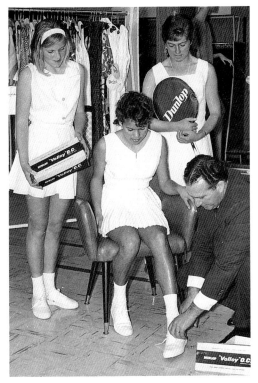 

Left: Sponsored by Dunlop, Trisha (left), Helen Gourlay and me *Right:* Aged 15 at White City

years. Several of the top girl players have, for one reason or another, lost their edge.'

Lesley Turner, Karen Krantzcke, Judy Tegart, Jan Lehane O'Neill and Kerry Melville were all good players, but, according to those who were concerned about such things at the time, none of them had the stamp of greatness. The next great player, these experts decreed, would come from the new generation of women players. These people had been tipping me to reach the top ever since Vic Edwards brought me to their attention in 1964, so I suppose it was only natural that they would look now at the void and repair to their typewriters with renewed vigour. Wrote Jack Kramer: 'But they [the top girls] will soon be joined by a teenager who many experts believe will become an even greater star than Margaret Court. Her name is Evonne Goolagong.'

Of course, not everyone was convinced. At the Australian women's singles at Kooyong in January 1968 Billie Jean King defeated Lesley Hunt 6–3, 6–4, while Margaret Court despatched me 6–3, 6–1. This prompted Billie Jean to declare Lesley the best junior player in Australia, a much better prospect than me. 'If she is willing to make the sacrifices Lesley could be a Wimbledon champion,' she said.

Mr Edwards gives me some pointers at VAETS

It had been only Margaret Smith that had retired; Margaret Court bounced back strongly, but during the latter part of 1967 and throughout 1968 a lot of trees perished so that the public might learn again and again about the little picaninny from Barellan who was bound for tennis glory. 'Wimbledon Here I Come!' trumpeted one newspaper. 'Evonne Moves Closer To A Place In Wimbledon Squad' claimed another. And my favourite for the year: 'The Strong Young Legs of Evonne, Our Bright New Star!'

This last was in *Pix* magazine, whose reporter, after watching me thrash Australian junior champion Lexie Kenny, wrote: 'Not by a toss of her short curly hair, not by an expression of nervousness in her flashing eyes, not by the slightest lessening of her lovely shy smile, not by any sign in her sturdy legs did she falter.' I wonder if he wrote as expressively about John Alexander, who was mirroring my achievements in the boys ranks. I suspect not, but at least the reporters were starting to spell my name right!

Towards the end of 1967, Lexie Kenny and I met three times in successive weeks: in the Queensland, New South Wales and Victorian girls championships. At Milton in Brisbane Lexie, who could hit the ball very hard at times, extended me by winning the first set of our semi-final 10–8. But she had little firepower left and I won the second 6–2, and went on to beat Judy Salome of Holland, the Wimbledon junior champion, in the final.

In the NSW championships at White City Lexie and I met in the final and she put everything she possessed into her serve to have me 40–0 in the first game. Then something inside me twigged. I knew this girl's game. I knew where she would put the ball and where I needed to put my return. Lexie took only six more points from me in the match, which I won 6–0, 6–1. At Kooyong in Melbourne, I took her out 6–0, 6–0 in the semi-final of the Victorian titles, and then beat Jan Young in straight sets in the final.

After this treble, Australian tennis great Adrian Quist wrote of me, 'At 16 she is a completely natural player with very orthodox ground strokes. She swings smoothly at the ball and her timing is perfect. Furthermore, her approach to the game is excellent … She plays every shot to win the point and does not rely on opponents' errors.'

This was high praise indeed from the legendary doubles player, but I can't say it made much difference to me at the time. I still never saw a critique, nor even a match report, and it is only in reading over the scrap books of my early career that I can see how perceptive some observers were, and how fanciful were others. This reluctance to read my own press originated with Mr Edwards, but it has stayed with me all my life. In fact I never even saw myself on television until 1976, five years after my first Wimbledon victory was seen live around the world. I was just too embarrassed!

In early 1968 I was the top-ranked girl in New South Wales but on the national stage a three-way tussle for supremacy had developed between Lesley Hunt, new star Brenda Jenkins of Victoria and myself. This meant very little to me, I must say, because Mr Edwards didn't hold much store in rankings. He had a very firm idea of what constituted a champion, and while he was never shy about putting this view to the tennis media, opinions to the contrary didn't bother him. Nevertheless, I didn't do my own cause much good in January when I went down to Kerry Harris, ranked number three in Victoria, in the Australian girls titles at Kooyong, nor when I was beaten convincingly by Lesley Hunt in the Wilson Cup at Kooyong a few days later.

Lesley said after the match, 'I didn't have any plan to beat her, but I'd been told she didn't play well against somebody who attacked the net. I did this, and she made the mistakes by driving the ball into the net or over the baseline.'

Despite these losses I was expected to be an automatic selection — after Lesley Hunt — in the six-player team to be sent by the Lawn Tennis Association of Australia on an overseas tour during the northern summer of 1968. But Mr Edwards had other ideas. The moment my selection was mooted, he declared, 'Evonne will not be going overseas until 1969 or 1970. This year she will be completing her schooling in Sydney.' There was no argument about this. Mr Edwards knew best. My job was to play tennis.

That summer, playing at Kooyong for the first time, I had been invited to attend a charity evening in Melbourne at which the singers John Farnham and Olivia Newton-John were to be guests of honour. The charity was a children's fund, and, as the new Victorian junior tennis champion, I was invited onto the stage. I wore a lime-green evening dress and felt every bit the star as I was presented to John and Olivia. After the formalities my 'minder' for the evening (the only time I ever had one) took me to the home of one of her friends who also worked in music and television.

Lesley Shaw was four years older than me and she was everything that I wasn't. She was loud, brash, confident and worldly. Not yet out of her teens, she knew her way around town like a veteran. Her flat was decorated with concert posters, loud music played all the time and people seemed to use the place as a thoroughfare. Lesley presided over this madness with a kind of lovable authority. She took me aside and surprised me with her knowledge of tennis.

'I love it,' she said. 'Never get a chance to see a match these days.' We made a pact. I would get her tennis tickets and make sure she came along to see me play; she would get me concert tickets whenever I was in town, and keep me supplied with rock tapes. Such was the beginning of a friendship which has endured over more than a quarter of a century, through fame and fortune, marriage, children, heartaches and hassles. While I made my name in the tennis world, Lesley's career progressed in leaps and bounds. She produced television shows then branched into live shows working with promoter Paul Dainty.

Yet no matter what Lesley is doing in her career, she is never too busy to come to the aid of a friend. She has always been there when I needed her, particularly during the early years in Sydney, often with the solution to the problem. If I was feeling low, stuck in a hotel room over Christmas, Lesley would be there with the tree and the decorations. 'Are you going to sit around and mope or are you going to help me tart this place up?' On one occasion I felt ill just before a final. Lesley asked me what was wrong. Her face screwed into a ball when I told her it was diarrhoea, but in a flash she was off. When she returned she had the remedy which allowed me to get through the match.

Whenever I needed time away from tennis Lesley was there to take me into her mad, magical world of entertainment. When Mr Edwards thought otherwise, she was the only one who would stand up to him and force the point. 'Whaddya mean she can't go out tonight? She's almost 18 years old!' Mr Edwards would usually end up laughing and agree to let me go.

Likewise, over the years I lived in America, when Lesley needed a place to hide out away from the madness, she would come and stay with us.

During my last year at school in 1968 my interest in boys intensified, although not in the same way that Trisha's did. She was a year younger and quite a small, dainty girl, but she had blossomed into womanhood a lot faster than me. I marvelled at the development of her breasts, compared with my flat, little-girl chest.

In ways other than physical she seemed to change too. Always a serious girl, conservative by nature, she talked more and more about marriage and raising a family, and less about tennis, which increasingly seemed to be something she pursued for her mother's benefit.

Mrs Edwards had given birth to seven children, two of whom — including the only boy — had died in infancy. The five surviving girls had all had brief flirtations with tennis, but only the youngest, Patricia, had pursued it. One would have thought that the parents — one the master coach, the other a former schoolgirl champion — would be delighted to see their last child progressing in the game. But as Trisha recalls it now, Mr Edwards never actively encouraged her to play. 'In fact,' she says, 'if Fred Stolle and Marty Mulligan hadn't encouraged me to get on the court and have a hit, I'm sure I would never have taken it up.'

Mrs Edwards, on the other hand, was delighted and offered quiet words of encouragement whenever Trisha played. She loved to see us as a doubles team — which was basically every second year, when we were within the same age division — and fussed over the design of our 'tennis twins' dresses, which she had a dressmaker run up. Somehow Trisha always looked more at home in the fancy frills than I did.

For all her seriousness, however, Trisha and I sometimes had fun together, and often it involved boys — in the most innocent ways, of course. Mr Edwards saw to that, with rules, regulations and curfews. Our social lives revolved around tennis. We played for Chatswood in the Northern Suburbs District Competition and when we got lucky we would be paired in the mixed doubles with a couple of guys who had sports cars. Nothing ever happened, but just zipping around in an exciting car in the company of a boy, and maybe stopping for a milkshake on the way home, was a thrill.

Throughout the winter of 1968 schoolwork took precedence over tennis. Trisha and I still trained every day, of course, but Mr Edwards was insistent that we attain the best possible results in the School Certificate. In Trisha's case there was a definite goal in mind. She had decided to become a speech therapist, once we had done 'the tour' and gotten tennis out of our systems. My own future was firmly linked to tennis. All I could imagine myself doing was playing tennis. But Mr Edwards' view was that we both needed a 'back-up', a career path we could fall back on should we break a leg, or worse, fail to make the grade at the international level. Thus it was decided that we would make our first European tour in 1970, leaving 1969 clear to complete secretarial courses at business college and achieve peak fitness in preparation for the year ahead.

All of this made perfectly good sense to me. Tennis was for fun, not money, and you had to earn a living somehow. I had no idea that events on the other side of the world that year were changing the whole structure of tennis, and of my future.

At the top level, amateur tennis was a sham by the late 1960s. Since 1926 a dribble of tennis players each year had decided that they needed money as much as glory and had gone off to play exhibition matches as professionals. But these players were considered outcasts and were shunned by the International Lawn Tennis Federation (ILTF). In the 1950s hard-nosed pros like Jack Kramer and Pancho Gonzales brought more attention (and credibility) to the renegade pro tour, but they were only interested in players who had

Rising stars. Trisha Edwards and me in 1968

already reached the top as amateurs. The reality, however, was that few players could afford to travel the world each year for the hell of it, and tournament organisers were forced to pay the top players under-the-counter 'expenses' and 'appearance fees' to ensure their attendance.

It was an absurd situation and it was coming to a head when Billie Jean King won Wimbledon for a second time in 1967. Nothing if not forthright, she told the world how stupid she thought a system was which allowed her to make as much as $US1200 a week from playing tennis while claiming to be an amateur. 'I'm not an amateur, for Chrissake! I'm a professional tennis player and it's time we were recognised as such.'

Faced with massive insurrection from the world's leading players, the ILTF agreed to sanction 12 open tournaments in 1968. The first completed match of the open era, at Bournemouth in April, was won by Owen Davidson, an Australian pro who had given me the thrill of my life at Albury a few years earlier, when he had asked to partner me in the mixed doubles.

Still, the birth of open tennis was not exactly a momentous event at VAETS in Roseville, NSW, nor at Willoughby Girls High, where I continued to cram for the final exams. And if Mr Edwards suddenly saw a brave new world in which his leading protégée, Evonne Goolagong, would bring home bags of money to make his retirement a well-deserved joy, he did not say so. I think it more likely that he was prepared to wait and see how the new world order worked out. I don't believe that making money out of my ability was his primary concern. Certainly, my continued success and high media profile kept the students pouring through the gates of VAETS, but Victor Allan Edwards was cut from the cloth of an earlier time — a time when the challenge was everything. And Mr Edwards' challenge was the creation of a champion.

Although Trisha had severe misgivings about our impending European tour, I was thrilled by the prospect. I loved nothing better than our excited chatter over the dinner table about what we would do and see, where we would play, who we would meet. It was *Princess* magazine in real life, and I couldn't wait for it to begin. These conversations usually took place in front of the entire family, and Jenifer and I would tease Trisha about her nervousness, and try to imagine what London would be like … or Paris. 'Come on, girls. Enough chatter, eat up.' Mrs Edwards would bring us back to the here and now when our flights of fancy became too much, but Mr Edwards would encourage me in my naive vision of the grand adventure.

I was not particularly surprised, therefore, when he took up the theme several times when we were alone. The talk was generally in the form of advice about what to expect, what we might encounter on the courts and off, offered in the most fatherly manner. He took me aback one day, however, when he suddenly turned the conversation around to boys and my social life, such as it was.

'If there's anything you need, anything you want,' he said, clutching me by both arms, 'you come to me, honey. Do you understand? Come to me.'

I was confused. I shook my head.

'About sex. Come to me.'

I felt sick to the pit of my stomach. What did he mean? No, he didn't mean that. I was taking his words the wrong way. I stared at my coach, my mentor, my guardian, my second father … and I might have cried had I not seen another way out. I laughed. Mr Edwards was making a little joke. He grinned, briefly. Everything was all right. It was just a misunderstanding.

Everything was okay, but it would never be quite the same.

Chapter 10

*I*N 1964 THE FOUNDATION FOR ABORIGINAL AFFAIRS had been established in Sydney in response to the growing need for city-based Aborigines to have some kind of social, cultural and administrative centre. A public appeal supported by community groups and churchmen like the Reverend Ted Noffs of Sydney's Wayside Chapel had raised enough funds to purchase a dilapidated old building next to the Lotteries Office in Railway Square.

While this was not the most salubrious part of town, it was a short walk from Central Station and only a slightly longer walk from the large Aboriginal community in the inner-city suburb of Redfern. Moreover, its very existence was a long way from the attitudes which had prevailed in Australia throughout the 1950s. In 1959 Aborigines had been declared eligible for Commonwealth welfare payments — except for unemployment benefits (the dole), since it was more than most Aborigines earned — but it was to be another eight years before the big breakthrough, the 1967 referendum in which 90 per cent of Australians voted in favour of recognising that we were people, too, thus allowing us to be included in the Census, and handing jurisdiction over Aborigines back to the Commonwealth.

In the meantime, however, the first generation of educated Aborigines had emerged, angry with their lot and articulate enough to give voice to their frustrations. Primarily concerned with the squalid living conditions of the majority of Aborigines, and the opportunities denied them and their children, these people had formed themselves into organisations like the Aboriginal Advancement League, the Australian Aboriginal Fellowship and the Federal Council for the Advancement of Aborigines (later extended to include Torres Strait Islanders). They took up such causes as the Yirrkala people's fight against the leasing of their land to the Nabalco mining company, the grazing leases which had been granted on Cummeragunga Reserve; and the now-historic wages claim of the Gurindji people of the Northern Territory.

The cattle industry of northern Australia — a string of vast and isolated empires increasingly under the control of a small number of multi-national corporations — had been reliant for almost a century on the work of Aboriginal stockmen. These hardy characters, who rightfully fill the pages of Australia's folklore, were for many years paid in tea and tobacco. Later the pot was sweetened to include rum and beer, and sometimes a roof to sleep under. But during World War II Aboriginal diggers (soldiers) received equal pay, and in the post-war years demand grew for the cattle barons to pay fair wages. The days of tea and tobacco were over, but the cattle industry refused to consider equal pay, claiming that it would ruin them.

In 1965 the Australian Council of Trade Unions had accepted Aboriginal stockmen as members and, after a case before the Arbitration Commission that year had confirmed that industrial law must be for 'all Australians', the pastoralists had been told to introduce equal pay immediately. But a delegation from the industry had managed to convince the Commission that immediate equal pay would have a devastating effect, and the ruling was deferred for three years. Fed up with waiting, the Gurindji stockmen and their families walked off Wave Hill Station, the 15,500 square kilometre (6000 square miles) property then owned by the British company Vesteys, in August 1966. They camped in a riverbed with a growing number of supporters, black and white, from all over Australia. The strike attracted world attention, and when the Gurindjis moved to their Dreaming land at Wattie Creek and refused to budge, it became the first Aboriginal land rights claim of the modern era.

This was the climate in which the Foundation for Aboriginal Affairs had been born — a time of great frustration, unfulfilled promise and unconcealed anger. Yet it was also a time in which hope replaced despair in many places, because in small ways Aboriginal people could see that they were starting to get somewhere. Vincent Lingiari of the Gurindji declared, 'On August 22, 1966, the Gurindji tribe decided to cease to live like dogs.' Charles Perkins, the first manager of the Foundation, established welfare officers, counsellors and administrators in one part of the building, and turned over the rest to a social and cultural centre. Then he had set off on his Freedom Ride exposing racism in the country towns of western New South Wales.

I can't remember who first mentioned the Foundation to me. It may have been Mr Edwards or it may have been my own family. Certainly Mr Edwards encouraged me to go there and mix with my own people, and since we were 'sisters' he also encouraged Jenifer and Trisha to go with me. There were regular Saturday night dances and it was at one of these in the summer of 1968 that I first met Isabel Hansen, and through her, yet another 'family'.

Isabel was a dark-eyed Aranda girl who'd grown up on Glen Ormiston Station in the Queensland Channel Country near the Northern Territory border. Both her parents worked on the station and had become friendly with the overseer's family. The overseer, recognising that there were no opportunities for young people in that remote part of the country, offered Isabel a place to stay in Sydney, should she wish to investigate a future there. When she was 16 Isabel went to Sydney to have a look, that was all. She phoned her parents and told them she was going to look for a job. She found one, with Charles Perkins, a second cousin, at the Foundation for Aboriginal Affairs.

By 1968 Charlie Perkins was developing into one of the key Aboriginal leaders, a man of great passion and commitment who could inspire the young people around him to work long and hard for the cause. His manner, however, was often abrasive. He tended to call a spade a shovel, and to engage his vocal chords ahead of his brain. Nevertheless, he was widely respected at the Foundation, and within Isabel's social group he was almost revered.

I had never met people like Isabel and her friends. They were young and full of fun, but their approach to life was underlined by a deep understanding of the politics of being black. Two of them, Bob Morgan and Michael Anderson, had been in Walgett when Perkins came through with his Freedom Riders in 1965. Like other young Aborigines who witnessed those confrontations, they thereafter understood the power of direct action, and yet they were not slogan-shouting activists.

Bob and Michael were cousins who had come to Sydney just a couple of weeks apart and shared a flat in Glebe at the western edge of the city. Michael enrolled in a business course at Sydney Technical College but both of them worked at the Foundation most of the time, where they built up a strong core of young Aborigines who were committed to advancing the cause. One day in 1967 Bob, Michael and a small group of these people walked up to the Great Southern Hotel in George Street for lunch. They were refused service. Incensed, Michael phoned Trades Hall and the *Sydney Morning Herald*. By the end of the afternoon a liquor ban had been imposed on the hotel and the *Herald* had a front page story.

At that stage of my life I had no interest in, and no understanding of, racial politics, but that didn't seem to concern my new friends. Soon after our first meeting I told Isabel, 'I'm just not political.' She responded, 'You were born black, that's political.'

There was no pressure on me, however, to take part in the rallies or to familiarise myself more with the issues they considered so important. Isabel says that I wasn't ready. It was as simple as that. I didn't know the issues and I couldn't understand them. There were people behind the scenes pushing me to become politically active because I was already famous as a tennis player, but to them I was just a friend. Tennis didn't mean that much to them. They used to like to go down to Manly Beach and throw boomerangs.

Most of the pushing to involve me politically came from Charlie Perkins. Although I had very little to do with him at a personal level, he made known his feelings. To him there were no grey areas. You were either part of the solution or you were part of the problem. In hindsight I would tend to agree in principle, but in the late 1960s Charlie could not — or would not — see that I was a teenager who had been brought up from a very early age with her entire being centred on one goal: to become a world tennis champion; to become the first Aboriginal world tennis champion. Charlie couldn't see that perhaps this would do as much for our cause as me walking down George Street holding a placard.

After I left school that summer of 1968 I took up with Bob Morgan. Nothing serious, mind you. We dated in groups most of the time, but I suppose he was my first real boyfriend. Bob was a few years older than me, a lovely, gentle Aboriginal man who enjoyed working with his people, as he still does. (He is now the director of the Koori Educational Centre in Sydney.) In fact most of the members of that group have devoted their lives to improving the lot of Aboriginal people in one way or another. Isabel is now married to Ramon Tarrago and heads the social and cultural division of the Queensland Aboriginal Affairs department. Another of the group, Tom Briggs, became the first Aboriginal policeman in New South Wales, and Michael Anderson is now a lecturer in Aboriginal Studies at Newcastle University and working towards his Master's degree in social anthropology.

We spent a lot of time at the Foundation, but the Edwards family also made Isabel and Bob and the others welcome at their home in Roseville. Isabel can remember sleeping top-to-tail with me on many occasions, and often, if we were all going out to a dance — Jenifer included, for she too had become part of the group — we would have a casual supper with the Edwards first. Isabel remembers Mrs Edwards as 'lovely, very caring', but Mr Edwards frightened her. 'He was so abrupt, so arrogant, that you got the feeling we were intruding, interrupting Evonne's training program or something. But I know he didn't really feel like that. It was just his manner. I know he wanted her to spend time with us Kooris.'

Michael Anderson has similar memories: 'We had good times at the Edwards' place, but most of them were when the old man wasn't around. He always seemed to me to be worried about our influence on Evonne, but Mrs Edwards, she was another story. She was from Angledool and she'd been there in 1939 when they sent the Kooris on the long march to Brewarrina. She knew our families and she understood our people.'

In *Evonne*, the book American tennis writer Bud Collins wrote about me with Mr Edwards in 1975, he quotes me as saying, 'The Edwards' outlook wouldn't coincide with that of the young activist Aborigines. It couldn't. Age and background are against it.' That's not quite true. For one thing, the 'activists' the Edwards family came into contact with through me were in fact moderates — at least they were in 1969. And for another thing both Mr and Mrs Edwards had, in my opinion, quite a liberal outlook on black/white relations for people of their generation. Unlike many of their peers, both of them had lived in the bush and worked with Aborigines. Sure, they were paternalistic in some unthinking ways, but I never heard or saw either of them treat a person of my race with anything other than respect.

In the book Bud Collins quotes from 'Vic Edwards' journal': '... must guard against her exploitation ... even by Aborigines, which may seem harsh, but she mustn't be diverted from her job ... from time to time Black Power-type Aborigines try to use her ... several extremely intelligent and well-educated ones have befriended her, and I'm glad for that, even though I know they believe Eva and I are making her "too white" and are keeping her from her people ... so be it ... people may believe what they will.'

I saw Bob less frequently as the tennis season wound up to its January peak, but I thought of him constantly. It wasn't love, but I was very fond of him, and of the whole group. They made me think of 'home', but not of Barellan; rather of those carefree days playing by the river at The Murie or Three Ways. They reminded me of my people, but not in a way that made me homesick or fretful; instead they gave me a sense of feeling good about being an Aborigine. Proud, that was it! Proud to be an Aborigine.

In January 1969 I renewed my tussle with Lesley Hunt. We met first in the final of the Victorian girls singles, in what was the unofficial clash for the title of heiress-apparent to the throne of Australian women's tennis. While I had stayed at home to finish school, Lesley had toured overseas with the LTAA's representative team, and her game had improved a lot. I expected to struggle against her but in the event we were evenly matched. I took one set from her and the others she won by a service break. We met again a week later in the Wilson Cup and I evened the score over three tough sets. Lesley was the Australian junior singles champion still, but I was beginning to feel that when I played my natural game — not allowing my opponent to dictate play — I had her measure.

At the beginning of February Trisha and I began our courses at the Metropolitan Business College in downtown Sydney, not far from Circular Quay. I was enrolled in the basic shorthand and typing secretarial course (nothing appealed to me less) but Trisha was to learn comptometry, which apparently was an ancestor of computing. I had no interest in that either. The only thing that interested me about business college was the fact that it was only two train stops to the Foundation for Aboriginal Affairs. This was where you would find me as often as I was at the college.

I would sit and talk over coffees with people from Griffith and the Condo, people who knew my people, or at least knew someone who did. During Isabel's lunch hour we would sit in Belmore Park with our sandwiches and tea cakes, or we would walk across to Paddy's Market in the Haymarket district, and look at the stalls and the characters who manned them.

During this period Mr Edwards' training program intensified in preparation for our overseas tour in 1970. Several mornings a week we would drive to Dee Why Beach and run along the soft sand towards Long Reef, building up the strength of our calf muscles and our overall stamina. We worked out on the back court and we played a lot of tennis. But Mr Edwards seemed to be at pains to avoid the 'burnout' syndrome. The majority of our matches that year were not of the highest standard, but against a wide variety of opponents. We played against kids younger than ourselves, against power-serving men, and middle-aged women to whom placement was everything. Often the object of the exercise was not to beat the opponents into submission, but to learn how to counter anything that might be thrown against us, from moonballs to top spin to smashes and drop shots. Club players could be just as crafty as anyone I later met on tour.

As part of this preparation Trisha and I played doubles in the regular White City badge competition twice a week. After one match in which we had comprehensively beaten two older women, we went to the net to shake hands with our opponents. As we shook hands across the net, one of the women turned to her partner and said, 'That's the first time I've ever been beaten by a nigger.'

Nigger. It took a while to sink in. At first I thought I had misheard. Trisha responded with a cutting comment of her own but it all seemed far away and as if it were happening to someone else. Then suddenly I was crying. We were both howling. Standing at the net long after the women had left the court, sobbing and hugging. I'm not sure why that word had such an effect. It was not one I had heard used too many times before, and was not even the language of Australian white supremacists. 'Nigger' had an air of cheap soap opera about it, of fake Scarlett O'Haras descending fake plywood staircases. It reminded me of daytime television. But I couldn't deny the hurt I felt. Was this the way it was going to be out there in the mean streets of tennis?

At Kooyong in 1968

Had Mr Edwards' protective bubble given me a false and naive sense of security?

Still sobbing, I phoned Isabel at the Foundation. She said, 'You jump in a taxi and get here right now!'

By the time I got the Foundation Bob was there, too. He and Isabel both hugged me and listened to my sobs. 'It's okay,' said Bob. 'These things happen to us all the time. You just have to deal with it, and you can. You're strong.'

Isabel tells me now that 'we sat around and drank cups of coffee and talked it through for hours. I'd never seen you so upset. Unlike you, Bob and I had grown up with that sort of thing — not an everyday occurrence but we had come to expect racist attacks from time to time. For you, this was coming from another world, an ugly, vicious world. If it happened today that woman would be in the courts, but back then all we could tell you to do was to put it behind you, to move on.'

Trisha had beaten me home by several hours and Mr Edwards knew all about the incident. He had informed the NSW Lawn Tennis Association by phone and was in the process of writing an official complaint. He appeared very matter-of-fact about it, but I suspect this was his way of dealing with a deep hurt. He was usually quick to anger, but unless he had already passed through this phase before I arrived home, he kept his anger to himself on this occasion. He told me, 'We have to deal with this in the proper manner, through the correct channels.'

I don't know what happened as a result of the complaint. I never saw the woman at White City again and she certainly never again had to suffer the ignominy of being thrashed by this 'nigger'. And I never again had to suffer such an indignity on the tennis court, although strangely enough, I was in the company of Bob and Isabel a few years later in 1974 when racism did rear its ugly head.

We had all flown up to Queensland for a holiday with Jenifer Edwards, who was then touring Australia with her boyfriend in a double-decker bus. We spent some time sightseeing with them around Coolum on the Sunshine Coast, then drove back to Brisbane to spend our last evening together. After dinner we decided to go on to a nightclub to dance the night away. Afro hairstyles were *de rigueur* for black activists at the time, and Bob had a beauty. Perhaps it was the hairstyle rather than the colour of his skin that induced the doorman at Chequers Nightclub to refuse him admission. We were waiting on the footpath when he came out shaking his head in disbelief. 'No Kooris allowed,' he said. This was Brisbane 20 years ago.

I was a touring tennis professional by this time, and I had a good deal more self-confidence than I'd had that day at White City. I wanted to storm the Bastille, but Bob counselled otherwise. 'You could end up in a lot of trouble in this town,' he said. (Brisbane in those days still had the reputation of a country town.) 'There are other nightclubs.'

We walked to Lennons Hotel and, still furious, I went straight to the doorman. He recognised me and could see I was upset. 'We just had a problem at Chequers. They don't let Aborigines in. Is that your policy too?' We were shown in immediately.

In May 1969, I made my debut at a debutantes ball at the Round House at the University of New South Wales. Although the ball was strictly speaking for pupils and former pupils of Catholic schools and I had attended a state school, an exception was made in my case by Madam Hagney, one of the ball organisers and the speech mistress who had laboured so hard at Monte Sant'Angelo school to make me walk and talk like a lady. The preparations were endless — ball gown fittings, rehearsals, dancing lessons. At home Mrs Edwards taught Jenifer, Trisha and me how to curtsy while clutching a posy. Mr Edwards sometimes shook his head as though puzzled by all of this, but in fact he approved wholeheartedly. He was old-fashioned enough to believe that 'coming out' was an essential part of a girl's transition into womanhood. I think he also believed that the formal bowing and scraping would be useful training for what was to come, just as the elocution lessons had given me the confidence and vocabulary to make a thank-you or acceptance speech.

The Goolagong family was invited to attend, and Mum made a special trip to Sydney for the occasion, arriving the day before the ball so that she could spend all day Friday making adjustments to a dress loaned to her by Mr Edwards' assistant, Barbara Worthington, and having her hair set for the first time. We went to the hairdressers together. When Mum was placed under the big drier she looked around nervously at the contraption. 'What are they going to do now, Mooch?' she asked. 'Send me to the moon?' The moon was very much on Linda's mind at the time. The first moon landing was only a month away and Mum had the concern of a fundamentalist Christian that this was an unnecessary and perhaps dangerous disturbance of the order of things in God's universe. But for the big night she was prepared to put these worries to one side. It was, after all, a highly sociable winter for the Goolagongs, with me coming out in May and Barbara set to walk down the aisle with Bill Bevan in July. ('And not before time,' Kenny would growl under his breath.)

I can't remember who partnered Jenifer, but Trisha was with her new 'steady' Mark Davis, and my partner was a friend from the tennis club, John Vickery. We had a wonderful night. I don't think I missed a single dance,

Left: Making my debut in 1969, with Jenifer Edwards and my partner John Vickery *Right:* Being presented to Bishop Muldoon

and the formalities were mercifully bungle-free. I curtsied perfectly and kissed the bishop's ring without giggling. As a newspaper noted the next day, 'While the orchestra played "When Irish Eyes Are Smiling", she was presented to Bishop Muldoon of the Archdiocese of Sydney.'

In the spring of 1969 Mr Edwards organised an exhibition match tour of the Riverina to help raise funds for my overseas travel. Trisha and I were joined by two of the leading junior men, Bob Giltinan and Sid Ball, for social tennis evenings at Leeton and Barellan. The tour was fun and helped to raise a good sum of money, but in some ways my return home was distressing. There seemed to be a tension in the Goolagong household that I'd never noticed before. Dad was out of sorts and drinking more than I'd remembered, and he and Linda seemed to fight more often.

Part of the problem may have been hard times — since Frank Gladman had left the district, shearing work had seemed harder to come by, and Kenny had resorted to all kinds of odd jobs to keep the wolf from the door. Sensing that his self-esteem needed a boost, I begged him to take me along to watch him shear as soon as the opportunity arose. This was a side of his life that he had always wanted to share with me, particularly when I was small and idolised Frank Gladman's gun shearer. But something had always come up and I had never seen him in action.

So I went along to the shed with him and watched. He was 42 now, but still fit and strong, and he put his back into his work. Years later I was reminded of that day, watching Kenny at work, when his great shearing and drinking mate John Emerson told me about the time Kenny sheared a district record. 'It was a hot summer's day, too, and Goolie went at it like a bastard. I thought he was gonna do himself an injury. When we sat down for afternoon smoko, he rolled himself one and said to me, "I'm buggered, mate." He was, too, but I told him he had a few left in him if he put a bit of sweat into it. Well, that got him going. He shore two to my one that afternoon, and at the end of it he just slumped down in a corner of the shed and he was unconscious.'

It wasn't just the strain of tight finances causing problems in my parents' home, although I wasn't aware of anything else at the time. Years later, while researching this book, I discovered that Kenny, and several other Barellan men — notably Clarrie Irvin — had begun to feel that Vic Edwards had taken over too much of my life. Kenny felt this quite strongly, while Linda could only see the good that living with the Edwards was doing for me.

Paramount amongst the concerns of Clarrie Irvin and others at the tennis club was the virtually open-ended management contract which Mr Edwards had got me to sign shortly after my eighteenth birthday. Although none of them had actually seen the contract, their feeling was that I was too young to make such a commitment without professional advice. In this they were almost certainly right.

Clarrie Irvin told me in 1992, 'Mr Kurtzman wouldn't say anything against Vic. He had too much respect for him. And there was no doubt Vic knew what he was doing. I've trained trotters and I've won at Harold Park. I know what a difference a tenth of a second can make, so I understand why he needed 100 per cent of you all the time, but it hurt us a bit that he cut you off from us. It hurt a lot.'

As our overseas trip became imminent the Australian media began to take great interest in me again. While I was still frequently described as 'Aboriginal tennis star', or worse, 'coffee-coloured youngster', the initial fascination with my Aboriginality had worn off a bit. Some commentators even went so far as to explain that I wasn't really an Aborigine anyway! 'In fact she is only one-quarter Aborigine,' Jack Kramer wrote, revealing a more intricate knowledge of the Goolagong and Ingram lineage than I have been able to trace in more than a year of research.

The line that many writers now took was that my lapses in concentration on the tennis court could be ascribed to my Aboriginal blood lines. They even gave it a name which they took to be Aboriginal — 'Evonne goes walkabout!' The term 'walkabout' is, in fact, an English word made up by Aboriginal stockmen to explain to their bosses why they sometimes didn't turn up for work. Such behaviour was — and still is — part of our free-wheeling nomadic tradition, a cleansing of the spirit by moving to another place for a time. It is the feeling known by young adventurers the world over.

In its new tennis context 'walkabout' meant me dropping a set, or even losing a couple of serves when my game went on to auto-pilot. There is no point me denying that my tennis always did suffer — and some would say benefit — from lapses of concentration. My mind wasn't always on the job. It was an honest failing. I was a dreamer, so shoot me! And I think on balance this flaw won me as many games as it cost me, because when I realised I was playing badly, I invariably snapped to attention and gave the next game everything I had, and more. A study of the important three-set matches I won would reveal many scorelines that read 6–3, 4–6, 6–1. I never said anything about it at the time, of course, but saying that I went 'walkabout' was just another way of implying that Aborigines were underachievers who lacked the will to win.

I had the will to win, and the ability, but I could only win my way. Mr Edwards had been a coach long enough to know that he couldn't change that, although he never stopped trying.

On the eve of our departure for London I had almost 60 age and junior titles to my credit but I was still not the automatic selection as best junior player in Australia. While more was made of my prospects overseas, some commentators still gave Lesley Hunt the edge over me. She was national junior champion, I was national hard court champion. There wasn't a lot in it, but by now I was confident that I 'had her number'. Time would tell.

In the meantime I desperately wanted to perform well on the European tour, as much for all the people who had helped me along the way as for myself. Throughout March 1970, I received letters, cards and telegrams from well-wishers, including some particularly touching ones from the folk at Barellan.

Then, towards the end of the month the waiting was over. There was a huge crowd to see us off at Sydney airport. Mum and Dad and some of the kids had come up from Barellan, and Mrs Edwards was there, of course, with the older Edwards girls. Patricia was locked in an embrace in a corner with her steady, Mark Davis, and Kim Warwick's family was there too. Kim was a fine young player also coached by Mr Edwards and having his first tilt at the tour, too. The plan was that the three of us would play singles and I would partner Trisha in the women's doubles and Kim in the mixed.

When our flight was called Kenny gave me a quick hug and turned away. Linda had promised not to cry, but when we embraced I could feel her sobbing quietly on my shoulder, and I started, too.

Five months was a long time and the world was a big place. I shouted a brave goodbye and got on the plane. Trisha, who didn't want to come and had left the love of her life behind, cried all the way to Singapore.

PART 3

Champagne and Strawberries

Celebrating with Mr Edwards in 1970

Chapter 11

$\mathcal{T}$HE CRYING WAS LONG OVER by the time we landed at Heathrow Airport in the last week of March 1970. It had been replaced by a torrent of nervous energy.

I had never seen anything beyond Australian soil before, and more than a year of excited chatter about what we would see, what we would do, had created in me a build-up of anticipation that fluctuated between nausea and giggly hysteria. Some people may have considered me a rather immature 18-year-old, but I regarded myself as sensible and self-assured. But this was the big one — we were on the tour at last! On the one hand I couldn't wait to pit my skills against the best players from around the world; on the other hand I was fearful that my dreams of fame and fortune on the Wimbledon Centre Court would be shattered.

We checked into the Majestic Hotel in Cromwell Road, South Kensington, to rest and recover from our jet lag before the first tournament. I couldn't believe the enormity of London, nor could I get used to the sight of the white-skinned Londoners, rugged up in their Afghan jackets against the spring chill. We had come directly from an Australian summer, and so different was our look and general bearing that we might have come from another planet.

'My goodness, luv,' said the lady in the corner store where we bought toothpaste, 'you're almost black!' The irony of her remark probably escaped her, but it was essentially true. Mr Edwards and Trisha, both relatively fair-skinned, went from pink to nutbrown in the course of a summer on the tennis court. I started at nutbrown and went black. In those days we were much less conscious of skin protection and I would occasionally get too much sun and my skin would peel. This was a great source of amusement to some of the other players, who discovered that I wasn't black underneath after all.

The 'Swinging Sixties' were over, but London still pulsated with excitement in 1970. The Beatles were feuding but still together. Carnaby Street was in decline but the Union Jack was still stamped on world fashion. Youth culture ruled and its icons were Twiggy, Terence Stamp, Donovan Leitch and Mick Jagger. I walked along Kensington High Street and marvelled at the vibrance

Dolly Birds in swinging London — Trisha and me

of the place. Old buses and taxis, new fashion, new ideas … and everywhere young people with long hair, flaired trousers and stacked heels.

And then we went to Southport. This dull Lancashire town was particularly grey and dismal the week I made my professional debut in my first British tournament. This was the first of a series of relatively small tournaments sponsored by the En-Tout-Cas tennis court company, held away from the limelight and at the end of the winter. Spring was theoretically with us, but everyone trained in track pants and pullovers and still froze. Mr Edwards hurriedly organised warm-up suits for us.

Mr Edwards had spent more than two years planning our first British campaign, and it was no coincidence that, thrown into a strange climate, I was 'blooded' against some fairly ordinary players. Many of the top women players were playing in South Africa at the Open, but had they been in England it is still unlikely that they would have chosen to play Southport. In those early days of open tennis there was no satellite or qualifying tour as such, but there were minor and major tournaments, and the Margaret Courts and the Billie Jean Kings had found they could live without the two-figure purses offered in the En-Tout-Cas. Nevertheless, as I progressed through the rounds I found myself up against some of Britain's quality players. In the semifinal Corinne Molesworth, England's under-21 champion, stretched me in the first

Winning my first tournament in England at Southport

set and I was expecting to struggle against the Wightman Cup player Joyce Williams, ranked number five in Britain, in the final. But it was over in straight, painless sets and I won my first professional purse — 40 pounds Sterling. In addition to this, Trisha and I won five pounds for making the semifinals of the doubles.

Flushed with this success, we moved on to the indoor tournaments at Poole and Staleybridge. It was just as well that the tournaments were indoors because at Staleybridge I saw my first snow. Excited, Trisha and I collected it from car windscreens in the car park and walked into the sports centre holding giant snowballs. Again these tournaments were smalltime stuff, with 'name' players few and far between and the majority of my opponents, like me, learning the ropes. I found it strange playing indoors for the first time, looking up to serve or for an overhead smash, and staring at the crossbeams and banks of lights. It was something I had to get used to, but for me the joy of tennis was never quite the same indoors.

We travelled back to London in our rented car to prepare for the start of the hard court season. I loved to drive along, admiring the scenery, and in England it never seemed to take very long to get from one place to the next. But the group dynamic inside the vehicle was sometimes a little strained. Trisha and her father were constantly at loggerheads over everything from the smallest detail of our itinerary to the fundamental problems in their father-daughter relationship. Their arguments never spilled over into the car, but nevertheless, you often could cut the atmosphere with a knife.

Trisha has said in more recent years that she had to bear the brunt of any of her father's displeasure with me, in the way a parent will invariably chide his own rather than someone else's child. But she brought her own tensions to the relationship that summer too. Essentially conservative, she believed she had left behind in Sydney the love of her life, possibly her one chance for marital bliss. She had begun dating Mark Davis the previous year, and clearly she believed, after several weeks' absence, that she was forsaking true love for a tennis tour in which I was almost certain to be the major beneficiary. She believed she was along for the ride, the doubles, and the adventure of it all, and she was not very happy about it.

I won the Cumberland hard court tournament in Hampstead and moved on to Sutton in Surrey, where we were billeted out at homes of the stalwarts of the Sutton Tennis Club. This was the homely nature of the tennis tour in England in those years. I had won two minor tournaments and was starting to attract some attention in the lead-up to the bigger events, but in Surrey I was just another little girl a long way from home. Trisha and I stayed with

Mr Edwards with his two girls. London, 1970

a family called the Grovers. I liked old Mr Grover and nicknamed him 'Groovy' Grover. We were now almost into May but the evenings were still cold and when we went to bed Mrs 'Groovy' would knock on our door with hot-water bottles for our feet.

By this time a subtle change had come over Trisha. She had decided that there was no cure for a broken heart like the company of another man, and there was no shortage of them on the tour. She became very friendly with the Australian player Ross Case, then at Sutton she took up with an English player named John Paish. Trisha was extremely attracted to him, but the relationship was fraught with difficulties from the start, for not only was Paish seriously involved with the soon-to-arrive Wendy Gilchrist, another Australian player whom he would eventually marry, but Trisha's beau Mark Davis had decided to come over for Wimbledon with his family. On top of this there was not much opportunity for serious dating, because Mr Edwards imposed a curfew on us most of the time, but with me covering for her, Trisha escaped as often as she could.

At one point during the Sutton tournament I remember walking past the club bar and seeing John Paish deep in conversation with a young man with longish hair and a charmingly roguish air about him. I was on my way to a match and had no time to stop and talk, but I took another quick look as I passed through the doors and our eyes met. I can't say that this episode meant much to me at the time — there was no shortage of men to look at at any of the tournaments.

One of the most charming men I met in 1970 — or any other year I played tennis, for that matter — was most certainly not available. For one thing, Teddy Tinling was about 40 years older than me. He was an extraordinary-looking fellow, more than 2 metres (6 feet) tall and thin as a rake. In tennis, Teddy was couturier to the stars. He had been the last word in tennis fashion since he designed American player Gussie Moran's lace panties that caused so much trouble at Wimbledon in 1949. Now each year he selected a group of women — some of them established stars, some rising — and designed a range of tournament dresses for them.

After I'd won a couple of minor tournaments in England, Teddy contacted Mr Edwards and arranged for a fitting session at his studio in London. I was knocked out by the man. He was absolutely charming and he knew everything there was to know about women's tennis. He boasted he had dressed 'every Wimbledon champion from Suzanne Langlen to Evonne Goolagong'. I laughed, but he said, 'Your day is coming, my dear.'

The British Hard Court Championships at Bournemouth had been the scene of the birth of open tennis in 1968, and two years later they were firmly established as the beginning of the serious stuff. All the top players were there, many of them just in from the Italian Open — Billie Jean King, Rosie Casals and Julie Heldman from America, Kerry Melville and Margaret Court from Australia, and Britain's Virginia Wade, Ann Jones and Winnie Shaw. In the second round I was up against Casals, the tiny, tough-talking American who was one of the original 'grunters'. I downed her 6–2, 6–3, and, growing in confidence, defeated Julie Heldman in the quarter finals. The world number five wasn't an easy opponent. She went straight through me in the first set, then, after I returned the favour in the second, took me to 13–11 in the decider of a match which lasted two-and-a-half hours.

I was now only one match away from the final, but it might just as well have been 101, because I was up against Margaret Court, the best player in the world. Margaret obliterated me in the first set, but I pinned her back in the second and led 4–1. There was a sniff of an upset in the air, but not in Margaret's mind. She pulled herself together and didn't let me win another game.

Straight after Bournemouth we went to another hard court tournament at Guildford on the outskirts of London. Again we were billeted — this time

Left: With Mr Edwards at Guildford, 1970 *Right:* A happy moment with Mr Edwards in 1970

in the same house as Mr Edwards — and again Trisha used me as a cover while she spent time with John Paish. To this end I was reluctantly dragged along to a wine and cheese party at the tennis club.

'You don't seem to be having a terribly good time. Can I get you something?' It was John Paish's friend, the man I had seen him with in the bar at Sutton. Naturally, I was mortified. Of course I was having a great time ... why wouldn't I be, standing in a tennis clubhouse in Guildford nursing a soft drink and being roundly ignored while I waited for Trisha to finish whatever she was doing outside!

I answered, 'No, I'm fine, thank you.' He introduced himself as Roger Cawley. He told me he had played on the British tour for a few years and that he'd seen my photo and read about me in tennis magazines. That was how he had recognised me at Sutton. It sent shivers down my spine to think he remembered that momentary encounter. We talked easily, about tennis, about his life in London and mine in Australia.

Eventually we found Trisha and John in the car park arm-in-arm. It was getting late but Trisha had had a few drinks and John thought it advisable to let her get some air before he took us home to Mr Edwards. The four of us took off down the country lanes in John's Morris 1100. At some point in the blackness of that May evening John pulled up by the side of the road and put his arm around Trisha. Roger leaned over and whispered, 'I think they'd like some privacy.'

We wandered up an embankment and onto a patch of grass. It was cold and Roger put his arm around me for warmth, but we just strolled and chatted. He suddenly stopped. 'Do you know where we are?' he asked. I shook my head. 'This is the seventh green of the Guildford golf course.'

We both laughed, then he grabbed me and started to waltz me around the green. It was crazy, but I couldn't remember having such fun. We looked up from the dance and discovered a cow gazing at us with a puzzled expression. Then the car horn sounded and we were summoned to join the others, who were no longer alone. The police had invited them to move along. We bade goodnight to the constable, clambered into the back seat and we were off.

Trisha and I crept into the house that night, past Mr Edwards snoring on the lounge. It was by no means late — well before midnight — but our hosts were asleep too. Trisha winked at me as we climbed into the twin beds in our room. Sisters in crime now. But I was convinced that was the last I would see of Roger Cawley. Through his friendship with John Paish he still mixed from time to time in the tennis world, but he had another life quite removed from anything I knew or understood. He operated his 'office' in the bar of a London pub, and there he wrote romance stories for women's magazines.

However, later that week at Guildford Trisha told me that Roger wanted to see me again. He was driving down to Guildford from London with John, who had been eliminated from the tournament, and they wanted to meet us for lunch at a riverside pub. I suppose I was pleased, but I was also shocked. This was a date. The other night on the golf course had just been a set of circumstances beyond our control. Trisha and I won the doubles and, still holding the bouquet of roses, I arrived at the pub late and full of trepidation.

I sat through the meal and barely spoke a word, which didn't seem to concern Roger. He remained attentive throughout and he and John — or 'Fish' as Roger called him, after the French court announcers' pronunciation of his surname — kept us amused with jokes and stories. I remember at one point gazing intently at some ducks on the water. Something scared them and they flapped their wings and were gone. I turned back to the table. 'Do ducks fly?' I asked, quite innocently. The group cracked up.

Roger has said to me since: 'I thought to myself, Jesus Christ! This one's a bit different.' And he asked me out again.

The next week I looked into the small crowd watching the second round of the London Hard Court Championships at Hurlingham and saw Roger. He waved his fingers briefly, in what might have been taken for the great Aussie 'blowfly' salute, had it not been accompanied by a warm grin. This was probably just as well, because Mr Edwards was sitting courtside not far away. I grinned back, then I grinned at Mr Edwards, just to allay suspicion. The spectators must have thought I was a complete idiot, because I was not playing my best that day.

After the match Mr Edwards made for the bar and I showered and came back and sat with Roger. We had been chatting for a while when a woman came up to us and congratulated me on progressing to the quarter finals. 'And is this your little brother?' she asked, offering her hand to Roger. 'How nice of him to come all this way.' I suppose we did look a little alike, but a Wiradjuri Aborigine Roger wasn't. We held our composure until she had moved on, but only just.

During that week at Hurlingham Roger's romance writing took a back seat to his own affairs of the heart. He came to the courts every day and when I was not playing, we were inseparable. Mr Edwards smelt a rat. He was already hostile towards Trisha over her fling with John Paish, and now here was I, gazing adoringly into the eyes of a young man who was, in all probability, as much of a rogue as he believed Paish to be. Vic Edwards would have been furious about any men who came between Trisha and me and our tennis, but he had a special resentment towards John. He believed he knew his type only too well — a professional but a rebel, as interested in winning hearts as in winning tournaments. And wasn't he the fellow who was involved with the Gilchrist girl?

Of course Mr Edwards knew nothing about John Paish, and even less of Roger, but no doubt once he had become aware of our friendship he would have asked questions at the bar. Not that the answers would have made much difference to him; he had already made up his mind about any prospective suitor of mine. Like John Paish, Roger was regarded as something of a tennis rebel, a promising young player who had refused to conform, then had worked out the odds of his winning Wimbledon and had hung up his racquet the previous season. Now, who knew what he did for a living? Not much, by the look of it, would have been Mr Edwards' response to that rhetorical question.

A couple of days before the tournament ended, Roger asked me to have dinner with him on the Saturday night, after I'd finished playing for the week. John and Trisha would come, too, the four of us would have dinner and go dancing at one of the West End clubs. It sounded wonderful to me. I knew

Mr Edwards' rules, but Sunday was our day off and there was no tournament the following week anyway. Trisha and I tackled him in the bar at Hurlingham when he was in an expansive mood on the Friday evening. Our request brought him crashing down from his scotch-induced high. He scowled and harrumphed, and eventually he said, 'You can go, but I don't think it's a very good idea.' This was one of Mr Edwards stock answers, designed to present the illusion of freedom of choice. But this time I was determined.

We made arrangements with the boys to meet in the foyer of our hotel in Cromwell Road for dinner at eight. Around six, Trisha and I packed up our tennis gear and made for the club bar. Mr Edwards was holding court with the usual collection of tennis writers and club officials. He said, 'I'm just in the middle of something. You'll have to wait a bit.' So we waited … and waited. Trisha and I became more furious with every new round of drinks he bought. We could have made our displeasure known or we could have left without him, and either of these courses of action would seem perfectly reasonable to most people. But to Mr Edwards they would have represented not only gross disloyalty but a very public humiliation, such was the curious code of conduct on which his tennis empire was built.

So we waited and said nothing. We eventually left the club after nine and did not present ourselves for dinner until after 10 p.m. I was terribly upset and apologetic, but Roger shrugged it off. 'Not your fault. Let's put it out of our minds and not let it ruin our evening.'

It didn't. We had a marvellous time and danced the night away at a little club where they played black soul music — my favourite. I guess it was 2 a.m. — certainly no later — when Roger and John dropped us back at the hotel. I remember him kissing me lightly on the lips for the first time, and how wonderful that felt. Then they were off in the Morris and we walked into the hotel.

Mr Edwards was sitting in the foyer, glowering. He made an exaggerated theatrical gesture of looking at his watch, then turned his black look on each of us. He didn't lecture us. He just said, 'I'm not going to let this happen to you', and marched us up the stairs to our rooms. He was in a foul mood all day Sunday. During a row with Trisha he actually threw some of her clothes out of the window. Then he said, 'I'm not going to put up with this. I'll take the whole team home.' Presumably he meant Trisha and me and poor Kim Warwick.

On the Monday, still hopping mad, he demanded the phone number at the flat John Paish and Roger shared. Patricia rang and warned them that her father would be calling, none too pleased. John and Roger discussed this and decided that because John was trying to make a living out of playing tennis, it would be better for Roger to catch the flak. Mr Edwards did call and began a tirade of abuse in which his central theme seemed to be that Roger's involvement with me was 'ridiculous'. The profanity with which he surrounded this statement astounded Roger, particularly as it came from someone he didn't know. Roger was told that if he and John went near us again Mr Edwards would take the entire team home. Roger apologised for bringing me home so late, but pointed out that the beginning of the date had been delayed for two hours through no fault of his. This enraged Mr Edwards still more. Roger was shocked at the ferocity of his approach. Clearly, the battle lines were drawn.

A few days later Roger went to the Queen's Club to practise with John and was stunned to find that the tennis press knew all about our late night out. In Mr Edwards' mind it had become an international incident.

Roger and John went to Paris for the French Open — John to play, Roger to cover the preliminary rounds for a newspaper reporter friend — and we buried ourselves in practice. Slowly Mr Edwards started to come around, but there remained a tension between us which seemed to abate only when he'd had a few drinks.

He'd had more than a few when we were returning to the hotel one evening. I don't remember where Trisha was but there were only Mr Edwards and me in the car. He could be amusing when he'd had a few, and I think we were actually enjoying a good laugh when he leaned over and squeezed my leg above the knee. He said, 'You know I love you so much I could rape you.'

I was shocked, but it seemed such a bizarre and offensive thing to say, I took it more as an indication of his level of intoxication, than as a statement of intent. Later in the evening he came to my room and rapped on the door. He was very giggly and I tried to keep him out in the corridor, but he pushed past me into the room. His words in the cab came back to haunt me and I was suddenly very worried and not at all sure what to do.

I said, 'You've caught me at a bad time, I'm just running a bath.' I marched into the bathroom and did just that. Mr Edwards followed me in there too, and attempted to wrestle me into the bathtub fully clothed. I pretended to match him giggle for giggle, hoping he wouldn't realise I was on the edge of panic. When I could get free I ran through the room, opened the door and did something completely out of character. I screamed the house down. Not the screams of someone under attack, but a cacophony of shrieks and howls and goodtime noises that I knew would bring the conservative management of the Majestic Hotel running in no time at all. Mr Edwards gleefully joined in the noisemaking as he tried to haul me into the bath.

The phone rang. 'Jonathon in reception, Miss Goolagong. Is everything all right?'

'Yes,' I said, 'Mr Edwards is just leaving.'

When Roger returned from France we continued the romance in secrecy. We would meet at a laundrette and find somewhere out of the way to have coffee while my clothes went around in the machine. I wasn't sure how Roger felt, but I knew I was falling in love. I seemed to spend more time being furtive and clandestine than I did playing tennis. Many years later I played in a celebrity event with the American actress Lucinda Crosby, who'd actually been on the women's tour in those early years and had stayed at the Majestic Hotel, too. She reminded me of our first meeting in the foyer. 'You rushed down the stairs, looked both ways and asked me if there was a back way out of the hotel. I wondered what you were up to.'

I was up to my ears in love with Roger Cawley. Roger, for his part, was spending lonely nights at home and lost days at the tennis, watching me play from a discreet distance, but never actually communicating with me in Mr Edwards' presence. It was a strange situation for both of us, but particularly for Roger who was only beginning to see Mr Edwards' obsessive protectiveness of me. Roger was 20 and I was almost 19, but we agreed to put up with this ludicrous state of affairs for the sake of my tennis. And sometimes the stand-off had its funny side. Once, when Roger's parents were up in London from Canterbury, he phoned to ask where Mr Edwards was taking us for dinner. He booked another table, in a direct line between our table and the men's toilet. Mr Edwards sat with his back to Roger all night, showed remarkable control of his bladder, and did not make a move to go until the Cawley table had departed.

At other times, though, his distaste for Roger could boil over and become quite nasty. Once, when I lost to the Scottish player Joyce Williams I showered and changed and, as usual, looked for Mr Edwards in the bar. He was talking to a man I'd never met, but he broke off to abuse me for losing. This was the kind of public humiliation Mr Edwards could not bear himself, and it was unlike him to inflict it on others. But on this occasion he just kept at it, and he said some very hurtful things. 'You played like a bloody C grade. Gutless. Your mind's not on the job. Why isn't it on the job? Well, we all know the bloody answer to that, don't we?'

I excused myself and only just made it to the locker room before I burst into tears. That was the first and only one of the few times I ever wept in

Meet the press. Queens Club, London, 1970

a locker room. Tennis matches did not usually reduce me to tears. I was trying to play by Mr Edwards' rules, but by God he made it hard.

As Wimbledon drew nearer I saw less of Roger. I phoned him every day but he felt it best to stay away and allow me to concentrate on the most important part of the tour. He said, 'You don't need the pressure of me hanging around upsetting old Vic. I won't be there, but I'll be with you in spirit all the way.'

Despite the fact that I had now had several months to see how the British adored tennis, the carnival of Wimbledon took me by surprise. I didn't think I would be overawed by the pomp and ceremony of the All-England Club, nor did the hallowed turf mean all that much to me, although something happened at the pre-tournament cocktail party to change my mind. Bob Howe, an Australian who represented Dunlop in London in those days, and was a confidante of Mr Edwards and a good mixed doubles player who won Wimbledon in 1958, took me aside at the party and whispered, 'I want to show you something.' He led me upstairs to the Members' Enclosure next to the Royal Box overlooking Centre Court.

As we looked out over the court he said, 'This is the Holy Court of the Holy Grounds. To play here will be one of the greatest experiences in your life. There is nothing quite like it.'

Centre Court was perfectly manicured, ready for action. It was empty and eerily quiet, except for Bob's low voice, which sounded like it was coming from the pulpit of a cathedral. It gave me goose bumps. Corny perhaps, but true.

When I came out to play my first round match with the French number three Odile de Roubin, on Court 4, there was a big crowd watching Rod Laver and Roy Emerson in a doubles match nearby. The crowd around our court was even bigger, despite a breeze with a real nip to it that swept around those outside courts. Not that I was terribly aware of the weather, or anything else for that matter. I was shockingly nervous, but determined not to let my opponent see that.

I'd been sitting in the wrong locker room for ages, wondering when I was going to get the call. I'd been asked to use the number one dressing room, normally reserved for seeded players and past champions, but I was too embarrassed and went instead to the downstairs room with Trisha and the rest of my friends. An official finally found me and spluttered that the match had been due to start 15 minutes earlier and I was in danger of forfeiting. We marched promptly to the court, where Mme de Roubin was waiting impatiently. Odile de Roubin was apparently not used to being kept waiting. She was the daughter of a nobleman from Avignon, who had a castle and a tennis club, which was just as well for Odile, who was never going to keep herself in the style to which she had become accustomed by playing tennis. She had a few ground shots and might have been competitive on clay, but as soon as I got the pace of her game on grass, my nerves started to slip away. And it soon became apparent the crowd was on my side. They cheered enthusiastically for every point I won in taking the match 6–1, 6–2. As I walked back through the crowd with Mr Edwards after the match, I said, 'Well, it wasn't as bad as I thought it might have been.'

'Wait until you're on Centre Court tomorrow,' he replied.

Centre Court! For a newcomer in a second round match? The prospect was as alarming as it was unlikely. But for some reason the Wimbledon committee had scheduled my match against the American number four, Jane 'Peaches' Bartkowicz, for the show court. To this day I don't know whether Mr Edwards wangled this as a favour to give me a taste of the big event, or whether there was so much genuine interest in me that Centre Court was the only place that could handle the crowd. I'd like to report that I was so nervous that I didn't sleep a wink, but losing sleep over tennis was never my style. The nerves didn't hit me until the next morning.

When I was called I came down from the locker room and sat in the

Centre Court waiting room with my opponent. The purpose of the room was to ensure that nothing went wrong with the clockwork precision of the tournament schedule, but the reality of sitting in a small room with your opponent was quite bizarre and unique in world tennis. The waiting room was long and narrow, about the size of a bathroom. A tournament official checked our clothing to ensure that it complied with the 'predominantly white' regulation, then Peaches and I sat in silence for about 10 minutes.

When we eventually walked out on to the court I tried not to look at the crowd. I kept my head down at all times. Nervousness was the main reason for this, but I also knew that Roger would be somewhere in the crowd, and if I acknowledged him there might be trouble with Mr Edwards. So I kept my head down, and if I looked at anyone at all, it was Peaches Bartkowicz, who had the annoying habit of staring you down as though this was the gunfight at the O.K. Corral, and not just a tennis match.

Peaches had a good double-handed backhand and she knew her way around the baseline, but her main asset was that she was wily. At that stage she could run rings around me in the psychology of tennis. She knew the crowd was on my side and that I was as nervous as hell, so she didn't try to power me off the court. She sat back and watched my game in the first set, letting me dictate the play. Peaches took the first set 6–4, but I had shown 14,000 people that I was competitive, and I should have been growing in confidence. But Bartkowicz's strategy had the reverse effect. She had an answer for everything I threw at her, and I started to panic. She seized on my unforced errors and came in for the kill. I didn't win a game in the second set. I was on the Wimbledon Centre Court for just 34 excruciating minutes.

It was a start, but it wasn't a great start. Mr Edwards said very little about it, perhaps sensing that I had taken a very public fall and didn't need to be reminded of it.

I had been thrashed in a second round match by a player who wouldn't be going much further in the tournament either, yet the post-match press conference was jam-packed. It was embarrassing. They didn't want to know about my tennis, they wanted me to speak in Wiradjuri or throw a boomerang or something. I was that year's Wimbledon freak show and I didn't have a clue how to handle it.

Did I feel proud to be the first Aborigine to play Wimbledon? What did I think of apartheid? Was there racial discrimination at home? Would I be playing mixed doubles with Arthur Ashe? Mr Edwards mercifully brought it to a halt. 'Thanks, boys. Evonne's exhausted. That'll be all now.'

The first and second round losers at Wimbledon are put into a consolation play-off called the Wimbledon Plate. With all attention focused on the main event on Centre Court, the Plate is a very relaxed affair, rather like a country tournament. Playing in it was great therapy for my post-Centre Court trauma and I actually went on to win it. So I was in a party mood again by the end of Wimbledon fortnight and I was delighted that Mr Edwards had consented to Roger and John Paish escorting me and Trisha to the Wimbledon Ball. After his pronouncements on the matter of Roger and John a few weeks earlier, this was an extraordinary turnaround, although it was made somewhat begrudgingly. Yes, the four of us could go to the ball, but he didn't think it was a very good idea and he would not be going if it meant spending an evening in the company of the dreadful layabouts from London.

That arrangement suited us perfectly. We dressed to the nines and all met at Trader Vic's for cocktails before going on to the Grosvenor House Hotel on Hyde Park for the ball. We walked into the ballroom that night to make our first real public appearance as a couple. We had made a table with Stanley Matthews Jr, the son of the legendary soccer player and then a rising star on the British tour, and some other friends. It was a lively, happy table, but Roger and I spent little time at it.

Roger has since told me: 'We got up to dance and I don't think we left the dance floor for the rest of the night. You looked fantastic. I don't remember even seeing anyone else. I can honestly say that was the night — even the moment — that I fell head over heels in love with you.'

The feeling was mutual. The next day — Sunday — I sat in the back of our rented car while Mr Edwards drove us to Newport in Wales for the next event, the Welsh Open, and wrote in a shaky hand the first of hundreds of letters I would send Roger in the course of our long distance love affair. 'I really couldn't have cared who was watching us last night or what they thought. I was just so happy to be with you, and I think I fell in love with you all over again too. Sometimes when I'm with you I really wish I never played tennis. I'm missing you so terribly …'

Then we arrived in Newport, and had to rush to the courts to get some practice in before the welcoming function. The caravan had moved on.

Chapter 12

$\mathcal{B}$EING HEAD OVER HEELS IN LOVE must have agreed with me. In the weeks following Wimbledon 1970 I was on a winning streak, playing my best tennis of the summer.

When I beat the hot-tempered American Patti Hogan in the final of the Welsh Open, I got the best reviews of the season too. Lance Tingay, the respected tennis writer for the *Daily Telegraph*, wrote: 'Evonne Goolagong … had the finest success of her lawn tennis career when she won the women's singles … yesterday, beating the American Patti Hogan 6–0, 8–6 in the final at Newport. This was the entrancing Miss Goolagong's first open title, the most prestigious and the most rewarding. It earned her 500 pounds. She will probably earn bigger sums in the future since the talent of this part-aboriginal (sic) teenager cannot be denied. Her splendid backhand — a stroke of rare quality — her delicacy of touch, mobility, flexibility and ball sense make her outstanding. There are weaknesses as well, notably on the forehand, and a second serve which invites attack.'

It is strange to read these things now, so many years later, and have a long-forgotten tennis match come drifting back. Thank God I never read any of it at the time. I would never have played another forehand!

Every night at Newport I sat in my room and wrote to Roger. This wasn't entirely necessary since halfway through the tournament he caught the train down for the day and came to watch me play. Afterwards we had coffee in town and I walked him to the station. He had spent all day in a train just to share a couple of hours with me. I was ecstatic, Mr Edwards less so.

I wrote to Roger, 'Father Dear has not said a word to either of us (Trisha and me), but maybe that's better than his usual complaints.'

The next week, at Hoylake in Cheshire I beat Kerry Melville in the final of the North of England Championships and won another 500 pounds. This was starting to be fun, but when I went back to the hotel at night I closed the door on my blossoming professional tennis career and became a lovestruck teenager. 'I dreamt that you and I lived on an island,' I wrote to Roger, 'and we were the sole survivors of some disaster. Everything was just perfect, no worries about being seen together, no Father Dear hiding behind every tree … we were wonderfully happy in our own little world … [then] Mr Edwards knocked on the door. It seems all good things are interrupted by Mr Edwards, even my dreams.'

On to Leicester for the Midlands Open. Patti 'Happy' Hogan again in the final. Thank you very much, another 100 pounds. And a happy end to the British season for Trisha, too, when we won the doubles title.

When I look back on this, my first serious winning streak, I realise I should have been overjoyed, but in fact most of the time off the court I was dreadfully lonely, and although I tried to keep my feelings hidden, my misery seemed to infect the whole group. Trisha was an emotional wreck, not sure who or what she wanted in life. Now no longer in complete control of both Trisha and me, Mr Edwards was a picture of barely contained rage. Even when I was winning tournaments he seemed to find fault with everything Trisha and I did, unable to come to terms with the fact that we were just normal teenage girls who had interests beyond tennis. In fact, of our group only Kim Warwick seemed to have weathered the long, intense summer.

From Leicester we were heading to Europe in late July for a series of tournaments, then home. I had to see Roger again. He phoned and we arranged to meet in the BEA (British European Airlines) terminal at the airport. I told Mr Edwards immediately, hoping to give him enough time to control his rage. He was surprisingly calm about it. I guess he thought that he could put up with seeing Roger again, if the object of the exercise was to say goodbye forever.

We had just checked our bags when Roger and John Paish arrived. Everything happened so quickly. He handed me a little parcel, told me again how much he loved me, and then Mr Edwards bustled us through the security check and into the gate lounge. As the plane taxied Trisha and I could see Roger and John on the balcony of the terminal. I felt the tears welling up. I opened my gift. It was a little gold cross on a chain. I put it around my neck immediately and swore I'd never take it off. When we reached cruising altitude I went straight to the privacy of the toilet and bawled my eyes out under the protective din of the engines.

Years later I learnt that Roger had been similarly awash with tears that night, in a most uncharacteristic display of emotion. From Heathrow he and John had driven back to London and sought solace at The George Hotel in Belgrave Road. After several rounds of solace Roger began to sob. Not just a little catch of the throat, but full-blooded sobs. John took him by the arm. 'Pull yourself together, lad,' he advised. But it was no good. Roger had dropped his bundle. He went home, a lovesick loon alone in London.

Left: Phoning Roger from Hoylake *Right:* Concentration. European tour, 1970

'Seems like I haven't seen you for days already, and I miss you something awful,' I wrote from our billet at Hilversum for the Dutch Open. 'The people I am staying with are not much help either. They are quite old and not very talkative. [In fact they didn't speak any English!] Whenever there is silence I can't help bursting into tears. I can't stop thinking about you.'

I celebrated my nineteenth birthday by being bundled out in the quarter finals by Margaret Court in our first European clash. Then it was on to Germany, first for the Bavarian Championships in Munich, then the West German Open in Hamburg. I beat Karen Krantzcke in Munich to take the Bavarian title, but to be frank, I didn't enjoy competing in Germany. Perhaps the state of my heart had a lot to do with it, but I found the gamesmanship of some of the German girls aggravating. One girl in particular questioned every line call in a quite obnoxious manner. This was not the way we played the game at the Victor A. Edwards Tennis School in Roseville, New South Wales, but when her appeals started to bear fruit I was tempted to start protesting myself. I resisted the urge to question the umpire, as I did throughout my career.

The last couple of weeks of the European tour were somewhat up in the

Celebrating on the dance floor after the German Open in 1970: Tony Roche, Winnie Shaw and me.

air. Mr Edwards had planned it that way to give us some flexibility. If the homesickness had become unbearable, we would have gone early, but with me still on a streak, we were looking for tournaments. There was talk of Istanbul and some places I'd never heard of. I wrote to Roger, 'We're not accepted in Istanbul, so we're playing Percheck. Where's Percheck?' Before Roger had a chance to respond I had written again, 'Never mind about Percheck, we're playing Innsbruck instead.' (I still don't know where Percheck is!)

In another letter (I still wrote every night) I had complained about not seeing enough of the country, a familiar lament among touring tennis players. 'We haven't seen much of Germany. I think you'd better come over and show me the sights. Maybe you can tell me some of its history, that's if you know German history. In any case you can make it up. I don't care as long as I see you.' I enclosed a fairly childish doodle, meant to represent a knight in shining armour. Under it I scrawled, 'Sir Roger Cawley on his trusty white horse and dressed in his fighting armour and wearing glasses 'cause he can't see, rescuing Miss Evonne Goolagong from the horrible, disastrous, racketeering world of tennis.' Oh to be young and in love and lonely in Hamburg again!

Left: A spectator at the German Open, Hamburg, 1970 *Right:* Playing in the German Open

After Hamburg we played in minor tournaments in the beautiful resort towns of Kitzbühel and Innsbruck. Here my spirits lifted as we played in the shadow of great dark mountains with patches of snow glistening in the sun, and, for the first time since May, I started to think about going home. Not going home to Sydney, going home to Barellan. I wrote a long letter to my sister Barbara and, by the end of it, I had made myself quite homesick. Finally the tour was over. We were delayed a day in Zurich while Mr Edwards worked out some business details and that meant our planned shopping spree in Hong Kong had to be cut short. I had time to rush out and buy my brother Larry a cassette recorder for his twenty-first birthday, and that was about all. And then in September we were home.

A few weeks after our return the London *Daily Telegraph* published its unofficial world rankings, compiled by the paper's tennis correspondent each year since 1914 and on this occasion by Lance Tingay. Mr Tingay kindly noted that I was 'the most splendid newcomer on the international scene for many years', but I didn't make his top 10, which naturally enough began with 1970 Grand Slam star Margaret Court, followed closely by her arch-rival Billie Jean

King. The two best players in the world were still in a league of their own, but I noted with considerable satisfaction that of the other eight women — in order from number three, Rosie Casals, Helga Niessen, Virginia Wade, Ann Jones, Kerry Melville, Karen Krantzcke, Julie Heldman and Françoise Durr — there was not one that I hadn't beaten and beaten well.

As soon as I had put things in order in Sydney I packed a small bag and headed for Barellan. The plane ride was horrific. What irony, to have travelled all over Europe without a hiccup, only to come home and experience, on our little commuter airline, the worst flying conditions imaginable! I think I was the only passenger who hadn't been physically sick by the time the pilot attempted a landing at Narrandera. The high winds and poor visibility proved too much and he climbed again and made for Griffith. Here the weather was just as bad so we climbed again, lurching from one air pocket to the next, and this time made for Wagga Wagga. We finally landed, but the weather was so bad we couldn't get clearance to fly again, and the airline had to put us in a cab to travel the 120 kilometres (75 miles) to Narrandera.

When we eventually pulled into the airport car park I was so thrilled to see my family that I left Larry's cassette recorder in the boot of the cab. Mum was in tears and Dad struggled to keep his composure. Mum said, 'Look at you, you've lost weight. Better get some damper into you? Bet you're still as silly as ever though.' We walked arm-in-arm to the old family car, my not-so-little nephew William (Barbara's son) tugging at our skirts and screaming for attention.

The younger kids all seemed so big, even Mully, the youngest. And Kevin, who was 17 now, was an adult. 'Come on, Mooch,' he said, 'I'll take you to the pub.' He loaded up the car with his mates and off we went to a pub in another town, to drink beers and play the juke box.

Kenny Goolagong didn't look a day older than when I had left, but there was something about his manner that seemed different. Most of the time he was even quieter than I had remembered, but when he was drunk — as he was on my second night home — he was shockingly maudlin. He cried and he almost had me in tears too as he told me how much he missed me. 'We're all so proud of you, Mooch ...' the sobbing would start ... 'but we wish you could come home again.' I just hugged him until it passed. Mum told me he sometimes made a nuisance of himself at the Commercial Hotel, bragging drunkenly about the tennis tournaments I'd won. 'Best bloody tennis player in the world, my little Eve. Don't you worry about that, mate. Now, what about buyin' me a beer?'

Linda just laughed and shook her lovely head of hair. 'He don't mean no harm, Kenny,' she said. 'There's just this little hole in his world since you went away, and he knows it's never gonna be fixed up right again.'

Linda Goolagong was a wise woman and I loved her more than I could ever hope to express. She was the same age that I am now when I wrote to Roger, 'I told Mum all about you and even showed her your photos. She was the one who got your three letters from the post office yesterday and straight away asked me if they were from you. She's a good old Mum. She always listens ... I told her about Mr Edwards and how he felt about you. Mum came to the conclusion that Mr Edwards seems to run the people in his life like he runs his business ... She wasn't annoyed with him or anything. She just discussed his side of the story, rather than mine.'

On Saturday Larry came home from his job in the wheat silos at Hillston, thinking that there was to be a party for me. We turned the tables on him and instead had a joint birthday party for his just gone, and mine at the end of July. Friends and relations filled the house to overflowing, the guitars came out and the beer flowed. At one point I had to break up a fight between two rowdy cousins. I pulled them apart and said, 'Please don't spoil the night for us.' They hung their heads and walked off in opposite directions.

There were official engagements too. One afternoon I had to model my Teddy Tinling tennis dresses for the Country Women's Association at the town hall. I didn't have any tennis shoes with me so I paraded around in white socks, holding a borrowed racquet. When I put the racquet down to change dresses backstage, someone's little darling grabbed it and took off. Feeling really stupid now, I paraded again with no shoes and no tennis racquet. When the Country Women had oohed and aahed long enough I nicked out a side door and picked up the racquet lying on the road.

Then we had the official welcome home party. The War Memorial Tennis Club put this one on for me at the Church of England hall — with tea and cordial and all the ladies bringing a plate. There were about 80 people present to hear a long line of speakers say how proud of me they all were. I was never too thrilled about politicians I didn't know making a big fuss over me, but when my old tennis club friends took the floor, it was a different story. It was lovely to see old Mr Kurtzman so thrilled and proud. He said, 'We never thought she'd do so well. Wimbledon scared her a bit, but then it scares everybody!'

Clarrie Irvin recalled driving me to Albury to meet Margaret Court. 'Margaret said then that she'd better think about retiring when Evonne grew up. Well, I think that time has come.'

At the end of the evening I was led on to the dance floor by nine-year-old Ian Goolagong, for an enthusiastic jazz waltz that took at least a year off the life of my brand new Carnaby Street platform shoes.

Back in Sydney at the end of September, my life fell into a familiar pattern. I trained and did chores by day and wrote letters to Roger by night. Although I could never discuss my long distance love affair with Mr Edwards, in Mrs Edwards I found a ready ally. She had been through this sort of thing several times before, and knew how to handle a young girl in love. 'Show me his picture,' she ordered. 'Mmm, very nice-looking lad. What does his father do?'

I was so smitten with Roger that I had no interest in going out with boys in Sydney, but one night my Aboriginal friend Michael Anderson phoned and asked me to come to a concert at the Foundation for Aboriginal Affairs. He had organised for Bobby Stephens and the Checkmates, a black American group who were touring Australia at the time, to perform a special concert at the Foundation. I went along and had a wonderful time. I met the band and the young Aboriginal actor Athol Compton, who had just starred in a movie called *The Games*. For the first time in a long while I thought of myself as Aboriginal. While my colour had been the subject of endless interest at post-match press conferences, Aboriginality had seemed a very distant concept. Now it was staring me in the face. Aboriginal was what I was, proudly.

I had a warm, wonderful feeling about that night for weeks to come, not knowing that within a couple of months I would be ostracised by many of my people, Michael Anderson among them, and made to feel like a traitor to my race.

Around the time in England that I was starting to have hot flushes every time I thought of Roger Cawley, we received word from the Lawn Tennis Association of Australia that I was urgently required to take up the third place in Australia's Federation Cup team in Freiberg, West Germany. Australia's team had been decimated by injury. First Kerry Melville had withdrawn and been replaced by Karen Krantzcke. Then, almost on the eve of the Cup, Margaret Court had withdrawn with a neck injury. That left just Karen and captain/manager Judy Dalton.

Naturally I was delighted to be asked. The Federation Cup was the Davis Cup of women's tennis, and since its inception in 1963 there had been some fantastic tussles between the twelve playing nations. But no sooner had I been asked to play, than the Cup referee turned down Australia's late team change. I stayed in England while Judy Dalton and Karen Krantzcke heroically won the Cup for Australia in a 3–0 finals rubber against the host team.

Now Australia was to host its second Federation Cup defence in Perth between Christmas and New Year. I desperately wanted to be selected to

represent my country, but I knew that what had happened in May would have
no bearing on the matter. The selection in December would be made on the
basis of form and performance during the Australian spring tour. Basically
this meant some early-season tournaments in Sydney followed by some steamy
events in Queensland.

First Trisha and I went to Townsville for the Queensland Hard Court
Championships. We were unchaperoned and, away from Mr Edwards for the
first time on tour, we had a good time. The boys on tour — Bob Giltinan
and Sid Ball to name two — were quite partial to a few beers and a bit
of yahooing, which was fun. But I was on a mission. I had to impress the
selectors. In stifling heat, American newcomer Patti Reese took a set off me
in the final, but I won quite comfortably and went on to the milder climate
of Toowoomba for the Australian Hard Courts full of confidence. In the rarified
atmosphere of the city of gardens I seemed able to do no wrong, and made
a clean sweep, taking out the singles, the doubles with Trisha and the mixed
doubles with Bob Giltinan.

At the Milton courts in Brisbane for the Queensland Open we capped the
Queensland tour by repeating the hat-trick. For winning the singles I received
an iron, while Bob Giltinan received a toaster for winning the men's. It wasn't
quite the $1000 I'd won at Newport or Hoylake, but I didn't think of it in
those terms. I was delighted with my iron — it would make a perfect Christmas
gift for Linda.

In early December the Federation Cup team was announced and I was
on it! After Queensland I suppose I shouldn't have been surprised, but Australia
had a lot of depth in women's tennis at that time, and it was hard to imagine
the selectors leaving out the experience of Judy Dalton, Karen Krantzcke and
Kerry Melville. In the event all three of them were overlooked not just because
of form, but because they had refused to give the LTAA assurances of their
availability for Australian tournaments in January.

Margaret Court, the Grand Slam champion, was naturally the first selected.
On current form I was next, and the selectors opted for Perth local Lesley
Hunt as a controversial third pick.

I wrote to Roger, 'My wish has come true … now I'll definitely be spending
Christmas in Perth with Margaret Court … Arrangements have been made
for me to leave on 21 December and have a few days' practice before the
big moment. I'm going to be scared stiff knowing I'm not just playing for
myself but for Australia.'

During the British tour I'd come to know Margaret and Barry Court
reasonably well, and the more I played against Margaret the more I was in

Left: Winning the Australian Hardcourt titles, Toowoomba, 1970 *Right:* At the Federation Cup in Perth, 1970

awe of her power and authority on a tennis court. At that stage of her career Margaret had largely overcome the nerves which had plagued her for so long, but she was still a nervous starter. It took her some time to warm up, and the ideal situation for her was a succession of progressively tougher games leading into the semifinals. Indeed, that was the way the draw was supposed to work but often didn't. In the case of the Federation Cup, Australia was not even to play until the semifinals! This bizarre situation occurred because the Australian government refused to issue visas for the Rhodesian team in line with United Nations sanctions, and the Yugoslav team withdrew at the last minute. So, much to the disgust of the US and French teams, we were straight into the semis.

This, however, didn't suit Margaret's game at all, so she asked me to come to Perth early as a house guest and work out with her. The Courts were easy going and fun to be with, and I settled in quickly, practising with Margaret for hours each day on their back court. I wrote to Roger, 'Margaret and Barry are just great fun and I find myself quite at home here. They even have me putting up wallpaper and doing the washing ... [The Courts] are definitely setting me on the wrong road. Now they've started me on shandies, and lately they seem to be getting stronger, and do you know what? I don't mind them at all … Christmas wasn't too bad. We had champagne breakfast, then visited several relatives of Margaret's who naturally gave us champagne. So, for the first time in my life I had a headache from too much alcohol … not a very good feeling.'

(In defence of the Courts' lifestyle in the days prior to their Christian renewal, I must say that a little alcohol went a long way with me in those days, and still does. What seemed like a lot to drink to a fairly naive 19-year-old probably amounted to a schooner glass of shandy after a workout on the court and a couple of glasses of champagne on Christmas Day.)

When we finally took to the court in the Federation Cup at Royal King's Park it was ridiculously hot. France had made it through to the semifinals and I met Françoise Durr in the first match. It was a typical Goolagong match in which I paid dearly for a lapse of concentration in the second set and let it go to a third. With the heat taking its toll, something told me I had to get off the court as quickly as possible. Six-love was pretty quick. Margaret went through Gail Chanfreau in straight sets and, rested, we came back on and took them out in straight sets in the doubles.

For the Cup final against England the next day, Perth turned on an absolute scorcher. The on-court temperature was over 45 degrees celsius, which was apparently supposed to favour Australia, since Margaret and Lesley lived under these conditions all the time, and I was an Aborigine! Well, it didn't. In the first set of my singles match against Virginia Wade I got quite dizzy and felt that I might pass out. Despite her formative years in Durban, South Africa, Virginia felt the heat even more than me. In the rests she had her team-mate Winnie Shaw drape wet towels over her head and shoulders, but it didn't help. She was a spent force in the second set.

Margaret had a slow start and the former Wimbledon champion Ann Jones actually beat her in a long and torturous first set. But hell hath no fury like Margaret Court scorned. She ignored the heat and cranked up the old power engine to take the next two sets and win the Cup for Australia.

Strangely, considering the strength of our team, Australia had gone into the Federation Cup finals very much the underdog. I was supposed to go 'walkabout', Margaret would choke, and Lesley just hadn't had enough experience at this level. That was the story. We proved the pundits wrong and press and public regarded it as a famous victory. I was thrilled at the way I had played in my first outing for my country. Moreover, I was thrilled to be considered the team-mate and equal of the great Margaret Court, the best tennis player in the world.

Now, all I had to do was beat her.

Chapter 13

I STAYED ON IN PERTH with Margaret and Barry Court after the Federation Cup, ostensibly so I could play in the West Australian Championships, but really so we could have some more fun.

In researching this book I've read press reports describing Margaret as dull, both in her style of tennis and in her personality, but I cannot agree. Certainly in those days she and Barry were a barrel of laughs. Particularly Barry, who was the more outgoing of the two. He took me sailing a couple of times and had me laughing so hard I almost let the boom hit me in the head.

Most of the time Margaret was quieter and harder to know, but as our on-court relationship developed, we established an easy rapport off the court too. She'd often joke about 'grooming' me to take her place as the queen of world tennis, and that was the way the press saw it. But Margaret had no intentions of retiring just then. She was more interested in the world's number one tennis player teaming with the hottest prospect in women's tennis to form an invincible doubles pair.

But it didn't start out that way, I can tell you. In our first practice sessions on Margaret's back court we were hopeless together. I couldn't see any future in it, but Margaret persisted and in the Federation Cup we played well enough together to take out the French doubles team in straight sets. (Against England in the meaningless doubles rubber of the final — the Cup had already been decided — I sat out the heat while Lesley Hunt teamed with Margaret.)

So, still in bliss after the Cup victory, I went straight into the singles at the WA Open ... and came straight out again after a shocking match against Holland's Betty Stove — a monumental let-down. Then Margaret and I teamed well to win the doubles title. 'Yes,' she said after the final, 'this is working. We should play together more often.' And Mr Edwards immediately made arrangements for me to join Margaret in the major doubles events throughout the 1971 tour of Europe and the United Kingdom. This was perfect for me, since Trisha had already decided against touring again. But, as I was to learn many years later, there was at least one voice of dissent at VAETS in Roseville. Faith Martin who, with Colin Swan had really 'discovered' me at Barellan

Federation Cup winners Lesley Hunt, Margaret Court and me

in the early 1960s, was totally against the pairing. 'You don't team up with your greatest rival,' she said. 'Not if you want to be champion.'

We two great rivals went off with Barry Court to Rottnest Island for a holiday to clear our heads after the pressures of the Federation Cup. We swam and fished and cycled around the island. It was just wonderful. Everywhere I rode my bike I was followed by a tribe of little kids and Margaret and Barry started calling me 'the Pied Piper'. When Margaret and I had a hit on the cement court near the hotel, the entire population of the island came down to watch. Soon we had about 50 ball boys. And in the evenings we popped shandies and toasted each other's health. We were enjoying each other's company so much, the thought never crossed my mind that the time was fast approaching when the woman sitting opposite me would be the last and only obstacle between me and the world championship of women's tennis, that in a matter of months — maybe only weeks — I would have to topple her and seize her crown, or live in the knowledge that I'd never quite made the top of the pile.

The time came much sooner than I had anticipated.

Margaret had held the Victorian women's singles title from 1961 to 1966 and again from 1969. She took great pride in holding the title of her old home state, and if you were ever going to topple Margaret Court, you wouldn't choose the Victorian Open as the place to start. But I had a dream run through the rounds, while Margaret couldn't seem to fire. My rain-interrupted semifinal against England's Winnie Shaw went into finals day for the deciding third set, and there was virtually no one in the stands at Kooyong to see me take it 6–2 to go into the final. It was probably the perfect practice session, and when the final began, an hour-and-a-half late, I felt loose and confident. I certainly had nothing to lose.

Margaret seemed tentative, while I attacked at every opportunity, but she stayed with me and, under new rules, the first set had to be decided by a nine-point tie breaker. It went my way.

In the second I attacked her even harder. Margaret ran me all over the court with her steady, deep volleys right on the lines, but I had an answer for almost everything she threw at me. Another tie breaker with the same result. I had broken through a four-minute mile called Margaret Court!

We had become so close in recent weeks that I was a little surprised at her reaction to losing to me for the first time. At the net she was almost surly, and at her press conference she played down my victory, saying, 'I let her play well because I served so badly ... My mind wasn't with it, I couldn't get interested in the match.'

Well, it was just one match, and many more would go her way, I was sure. But the princess had sniffed the throne, and the queen was rattled.

At Kooyong that week I had been reunited with friends from the European tour, Brenda Kirk and Laura Rossouw, both of South Africa, whose matches in the Open were frequently marred by the appearance of anti-apartheid demonstrators in the crowd. During one of Laura's matches a demonstrator actually ran on to the court and tried to stop play, and every time the South Africans played they were booed and jeered by a small but volatile group of students.

South Africa's apartheid policy had become the biggest issue in international sport in 1970, with the introduction of United Nations sanctions against the white supremacist regime provoking a world-wide campaign against sporting ties with the country. South Africa was becoming increasingly isolated in the world of sport, but in Australia the conservative government had so far made no moves to sever ties. Indeed, a rugby tour of Australia by the South African Springbok team was planned for the winter and had strong support from many sections of the community. This was to be followed in 1971–72 by a South African cricket tour in which Australians were looking forward to seeing Barry Richards, whom many considered the world's best batsman at that time.

So while there was clearly an international movement gathering the momentum which it thought would force South Africa to rethink its racial politics, there was not a concerted campaign as far as sporting ties were concerned. In fact, it was difficult to find two countries whose governments could agree on the best approach to the issue.

I knew next to nothing about South Africa, let alone its government's policies, when Mr Edwards first told me in early January 1971, that the organisers of the South African Open in Johannesburg wanted to invite me to play. Still buzzing from the Federation Cup victory, I don't think I even registered a reaction. If there was one, it would most likely have been along the lines of, 'Oh, good! Maybe I'll get to see some lions and tigers and giraffes and things.'

In what may have been a ploy to test international reaction, the story broke in a Johannesburg newspaper well before we had received an official invitation. The report said that my 'racial origin need pose no problems to the South African government, which was not expected to oppose her entry. She would be viewed in the same light as the New Zealand Maoris who were included in the All Blacks rugby side which toured South Africa last year.'

The 'problems' referred to was an oblique reference to the black American tennis player, Arthur Ashe, who had spoken out against apartheid and had subsequently been refused a visa to compete in the country. Mind you, Arthur not only wanted to be let in, he wanted to be let in on his own terms, which included the right to address political rallies.

All hell broke loose in Sydney even before the invitation arrived, and when it finally came things got worse. Under pressure from the media and wanting to protect me from constant harrassment by reporters whenever I showed my face, Mr Edwards organised a press conference on 13 January. 'Any nonsense [in South Africa],' he told the packed interview room, 'and we'll be on the first plane out of there.' I suppose some reporters must have felt he had totally missed the point, but in his mind tennis was tennis, politics was politics. The rest, as Vic Edwards would say, was bullshit. All that mattered was that this little Aboriginal girl should be protected from any nastiness. He went on, 'All we want is the same treatment for Evonne as the other players in the tournament. I certainly don't want any of this business where Evonne has to eat in a different place, travel in a different section [of the bus or plane] or use a different lavatory to the whites.'

I sat through all of this a little shell-shocked. Different lavatories! What was he talking about? When the questions were directed to me I reiterated what Mr Edwards had said. 'As long as I'm treated like any tennis player in any part of the world, then South Africa will not worry me. I'm going to South Africa to play tennis and to see the country, and that is as far as it goes. Apartheid? Well, I don't want to talk about that.'

I couldn't talk about it! I knew nothing about apartheid other than that I, a black Australian, had white South African friends who treated me as an equal wherever we met. Would they be different in their own country? I doubted it. But as the weeks went by I was shocked by the hostility of some of the reactions, and the ones that hurt most were those of my own people. Although I hadn't seen much of them since my return from Europe, I talked regularly with Isabel Hansen and Bob Morgan. The romance had pretty much gone out of my relationship with Bob, even before I had gone to England, but we remained close in spirit, or so I felt. And Michael Anderson, the political radical of the group, had been with me at the Checkmates' concert in the spring.

I sensed that Isabel and Bob were uneasy about South Africa, but I think there was also an element in them that thought, why not? If both black Africans and black Australians are treated as second-class citizens, why is it okay for me to play tennis here but not there? But whatever their innermost thoughts on the matter, they both supported me as friends. Michael, on the other hand, was running around in his black-power gear demonstrating against me.

The demonstrations came to a head at Kooyong at the end of January and, as far as I was concerned, took much of the gloss off my victory over Margaret Court. I became infuriated with the treatment of my friends Laura Rossouw and Brenda Kirk. It just seemed to me that they were tennis players trying to play tennis, and no one had the right to interfere with that. I wrote to Roger, 'They [the demonstrators] were calling out and clapping every time Laura lost a point. The rest of the audience was barracking for Laura. They felt so sorry for her and so did I. Actually, I was really mad. After the match, reporters came up to me and asked did the incidents change my mind about going to South Africa. The only answer I ever give is that I'm just going to play tennis. Even some of the Aboriginal groups are against me going, but they just don't realise that I'm just like Laura and Brenda. Wherever my tennis takes me, I'll play.'

Late in February the respected tennis writer Alan Trengove published an article in the Melbourne *Sun* headed, 'Just a Moment, Mr Edwards.' In it he voiced the most trenchant opposition to our South African tour imaginable. It must have placed Mr Edwards under immeasurable pressure. I know that during this period I felt closer to him than I had in a long time, despite our differences. I wrote to Roger, 'It may be hard for both of us, but I just couldn't have any more arguments with Mr Edwards [on the coming tour]. I care for him, too. Sometimes he's like a little child, therefore I have to handle him a certain way.'

In his article Mr Trengove wrote of me, 'I fear she is about to destroy herself; I believe her coach, Vic Edwards, has committed the greatest misjudgment of his life … Those are not easy words to write about a 19-year-old or a man who is widely respected as a coach and who has been a friend of mine for many years. But even at this late stage I can't urge him strongly enough to cancel this trip. It is regrettable perhaps that a sporting coach may now need to be as much aware of world politics as sporting technique and tactics. It is nevertheless a fact.'

For the most direct criticisms of me, Mr Trengove found one of my own people who was willing to express the most radical view of a broad range then circulating. John Newfong, a member of the staff of the Aborigines Advancement League of Victoria (and later a stalwart of the Aboriginal tent embassy in Canberra) was quoted as saying, 'What she is about to do will never be forgotten. She will not be remembered for her tennis, but as one who sold out responsibility to her race for the prospect of being a white for a week. She will never command respect either among her own people or white people.'

Fortunately I didn't read those words in 1971, for even today I cannot read them without the tears welling up my eyes, not for what Mr Newfong said, but for the bitterness with which he said it. Perhaps I was naive in my view that going to South Africa was the right thing to do. Certainly, over the many years since then people have suggested that to me, particularly since I began to research and reappraise my own Aboriginal identity. But I am unrepentant. I went to South Africa because Mr Edwards said I should play in the South African Open, and I will always be unrepentant.

At the time I was very impressed with the achievements of Lionel Rose, who in 1968 had beaten Fighting Harada in Tokyo to become the first Aboriginal world boxing champion. Lionel fought his way to the top against boxers of all nationalities. I felt very proud that an Aborigine had proven he was the best in any company, and in a small way it made me think of Kenny and Linda moving away from the fringe-dweller settlements and right into the middle of a white man's town. And why not? My parents were just as good

The Aboriginal tent embassy in Canberra. Michael Anderson is on the right

as any white people, and could prove it.

In my own sporting career I never wanted to be restricted to playing a certain level of opponent. I wanted to show that I was good enough to mix in any company, and once the fuss about South Africa set me thinking about that issue, I welcomed the opportunity to show white South Africans just what a black athlete could do, given equal opportunity. And I believed then, as I believe now, that sport can bring people together. After my 1971 visit the racist visa policy was loosened a little, and in 1972 when I went back, I was in the company of black American Bonnie Logan and black New Caledonian Wanaro N'Godrella. That year a black South African named Dan Beuke was allowed to enter his homeland's championship. These were very small advances, I know, but they were advances.

However misguided John Newfong may have thought I was, I believe he showed a complete lack of compassion for an Aboriginal sister. When I think

Arthur Ashe, the great American tennis player. The refusal of the South African government to give him an entry visa caused great controversy

of his remarks I am reminded of the black South African poet Don Mattera who, when Arthur Ashe was finally admitted to the country on his own terms and amid huge controversy in 1973, wrote a poem which summed up beautifully the mixed emotions surrounding his visit.

Anguished Spirit — Ashe

I listened deeply when you spoke
About the step-by-step evolution
Of a gradual harvest, Tendered by the rains of tolerance
And patience.
Your youthful face,
A mask,
Hiding a pining, anguished spirit,
And I loved you brother —
Not for your quiet philosophy
But for the rage in your soul,
Trained to be rebuked or summoned ...

My acceptance of the South African invitation and the subsequent issuing of a visa created a major headache for the South African government, about which I was quietly glad. Arthur had been knocked back in 1969 and 1970, but now, with a precedent established, he applied again. He had considerable support within South Africa too. South African Lawn Tennis Union (SALTU) president Alf Chambers urged the government to rethink its position. Top South African player Cliff Drysdale said, 'I do not necessarily accept the American policy in Vietnam yet this does not exclude me from going to America to play tennis.'

South African Open tournament director Owen Williams, a lovely man with whom I would form a lasting friendship, said, 'My own feeling is that Arthur should get that visa, but I don't think he will.'

He didn't.

At the end of March we flew to Johannesburg, then on to Durban for the Natal Open. I don't know if it was the pressure of the last few weeks, the jet lag or what, but I was bundled out of the quarter finals by unseeded Heidi Orth. We stayed privately in Durban and I had my first taste of South African family life. During tournaments it was always my practice to come home after a match, hand-wash my tennis clothes and hang them out. Here when I asked the black domestic to direct me to the laundry she was horrified. 'Oh, no! You don't have to do that.' I protested that I always did it, but my washing was hurriedly whisked away.

In Johannesburg the following week for the South African Open, Mr

Edwards and I stayed with Bob and Delaille Hewitt and Delaille's parents. Bob had been a protégé of Mr Edwards who looked like becoming a very good player for Australia until he fell out with Davis Cup captain Harry Hopman. 'Hop' had many good points, but if you got on his wrong side your options were so limited and you might as well leave the country to further your tennis career. In this manner Ken Fletcher had wound up in Hong Kong, Marty Mulligan in Italy, and Bob in South Africa, where he had married and made a new home.

I shopped with Delaille, saw the sights with the family and often wandered around town by myself. At no stage was I ever treated other than with hospitality. So it was with some shock that I ventured into a packed Ellis Park for the Open and saw for the first time toilets signposted for blacks and whites. When I looked more closely at the packed stands it soon became apparent that some were for whites and some were for blacks. They all seemed happy enough with the arrangement, and I wondered if the blacks would bother to move if they were allowed. But the toilet signs sent a jolt through me. I was suddenly reminded of the time my sister Barbara had discovered why there was a rope across the aisle at the cinema in Condobolin. It was a symbol of an oppression from which I had obviously been shielded.

There was only one women's dressing room for the players, and I was allowed to use it. In fact I wasn't the only black in there. During the course of the tournament I became friendly with the lady who distributed the towels, a beaming woman who reminded me of my mum.

I received a tremendous ovation from the Ellis Park crowd when I went out for my first match, and it inspired me to play very good tennis throughout the tournament, culminating in meeting Margaret Court in the final. (Ken Rosewall and Fred Stolle fought out the men's singles, making it an all-Australian affair.) But I had obviously used up all my juice. Margaret, the defending champion, thrashed me in straight sets in 45 minutes. I was to go on and win the doubles title playing with Margaret, but such an anticlimactic final must have been a disappointment for the black South Africans in the stands. The first South African Open title to go to a black would have been such a milestone, but for that they would have to wait.

Straight after the match the South African sports minister Frank Waring stepped on to the court to make the presentation. Booing and jeering broke out from both blacks and whites around the arena, and it went on for endless minutes. Margaret and I looked at each other and wondered whether anything more drastic would happen. Waring had been at the centre of an apartheid controversy for several weeks because he had refused to allow non-white cricketers to be considered for selection for the team to tour Australia later in the year — a tour that would have to be called off because of anti-apartheid demonstrations.

Mr Waring presented us with medals and cheques and walked off. At the press conference a reporter asked us if we had been surprised by the reaction. I admitted I had, but Margaret said, 'No, I expected it. Something has to happen in sport in this country, and this might be the turning point.'

After the Open, Margaret, Bob Hewitt, Italy's Nicky Pietrangeli and I piled into a limousine provided by tournament director Owen Williams and took off on an exhibition tour. This was a great excuse for sightseeing in the magnificent South African countryside, but Owen and SALTU officials had also engineered some brief glimpses at various aspects of South African life for my benefit.

We spent a day at a women's prison where apartheid apparently didn't exist. All the women, black and white, were bundled in together. They set up a makeshift court in the prison quadrangle and, after we'd played a couple of sets, several of the women joined us in doubles. At the end of the visit one of the prisoners, a lovely, softly-spoken young woman, presented me with a pencil sketch of a charging elephant. It was quite beautiful and I was very touched by the gift. I asked later what on earth she had done to find herself in prison. I was told she had murdered her husband.

The tour was an educational experience for me, but it had its funny moments as well. One evening we were playing under lights and Margaret was annoyed about something — I think she'd had a fight with Barry. We played our singles matches, then had a break before the mixed doubles. During the break we uncorked a bottle of wine and, giggling like schoolkids, we swigged it down from the neck of the bottle.

When we went back on court I could do no wrong. The ball was bigger than a football and my strokes were close to perfection. Margaret, on the other hand, couldn't hit the ball in the court. It was very funny until halfway through the second set, when I realised I was busting to go to the toilet. I told Bob Hewitt, 'If this goes to three sets I'm going to pee myself, so do the right thing.'

Naturally, that was red rag to a bull. We played three sets, me cross-legged for the last of them, and Bob and Nicky laughing hysterically at my predicament.

At Capetown we played an exhibition in front of an all-black crowd. They loved tennis, and cheered enthusiastically through the first couple of games. Often in these exhibitions we'd contrive a close match for the benefit of the crowd, but in the break Margaret and I put our heads together. She said, 'This crowd is fantastic.'

'Yeah,' I replied, 'let's give them something to remember.' What followed might have been a Grand Slam final. We both gave it everything we had through long rallies full of drop shots, lobs and diving returns. We were exhausted but thoroughly elated after the three-setter. I can't even remember who won.

After the match we met the local people at a reception in our honour. They were very friendly and appreciative of what they had seen. One blue-black woman with a mischievous air about her came up to me and looked me up and down before speaking. 'I can't see what all the fuss is about,' she finally said. 'You're not even black!'

Chapter 14

WE LEFT THE WARM VELDT for a chillier climate, in more ways than one, I feared.

Although he had dominated my off-court thoughts these past nine months, I barely knew the love of my life, this Roger Cawley. We had spent a dozen afternoons and a mere handful of evenings together. We had held hands and cuddled, but the physical side of our relationship had progressed little beyond that. For most of the summer we had met briefly and in public, and yet I believed that we were kindred spirits, that our souls had reached out for each other, and in the 50 or so letters I had sent him since that sad farewell at Heathrow, I had never stopped telling him that my love was sure and true.

He had turned 21 in my absence, I was 19. We were kids, and I was a fairly immature one at that, although at the time I would never have conceded this. I believed in the signals that came from my heart, and, for most of the time we were apart that southern summer, I believed in the signals I got from Roger's heart, too. His letters were newsy, funny, sometimes a little zany but always underlined with the warmth I felt every time we had been together.

And then in the New Year they started to change in small ways. It wasn't so much what he said as what he left unsaid. He seemed to me to be preoccupied. With what? Another woman? Or was the prospect of playing hide-and-seek with Mr Edwards again this summer simply too much for him to contemplate?

I wrote: 'Patience may pay off, I don't know. But honestly, if times do get a bit rough with the three of us, I want you to know if you want to get out of it I will not stop you, as I told you before. I believe that if one [partner] loses interest then the other must accept it willingly.'

During the African trip I barely had time to think about anything other than the next match, the next town. So everything was on hold until my arrival in England. I had sent Roger a tentative tour itinerary as soon as Mr Edwards had planned it. It looked like my first English tournament would be Guildford, where we had met the year before. I scribbled on the bottom of the copy of the itinerary, 'I'll be seeing you again at our meeting place, my love.'

In fact Mr Edwards and I flew in the week before and I started the tour at Sutton. We went straight from the airport to the courts, but rain had delayed the start and I had the afternoon free. As soon as we had settled in I phoned Roger's London number. There was no reply. I wasn't entirely surprised. I knew that he was working regular hours now in his job in the printing industry and couldn't get away as he pleased. And he wasn't expecting me to arrive until Guildford. I was disappointed but I put it out of my mind and went on at Sutton win my fifth British title in succession. The African tour seemed to have loosened me up and I felt strong and confident in the cool English spring. With every match I played I grew in determination, and with every passing day I began to wonder more about Roger.

I won at Guildford, too, but for most of the tournament I had one eye on the stands, hoping to see Roger arrive and give me his supportive wink. I had phoned his number several times during the week and received no reply. We moved on to Hurlingham where Australia's Judy Dalton made me realise I wasn't invincible and Roger Cawley made me realise I was a fool in love. Moping around after Judy had knocked me out of the quarter finals in a torrid three-setter, I phoned a number I had for Roger's sister Alison.

She told me Roger had moved in temporarily to another flat and gave me a new number. I hung up and dialled it. A female voice answered.

'May I speak to Roger Cawley?'

'He's not here right now. Shall I ask him to call you when he comes in?'

I said that would be a good idea and gave her my name and number. When I put the phone down a completely irrational surge of jealousy ran through me. Alison had said he was sharing with a group of people, after all. There was absolutely no reason why one or all of them might not be women. (Indeed, I later found out that Roger's flatmates were all women!)

In a while Roger called back. He was full of excuses about workload and deadlines, all of them quite plausible. I wanted to believe him but I couldn't. The conversation was dotted with awkward silences and embarrassed rushes of small talk. He seemed to want to tell me something, but when the openings were presented to him he did not respond.

Finally, he said, 'I'll make some time during Wimbledon. Can you leave some tickets for me and some friends? Perhaps we'll have a chance to chat then.' I held the phone away from my ear and his voice trailed off. A chance to chat. Hell would freeze over, Roger Cawley, before I gave you another chance to do anything.

There may have been a tear in my eye as I replaced the receiver, but I had toughened up in a year. Perhaps I'd been deceived, or perhaps much too much of it had been the fantasy of a young girl from the bush who wanted to believe the world was like a story in *Princess* magazine. But now I had to face reality.

I took a long walk and when I came back I had scrubbed Sir Roger Cawley and his white steed from my mind. Or so I hoped.

With neither Roger nor Trisha around to fan the flames, my relationship with Mr Edwards was much easier this tour. He still propped up the bar at every tournament, but he seemed much more focused on my tennis, rather than on what I did off the court. Perhaps this was because I wasn't doing anything off the court! Or perhaps he had begun to realise that I had grown up, that a few weeks after Wimbledon I would no longer be a teenager. I still harboured doubts about him as a result of his amorous outbursts, but for the good of the relationship I had buried them deep in the back of my mind, and they were not to resurface for several years.

In the British Hard Court Championships at Bournemouth, I met Margaret Court in the final and she gave me another lesson in power serving. A change had come over Margaret in the months since our holiday together on Rottnest Island. Then I was the heiress to her throne, waiting for her to step down. But since I'd beaten her in the Victorian Open it had become a whole new ball game. Margaret hadn't been quite ready to step down, but suddenly it became just possible that the throne might topple. Now when we met on court she took no chances, and if beating me in the Australian Open in March and the South African Open in April had allayed her fears, she gave no indication of letting up at Bournemouth. I was leading 4–1 in the first set when she turned on the firepower, and I was lucky to win two more games.

None of this worried Mr Edwards. For years he had maintained that I would be the Wimbledon champion of 1974, an estimate he had revised from his original claim of 1970 after the introduction of the stronger competition of open tennis in 1968. He believed I was on target for this goal and that I would be doing very well indeed to be the third best player in Europe in my second season. In time, he felt, I would get the better of Billie Jean King, and Margaret would retire. But then we went to Paris and everything changed.

I was seeded number three for the French Open, but neither Mr Edwards nor I believed that to be an accurate reflection of my chances. This, after all, was my first time on the slow clay of Stade Roland Garros in the Bois de Boulogne. The slower pace of this European style of tennis brings out a variety of approaches to the game that are seldom replicated anywhere else. Some are very odd indeed, but most are effective, and in the home of the high lob and the low slice, a touring pro just has to adapt. My initial experience of European clay in 1970 had been very strange indeed. At Hilversum in the Dutch Open I had struggled with the slow surface but by Munich I had learnt to adjust the tempo of my game and found that I enjoyed the variety of shots that clay encouraged. I began to experiment with my game, covering a lot of court and skidding into my shots. Now, in France, the heavier, unpressurised balls further accentuated the slower, patient game, but I knew if I could adjust quickly, I had the shots to play well.

I fell in love with Paris immediately, the shops, the smells, the people, the cobblestones. I took to wandering the Champs Elysée in the evenings, stopping at a cafe for an onion soup, savouring the sights … It was the city of romance, and I was in love with the idea of being in love. I struggled to keep Roger out of my thoughts, unsuccessfully at first, but once I was absorbed in the tournament, tennis took over, although when I played Wendy Gilchrist, John Paish's girlfriend, in the first round, I was tempted to ask after Roger. I thought better of it.

After Wendy I met Italy's Lea Pericoli in what was a classic example of the anomalies of the clay court game. Virtually unknown outside Europe, Lea had been Italy's top woman player for 15 years, and at Roland Garros she was considered a huge threat to me. Her secret weapon was the high lob, delivered again and again until her frustrated opponent smashed into the net, but this time it wasn't enough.

In the quarter finals I met Françoise Durr, French champion in 1967 and the crowd favourite. Gail Chanfreau had eliminated Margaret Court in a surprise result on the other side of the draw, and suddenly France's only home-grown women's champion since 1948 was a good bet for the title — if she could get past me. The odds were with Frankie. Only Maureen Connolly in 1953 and Althea Gibson in 1956 had ever won the French title on first appearance at Roland Garros.

I had played Frankie a bit, notably in the semifinal of the Federation Cup in Perth when I came back after losing the second set and demolished her to love in the third. But I knew she would be a tricky customer on her home turf, and so it proved. Her cream puff serves were deceptive, her court coverage quicker than it looked. We were even after six games when I turned the power on. I suddenly had the feel of the court and everything seemed to click. I won nine straight games from the stunned local hero.

Mr Edwards was ecstatic when I came off the court and I could barely contain my excitement either. It wasn't that I had beaten Frankie Durr — I beat her in Perth, too. It was that I had played one of those matches a tennis player dreams of, a match where you can do no wrong, where you fly with the angels. Mr Edwards was still bubbling away in the bar when I came back from the locker room an hour later. 'I think you can win from here, pet,' he said. 'My bloody oath I do.'

I was in the final four and the press went beserk. The French had lost their favourite daughter so they replaced Frankie with me in their affections. 'La Belle Evonne', the Paris papers announced. (At least they spelt my name correctly.) The English went a bit overboard too, even my old mate Lance Tingay from the *Telegraph*, who wrote: 'Every now and then in lawn tennis one sees a gem of a performance, and it was such when Miss Goolagong, as near faultless in her game as a human being could be, beat Miss Durr ... in an entrancing performance.'

I felt as if I'd already won the French Open, but there was the small matter of a semifinal and, hopefully, a final to come. Marijke Schaar of Holland was one of the most unusual players to ever reach the top four of a major tournament. She had no backhand at all but threw her racquet from hand to hand ambidextrously. You had to struggle not to watch her hands, rather than the ball, but once that was mastered, so was she. I moved on to the final against Tasmania's Helen Gourlay, who had staged an upset in knocking out American Nancy Richey-Gunter. I thought I had Helen's measure, but in some ways I would have preferred to play Nancy. Helen had learnt her tennis from Vic Edwards and, just before I came to live with the Edwards family at Roseville, she had been the regular boarder.

I knew Mr Edwards was excited about me winning my first major title, but it was difficult for him to will Helen to lose. He felt a keen sense of divided loyalty and I think he was relieved as much as he was overjoyed when I beat her in straight sets in something of an anticlimax. Lance Tingay described it as 'a nice match between two modest girls'.

At our hotel that night Mr Edwards phoned his wife in Australia. 'I think you'd better come over as soon as you can,' he said. 'This could be her year after all.'

I was seeded number three for Wimbledon and, in the wake of my French Open victory, I was the centre of attention in London in the lead-up to the climax of the season. It was an enviable position to be in, and I'm sure this was not lost on Margaret Court nor Billie Jean King, for they had been there once too. There comes a point in the career of every major player where you have nothing to lose and everything to gain. At 19, defeat would be considered heroic, victory a bonus. And, although I would be fortunate enough to have the blessing of the crowds throughout my career, I would never again be so free of the pressure to perform that comes with sporting fame.

I had done several interviews the previous season, but now I was inundated. Mr Edwards carefully monitored the flow of reporters and photographers so as not to try my patience, but I was rarely bothered by the press. They all asked the same questions, I gave the same answers and they seemed to go away happy. I never read the results at the time, but it is notable now that the more interesting articles were written by people who did not talk to me, who formed their impressions through some oblique study of the 'Aboriginal problem'.

One such was a profile which appeared in the *Observer*:

> Although at 19 an unusually controlled young woman, Miss Goolagong is apt to show signs of irritation when questioned about her descent. [This reporter had never questioned me about anything!] Reasonably enough, she wishes to be thought remarkable only for her tennis. It is also self-evident that, having committed herself to a fiercely competitive way of life, she must wish to give the whole of her young mind to the game. She could scarcely involve herself directly, just as her career is blossoming, in the affairs of her ancestral folk, even though in the last few months startling accounts have been published of their depressed condition and of the forlorn fight some of them are putting up for their rights.

When I read this recently in a scrapbook, sent to me many years ago by an elderly British fan, I thought of my time on The Murie at Condobolin, and at the Three Ways mission, and throwing boomerangs on the beach with my friends from the Foundation; and of the busy two-way street running between me and my family, whose only traffic was love and support for all those years when they needed the support, and I needed the love. I thought about all those things as I read the article, and I wondered how much time the builder of those beautifully-constructed, completely meaningless sentences had spent with his own ancestral folk, ladling soup and dispensing rugs on cold winter nights in the East End.

Mrs Edwards arrived a couple of days before Wimbledon and joined us in the flat Mr Edwards had rented at Park Walk, just off the Fulham Road in Chelsea. I had skipped the Queen's Club tournament in order to be completely match-fit for Wimbledon, and had even scaled down my training in preparation for a tournament in which state of mind would be more important than state of body.

That left plenty of time for shopping and sightseeing. It was Mrs Edwards' first visit to London and she enjoyed herself immensely from the moment she arrived, but I think that had as much to do with me as it did with the excitement of experiencing a new place. She was loving and attentive and very careful to see that I was happy at all times. I don't know what, if anything, Mr Edwards had told her about me and Roger, but she knew enough not to mention the subject.

When the tournament began I realised a lot had changed in just 12 months. What had seemed an awesome prospect in 1970 was perfectly normal in 1971. Of course, the jitters would come if I got through the early rounds, but I felt no pain at all in cruising through the Americans Patti Hansen and Kristian Kemmer to reach the third round and their compatriot Julie Heldman.

Julie, then rated fifth in the world, had been considered one of my great conquests of the previous season, but her game had seemed to slip in inverse proportion to her financial demands. She, Billie Jean and Rosie Casals were at the forefront of the 'Women's Liberation players' (the 'Libbers') that year, a group of players orchestrated by Julie's mum Gladys Heldman, who were in the throes of setting up a separate women's tour and were demanding equal purses with the men. Somehow Margaret Court and I had been lumped on the opposing side. Margaret had made the fatal mistake of saying that men played better tennis and were worth more, but I'd never said a word on the subject. I had enough to worry about with the anti-apartheid demonstrators, who had threatened to bombard Centre Court with cream buns, with me as a principal target. If this eventuated I hoped it would happen during the more casual play of the mixed doubles, where I might be tempted to use my free hand to catch them and eat them!

Anyway, Julie wouldn't have beaten too many men that day — I won 6–3, 6–3. I went into the next round against my Federation Cup team-mate Lesley Hunt, who took the first set of the tournament from me and gave me a scare before I hit back. Then Nancy Richey-Gunter succumbed in the quarter finals and suddenly I was into the final four.

Linda and Kenny still didn't have the phone on at home in Barellan — that was something I was planning to rectify as soon as I could talk Mum into it — so I phoned the post office.

'It's Evonne!' I heard the postmistress cry. 'Nick down the road and get the Goolies.' And then into the phone: 'Now what's it like over there in England, love? Have you seen the Queen and them yet?' I was worried that we'd be up to the well-being of the characters in 'Coronation Street' before the family could be rounded up! 'Oh, look, here's your Mum and them. I'll put her on and that.'

'Mum, I'm in the final four!'

Warming up for Wimbledon, 1971

'Don't you think we know that? We've got the telly, you know.'

'Are you excited?'

'Of course we are. John Emerson says we've got to have a big party when you play the final.'

'If I play the final.'

'Yeah, well, Dad says to wish you luck. He's had a couple and he'd get all teary if I put him on. Here's Kevin ...'

And so it went on, through a succession of brothers and sisters, friends of the family. I didn't always miss the simple life of Barellan, but whenever I heard those Australian voices again something gnawed at my heart. I promised I'd wave at the television cameras for them and rang off with tears in my eyes.

Billie Jean King. The Old Lady, they called her, although she was younger than Margaret. Our paths had never crossed, except when I was a kid and she thrashed me at the Milton courts in Brisbane years in 1958, but I'd watched

Billie Jean King and I march out to do battle on Centre Court. Wimbledon semifinal, 1971

her play Margaret in that brilliant 1970 Wimbledon final, and I'd been struck by how much larger than life, how intimidating she seemed for such a small woman. She fascinated me, and in all the years I played her I don't think I ever got used to the sight of her prowling the baseline. Now she was the fiercest Libber of them all, a loud and sometimes abrasive woman who seemed to be playing for her life in every match. When she made an unforced error she stomped across the baseline, cursing and muttering to herself. In style and temperament, Billie Jean was a world away from me, and players like that were always the most dangerous because they could be difficult to adapt to. And, of course, she was the second seed, widely recognised as the best player in the world after Margaret.

The smart money was on a Court–King final. The theory was that Billie Jean had the guile and experience to throw me off, no matter how poor her form nor how good mine had been. She had, after all, been here before. Margaret had beaten Billie Jean in the final in 1963 and again in 1970, but in between times Billie Jean had won it three years in a row against Maria Bueno (Brazil), Ann Jones (England) and Judy Dalton (Australia). At Wimbledon her nemesis was named Court, not Goolagong.

All of this worked to my advantage. Margaret seemed to have a ticket to the final in Judy Dalton, a fine player but not in her class. So I had absolutely nothing to lose from here, a set of circumstances which often resulted in my best tennis. Mr Edwards took me aside before the match and told me what I had already figured out. He said, 'Give it your best, sweetie, but there is no pressure on you at all. I'm just thrilled that you've come this far.'

I started the match by breaking Billie Jean's service, then going to 2–0. I felt good and strong, and even my second serve was working. Billie Jean retaliated by returning everything to my backhand. Where was the guile in that? Hadn't the Old Lady heard that this was my greatest strength?

Then something happened. I double-faulted and my game started to fall apart. Billie Jean took a 3–2 lead and I had to claw back again, breaking her service to regain the lead at 4–3. I held serve to take the set, then got the break I needed in the fifth game of the second set. I was into the final!

Billie Jean was a study in cool at her post-match press conference. 'I couldn't get any sting in my game, and Evonne's been around long enough to know what to do and she took advantage of my mistakes … I'm pleased for her … She's just what women's tennis needs.'

By contrast, at my press conference I was so excited I could barely speak. I blathered something about 'the greatest moment in my life' and then said success wouldn't spoil little Evonne, I'd be back at the kitchen sink washing dishes in a couple of hours. Something silly like that. It was a very silly, excited press conference. The photographers wanted me to wink. I could never wink, that was Roger's forte …

Roger. Somewhere in the midst of my euphoria that hit home, and I faltered. He had phoned me a couple of days earlier, full of nervously cheerful small talk and wanting tickets for himself and some friends. Sure, why not? It was all over between us. There was no point in harbouring a grudge. I had even said yes to a date with the friend of one of the Australian players. But every time I thought of Roger …

Sensing that my emotions had gotten the better of me — as his had when I'd hit the winner against Billie Jean — Mr Edwards whisked me out of the press room and back to the hotel.

'Are you all right, pet?'

'Of course. Just a bit overcome by it all.'

I woke early on the morning of Friday 2 July and my first thought was not of Wimbledon but of Roger. I put the thought out of my mind immediately and chastised myself severely for being so stupid. Grow up, Goolie! Get on with your tennis!

Half a world away in Barellan, shearing mates John Emerson and Kenny Goolagong were organising a party. Nothing flash. A dozen bottles of beer, some fish and chips and a bottle of tomato sauce. Then they planned to sprawl out in front of the telly and watch the big match. John would rather have been settling in for a Sydney rugby league grand final, of course, but then, this was their Mooch, playing in front of the Queen or the Duke or some bloody bigwig all the way over there in Pommyland!

When they pulled up in front of the house with the case of beer and the fish and chips they noticed two cars parked opposite. Out-of-towners. In a town the size of Barellan, you notice such things. John Emerson grabbed the beer and got out of the car, wondering who the late visitors might be. A man got out of one of the other vehicles and strode across the street. 'Excuse me, I'm Bob Johnson from the Melbourne *Sun*. Is this the Goolagong residence?'

Within hours Barellan was swarming with pressmen, all hoping to see some yokels and 'bushies' which would underline the perceived irony of someone like me appearing on Centre Court at Wimbledon. I hope that this doesn't sound bitter, because, despite the hoops the press have had my family jump through over the years, our reaction has always been to have a good laugh about it all later. 'Now Mrs Goolagong, could you be rubbing the sticks together while Mr Goolagong attempts to light his cigarette?' That sort of thing.

The official Daimler picked us up from the flat in Park Walk around midday,

Wimbledon final, 1971

a couple of hours before Margaret and I were due on Centre Court to play the first all-Australian final in the 87-year history of women's singles at Wimbledon. On the ride out of town neither of the Edwards, nor their friend, the Australian freelance journalist Alf Chave who was staying with us, said much that made sense. They just chattered excitedly about the weather and how big the crowd might be. It was too late for serious coaching advice now, and Mr Edwards knew it. I would be the underdog, the crowd favourite ... nothing to lose.

Nothing to lose ... that was my mantra as we arrived at the Doherty Gate and I waved to the fans. Nothing to lose as referee Captain Mike Gibson led us onto Centre Court and Margaret and I curtseyed to the Royal Box, while the band played 'Waltzing Matilda'. Margaret to serve first. Nothing to lose as I paced on the baseline and waited ... Nothing to lose as I broke her first serve and the Centre Court crowd cheered themselves hoarse. Time, and the crowd, were on my side.

'Up Barellan! Up the Goochas!' yelled John Emerson, the bodgie of Barellan, when I won the first set 6–4. Protracted negotiations with reporters in cars had resulted in John allowing one, Adrian McGregor of the *Australian*, to join the family in front of the television. I have Mr McGregor to thank for this account of the second set:

> Mr Goolagong chuckled each time (John Emerson shouted) and rolled a cigarette. His eyes never left the screen. At 3–1 he said, 'Margaret must be worried, I reckon.' Evonne slammed a first service into the net. Kevin said it had plenty of sting. The rest of the room groaned.
>
> Mr Goolagong's commentary continued: 'If only she can get this one — hit it, hit it!'
>
> At 5–1 Mrs Goolagong turned and looked at her husband. He said quietly, 'I think she's going to win it.' Two points to win it. One point to win it. Margaret served a fault. Mr Goolagong said, 'Now, if she hits this next one into the net, Evonne's won it ... She did! She did!'
>
> People rushed about hugging and laughing. Mr Goolagong, handed a beer, kept repeating, 'Beaut, just beaut!'

PART 4

Australia's Sweetheart

A welcome home kiss from Mum and Dad

Chapter 15

SIXTY-THREE MINUTES. It wasn't a long Wimbledon final but it was long enough to change forever the course of my life.

Those first few minutes of my Wimbledon reign are a blur on which it is difficult to focus after so many years. I can remember Margaret Court congratulating me at the net. She didn't exactly fall all over me with praise, but that was never Margaret's style. She was pregnant, we were both to find out later, and her body was planning a future of its own. In those chaotic moments, however, I don't think I thought deeply about Margaret's future, nor my own for that matter. I know I waved triumphantly to Mr and Mrs Edwards, sitting behind Barry Court in the players' box, both of them struggling to control their tears. And I may have aimed a smile at Princesses Margaret and Alexandra up in the Royal Box with British Prime Minister Ted Heath, but I don't remember that either.

The ball boys in their green and purple shirts formed a guard of honour along the green carpet which led onto the court. Then Princess Alexandra walked the slow royal walk, stopping to chat to the ball boys, before taking her place for the presentation. I curtseyed and she presented me with the famous golden platter. I'm sure the Princess and I exchanged pleasantries but you'll have to wait for her book to find out what they were. I haven't a clue. The newspaper photos of the great moment tell me I held the platter aloft in the grand winner's style, and that part I have no trouble remembering.

The press conference seemed to go on forever. 'Evonne, how does it feel?' 'Evonne, do this please.' 'Evonne, do that please.'

When it was finally over, Mrs Edwards grabbed me and dragged me free of a clutch of photographers. 'Come on, let's go and watch Kim play.' Kim Warwick, my friend and sometime mixed doubles partner, was playing in a semifinal of the Plate consolation event on Court 1. Heads down and giggling all the way, we snuck through the crowds of well-wishers and sought refuge in the stand. We watched Kim play in complete silence for a while, and then it struck me. 'I've won it!' I cried. 'I've won it!' I almost hugged the life out of Mrs Edwards.

Left: Receiving the plate from Princess Alexandra *Right:* The Wimbledon champion, 1971

That was the last time for 15 years that I would be fortunate enough to sit in the stands at Wimbledon and watch the tennis. Fame is a mixed blessing and at Wimbledon it can make you a prisoner. Until a few years ago, when I took my children to Wimbledon and was anxious to watch the juniors on the outer courts, I watched all the tennis from the dressing rooms.

Mr Edwards and Barry Court had made a pact before the final. No matter who won, we Aussies would party the night away. We did, at Knights of Knightsbridge, but the Courts didn't show up. I was too busy having a good time to take much notice, but if Mr Edwards was miffed by their non-appearance, then he didn't show it, and I'm sure when he later heard about Margaret's pregnancy, that would have explained everything.

I remember dancing in my knee-high boots and Teddy Tinling hot pants — he had made them for me to wear on-court rather than off, but I know he would have approved — but I don't remember the formalities of that evening as well as Alf Chave, whose account I shall rely on: 'About midnight Vic asked me to propose the toast to Evonne. For me it was a proud moment. Evonne in reply was so modest and yet so confident that everybody in the place stood up and cheered when she finished. I looked at Vic. There were tears streaming down his face. I felt my old weatherworn face. It was moist too.'

Not a dry eye in the place! No wonder I got out while I could and took a taxi back to the flat. It was morning in Barellan now, so I phoned the post office. Eventually Mum came on the line and added her tears to the international flood that my victory seemed to have created. But it wasn't a long conversation. I'd been congratulated and wept over by barely half the family when I simply had to go and lie down. The new Wimbledon champion was absolutely knackered.

The next afternoon I was back on Centre Court for what was probably the strangest tennis match I've ever played. Margaret and I were in the doubles final against Billie Jean King and Rosie Casals. Billie Jean and Rosie had been playing efficient — sometimes inspired — doubles for a lot longer than Margaret and I had been paired, but winning or losing was not my concern. It was how to handle Margaret!

She was my friend, in some ways my mentor, in other ways my idol. She was — and is — the greatest women's tennis player in history, and 24 hours earlier a sellout crowd had gone berserk while I made her look human. The London tabloids had gone completely nuts that Saturday morning. 'Evonne is new Miss World!' screamed the *Daily Mail*, confusing the event with something completely different. 'The babe from the bush is champion!' shouted another, apparently unaware that both Margaret and I were 'babes from the bush'. 'Bold and brash, brilliant and booming, that was Miss Goolagong as she burned to the title, her arrogant game sending the new generation to the crown in place of the old. For Mrs Court, three-times Queen of Wimbledon, it was the end of the road.'

At just 28, happily married, pregnant with her first child and with a lot of tennis left in her yet, Margaret may have been forgiven for believing that there was a little bit of road ahead of her. But this was what I came to love about the Fleet Street tabloids — their thoughtful analysis of the situation. Margaret had beaten me in Johannesburg a couple of months earlier, she would beat me in Dublin the week after. On the day I was the better player, that was all.

None of this helped Margaret's blues when we came out to play the doubles. I wasn't about to apologise and I suppose there was not a lot to say. We went through the motions — and lost in two uneventful sets.

Mrs Edwards and I went straight from Wimbledon to the hairdressers, where we had ourselves made ready for the Wimbledon Ball that night at the Grosvenor House Hotel. For me, winning the tournament had little to do with the excitement of the ball. At my first Wimbledon Ball the year before I'd had the most wonderful night of my life with Roger. This year,

The morning after — Margaret and I playing the doubles final

without him, I was going to have an even better night. I'd bought a marvellous silver lamé gown on the Kings Road and teamed it with silver shoes and an evening purse I'd borrowed from tennis legend Frank Sedgman's wife.

My partner for the evening was Colin Dibley from Sydney, who'd astounded a lot of people by reaching the quarter finals. When I asked Col to partner me he'd protested, 'But I haven't got a suit!' He got one. Men's singles champion John Newcombe danced the first waltz with me and managed to keep off my new shoes despite the atrocious rhythm of 'Tie Me Kangaroo Down Sport' — Rolf Harris had a lot to answer for in those days.

Then came my first big speech. I stumbled through a few thankyous at first, then explained that I was still in a bit of a daze. At Wimbledon that year there'd been numerous arrests of spectators for indecent behaviour, mostly for the heinous offence of bottom-pinching. I said: 'I feel like someone should pinch me to make sure this is not a dream. I guess I'd just have to walk around Wimbledon to find out.' My little joke brought the house down. When I sat back down Mr Edwards grinned at me and leaned over and whispered, 'Very good, but don't give up your day job.'

Wimbledon 1971 had finished but the party was far from over. We flew to Dublin for the Irish Open, the kind of tournament where they had the great good sense to play the important matches in the early evening, after the Guinness had had time to work through the system. Margaret beat me in the final, but what I really remember about Dublin is the disco! Then on to Hilversum again for the Dutch Open. At home on clay now, I celebrated my twentieth birthday by winning the tournament. After the final I was presented with a Dutch doll and a birthday cake, then the entire audience stood and sang 'Happy Birthday' in Dutch.

Mr Edwards had resisted pressure from the Americans to have the Wimbledon champion play the US Open at Forest Hills, but we still had to cross the Atlantic for one more playing engagement before heading home. I wasn't much interested in the Canadian Open, but our brief stopover in New York was another matter.

Earlier that year in London we'd signed with the agents Bagenal Harvey who were instructed to explore my commercial potential as a top-ranked professional tennis player, and one of the first deals they'd done after my Wimbledon win was with the clothing designers, Ginori of New York. We had to stop by and shake on it, which seemed to me to be a reasonable enough thing to do. Mr and Mrs Edwards and I checked into the Manhattan hotel Ginori had arranged for us, and in no time at all I'd been whisked off for fittings and to have my hair done by Vidal Sassoon. When I reappeared at the hotel Mrs Edwards dropped her magazine and stared at me in horror. 'Oh my goodness! What have they done to you?'

Mr Edwards was all for taking legal action. He later wrote: '... a free haircut from a so-called world-famous hair-stylist, and this fellow made a mess of Evonne's hair and upset her ...' Upset me! I thought I looked great. Sassoon had cut my hair short and severe in the Paris/New York style of the early 1970s, and lightened the colour a little. Certainly the man from Ginori wasn't offended by the look when he came to pick me up for dinner and dancing. This outing was another thorn in Mr Edwards' side. He told me later he was concerned that people would 'take over' and make me do things I didn't want to do. I suppose there was an element of truth in this, but in professional sport it was also the nature of the beast, and I think what concerned him most was to see control of my life slipping away from him.

The night on the town in Manhattan was innocent enough — a group of us danced until dawn at a discotheque called Hippopotomus — but I drank a few too many cocktails for the first time in my life and paid the price. I remember being steered through the airport by the none-too-happy Edwards for the flight to Toronto, the extent of my suffering hidden behind dark glasses.

I didn't want to be in Toronto, and I suppose I made my feelings plain enough to Mr Edwards, but I had never been a spoilt or indulged child and I don't believe I developed these traits as an adult. I wanted desperately to go home and share my glory with my family, but I had a job to do in Toronto and there was no question of me not fulfilling a commitment. So what happened there, and Mr Edwards' reaction to it, disturbed me greatly.

I played well within myself and was lucky to beat Virginia Wade in the semifinals, coming back from a shocking start. Then I met Françoise Durr in the final. Since I had beaten her in the quarter final of the French Open a couple of months earlier, Frankie and I had become mates — we'd had a couple of meals together in Toronto — and for me friendship is a distinct disadvantage when you're looking at someone across a net. I didn't play badly on the clay, I just didn't think about my game as keenly as Frankie did hers, and she took the title in straight sets.

Win some, lose some. That was my reaction. Mr Edwards' reaction was unbridled fury. It seemed he'd allowed me the luxury of goofing off in Dublin and at a couple of minor tournaments, but now the time had come to face up to the awesome responsibility of being Number One, world champion, the

Practising for the Canadian Open under the watchful eye of Mr Edwards

Big New Thing. He ranted and raved, and later he wrote, 'Evonne's becoming conscious of money, although it still means little to her ... the first time I brought it up was when she lost the Canadian Open to Françoise Durr in a lackadaisical performance ... that cost her $2000 and I thought she should know that while the money isn't utmost ... a little extra concentration can be very worthwhile ...'

I just wanted to go home. Couldn't he understand that?

And finally, in August, I *was* home. To a ticker-tape parade through the streets of Sydney and a Lord Mayoral reception. Of course I was honoured, but I couldn't help wondering why. John Newcombe had won Wimbledon for two years running and hadn't been so honoured. Margaret Court had three Wimbledon crowns to her credit, but no ticker-tape parades. Why me? Wasn't I the same Evonne who had been ostracised by my own people six months earlier for daring to play in South Africa? Wasn't I on the verge of destroying myself?

At the time I didn't allow these small doubts to stand in the way of a very good time. It was exciting and quite moving to stand in an open-topped car and soak up the warm applause of my countrymen as the motorcade circled

The welcome home parties: with the Lord Mayor in Sydney and Barbara in Barellan

204

the city. It was only much later that I attempted to put into some kind of historical context the extraordinary welcome home I received.

Racial politics had reached boiling point in Australia during the winter of 1971 with the attempts of anti-apartheid demonstrators to disrupt the South African Springbok rugby tour. In Sydney and Brisbane there had been unprecedented scenes of civil unrest as thousands of students jostled with police at the playing grounds and on the streets. While the majority of Aboriginal activists wholeheartedly supported the anti-apartheid cause, there was also a strong feeling that the real issue was the oppression of indigenous peoples all over the world. And, while the McMahon Liberal government in Canberra had paid lip service to equal rights, nothing was being done. Some Aborigines believed that unless the Australian government moved soon to implement the good intentions of the 1967 referendum on equality, then civil disturbances and clashes between blacks and whites would become the norm in urban Australia.

As this frightening prospect took root in the psyches of middle Australia, a black Australian curtseyed before royalty, then went on to prove that Aborigines could make it to the top, could strive for the same goals as white Australians, and achieve them.

Of course I would be naive to deny that the way I played tennis and the way I approached life had struck a chord with a great many Australians. But underlying this attachment to me as someone who seemed to cherish the warm old values in the cold new world of professional sport, was a kind of racial relief — a feeling that somehow my achievements proved that Australia was a land of equal opportunity. Perhaps some people murmured to themselves, 'Thank God one of them has made it to the top. Now, if the rest of them would follow her example and stop bloody whingeing...'

I'm not suggesting all Australians felt that way, nor am I ungrateful for the support I've received over the years from so many who have never even met me. But I do believe that whenever an Aborigine succeeds in any endeavour in open company, there is a tendency, perhaps unconscious, for Australians to say, 'See, we're not holding them back, we give them every opportunity.'

Having received the keys to Sydney, I flew to Narrandera to be welcomed home all over again. I was a little annoyed about the sequence of events here. I'd played tennis in Narrandera, and it was where I caught the plane, but other than that I had no particular attachment to the place. Everyone who'd ever helped me was 30 kilometres away in Barellan. Nevertheless, the moment I walked down the gangway to be gripped by the diminutive Member for Riverina, Mr Al Grassby, I was in the hands of the town's civic authorities.

I managed to slip out of their clutches for long enough to hug and kiss

Home with the family. From left: Mully, Ian, Gail, Barbara and son William, Larry, Mum

the family — everyone was there from Kenny down to Barbara's little boy, William. We all kissed and cried and started to talk at once, until I was recalled to duty. Another motorcade, another reception. Finally we made it home to Barellan and talked away into the night at the house on Yarran Street. But not too late. In the morning there was another welcome home.

Under the command of Bill Kurtzman, the Barellan 'Welcome Home' Committee had worked for several weeks to ensure that this was Barellan's greatest day. There was to be a float procession, an official reception, several morning and afternoon teas, a sports carnival and a victory ball. I nearly choked on my cereal when I was given the schedule for the day, but with brothers and sisters to provide moral support, I prepared myself.

There were about five times as many people as I'd ever seen in Barellan, lining the streets and cheering that morning as our procession made its way to the recreation ground. My tear-stained memory of that morning is a little hazy, but the *Times-Leader* of Ardlethan and Barellan reported:

It is doubtful if there has ever been such spontaneous out-pouring of effort and energy in any town. It would be hard to name an organisation or sporting club

Signing the council's vistors' book in Narrandera

in the town and district of Barellan which had not played its part in doing honour to Evonne ... Over 20 gaily decorated lorries, each with a special motif, followed in gay procession behind the smiling Evonne, with her little sister Janelle standing proudly beside her as she acknowledged the plaudits of the crowd ... The procession wended its way to the football ground where the floats encircled the official enclosure. Evonne was able to move freely around among her friends, shaking hands, signing autographs and obviously being very much at home among the old faces, people who had watched her career from a very small girl to the Women's Tennis Champion of the world.

The official welcoming speeches were made from a specially erected dais where an obviously delighted Bill Kurtzman, as chairman introduced ... speakers ... For Bill ... it was an occasion to cap the memories of a lifetime.

Indeed it was. Mr Kurtzman, God bless him, was nearing the end of his life and, although Mr Edwards had become in the eyes of the world my 'mentor', in Bill Kurtzman's eyes I was forever the property of the Barellan War Memorial Tennis Club. In fact, many years later, when Mr Kurtzman was long gone and Mrs Sissy Kurtzman was seeing out her days in a nursing home in Griffith, she clutched me to her one windy Sunday afternoon and whispered in my ear, 'You meant everything to him, dear. He lived to see you succeed.'

Bill Kurtzman led a full life, and when he died at 78 it had only been a decade since he had seen me hitting balls against the wall in Barellan. Nevertheless, he gave that last decade of his life unselfishly and I will always treasure my memories of him.

During the sports carnival in the afternoon Pastor (later Sir) Doug Nicholls from Cummeragunga mission showed up to wish me well. Doug, a great footballer and runner in his day, had recently been appointed chairman of the Aboriginal Sports Foundation, and had driven out of his way to see me en route from Melbourne to Sydney.

That extraordinary day in my home town will live forever in my memory, from the procession of funny floats through to the last dance that night in the crowded Memorial Hall, but unfortunately the only documentary film of Barellan's welcome home set out to belittle the town, its people and my family. I suppose the intention of the crew from the ABC's 'This Day Tonight' program was to illustrate beyond any shadow of doubt the rags-to-riches element of my story. Kenny and Linda had already become quite used to this sort of thing and took no offence at being portrayed as battlers, but 'This Day Tonight' searched the district to come up with a couple of rusting car bodies and tractor parts, through which they filmed most of the action. All the tennis I ever played in Barellan was on the immaculate courts at the War Memorial Tennis

Left: Linda in a jam: Narrandera homecoming *Right:* Dancing with Kevin: Barellan homecoming

Club, but the ABC reinvented my history so that the doctor's disused backyard court at our new home on Yarran Street became the birthplace of the legend.

I had become media-aware enough to realise what was going on, but I had no idea how to stop it without antagonising the film crew. Mr Edwards would have had no problems with this, but he was back in Sydney. I finally lost my cool when I answered the door one morning with my hair in rollers and found them filming me.

When the segment went to air there was an uproar in our little part of the world. Maybe elsewhere they got a giggle out of it, but the proud folk of Barellan were incensed. On behalf of the Welcome Home Committee, Bill Kurtzman wrote a letter of protest to the ABC: '... It is our feeling that this film was degrading and humiliating to Evonne and her family and emphasised the fact that they are part aboriginal (sic) and as such could be inferior, instead of which they are accepted as equals in the community ...'

The NSW Lawn Tennis Association added its voice to the protest and the NSW Minister for Aboriginal Welfare, Mr Waddy, protested to the Postmaster-General (the Minister responsible for the ABC) Sir Alan Hulme. The ABC's

Home again, 1971

only response came in the form of anonymous comments published by a Sydney television writer. 'When our crew went to Barellan to film the welcome-home celebrations, some technicians were given the impression that the Goolagongs were treated as second-class citizens by the locals. One ABC member was told that the the town's civic-minded citizens decided to call together a working bee to clean the place up just to make it look good for the visitors. If you couple that with the story that the local authorities put on the electricity to the house the night before Evonne's homecoming so that the family looked like it was coping with its circumstances reasonably comfortably, you have another side to the story of the badly-done-by people of Barellan.'

At the time we Goolagongs remained silent on the issue, and I have never commented on it — until now. Times have changed. No television station would run a segment like that today. Yes, my family sometimes forgot to pay the electricity bill, and the phone bill, and a few others. No, we were never treated like second-class citizens in Barellan. I don't believe the ABC set out to denigrate the Goolagongs or Aborigines generally, but in selectively filming and even fabricating scenes they reinforced the Aboriginal stereotype. The Goolagongs may have been moving rapidly into the .middle class in 1971, but as far as the ABC was concerned, we would always be fringe dwellers.

Chapter 16

$\mathcal{F}$OR WINNING THE WIMBLEDON women's singles in 1971 I received 1800 pounds Sterling, plus another 150 pounds for coming second with Margaret Court in the doubles.

Not exactly a fortune for winning the most prestigious title in tennis, but it seemed like one then. With my French Open victory, several minor titles and quite a few seconds that season, my tennis earnings for the European tour were probably in the vicinity of $20,000, against travelling expenses of around $10,000. For the first time in my career I was in the black, so to speak. Throw in a few lucrative endorsement deals, like my long-standing arrangement with Dunlop-Slazenger and newer ones like Ginori, and I was starting to have a tax problem.

Of course, I never knew anything about how my finances were managed. That was entirely Mr Edwards' responsibility. I remember being relieved in 1970 when I thought I had probably made enough in prize money to pay him back for the London air fare — I had no idea that many of the costs associated with our trips in 1970 and 1971 were met by Dunlop. In 1971 all I cared about was being given enough money to shop occasionally for records, tapes, charms for my bracelet and glass figurines for my growing collection. My only other financial concern was to make life more comfortable for my family.

One of the ways I could do this was to buy the Yarran Street house for them. Dad was always having trouble finding the rent, and with that problem solved, he could use whatever spare cash he came by to fix the place up a bit. I got things moving with a few big and necessary items — like a new water tank, toilet, stove and phone — and thereafter I would always lend a hand whenever it was needed.

Not that my family developed extravagant tastes. Their needs were simple and basic and I was happy to oblige whenever they asked or I saw a need, knowing that if the situation were to be reversed, Mum, Dad, Barbara and Larry would be there to help me.

While I remained naive about money, Mr Edwards learnt very quickly how to exploit my new world champion status. Although he had coached

Racquet design. Dunlop factory in England, 1971

tennis champions for decades, I was his first in the age of open tennis. It was a time when rules were made to be broken, when no one was really sure how far all this would go. Despite the fact that tennis players had been playing for money since the 1930s, never before had anyone done better than to earn a living comparable with that of their contemporaries outside tennis.

The 'shamateurism' of the time, in which top players received 'under the table' appearance fees, was considered by the diehard amateur officials to be preferable to open and honest prize money.

In his excellent book *Kooyong: A Serve To Authority*, Richard Yallop recounts the story of a trip some Australian players made to Hamburg in 1964: 'Brian Tobin, who later became president of the LTAA, went overseas in 1964 as manager of a touring team including John Newcombe, Tony Roche, Margaret Smith and Lesley Turner, and he recalls going to the Hamburg tournament and being handed two envelopes, both containing $US 3000. The German official handed over the envelopes, saying, "This is for the association, and

this is for you." Tobin said: "I don't know if they were paying us twice ...
I didn't ask, but the money didn't go into my pocket." '

When tennis went open in 1968, the players were initially not much better
off, but by 1971 corporate sponsors were beginning to see the possibilities and
to pump money into the sport. By today's standards the amount was peanuts,
but after I won Wimbledon there was an expectation — of which I was
blissfully unaware — that if I planned wisely, continued to play well and put
my name on a variety of products, I could draw a comfortable income for
the forseeable future. That was all. Tennis millionaires were still for the future.

From the time I turned professional at Southport in 1970 to our eventual
split in 1975, Mr Edwards claimed he never took a manager's cut from my
income. He invested my earnings for me (by and large wisely) and managed
the working accounts so that I paid for all the touring expenses incurred by
our party — and admittedly the party got bigger and bigger as the prize
money escalated. But he always maintained that he never claimed a percentage,
believing that the business that my fame brought through the doors of the
Victor A. Edwards Tennis School was adequate payment. And VAETS did
boom, although Vic Edwards was rarely there to oversee the development
of the next Evonne Goolagong.

Soon after my Wimbledon victory in 1971, Australian writer Harry Gordon
wrote in an article about me which was first published in the *New York Times*
and later, in a condensed version, in the *Reader's Digest*: 'Not a cent of her
earnings goes to Edwards. He already runs Australia's largest tennis school,
and the publicity Evonne earns assures him that it will grow larger still. His
fares are paid by tournament organisers when he accompanies her, and he has
already invested a chunk of her winnings in real estate.'

In the 1975 'autobiography', *Evonne*, compiled by tennis writer Bud Collins
from information provided by Mr Edwards, I am quoted as saying: 'Mr Edwards
has never taken a penny of my earnings. He'd be more than justified in
extracting a percentage from my prize money, as International Management
does from everything I earn. I'm sure many people believe he does take his
cut, and he'd be entitled to, if only to get something back from all he's spent
on me. But does a father take a cut from a daughter?'

I can't see why one wouldn't, and in fact this 'father' did. He had a
managerial contract with me from 1970, and in the year to 30 June 1974, when
the book was written, he had been paid $20,000 which corresponded to about
30 per cent of my winnings that year. This base rate was to increase by $5000
each year. To this day I do not understand why he felt he had to lie about
this perfectly normal business relationship, nor do I understand how he could

fabricate my words to support his fiction. The fact is that in 1975 I did not and could not have made the statements about our financial relationship — or lack of one — that appeared in the book. At that stage I had no idea what happened to my money.

But in view of the criticism Mr Edwards was to receive in the years to come, I think it is important to remember that for whatever reason he chose to be furtive about his cut, in financial matters he did what he did with my interests first and foremost in mind.

In September 1971 Lance Tingay published his world tennis rankings in the London *Daily Telegraph*. The two top-ranked players in the world were John Newcombe and Evonne Goolagong, the Wimbledon champions. I had gone from unrated to number one in 12 months. Wrote Mr Tingay: 'Miss Goolagong hinted at a claim to world leadership when she won the French title at a meeting where Mrs Court failed. She established herself undisputably (sic), in my view, as number one when she won Wimbledon, not only in taking the title but in beating both Billie Jean King and Mrs Court in the last two matches.' He went on to say that there was a huge gap between the top four women — myself, Margaret, Billie Jean and Rosie Casals — and the rest. Nevertheless, at number 10 he found space for a promising player from Florida named Chris Evert.

A few days after these rankings were published I received a firm offer to join the 'Women's Liberation' tour in America, the 11-tournament circuit which had just been set up, in opposition to official tournaments, by Julie Heldman's mother Gladys Heldman. Mrs Heldman was a promoter and the publisher of *World Tennis* magazine, and she had taken on board the complaints of her daughter and players like Billie Jean King and Rosie Casals that in open tennis the women were being treated like second-class citizens — the Aborigines of sport. Matters had come to a head when the leading women boycotted the Pacific Southwest Open in California in late 1970. This tournament offered women less than 10 per cent of the prize money offered to the men.

In 1971 Mrs Heldman sought and received financial backing from the Philip Morris tobacco company for a women's tour independent of the men and the circuit known variously as 'Women's Liberation', 'Lob' and finally, 'Virginia Slims' was born.

The Heldman offer didn't exactly come as a surprise. I'd gone along to a 'Libbers' meeting during the Hurlingham tournament on the English tour and had been sounded out, but because he believed participation would pit me against the powerful tennis establishment, Mr Edwards declined the offer. Conflict with the establishment was inevitable however, because he now began to seek appearance fees, or guarantees against prize money for my participation. Seen in the context of the evolution of tennis worldwide, this was not an unreasonable request, and the amounts he asked were by no means excessive. But in Australia, where footballers were still all basically amateurs and Test cricketers were expected to tour England for four months for glory and some beer money, there was outrage.

The view of the establishment, the Lawn Tennis Association of Australia, was that tennis had made Evonne Goolagong and now she owed it. When a New Zealand promoter offered me an all-expenses-paid trip and a $2000 guarantee against the possibility of picking up $7000 in prize money to play in two tournaments in Christchurch and Auckland, Mr Edwards agreed and matters came to a head with the LTAA. We were informed that as the tournaments clashed with the start of the Australian season in Brisbane, if I failed to play at Milton I would risk being declared a player 'not in good standing' and being barred from tournaments around the world. It was a fairly hollow threat because any ban on me was unlikely to be endorsed by tennis authorities outside Australia, but the risk was that I would be barred from the Australian Open and thus disqualify myself from Grand Slam contention.

Mr Edwards responded huffily that naturally he would prefer that I played in front of Australian crowds, but that I had to earn a living. My special discounted Australian price was $1500 a tournament. The LTAA wrote back and said they were not in the business of providing guarantees and that I would have to do battle for the prize money, which in the Queensland grass court titles was $275 for the singles champion and $50 each to the doubles champions.

The battle lines were drawn. I think that anyone who analysed the situation from the point of view of me trying to earn a living, could not help but conclude that the Edwards price was fair and reasonable, but Mr Edwards' aggressive approach created a substantial — if not tidal — wave of resentment, even from his buddies in the tennis press. The Melbourne *Sun's* Greg Hobbs wrote, 'Now she wants a pay cheque before she appears on the courts where she cut her teeth. I think Evonne's manager is playing the game too hard.'

Alan Trengove, who six months earlier had said I would be ruined if I went to South Africa, now spelt out what he regarded as my obligation to play in 'minor Australian tournaments that are made possible by little people'. LTAA president Wayne Reid said, 'We are trying to protect the game in Australia that has made many Australians famous — including Evonne.'

In the end a crisis was averted — at least temporarily — when the LTAA agreed to a compromise in which I was permitted to skip the Queensland hard court titles and play one tournament in New Zealand, and the Brisbane

Telegraph agreed to put up the $1500 guarantee for the Queensland Open. But the broader issue of the hard-edged commercial exploitation of my talents remained a subject of great discussion around the tennis club bars and boardrooms. Fortunately, I remained oblivious to all of this, and it was Mr Edwards who took the flak. He was the one believed to be manipulating me for his own financial gain, particularly, the press thought, by making ridiculous demands like $50 for me to talk to a newspaper reporter. As I have said, Mr Edwards' motives were essentially pure. But with the benefit of hindsight, I must say that his methods were a little heavy-handed.

In October I flew to Britain alone for the indoor Dewar Cup tournaments. Given the fact that I had longed to travel somewhere — anywhere — alone since my first frustrations with Mr Edwards in 1970, I suppose I should have been excited. But I was miserable. Britain would be cold and damp, I hated playing indoors and would be hard-pressed to live up to expectations, and finally there was the matter of Roger Cawley. In Australia I had started dating other men and had put Roger out of my mind, or at least into a seldom-opened drawer in the back of it. Now the drawer would be opened again.

I won the opening round in Edinburgh, but thereafter played some rather ordinary tennis over the six weeks of my stay. During the play-offs at the Albert Hall I spotted Roger in the audience. He motioned for me to join him and we sat and chatted for a while. He was as charming as ever, but the conversation was stilted and difficult. I didn't know what to make of him, and the meeting did little to cure my blues. To add to my misery I became ill with the flu, despite the fact that I wore almost constantly the kangaroo fur coat and hat given to me by the proprietors of our corner shops at Roseville. When I returned to Sydney in late November I was ordered straight to bed. The doctor diagnosed an acute respiratory infection and bronchitis. 'If she travels, she risks pneumonia,' he told Mr Edwards. 'Keep a close eye on her because Aborigines often have problems in this area.' I'm not sure that the doctor knew too much about Aboriginal physiology, but the New Zealand trip was cancelled immediately.

A week later I was still not feeling 100 per cent, but was well enough to win both the events in Queensland while Billie Jean cleaned up in New Zealand. After her Christchurch win she declared herself the best female tennis player in the world. 'In my heart I feel I am a better player than Evonne,' she said generously. This was just a small volley in a battle between the Lib girls and me, which was to intensify in the New Year and dog me through my toughest year of tennis. I may have been Australia's sweetheart in the minds of the public, but inside the often bitchy world of women's tennis, I was just another duck in the shooting gallery.

If 1972 was going to be a year of frustration and disappointment, it didn't start out that way. On New Year's Day 'Gong' got a 'gong'. In the New Year's Honours List I was awarded an MBE (Member of the British Empire) for my services to tennis. This honour, bestowed by the Queen — and actually presented to me by her at Buckingham Palace later in the year — was quite a thrill, but my Australian of the Year award, presented a few weeks later on Australia Day (26 January), meant more. Since the inception of the awards in 1960, only one Aborigine — Lionel Rose — had won. I felt that the award vindicated my trip to South Africa and adequately answered the critics who said I had betrayed my people. The Australia Day Council evidently didn't think I had betrayed anyone.

The *Land* newspaper, which services Australia's rural sector, said the Australia Day Council had shown 'rare judgment in selecting one of her race for the honour … The year 1972 could be a notable year for the Aborigines

Jenifer and I share a moment with HRH Elizabeth II after receiving my MBE, 1972

— that is, if the Black Power extremists do not alienate growing public sympathy and understanding of their problems. Everywhere in Australia there is a new (and overdue) awareness that something has to be done for the Aborigines one way or the other.'

That 'one way or the other' sounded a little ominous, and, as it turned out, on the very day that article was published a group of young Aborigines set up a 'tent embassy' on the lawns of Parliament House in Canberra, flying the black, red and yellow Aboriginal flag. One of the embassy's earliest custodians was John Newfong, the man who believed I had lost the respect of my fellow Australians, black and white. I watched the news of the establishment of the tent embassy in my hotel room in Melbourne, after the reception at which I was made Australian of the Year. Strangely, considering the views of at least one of the Aboriginal 'ambassadors', I felt great pride and empathy with the protestors. On Australia Day 1972, I thought we were both, in our own ways, advancing the cause of Aboriginality.

My old friend from the Foundation for Aboriginal Affairs, Michael Anderson, apparently didn't share this view, however, when he came to Kooyong to watch me miss out on my own national title again when England's Virginia Wade beat me in the final of the Australian Open. We'd spoken by phone in Melbourne and I'd arranged tickets for him. Since I'd last seen him Michael had totally embraced Black Power and turned up in full costume, sporting a badge which said 'Black Power Is Black On'. Later he told the press that I should refuse to accept my MBE and should become a Black Power spokesperson. 'But she has been brought up to think like a white,' he added.

My loss to Virginia prompted an elderly British fan who had monitored my progress with religious zeal, to write to Mr Edwards, 'Unless she uses her natural talents more intelligently and also cures the weaknesses so apparent to her opponents, I foresee a bleak year. While it is true she has time to mature fully, the longer she delays curing her defects, the more difficult eventually it will be for her to get rid of them.'

When I beat Virginia a couple of weeks later in the NSW Open he wrote again: 'Miss Goolagong's win rather takes the point out of my letter … but I am not sorry I wrote. My comments are, I feel, still justified as the lapse in the second set proves.'

I'm glad I didn't see the letter then or I might have been tempted to respond bluntly. I beat Virginia 6–1 in the first set in 17 minutes. She pulled herself together in the second and I won in a tie breaker. What did he want? Blood? Despite the fears for my future, I won four State titles that summer and felt reasonably happy with my form as we headed off overseas again.

In March 1972 I made my American debut at the $50,000 Maureen Connolly Brinker International in Dallas, Texas, an indoor tournament held at the T-Bar-M Racquet Club. This was an independent tournament put together by a woman named Nancy Jeffett, quite separate from the Virginia Slims tour yet featuring all the name players from it. In the lead-up to my third European tour, it would provide some excellent match practise. But there was another reason for being there.

In England the previous year I had heard locker room stories about a girl from Fort Lauderdale, Florida, who at 15 had beaten Margaret Court in a minor tournament. At the 1971 US Open, Chrissie Evert at 16 had taken out some good players before being stopped by Billie Jean King. Then, early in 1972, she had turned the tables on Billie Jean in a Virginia Slims tournament at home in Fort Lauderdale. The scoreline was 6–1, 6–0. Chris Evert was suddenly the name on everyone's lips.

Chris was blonde and pretty, still in school and apparently possessed of a cool temperament, a double-handed backhand and the daunting ability to hit them hard and to the baseline all day long. If I was the New Big Thing in women's tennis, she was the Next Big Thing. The promoters couldn't wait to get us on a court together, and to this end I was offered an appearance fee for Dallas that Mr Edwards couldn't pass up. The moment Chris and I appeared at the club there was a clamour of photographers to get us to pose together. We chatted and she seemed nice enough, but that was as close as we got to each other at the Little Mo tournament (named for Maureen Connolly).

Whoever had worked out the draw for that tournament must have been thinking about something else at the time. Billie Jean, Chris and I were all in the same half, and Billie beat Chris in the quarters and then me in the semifinals. So the great match between the 'super kids' had to wait. But I did get to see Chris play. I watched her torrid match with Billie Jean, in which Chris took the first set in a tie breaker, then suffered the revenge of the Old Lady and her gallery. Putting everything she had into it, and some more, Billie Jean wore Chris down, applying considerable pressure to her double-handed backhand, an awkward shot that I had never seen a woman use before. In the deciding set, Billie Jean's supporters went beserk, sensing the victory of Libbers over lovers. (Well, Chris hadn't quite become a sex symbol yet, but according to the media she was on her way.)

After the match I was in the locker room when Chris came in. She sat down and bawled her eyes out. There were a few players in the room but no one was taking any notice. I sat down beside her and touched her on the

Meeting Chris Evert for the first time, 1972

shoulder. I said, 'Don't worry about it, you've got a long way to go yet and you'll have plenty more chances against her. And hey, it's only a game of tennis!' That brought out a grin beneath the tears, but when I left her I thought how determined she really was. I mean, as far as I was concerned there was never any shame in being beaten by Billie Jean King.

A couple of months after my inauspicious US debut a cover story on women's tennis appeared in *Newsweek* magazine. Chris Evert was the cover girl and much of the article concerned her anticipated dominance of the women's game over the rest of the decade, but the writers eventually got around to me:

> As for Evonne, the wonder girl of last summer may well find Wimbledon considerably harder this year. For one thing, she has been off form at several recent tournaments; and because of her aloofness from the touring women, Evonne has found herself pegged, in Frankie Durr's words, as 'the one we all want to beat'. Like any protracted psychodrama, the rise of Women's Lob has produced its own heroines and villains — and, largely because of her manager, the personally pleasant and engaging Evonne seems too often cast in the latter role in competition.
>
> When the [Virginia Slims] tour began, the two most notable absentees were top-ranked Margaret Smith Court and Miss Goolagong. Mrs Court, now sidelined after having a baby, demurred because she didn't want to give up the lucrative, extra financial guarantees she received as an independent; Miss Goolagong has stayed away under orders from her coach, Vic Edwards, who seems intent on charting her career along his own rigidly outlined course. Edwards drew the wrath of the other women when he brought Evonne to the richest tour event of this year in Dallas, then sought an appearance guarantee and refused to allow her to promote the tournament on television unless she was paid. He has continued to antagonize the press as well as the players by demanding money in return for interviews with his protégée.

I had no idea there was such antagonism amongst the Lob girls, although I did come to appreciate later that Billie Jean King would not have been pleased when, during her campaign for a bigger purse for women at Wimbledon, I remarked that I loved the tournament so much I'd play there for nothing! But if Mr Edwards had really set me against them, they kept their feelings to themselves in the locker room on those occasions when our paths crossed. Most of the time at tournaments I kept to myself anyway, or in the company of a small group of friends. I didn't realise I was being aloof. I was just being me!

The criticism of Mr Edwards' sledgehammer approach to management may well be justified, but *Newsweek* got it wrong about Dallas. He didn't demand an appearance fee. The promoters, desperate to get me and Chris on the court together, desperate to host my American debut, offered it. A pity they didn't spend some more time working on the draw.

From Dallas Mr Edwards and I flew to Johannesburg for the Federation Cup and the South African Open. This might have seemed like a convenient way to avoid anti-apartheid demonstrators, but the fact of the matter was there were none. Sporting bans on South Africa would remain an issue for the next two decades, but in 1972 there was deafening silence from the protest lobby. No one in Australia said 'boo' as Lesley Hunt, Helen Gourlay and I, defending the Cup for Australia, made it through to the semifinals where we were bundled out by Britain in the deciding doubles rubber.

Perhaps the only indication that sporting tours of South Africa were officially frowned upon came from the Lawn Tennis Association of Australia, which failed to provide the Australian team with a uniform. Mr Edwards was horrified by the thought of us parading in 'civvies'. At the eleventh hour he contacted a dress designer who agreed to make something in green and gold. The hot pants and tunic uniforms were not my favourites, but they were ready an hour before the opening parade.

Federation Cup in Johannesburg, 1972. Helen Gourlay, me and Lesley Hunt

In Johannesburg I renewed my friendship with Wanaro 'Bill' N'Godrella, a black Frenchman from New Caledonia who had played Davis Cup for France and toured Australia with the French team the previous southern summer. Bill, America's Bonnie Logan and I were the only blacks competing in the Open and, naturally, there was a strong bond between us. There was also a bit more between Bill and me. He was the funniest man I'd ever met, an immensely lovable prankster who brightened my evenings as we strolled around the city. But when night fell, Bill would say, 'We'd better get off the streets before they arrest us!' He was only half-joking.

The South Africans billed the 1972 Open as the first 'multi-racial' championships, but black and coloured South Africans were still restricted to certain stands at Ellis Park, and they still had to use separate toilets. Bill, Bonnie and I were the token touch of multi-racialism which enabled SALTU to later make its pitch for staying in the Davis Cup — 'But things are changing in South Africa, look at our multi-racial championships, look at the Homelands championships where blacks are playing whites for the first time' — but that fact did little to dampen my feelings when I overcame the loss of the first set to overpower Virginia Wade in the final and become the first non-white South African singles champion.

The wild cheering from the black sections of the crowd continued for long minutes while I beamed and tipped my racquet to them. Sure, I accepted my cheque and trophy from a representative of a white supremacist government, but more importantly, in my view, I demonstrated to all South African tennis lovers, black and white, that being born black was no impediment to becoming a champion.

Chapter 17

RARELY IN MY PROFESSIONAL LIFE have I felt great pressure to perform. For most of the 20 years in which I made my living from tennis, I did what came naturally. As the American player Julie Anthony told the writer Grace Lichtenstein back in the 1970s: 'I don't think that Evonne can ever attain the stature of greatness of a Billie Jean (King) or Margaret (Court) until she gets a little bit more serious at discipline. But maybe, like a wild animal, if you tried to discipline her it would destroy the essence that's so great about her.'

Most of the time I played the game with abandon. I knew no such thing as safe tennis nor did I understand the percentage game. Some thought it was naivety in the beginning and senility towards the end, but I only ever knew one way to play tennis, and for that I offer no apology.

So, the pressure cooker I found myself in at the beginning of the European tour in 1972 was all the more distressing to me. I had not yet come to terms with Mr Edwards' new insistence that I win every tournament I entered, when I began to realise that the world's leading women tennis players were mounting a campaign to unsettle me and knock me off my fairly unsteady champion's perch.

I am not suggesting there was any personal malice involved — although I now suspect that there were some ruffled feathers over my refusal to become involved in the politics of the women's tour. Rather, it was simply a case of my opponents playing hardball, which was becoming the norm in professional sport at that time. I was the number one player in the world, but at least two other players believed they could beat me more often than I beat them. A third, Chris Evert, had yet to play me but was no doubt itching to find out if the same might be true of her.

I was the defending champion in two of the big four — Wimbledon and the French Open. I had nowhere to go but down and the press and the players well knew it. The screws were on and neither Billie Jean nor Rosie Casals — both of whom I liked very much — ever let a chance go by. At every press conference they remarked upon my recent poor form or my legendary lapses in concentration, and these comments were duly reported. I never read any of this stuff or watched it on television, but it filtered down to me through other players or, more directly, through the ire of Mr Edwards.

He seemed determined, however, to keep me healthy and happy in those vital few weeks between our return from South Africa and our departure for England. So Trisha and I were allowed to go on a two-week Pacific island cruise on the SS *Orsova*. (Trisha had taken up an office job in Sydney and now restricted herself to club and state level tennis, but we still played doubles together on occasion — and picked up a few titles.)

We imagined ourselves poolside by day and discoing by night, but when Mr Edwards came with us to make the booking he insisted that we travel first class where we would be away from any 'annoying riffraff'. Dancing the night away with some riffraff was exactly what Trisha and I had in mind, so we phoned the travel agent later and received an assurance that as first class passengers we would have the run of the ship, and would be free to mix with the younger people.

As it turned out we were not. We were mostly confined to the captain's table, the silver service and the company of much older people. It was the longest fortnight of my life and when we disembarked at Circular Quay I was extremely frustrated and ready to belt the sides off a few tennis balls.

It had been decided that Jenifer Edwards would take time off from her dressmaking business to accompany her father and me on the European tour. In many ways this was an ideal situation for both Mr Edwards and me. He could spend more time talking tennis in the bar with his mates, and I had a travelling companion who didn't give a damn about tennis and was ever-ready to whisk me away from the game and the players. On the long flight to London we planned our sightseeing tours and our nights out in London and Paris.

Having Jenifer along for the ride kept my mind off the important tournaments ahead, but somewhere in my subconscious I must have been worrying over my title defences, for during the second tournament of the tour at Guildford I came down with an attack of shingles. Initially this stress-related disease of the nerve endings simply created a mild discomfort when my tennis dress brushed against the blisters which are the trademark of the illness. But soon I was suffering from muscular soreness and even slight spasms. I still managed to win but I was feeling rather unwell when we flew to Paris the next week. In fact I had barely slept a wink in 72 hours, keeping Jenifer up all night with my whimpering. I had received a course of treatment from a doctor, but Mr Edwards was unusually casual about the whole thing, perhaps not understanding how painful the disease could be.

It was somewhat ironic therefore, that my old friend Mr Lance Tingay of the *Daily Telegraph* should conclude that the bedraggled wreck who emerged from the aircraft in France was 'Miss Goolagong At Peak For Paris'. Of course he knew nothing of my health and had only recent form to go on — I had won at Bournemouth and Guildford with relative ease. He wrote: '... Evonne Goolagong could hardly have had a better preparation for what is for her a novel task, the defence of a major title. A victor at Bournemouth nine days ago and ... at Guildford on Saturday, the Wimbledon champion is right in form. No one doubts Miss Goolagong's obvious genius, or her championship quality, but the test of a great champion is the ability to win from in front.'

Without playing at my peak, I cruised through the preliminaries at Stade Roland Garros without dropping a set to meet Billie Jean in the final. In the press, the concensus of opinion was that my semifinal win against local hero Frankie Durr was 'jaded'.

Perhaps I was a little jaded in the final too, but I offer no excuses for my straight sets defeat in just over an hour. After playing so well on clay in 1971, I fancied my chances against Billie Jean at Roland Garros. The French Open was the only major title which had eluded her, and I thought she might try a bit too hard to win on her serve, leaving me plenty of time and space to work my return. But there was no room for a game plan. Billie Jean was superb!

Lance Tingay reported: 'Miss Goolagong came for the first time and conquered a year ago. Her tenure as a defending champion lasted no longer than the shrewd and able onslaught Mrs King directed against her yesterday. Will it be the same at Wimbledon?'

Indeed. Or would Chris Evert despatch me before Billie Jean had a chance? Or would I go 'walkabout' again or maybe not even show up at the All-England Club? Speculation ran rampant and, despite the fact that I'd won the first two and finished runner-up in the third tournament of the tour, my Wimbledon price blew out with the London bookmakers and I, like many other one-time champions before me — Billie Jean among them — seemed certain to begin my world championship defence as the underdog.

During June Billie Jean and Rosie Casals stomped all over England, noisily asserting themselves as Womens' Libbers and Virginia Slimmers. At Bristol Rosie was ordered off the court when she turned up to play in a Slims T-shirt. She then got into further hot water when she gave a linesman the finger.

Still troubled by shingles, I played poorly in Bristol, but rallied the following week in Nottingham and played Virginia Wade in the final of the John Player tournament. She finally got the better of me in a long three-setter. Exhausted,

Above: Teddy Tinling and his teenage girls, 1972 *Left:* Scratching my head over what to do about Virginia Wade, Nottingham, 1972

I slumped into a courtside chair and sucked at my orange. I suddenly became aware of Mr Edwards, standing over me shaking his head. 'Well,' he said slowly, the quaver of great anger in his voice, 'you might as well have stuck a knife in my back, the way you played just now.'

I held myself together until I got out of his sight, but only just. And there I was, howling my eyes out in the locker room, just like Chris Evert. But there was a difference. Losing a tennis match couldn't make me cry, but Mr Edwards could.

Apparently this sort of 'encouragement' was okay in Mr Edwards' book, but the pressure tactics of the girls in the locker room were not. On the eve of my Wimbledon defence he gave a couple of reporter mates a 'scoop' about the 'nerve war' being waged against me. I'm not sure what end he thought this would achieve, but he was still smarting over the cutting remarks about him published in *Newsweek*, and held the Women's Libbers directly responsible. He told the journalists that I was being given the 'cold shoulder' in the dressing room. 'They'll stop talking when Evonne enters the room, or begin to whisper to one another, excluding her ... No doubt the other girls who desperately want to beat her are trying to worry her into not being able to concentrate on her play in the championships.'

This was a dreadful exaggeration, of course, but there was no denying that the Libbers had me 'under the blowtorch' and it was having the desired effect. A few days before Wimbledon began I told an interviewer, 'Billie Jean is a better player than me. I haven't reached my peak yet.' Oh boy!

At Wimbledon in 1971 Alf Chave claimed to have done some research and come up with the English translation of Goolagong — 'tall trees by still water'. It was a lovely, but totally inaccurate, interpretation. Nevertheless it was one that would be with me throughout my career, beginning with the signature 'landscaped' tennis dress that designer Teddy Tinling made with for my 1972 defence. As much as I loved Teddy, this creation, with its border of tree trunks and billabongs, was not one of my favourites. But the press seized on the Aboriginal connection again until something better came along in the form of a controversy of their own making.

When I arrived at the All-England Club in one of the 50 chauffeur-driven Leylands for the commencement of hostilities, the first noise I heard was a wolf whistle. Then some one called, 'Morning, Cuddly.' I wasn't used to such familiarity, especially at Wimbledon, and I was puzzled by it. All was revealed in the locker room. The London *Sun*, recently purchased by Australian Rupert Murdoch, was running a series of illustrations called 'The Naked Truth of Sport' by a cartoonist named Paul Trevillion. On this Wimbledon morning Trevillion had revealed what he imagined to be the naked truth about Evonne Goolagong.

Today I would probably laugh it off. Back then I was horrified and mortally embarrassed. Just in case his drawing of me from side-on and behind, clad in only tennis shoes was not offensive enough, Mr Trevillion had offered his thoughts on how sports stars take on the physical characteristics of the tools of their trade. 'Goolagong is round, soft, cuddly, bouncy — she's like a fluffy new tennis ball. Her cheeks are round like a tennis ball. Her whole body is rounded. She is a round tennis ball — a playful object.'

Oh, please! At least he didn't say I looked like my dog!

Mr Edwards was furious, and I have to confess that my anger grew with each new smart remark. I'm sure Mr Trevillion was guilty of no more than a lapse of taste — and this was later the finding of the Press Council — but it was hardly the thing for the hallowed home of lawn tennis. And that year I really didn't need to give the Libbers any more ammunition to fire at me.

The men's competition at Wimbledon that year was notable for the absence of 1971 champion John Newcombe and other top players such as Rod Laver and Ken Rosewall, who were declared ineligible as contract professionals after signing with Texas millionaire Lamar Hunt's World Championship Tennis. So the focus shifted to what was universally seen as a three-way battle for the women's crown. If you believed the bookies, I would get scuttled somewhere along the line and the final would be fought out between Big Billie and Little Chrissie. I don't know where the pundits would have placed Margaret Court, but she was back in Perth with her first-born baby Danny.

I struggled through the early rounds, dropping a set to the Russian Olga Morozova and surviving two set points to Frankie Durr. Mr Edwards noted in the bar (and was reported around the world): 'I can't understand it. Evonne doesn't seem to be concerned about her form, or want to do anything about it. Right now she doesn't seem to be bothered if she loses her title or not.'

The crown was beginning to wobble, the experts said. My semifinal would tell all. It was the long-awaited clash between Chris Evert and me. I couldn't see it was the huge deal that everyone seemed to think it was, although in the months since I'd first seen her play in Dallas, Chris had ripped through Billie Jean a couple of times and firmly established herself as the darling of the American press, a pony-tailed Miss America who managed to appear both wholesome and sexy at the same time — but the latter image was her preference. In Britain however, the tabloids had dubbed her the Ice Maiden for her robot-like court presence.

Over the next 10 years I was to learn a lot about Chris, and come to like and respect her. On the court our matches flowed easily, and we could have done without an umpire, such was the trust we had in each other's calls. No tantrums, no questions, we just played the game. I liked her family very much too, and Mrs Evert became very close to Mrs Edwards over the years. But for all that, off the court Chris and I were totally different personalities. Professional sportsmen and women have to make a choice very early in their careers as to whether they want to live their lives in a goldfish bowl, or to restrict their fame to the duration of their performances. I chose the latter path; Chris, even at 17, had decided to share her life with the readers of *People* magazine.

Although she lacked the electricity of Billie Jean, and didn't have my range of strokes, there was no denying the quality of Chris Evert's tennis. She had spent all her young life learning precision tennis, whacking balls over a net into a handkerchief on the baseline at her father's tennis school. She was good, she was more determined than anyone I had ever seen in my life, and she was unbelievably popular in America — so much so that the Forest Hills crowd had reduced Lesley Hunt to tears when she played Chris in the 1971 US Open. At that tournament the pro-Chris crowd even got upset when Billie Jean despatched her in the semifinals. Typically, Billie Jean responded, 'I don't mind. This is a 16-year-old kid beating the best people in the world. It's beautiful!'

It wasn't so beautiful to me at 0–3 in the second set, having lost the first 6–4. The Centre Court crowd was hushed. I don't think they felt the same way the Americans did about Chris's mechanical baseline game, but it was proving effective. I had to find an answer for it or be out of the tournament, and for the first time ever I resorted to following advice. Not that I was prone to ignore advice — it was just never given. Mr Edwards' usual instruction was, 'Play your natural game.' Before this match, however, he had suggested I draw Chris off the baseline by playing diagonally short to her double-handed backhand. This awkward shot tended to be rushed and off target when she had to move into it, so I started slicing my backhand to hers whenever I could. The tactic worked. I took the second set and, full of confidence now, chipped away at her until I had the decider.

At Wimbledon 1972, (left) against Frankie Durr, and (right) first match against Chris Evert

Into the final against Billie Jean, when we'd all find out if the psyche-out campaign had worked. I guess it had — 6–3, 6–3 in 50 minutes and Billie Jean had her fourth Wimbledon crown. My brief reign was over.

Billie Jean held her head in her hands and wandered around at the net in a daze, tears streaming down her face. It suddenly struck me as very funny. It looked like I'd won and she'd lost. I put my arm around her and said: 'Don't worry, Old Lady, it'll be all right.' Billie Jean cracked a grin and I felt better about it.

In many ways defeat was a great relief. The pressure valve was off, the steam was out. We could get on with life again, and I could resume my friendship with Billie Jean free of the hype. Just as Chris Evert and I were very different people, so Billie and I were like chalk and cheese, but she was an extraordinary tennis player and still is a genuinely nice person. Forget the mind games and the hype, whenever I really needed a friend on the tennis tour, Billie Jean was there with advice or a caring word. No doubt some people in tennis will remember her as a ranting, raving drama queen of the game; to me she will always be her own woman, someone who stood up for herself and the things she believed in.

At the post-match press conference I was asked if I was devastated by the loss of my title. (I think the reporters were hoping I'd cry.) I said, 'I don't worry too much about losing, but I am disappointed for all those people who get upset when I'm beaten. It's still just a game to me. I can forget defeat very easily ... What did upset me was the people clapping when Billie Jean hit a bad shot. I don't think that's fair.'

Although I had spent most of the English season in the company of Jenifer Edwards — hanging out, driving around in a rented car, being sisters — I had also seen Roger Cawley. We had gone out to dinner in a group on a couple of occasions and he had come to watch me play — staying well out of Mr Edwards' way. Once bitten, twice shy was my approach to Mr Cawley, but he seemed to have a new seriousness of purpose. I don't mean that he had become boring — far from it — but he seemed intent on making rapid progress in the business world. He was no longer the devil-may-care romantic fiction writer based in the back bar of a London pub. Perhaps he was even developing into the kind of young man of whom Mr Edwards would approve!

I gradually came to realise that the reason Roger had 'dropped' me was that he had had an attack of cold feet. The intensity of feeling during that summer of 1970, and in our subsequent letters, had frightened him, while at the same time he had felt alienated because of the physical distance between England and Australia. Coupled with my increasing media profile and Mr

Edwards' obsessive possessiveness, he shied away. When I'd arrived in England he'd felt awkward about approaching me. And as my fame and success grew proportionately that summer, so too did his reluctance to bother me. Thus he stayed silently away, not contacting me as he might have in 1970. My new found celebrity was scaring him off.

We were both young and sometimes you get it wrong. Boy, he certainly got it wrong that summer! We kept each other at a safe emotional distance. However, we talked a lot and began enjoying spending time together again.

When I left England at the end of July to start the American tour — having celebrated my twenty-first birthday at Hoylake with the Rothmans tournament crowd — I sent him a little friendship card with a list of contact addresses in America. The card said: 'We're friends to the end ... and there'll never be an end!'

Despite an up-and-down season in America — my first full tour there — I won a good deal of prize money and only slipped one place in the *Daily Telegraph* rankings. Mr Edwards wasn't too impressed when a virtual unknown

One of my 21st birthday parties. In Hoylake with Mr Edwards, Jenifer and John King of Rothmans

— American Pam Teeguarden, who later became a good friend — bumped me out of my debut US Open in the first round — 'you played like a bloody C grade!' — and Chris Evert showed she could beat me in our singles rubber in the Bonne Bell Cup at Cleveland, but she was ranked three behind me and Billie Jean. For the moment, at least, I was hot property despite the loss of my Wimbledon crown.

All of which must have prompted Mr Edwards to look for a new international agent to replace Bagenal Harvey. Professional tennis was changing fast, he wasn't getting any younger and I don't think he ever really understood the financial machinations of the business of the sport once it went beyond the plain brown envelopes stuffed with beer money. That was why we joined up with Mark McCormack's International Management Inc. that year. The Cleveland-based McCormack had started out in the 1960s managing golfing legend Arnold Palmer's business affairs, and had proved so good at making deals that he soon signed other top sporting figures like racing driver Jackie Stewart, soccer player Pélé, skier Jean Claude Killy, and tennis players Rod Laver, John Newcombe and Ion Tiriac. I was the first female tennis player to sign up, and McCormack's company — later IMG — managed my affairs for almost 20 years.

Under the terms of the agreement, Mr Edwards would remain my coach/manager, look after my tournament schedule and run my tennis career as he always had done. IMI, or more particularly, McCormack's right-hand man, H. Kent Stanner (known to all as 'Bud'), would handle all press, television, advertising and sponsorship deals. I was delighted with my Ginori clothing deal and I liked my Dunlop racquets, but beyond that I wasn't really interested in much of this stuff. However, I liked the casually authoritative style of Mark McCormack, and although initially he scared the hell out of this country girl with his raucous American business style, I later fell in love with 'Uncle' Bud Stanner, a man who would become friend, confidant and business guru to me.

Although my twenty-first birthday celebrations had begun in England, my actual birthday fell during the Bonne Belle Cup in Cleveland, and we celebrated there and yet again, later, in September, in New York. But the party I'd really been waiting for came two months later in September when the folks in Barellan put on an evening for me in the church hall. Just about everyone in the district came along for a 'ladies' plate' supper of sandwiches and chicken legs and a disco dance. All the relations from Condobolin and Hillston were there to watch Kenny Goolagong present me with the key to the door of life. With a tear in his eye Dad handed me the key and gave me a self-conscious hug, before retiring to the back of the hall for a surreptitious beer with John Emerson, while Mr Kurtzman — looking very old and frail — made an emotional and quite lovely speech.

That I had tried and failed in 1972 meant nothing to these people. Mr Kurtzman told me he believed me to be the best in the world and that he needed no further proof. Mum didn't care if I never played another tournament, let alone won one. I was home again, however briefly, and that was all that mattered.

Soon after my return to Australia a vital Federal election campaign began. After more than 20 years of conservative domination of Australian politics, a tall, charismatic man named Gough Whitlam was leading the Australian Labor Party out of the wilderness on a platform of social justice. In his policy speech he said, 'We will legislate to give Aborigines land rights — not just because their case is beyond argument, but because all of us as Australians are diminished while the Aborigines are denied their rightful place in the nation.'

Whitlam and Labor were swept into power on 2 December 1972. Some Australians may have been concerned with the dramatic agenda of change, but for my people there was a real glimmer of hope that the unfulfilled promises of 1967 would at last be kept.

Chapter 18

$\mathcal{T}$WO EXCITING THINGS HAPPENED that Australian summer, apart from the spectacle of Gough Whitlam turning Australian society upside down. The first was that Trisha Edwards got married to New Zealander Errol Hill in a beautiful ceremony at St Mary's Cathedral in Sydney. I was one of her attendants.

The second thing was that Margaret Court came back from her maternity leave with a vengeance, beating me in the final of the Western Australian Open in Perth, then again in an epic three-set final of the NSW Open at White City. Margaret had been on a roll since she'd made her comeback at the beginning of the summer, silencing all the critics who'd said you couldn't be a mother and a champion. In less than four months she'd made around $40,000 in prize money — more than my total for 1972 — and had increased her win ratio over me to 10 matches to two.

It seemed I was going to have more than just Billie Jean and Chris to worry about on the European tour in 1973. Not that 'worry' was the appropriate expression. Unlike Mr Edwards and everyone around me, I still didn't worry about losing tennis matches. 'It's only a game' continued to be my motto. But it was comforting to know that win or lose, for the top players in women's tennis the pay cheques were getting bigger by the minute.

For that we had Billie Jean King to thank in large part. People like Gladys Heldman kept the wheels moving, but it was Billie Jean's raucous presence on centre courts that put our game on the map. She rarely opened her mouth without complaining about the meagre prize money on offer for women, and by 1973 important people were actually listening.

As the rebel Virginia Slims women's tour rolled into its third season, prize money was nearing $US 500,000, but the flow-on effect from that tour was enormous. The United States Lawn Tennis Association (USLTA) had launched its own seven-tournament women's tour worth more than $200,000, and even the All-England Club had come to the party, announcing a Wimbledon prize money increase of 25 per cent to bring the women closer to parity with the men. In 1973 the women's singles champion would receive 3000 pounds,

Trisha's wedding to Errol Hill, 1973. The entire Edwards clan, 'Killarney Gran' seated

compared with 5000 pounds for the men's champion. The radicals in women's tennis would be satisfied with nothing less than equal pay, but the more moderate elements felt that 75 per cent of the men's purse would be acceptable. But at Wimbledon, traditionally a generation behind the times, 60 per cent of the men's kitty looked to be a pretty good offer.

Overall, in its sixth year open tennis looked to be in pretty good shape, with some $US 4 million up for grabs in open tournaments all over the world. The sport was not quite big business yet, but it was getting there, and key players were on their way to millions. Rod Laver, supposedly the first of the tennis millionaires, had already got there; Billie Jean was not far behind. And me? I didn't have a clue, but I didn't feel guilty about expenses any more.

In 1970, when I toured Queensland, hoping to bring myself to the attention of the Federation Cup selectors, I brought home a two-week expenses bill of $77 and stewed over it for a month before I could show it to Mr Edwards.

An indication of how we were going financially, however, is the fact that I had been able to buy my parents' house for them in 1971, and during the summer of 1973 Mr Edwards had apparently bought land on the New South

Wales central coast in our joint names. I am not sure if this was meant to be an investment or my retirement home. I approved the purchase but it was only later that I found out I was co-owner of the property with Mr Edwards, despite the fact that he had made no financial contribution.

Since Trisha had quit the tour after 1970, I had played with any number of doubles partners — Margaret Court in 1971, Helen Gourlay, Gail Chanfreau, even my arch rival Virginia Wade. In 1973, however, Janet Young came to America as my regular doubles partner on the USLTA tour.

Janet, from Melbourne, was the same age as me and had been around the game a long time. But her career path had been somewhat different to mine. She had put her tennis on hold while she completed an economics degree at Melbourne University, and was now as interested in the effect of the Watergate scandal on Wall Street stocks as she was in who was top seed for the next tournament. I found that refreshing and, although I didn't share her interest in American politics, we became great travelling buddies.

I beat Virginia Wade in the final of the US Indoors Championship, but apart from that, the story of that American spring tour was all about the player the press called 'Miss American Pie'. Chris Evert beat me week after week. It would have been frustrating had it not been so funny.

Mr Edwards couldn't see the humour in it but Janet and I could. She'd whip me in Sarasota one Sunday and in Miami the next. In between times we'd go through the motions of working our way through the draw, but there was rarely any doubt about who was going to play the final. The same thing was happening between Billie Jean and Margaret on the Slims tour. Would the public get sick of seeing the same match played over and over again? We hoped not. Although I won only one tournament on the seven-week tour I made more than $20,000 in prize money before I even got to Europe. In cricket, the parallel would be scoring 100 before lunch.

After the spring tour Mr Edwards, Janet and I flew to Germany to join up with Pat Coleman for the Federation Cup in Bad Homburg. Janet and I had a brilliant week in the doubles, not dropping a set as we marched towards the final against titleholders South Africa. But the real surprise package was Patti Coleman, a tiny (under 5 feet or 152.5 centimetres tall) but tough player with a two-fisted backhand, from Parkes in western New South Wales. She was a baseline basher a couple of years younger than me, and one of the few players who had ever beaten me in the junior ranks. In Bad Homburg she suddenly came of age. My South African friend Brenda Kirk gave her a tough time in her singles rubber in the finals, but Patti came through without dropping a set, and Australia retook the Federation Cup.

Doubles partners Goolagong and Young

Federation Cup winners 1973. Patti Coleman, Janet Young, me and Mr Edwards

The European season was notable for the emergence of a hot new Australian prospect in Dianne Fromholtz, and for our trip to Rome for my first Italian Open. If I loved Paris, I adored Rome, and so did Mrs Edwards, who had flown to London to join me on the tour. We spent hours and hours wandering the streets, sightseeing and shopping.

The tennis wasn't bad either. In the awful heat of the Foro Italico, I got back into the big league, probably just in the nick of time. I hadn't beaten Chris Evert since Wimbledon 1972, and people were starting to say she had my number. I felt I was the better player, but I was a human and Chris a machine. To borrow a phrase, when I was good I was very good, and when I was bad I was horrid. Chris rarely matched my best, but she never played as badly as I was capable of doing. Except in Rome.

The final of the Italian Open began predictably enough, with Chris breaking my serve and leading 4–2, before I put on my thinking cap and made her stretch on her backhand. But even when I pinned her back to a tie breaker for the first set she should have won it. At five points to three she seemed

239

The face of a champion. Federation Cup, Bad Homburg, 1973

to lose concentration completely, allowing me to win the set with four straight points. The second set was over in 13 minutes without Chris taking a game. I hoped she wouldn't cry as she tried to force a little smile at the net. I felt terrible about it, but not for long.

How could you feel terrible about anything for long at Il Foro Italico which, despite the heat and the slow clay of Centre Court, was the most magnificent place to play tennis? The Centre Court is reached from the dressing room via a long tunnel and the effect when you emerge is right out of a gladiator scene from one of my favourite movies *Spartacus*. Surrounded by the foothills of Monte Mario, with tall pines fringing the courts and statues staring down on the play, Il Foro is one thing that Mussolini left behind and could be proud of. (Unfortunately today the success of the Italian Open has meant that the statues are hidden under scaffolding supporting additional Centre Court seats, and sadly, are covered with graffiti.)

In Rome a couple of young Czech girls made it through to the doubles final against Virginia Wade and Olga Morozova, the pair who made a mockery of the Cold War. Since I was going to Prague to play in the Czechoslovak championships later in the year, I watched a bit of the match to see the standard of the locals. Renata Tomanova was a useful player who had been around a season or two, but her 16-year-old partner was brand new — a skinny, gangling girl who seemed to derive tremendous power in her shots from who knew where? She never once looked at the crowd but kept her head bowed as she engaged in constant lecturing of herself in her native tongue. A strange one all right, but she had the strokes. I made a mental note of the name: Martina Navratilova.

And so, back to London and Wimbledon. I felt good about my tennis in 1973. I was winning enough to keep Mr Edwards off my back and my game was consistent and thoughtful most of the time. The 'walkabouts' still happened, but less frequently. Moreover, my life had settled into a travelling routine. Nine months of the year I was a touring tennis pro, living out of a suitcase and eating in restaurants, but the rewards were good. The only thing I missed was the normal stuff a 21-year-old does, like hanging out with your girlfriends, going crazy on shopping expeditions, planning your life with a man.

Roger phoned soon after the Edwards and I had set up home in a Chelsea flat and asked me out. Mr Edwards made no attempt to dissuade me. I was an adult now. He said 'I don't think it's a good idea' only with his eyes.

Roger and I sat in a restaurant for hours after the last course had disappeared, sipping coffee and re-establishing the rules of the relationship. I felt we had a special bond, that I could love him and he could love me, but there was so much about him I didn't know or didn't understand.

'There's no hurry,' he said, looking into my eyes with that dreamy expression he gets, 'I'll be here for you when you're ready.'

Despite the good year I was having, Wimbledon 1973 was not exactly memorable. Billie Jean was on fire on her way to her fifth title, and she bundled me out in the semifinals. The caravan moved on again, this time to Dusseldorf for the German Open.

I had spoken to Roger again just before leaving England, and my heart was totally confused. I sat down to write him the first letter since my friendship card almost a year earlier. I wrote, '... At the moment you have me completely confused. I seem to be thinking about you a lot but it's not the same strong feeling as before ...' The letter was interrupted while I played the first round of the Open against Heidi Orth. I resumed a couple of hours later. '... It took three sets! I fell asleep in the second ... I couldn't think of that tune "Ain't No Sunshine When You're Gone".'

I changed my mind about it not being the 'same strong feeling' almost immediately and started to write another letter the next day, but I was interrupted by Mr Edwards, who'd received a telegram from Barellan. He sat next to me on the bed and said, 'Sweet, I've got some bad news ...'

Ill-health had forced Bill Kurtzman to resign as president of the War Memorial Tennis Club in February. He stayed on the committee and served on the grounds sub-committee, but as the Riverina winter descended on Barellan in 1973, the frail old man grew weaker and weaker. This lovely old farmer had made me his life's mission. The last clippings Mr Kurtzman had pasted into his scrapbook documented our triumph in the Federation Cup at Bad Homburg in May. I know that would have brought him joy. After that his unsteady old hand cut out occasional articles, which he put in the back of the book for placement and pasting later. The last article clipped told of the 'Aussie Day of Glory' when Margaret Court, Kerry Melville and I made it into the final eight at Wimbledon. A week later Bill Kurtzman was dead at 78. I wished he'd been able to go out backing a winner.

I was deeply upset and very angry — probably at myself for not having been a more dutiful daughter of the tennis club. I scrawled a disjointed letter to Roger. 'You know I wouldn't be here only for the help he has given me. Maybe I should have written more to him. Oh Roger, why do these things have to happen? I feel bloody rotten.'

Bob Howe, the London representative for Dunlop, accompanied me to Bratislava for the Czechoslovakian championships, my first foray behind the Iron Curtain. I celebrated my twenty-second birthday by beating Renata Tomanova in the singles and teaming with Bob to win the mixed doubles. We moved on to Prague to play an exhibition. The beauty of the city surprised me. I suppose, like most people in the West, I had been conditioned to believe that Communists lived in featureless grey apartment blocks and marched like automatons each day to featureless grey factories. Maybe they did, but along the way they would have passed some magnificent old buildings.

We holidayed briefly in Amsterdam before heading back to America for the rigorous fall season centred around the US Open at Forest Hills. I got off to a good start, beating Chris Evert on clay in Cincinatti. I wrote to Roger, 'I quite surprised myself because I played her at my own game for half the match, and her game for the other half.' The more we understood about each other's tennis, the better the contest between Chris and me became, drawing huge crowds to the tournaments. Our finals had become a much bigger drawcard than the battles between Margaret Court and Billie Jean in the Slims tour, and promoters set up their tournament draws and hoped and prayed that no one would get in the way of a Chris versus Evonne final. When some-

With Renata Tomanova after winning the Czech title in Bratislava

one did — like a girl named Marita Redondo, who beat me in the first round of a tournament in snowbound Akron, Ohio — the promoters were apt to get hostile. Not with the winner but with me. I wasn't allowed to have an off day, not when my appearance in the final meant bums on seats. I found that attitude rather disheartening, because tennis needs its Marita Redondos, the mavericks from left field who get up and beat the champions, just as an 11-year-old Aboriginal girl from Barellan had once startled Australia's number two player, Jan Lehane.

My form stayed with me and I won in Toronto, where I teamed up for the first time with the American girl Peggy Michel, and again in Charlotte, North Carolina, where Peggy and I won the doubles against Helga Masthoff and the Navratilova girl, who had put on lots of weight. 'McDonalds,' said Peggy, matter-of-factly. 'They come out of Siberia and go nuts on junk food. Who can blame them?'

From Charlotte, Mr Edwards and I flew to the industrial city of Pittsburgh, Pennsylvania, not to play tennis but to cut one of the biggest deals in the history of women's tennis. Bud Stanner flew in from Cleveland to join us in our final negotiations with Frank Fuhrer and his associates, the owners of the Pittsburgh Triangles, one of 16 city franchises in the new World Team Tennis league.

Larry King, Billie Jean's husband, was one of the people behind the league, and Billie Jean was to be the captain-coach of the Philadelphia Freedoms. The Triangles had already signed Ken Rosewall as their captain-coach, and wanted me as their star woman. Mr Fuhrer — I never, ever got used to that name, I'm afraid — had been pursuing us since Toronto, where he'd interrupted our dinner one evening to wave his cheque book. I didn't like him much and the whole concept of World Team Tennis — indoor tournaments, razzamatazz and another three months a year in America — didn't appeal either. But Mr Fuhrer was not easily deterred. He kept chasing us around the country waving his cheque book and adding noughts to the offer.

I was ecstatic when it was finally agreed that I would sign on — for almost a million dollars over five years, with a get-out clause for me after three years — not because I was looking forward to team tennis, but because Mr Fuhrer would leave us alone at last. The money was just a big number. It didn't mean much, except that I could afford to buy Linda Goolagong a much-needed new refrigerator. I wrote to Roger, 'The best part about going home is giving out all the presents. Guess what? I'm going to buy my mother a new refrigerator as a surprise ... I can't wait, every time I think about it ...'

I had six days in Australia before flying to Japan for a new tournament in Osaka. I couldn't afford to waste a moment. Flying to Narrandera I started to get very nervous. I'd been away so long, and it had been such a dreadful winter for Mum. She'd been terribly upset by Mr Kurtzman's death, my older sister Barbara had suffered a miscarriage and another sister had suffered personal traumas which would take years to get over. On top of all that, relations between Mum and Dad had become strained and he'd shot through to Hillston chasing work. Kenny was always shooting through for one reason or another, but this time Mum really needed his support and love, and he wasn't there for her. The stress was taking its toll on her health, and her blood pressure was dangerously high.

Barbara met me at the airport and we spent the night at her place catching up. In the morning we drove to the biggest store in town and I paid cash for the biggest and best refrigerator we could find. Then we raced the delivery man to Barellan, beating him by bare minutes. I later wrote to Roger, 'It was the greatest satisfaction I've ever had ... because Mum was just so excited and pleased she just cried ... She didn't know what to do with herself, so she just dashed to her room and didn't come out until the [delivery] men had left … Actually, she wasn't the only one crying. I feel so happy when I think of her reaction that day.'

In October I travelled to Japan for a tournament, but when I returned to Australia I took a much-needed holiday from tennis. I went to Coolum on Queensland's Sunshine Coast, where Jenifer Edwards was living in a double-decker bus with her boyfriend.

I wrote to Roger: 'Did I tell you that Jenifer had a motor bike? Well, the day I arrived Jenifer was in hospital through falling off her bike … She's all right now but very sore with bruises and cuts. If Mr Edwards knew he would just die. I had another surprise too. She's become engaged and she will have to break the news when she goes home for Christmas. Boy! It's really going to be hard for her.'

Then I got to the heart of the matter. 'I haven't heard from you for a while but I do hope you are well and happy. In fact I'm really looking forward to hearing from you again. In fact you bloody well had better write soon! Roger, I know you have told me you love me, but please if at any time you meet up with someone else who becomes kind of special to you, please tell me straight away. It would make things so much easier for both of us. Naturally the same goes for me, too.'

I left Jenifer to her bruises, her boyfriend, her double-decker bus and her idyllic 'beach bum' lifestyle (Mr Edwards wrote at the time that 'Jenifer is roaming as though she were the Aboriginal of the family') and flew back to Sydney to pack my bags for South Africa, where I was to defend my South African title. Fortunately for Roger, there was a letter waiting for me.

Chris Evert beat me in the final in Johannesburg to take away my title, and her boyfriend Jimmy Connors took the men's title after beating Arthur Ashe. Two nil for the white folks. But winning or losing wasn't the issue in Johannesburg that year, because equality was the winner. Arthur had finally been granted a visa on his own terms, and blacks were free to sit anywhere they liked in Ellis Park. How wonderful it was, too, that two of the four blacks in the tournament should make the finals. In the men's final there was pandemonium in the stands every time Arthur won a point, and it was a little disappointing that he wasn't able to go on with it and become the first black men's singles champion of South Africa.

Back in Australia I was immediately thrown into preparation for Australia's defence of the Bonne Bell Cup, an Australia versus USA trophy inaugurated in Cleveland, the home of Bonne Bell Cosmetics, the previous year. After his successes in Cleveland and Bad Homburg, Mr Edwards was named team manager, and now Kerry Melville, Janet Young, Kerry Harris and I had to keep the Bell Cup down under without the help of Margaret Court, who was having another baby. The best-of-nine series started badly at White City when Janet Newberry defeated Kerry Harris and I went 'walkabout' in the third set and succumbed to Julie Heldman. We clawed our way back and on the final day we launched a blitz.

Mr Edwards had a lot of emotional stock invested in this defence at home. I think he felt that his team management overseas had largely gone unrecognised, and in Sydney he was determined we should do well. But the pressure took its toll on him after our poor start. He chain-smoked as he watched our matches at courtside, and only decorum won over his desire to take reviving swigs from the whisky flask he sometimes carried. Janet and I took out the doubles and then Kerry Melville clinched the series for us by beating Julie Heldman. My clash with Chris Evert — the match everyone had been waiting for — turned out to be superfluous.

Nevertheless it was vital as far as Vic Edwards was concerned. It was the 'clean-up', Evonne versus Chris in front of all his mates. I felt I had the edge on Chris on grass and I was determined to play well. I breezed through the first set 6–2, but faltered in the second. At 1–3 and a point away from 1–4, Mr Edwards glared at me. In the break he said, 'You're representing your country, for Christ's sake! Your sister Barbara is here, your sister Jenifer is here … They don't want to see you do this. For their sake if not for mine, get out there and play the way you can!'

I didn't let Chris take another game. Mr Edwards was as emotional as I have ever seen him, including at Wimbledon. He kissed a disappointed Chris, then he embraced me in front of the cameras. He whispered to me as the cameras were clicking: 'Now let's go on and win the Australian. You deserve it, sweetie — 1974 is going to be the big one. I've always said that.'

The pictures of that embrace were wired around the world. We both looked so happy, and of course we were. But underlying the image of the kindly old coach and his star pupil was the knowledge that this could not go on. I was a big girl now — too big to be Mr Edwards' 'pet' for much longer, and when the time came I hoped he would recognise that.

PART 5

Advantage, Mrs Cawley

Mr and Mrs Cawley

Chapter 19

A

CCORDING TO VIC EDWARDS' prediction several years before, 1974 would be my greatest year. Since I'd already won Wimbledon, he now defined 'greatest' as winning the Grand Slam. Thus, in signing with the Pittsburgh Triangles in the World Team Tennis league the previous summer, he'd ensured that the contract allowed me time off to compete in the French Open in June.

But to have a chance at the Grand Slam I first had to win the Australian Open, a title I dearly wanted, but which had so far proven beyond my reach. After the Bonne Bell Cup victory, however, I felt more confident than ever before, and went to Melbourne after Christmas with fire in my belly.

It must have rubbed off on my tennis. While people in the crowd were passing out in the sweltering heat, I battled my way past Karen Krantzcke in three gruelling sets to reach the semifinals. Then, on New Year's Eve, I had another battle royal to beat Kerry Melville, this time dropping the middle set. Centre Court was like an oven in the Melbourne heatwave, and we both suffered cramps. Fortunately mine came and went in the second set, while Kerry's came and stayed in the third. She'd been popping salt tablets at each change of ends but obviously their effect hadn't reached her legs in time.

And so I began 1974 with my fourth consecutive Australian Open singles final, this time against Chris Evert. Margaret Court had kept me from the title twice, Virginia Wade once. I wasn't about to let Chris rob me of it again, not playing her on grass.

A crowd of 12,000 people overflowed from the Kooyong stands for the New Year's Day final. There was a heat haze in the sky and a real electricity in the air. Since my victory over Chris in the last match of the Bonne Bell Cup, I'd become the bookies', as well as the sentimental, favourite. I would say 11,999 people at Kooyong that day were willing me to win, and who could blame the other — Jimmy Connors — for being in his new fiancée's corner?

The first set went my way in a tie-breaker but I never really felt I'd lost control. Beating Chris in a Grand Slam event was not meant to be easy, and I was satisfied that I was wearing her down. Then in the second set it happened

On my way to my first Australian Open title against Chris Evert, New Years' Day, 1974

again. Mesmerised by the ball-machine pumping them back to me from the baseline, I let Chris dictate the play. I hung back and played her game, dropping service twice before I broke back. But Chris held her serve. One each.

Chris and I had pulled out all the stops for almost an hour and a half, running every ball down in the heat. Appreciating the competition, the crowd went beserk as we towelled down before the decider.

According to the newspaper reports, Mr Edwards grabbed me in the break and said: 'Believe in God, believe in yourself and believe in me!' Pretty enigmatic words I suppose, but it shocked me to hear him say it, especially as he wasn't a religious man. I felt he should be believing in my ability to go on and win, rather than me believing in him! Maybe I was as emotional as he was, but I don't think so. I was wide-awake and focused on winning my first Australian title. Chris, the Little Miss Cool who once declared, 'No point is worth falling down over,' looked like she'd just come out of the make-up room. Barely a hair was out of place, whereas I was a lather of sweat. But I'd played her often enough to know that she was hurting on the inside. It was time to grab the match by the scruff of the neck.

She won just ten points in a 6–0 drubbing that was over in 18 minutes. The stunned crowd took a moment to appreciate that it was all over, then they stood and gave me an ovation that was almost as long as the final set. For the second time in a month, Mr Edwards stood at courtside with tears rolling down his cheeks. At such times I came as close as I ever got to loving this over-bearing, belligerent, difficult but essentially well-meaning old man.

He sat at the back of my post-match press conference sipping a beer and beaming with pride. I felt so happy for him. As I later wrote to Roger, 'Mr Edwards was just so thrilled, which meant more to me than actually winning.' The press lapped up the image of the 'gruff coach' who had become 'second father' to this dutiful Aboriginal daughter. It was part of the Evonne Goolagong

The prize is mine — Australian Open title

legend, but even in these highly-charged moments during our long association, nothing was quite as it seemed between Mr Edwards and me. Ours was not a father-daughter relationship, never had been and never could be.

Kenny Goolagong had come home from his wanderings before Christmas and all was forgiven. I decided to shout them a family holiday. Kenny and Linda had watched my big matches on television, but they hadn't come to the court to see me play since I was about 10 years old. The time had come. I booked them into a Double Bay hotel handy to White City for the NSW Open. But the Goolagong tribe doesn't do things by halves — Mum and Dad showed up with my sisters Gail and Janelle, brothers Ian and Martin, and Larry's wife Loris.

I had a wonderful time showing them the sights and taking them to restaurants, but before the start of the tournament the blisters on the soles of my feet became so painful that Mr Edwards insisted I see a doctor. I'd been troubled by blisters since the first time I played on concrete courts in South Africa, and when I played on hard surfaces in very hot weather they could get quite nasty. The doctor advised me not to play, but that was out of the question. 'My family's come all the way from Barellan,' I explained.

I hobbled my way through to the final that week, watched attentively by at least two people who had no idea whether I'd won or lost. Dad had some inkling of the game, but without the television commentary Mum was lost. In the end Karen Krantzcke won in straight sets in a fairly lacklustre final. Gail ran down to the courtside to meet me as I limped off. 'Mum's crying,' she blurted.

'Why? Because I lost? Tell her to stop being silly.'

'No, it's because you've won the *Sun* Sportsman of the Year award!'

As soon as my blisters had healed I was off to New Zealand again, this time with my new doubles partner, Peggy Michel, a fun-loving college graduate from Los Angeles. We blitzed the New Zealand Open, with Peggy and me taking out the doubles, and then me beating her for the singles. The real fun, however, was a few days' holiday afterwards at the Bay of Islands. Bill N'Godrella, my friend from the French Davis Cup team was on the tour, and we saw quite a bit of each other. I locked my mixed-up emotions in my suitcase and had a wonderful time, but on the plane-ride back to Sydney I found myself writing to Roger, 'Don't worry, it's nothing serious … but I just wanted to tell you because I feel I want to tell you everything.'

On April Fools' Day Mr Edwards and I flew back to America to start the Virginia Slims women's tour. After three years of operating outside the aegis of the USLTA, the hugely successful Slims tour had at last been recognised by official women's tennis, which meant that Chris Evert and I would be sharing finals duty with Billie Jean and Rosie again, if not with Margaret Court, who was still off the circuit.

I had limbered up for the start of the tour by hitting the Melbourne nightspots for a week with my friend Lesley Shaw, so I was raring to go. In those days the best possible preparation for me was to get as far away from tennis as I could, and dancing all night in smoky discotheques with Lesley and her friends was a pretty good distance. But as we crossed the Pacific again, I went over my playing schedule for the year and felt the energy begin to drain out of me.

We had become an industry. I seemed to have commitments almost every week, and when I wasn't playing I was on show in department stores or visiting boardrooms to shake on a deal.

The Slims tour moved from Florida to Philadelphia, then we flew back down the eastern seaboard for the *Family Circle* Magazine Cup, the first of the season's outdoor tournaments on Hilton Head Island. I had first visited Hilton Head the previous year for the inaugural World Invitational Tennis Classic, a made-for-television tournament devised by International Management's Mark McCormack. That first year Billie Jean, Margaret Court, Chris and I represented the women, and John Newcombe, Rod Laver, Stan Smith and Arthur Ashe the men. It was a great concept in which 10 singles, doubles and mixed doubles matches were played and individuals accumulated points for each win. Invariably it came down to the last mixed doubles match in which either a man or woman could triumph.

McCormack had also introduced a lot of razzamatazz, with cars being offered to the player who could serve the most aces. I actually aced John Newcombe in the first tournament but cross-gender aces were disallowed!

Billie Jean King had been the touring professional for the Hilton Head Racquet Club where the Invitational was first held in 1973, but her contract was nearing an end and the owners approached Bud Stanner about me taking over. The concept of 'touring pro' was quite new to tennis and very new to me. The Hilton Head Racquet Club would now become 'home', conveniently forgetting Barellan and Sydney. Contractually I would be required to hold clinics and hob-nob with company executives. Each time I played, the court announcer would brazenly tell the crowd: 'Miss Evonne Goolagong, touring pro for the Hilton Head Racquet Club, has won over $100,000 in just twelve weeks so far this season ...' I thought this was rude in the extreme, a gross invasion of privacy. On the other hand, with my growing commitments in America I really needed somewhere to hang my hat, to take my clothes out of the suitcase and let them air. The deal was struck during my absence in Australia, and we were to sign during the Family Circle tournament. I was given the use of a condominium in the Shipyard Plantation resort which was hastily decorated with a pair of crossed racquets and a sign which said 'The Evonne Goolagong Villa'. This was indeed a great honour, although I was to discover over the next couple of years that I didn't automatically get the use of the Evonne Goolagong Villa just because I was Evonne Goolagong. It was frequently booked out to tennis-mad guests.

My new American home was on the second-largest island of the country's eastern seaboard, some 30,000 developable acres in the midst of pine forest reserves and protected wetlands, connected by bridge to the mainland just north of the border of South Carolina and Georgia. Hilton Head had once been a private hunting reserve for wealthy southern families, but since the shooting had stopped the deer had returned to roam free over much of the island. In the 1950s Charles Fraser, the first man to graduate from Yale with a degree in 'resort development', applied what he had learnt to the strictly-controlled development of Hilton Head. Traffic lights, gaudy signs and buildings above tree level were among the no-nos. The result was a naturally beautiful resort island, dotted with small and quaint shopping villages. I loved it immediately, although the sporting spotlight that residents like Stan Smith and me were to place on it inevitably changed it over the years.

When I set up camp at Hilton Head in 1974, there were about 3000 residents. When I left a dozen years later, there were 80,000 residents and more than a million visitors each year, drawn to the island by its fame as a sporting paradise, which at its peak hosted a couple of dozen nationally televised sporting events.

Unfortunately I had little time to get accustomed to my new 'home', because I also had a new job more than 1000 kilometres (600 miles) to the north in Pittsburgh. World Team Tennis (WTT) was due to start in 16 cities across America in early May, and I had to go and meet the other members of the Pittsburgh Triangles. The team was based at the Monroeville Racquet Club outside Pittsburgh in the lovely Pennsylvania countryside, and the players were housed in an apartment block next door. Peggy Michel and I shared an apartment; on another floor was Vitas Gerulaitis, a long-haired New Yorker who was to become a great friend; and on another floor again was the veteran Ken 'Muscles' Rosewall, who seemed to spend most of his time wandering around Pittsburgh with a quizzical grin on his face. 'Muscles', our captain-coach that first year, could never quite believe that tennis had come to this!

And team tennis was different, that's for sure. The franchise owner Frank

Fuhrer was a great believer in the power of promotion, and when we weren't on court he had us in shopping malls or used car yards, waving the flag for World Team Tennis. He was also big on motivational lectures. During one of our early practice sessions he burst into the players' room with a prepared speech, but he was only a couple of paragraphs into it when Muscles gave him both barrels. 'This is private in here,' he said. 'If you've got something to say you invite us into your office at an appropriate time!' Chastened, at least momentarily, Fuhrer left the room.

When my Triangles contract had been drawn up, Mr Edwards had asked Bud Stanner to build in a role for him. He became a 'player director', mainly working with the women on the Triangles team. This was quite a good arrangement for me because it gave me that little extra distance from him that I seemed to need more and more.

We played our first match against Billie Jean's team, the Philadelphia Freedoms, in a half-empty indoor stadium in Philadelphia. A brass band played us onto the court and the fans were encouraged to cheer the home side and boo the visitors. Bells rang every time the Freedoms won a point, and when they finally beat us, hundreds of balloons cascaded down from the ceiling. It wasn't much like Wimbledon, and our initial reaction as players ranged from amusement to horror. Mr Edwards wrote in his VAETS newsletter: 'Quite candidly, I just can't see what this is going to do for tennis … however we are told this is what the American public want.'

Over the season I came to like the one-set, sudden death format of the WTT game. Every point counted and every game you won went to your team's tally, so even at 1–5 there was no excuse for playing below your best. Quite apart from all the ballyhoo, I found the pressure of the contest helped my concentration enormously, and was a contributing factor in the all-round improvement in my game in the mid-1970s.

But the travel — oh, the travel! The 16 teams in the league that first year were spread all over the continent and beyond. We played three, sometimes four matches a week, and often our schedule would have us playing in Honolulu one night and Cleveland the next, so we had to battle not only jet lag but also climate lag. The frequent exhaustion brought on emotional outbursts and clashes of temperament. One night I played a home game in Pittsburgh, then went straight to the airport where a private jet was waiting to fly me to Boston. I got to my hotel at 2 a.m. and slept until 7, then I conducted a tennis clinic arranged by my managers, IMG, until 4, went back to the airport and jumped onto a plane for Honolulu, arriving an hour before the Triangles were due to play. This was like the baseball tour — you didn't think about it, you just got off the plane, played, and got back on the plane. That night I think we beat the Hawaii Leis, but I couldn't be sure. I do know that the next morning we were on a plane back to Phoenix for another match, then on to Cleveland the next night. I lost 6–0 to Martina Navratilova in Cleveland and walked into the net post coming off. Frequently Peggy Michel and I would get back to our apartment in Pittsburgh after touring for a week, get under the hot shower and bawl our eyes out for emotional release.

Sometimes the entire team would be punch-drunk and we'd get the giggles for absolutely no reason. In Phoenix one night Vitas Gerulaitis was being thrashed within an inch of his life. Normally he would have been upset with himself, but after every bad shot he laughed out loud. Pretty soon we were all hysterical! God knows what the audience thought.

The upside of life with the Triangles was that a real team spirit evolved. I had always enjoyed playing in Australian teams in the Federation and Bonne Bell cups, and World Team Tennis was in some ways a natural extension of that. While I was never one to hang around the courts longer than I had to, with the Triangles on tour there was nowhere else to go, and none of us would have ever considered not being there to cheer our team-mates on. In fact it was mandatory. It was fun, it was exciting!

Beyond that, representing Pittsburgh meant that we all became involved in the community, which is rare for a touring tennis player. Vitas, in particular, when he wasn't touring or partying, became involved with Pittsburgh's street kids, running clinics for them and getting them free tickets to the home games. The 'G-Men' became his own personalised cheer squad.

I took a week's break from the Triangles and flew to Naples to join the Australian team in the Federation Cup. We beat the Americans in a wonderful finals rubber, but for me the highlight of the trip was to have been seeing Roger during our London stopover. Unfortunately the way the flights worked out I spent only two hours at Heathrow and only managed to speak to Roger briefly on the phone. But this was of no great concern. I was looking forward to seeing him in Paris during the French Open. When Roger read this in my letters he scratched his head. The rest of the world knew that all World Team Tennis players had been banned from the French Open. I didn't.

Philippe Chartrier, head of the French Tennis Federation (FTF) and later to become president of the International Lawn Tennis Federation (ILTF), regarded World Team Tennis as a major threat to the future of the European tour. Not only did the summer schedule run right through all the European tournaments except Wimbledon, but WTT also offered lucrative salaries, win or lose, as opposed to the modest purses offered by the French and Italian

Open tournaments. Chartrier felt he had to take a stand or be wiped out, and the ILTF and the Commercial Union, an insurance company which sponsored both the French and Italian Open tournaments, agreed.

The players with the most to lose from the ban were the Australian Open champions, Jimmy Connors and me, both of us in the hunt for the Grand Slam. Jimmy's manager, the Las Vegas promoter Bill Reardon, decided to take Chartrier on in the courts, and Mr Edwards tacked my name onto the lawsuit. In addition to this World Team Tennis filed on our behalf a suit against Commercial Union and its agents, Jack Kramer and Donald Dell, seeking $US 10 million damages.

It was totally against Mr Edwards' nature to take on the tennis establishment in this manner, but he clearly believed that I was playing well enough for the Grand Slam to be a real possibility — and we had nothing to lose. He expressed his distaste for the whole legal quagmire when he wrote in his VAETS bulletin: 'It is all very worrying. I never liked or was mixed up in the politics of tennis and never wanted to be … my job in life has been to coach, encourage, advise, guide and manage players — not to get them mixed up in the politics and unsavoury aspects of this game . . .'

(The action was dropped within the year when Chartrier realised that WTT wasn't the threat that he had feared and revoked the ban. But it still may have cost Jimmy Connors a Grand Slam in 1974. He went on to win both Wimbledon and the US Open.)

Mr Edwards, Peggy Michel and I flew to London a few days before the start of Wimbledon and set ourselves up in a flat in Victoria. As soon as I could I contacted Roger and went to see him at his flat. Our reunions were no longer awkward, rather they were like two old schoolmates getting together once a year. It took us time to show affection again, never quite certain how far the other wanted to take the relationship.

We saw each other a few times during the fortnight, but by the time Kerry Melville knocked me out in the quarter finals — my least impressive Wimbledon singles performance since 1970 — we had barely scratched the surface of our emotions. Perhaps it was better this way, I was beginning to feel. Maybe I needed a friend more than I needed a lover, particularly one who lived on the other side of the world.

Once I was out of the singles we dated more often, although there could be no late nights as Peggy and I (in response to the earbashing I'd received from Mr Edwards after my singles performance) were on our way to winning the doubles crown. Our victory was an enormous triumph for Peggy, who played brilliantly, and a great relief for me.

Our friend John Russell took this photo, one of my favourites

On the Friday night before the men's final Roger took Peggy and me to see a movie. When we had a nightcap afterwards he seemed to become hyperactive, prattling on about nothing and every so often he would look at me and just glow. Months later he was to write, 'I had come to the conclusion that I was still in love with you … when I saw you after the cinema with Peggy, it shook me rigid just how true that feeling was. The result at the time was that I talked and talked and talked about anything that came into my head, because inside I was in utter turmoil!'

I was flying back to America on the Monday, so we arranged to have dinner on the Sunday evening. We walked into a crowded restaurant and left an empty one. In fact the owner had kindly kept open to accommodate us while we talked — or I should say while Roger talked and I listened. He later wrote, 'I decided to tell you, hence our (or rather my) talk on the last Sunday. I didn't want to write and tell you later in a letter — I had to tell you to your face. Perhaps it wasn't the best, but neither was it the easiest thing to do.'

Roger told me how much he loved me and that he wanted to spend his life with me. I suppose it was a proposal, but it left me confused and more than a little scared. Did I still feel the same way? I didn't know. So much had changed since that summer of 1970. Roger was now a businessman working in the metals market and I was one of the most famous sportswomen in the world. Moreover, we were both adults with our own established paths in life. Maybe, just maybe, the moment for us had passed.

Flying back to Pittsburgh I went over and over my relationship with Roger. The more I analysed it the more I realised that in the four years we had known each other we had spent so little time together that I barely knew him. I couldn't marry a man I didn't know! Back in the Monroeville apartment I started several letters and ripped them up. In one I got eight pages into it before I realised that I was writing the things that Roger would want to hear, not necessarily from the heart. So, in the end I was so confused that I didn't answer him straight away.

We finished the WTT season as runners-up to Philadelphia — a pretty satisfactory result, we all thought, but Frank Fuhrer kept screaming about his bank balance. There was also some mild discontent in the camp surrounding Mr Edwards' appointment of a young Pittsburgh girl named Gere Kitch as his personal assistant. Gere was a brash and brassy girl about three months my junior, but she treated me and the other players like errant children. 'Gee, thanks Mom,' Vitas would say in his best 'Beaver Cleaver' voice when she handed out the boarding passes at the airport. It is fair to say that Gere and

The Pittsburgh Triangles take a bow, 1975

I disliked each other with about equal intensity. I don't know about her, but it was rare for me to feel that way about anyone.

After the final match of the season in Pittsburgh, the entire Gong show moved on to New York for the US Open. Having missed the French, I was out of the running for a Grand Slam, but the US title was one Mr Edwards believed I could win, now that I had worked out Chris Evert. But the draw pitted Chris against me in the semifinals. I beat her and went into the Forest Hills final against the Old Lady — Billie Jean King improving with age.

Of all the great matches I played in 15 years at the top of world tennis, few were better than the 1974 US Open women's final. We took a set each, going flat-out, running every ball down, to the delight of the enthralled crowd. I was up 5–3 in the third, with the championship within reach, when suddenly winning didn't seem important any more. It had nothing to do with a lack of 'killer instinct', nor with going 'walkabout'. Quite simply, I believed that our tennis had transcended the scoreboard. Our rallies seemed endless, and after an exchange of impossible returns I felt goose bumps rise on my flesh as the crowd roared its approval. History records that Billie Jean beat me that day, but no one who saw the match would have believed I was the loser.

It had been a hard, cold winter in Barellan with little shearing work about. Kenny Goolagong had been forced to take to the road again to find jobs, and, inevitably, this had led him back to Hillston. During the winter Dad had written me a long letter in which he had asked me to buy him a car. The old one had too many bush miles on the clock. I had to have time to think about that, time to pluck up the courage to ask Mr Edwards for the money.

One warm evening in early October Kenny Goolagong stepped out of the pub in Hillston and started the walk up past the school to the house where he'd rented a small room. I imagine the beers he'd drunk filled him with good cheer, and as he picked a path along the edge of the road, he was probably singing his song: 'I've got the bull by the tail and a downhill pull ...'

Mrs Jean Sommerville, the wife of a schoolteacher who'd only recently been assigned to the Hillston school, was setting the table for dinner when she heard the roar of the cars and the screech of brakes. She ran out through the front door and looked up the street into the twilight. She could just make out the figure of a man lying at the edge of the road. Several people were running to his assistance but he seemed very still.

'Bloody kids,' said one of the neighbours. 'That's what it was. Bloody larrikins racing their cars down the road. Knock a poor bloke for six.'

After the Bonne Bell Cup in Cleveland — we lost — Mr Edwards flew back to Australia and Mrs Edwards came along with Peggy and me for the resumption of the Virginia Slims tour. I got off to a good start, beating Chris Evert in the final in Denver. We went on to Houston increasingly confident that I was looking a good prospect for the Slims Championships in Los Angeles, which carried the biggest purse in the history of women's tennis.

In Houston I played well again, and later came down from my hotel room to meet Mrs Edwards, raring to go in my semifinal against Chris. Mrs Edwards looked unusually grave, and was deep in whispered conversation with two of the organisers of the tour. I sensed something was wrong when I approached the group, but Mrs Edwards bundled me into a car and we drove to the tournament. There she took me into one of the offices, closed the door and hugged me.

'What is it? What's wrong?'

'I didn't know how to tell you last night, love. I don't know now ... It's your Dad. Kenny's dead, I'm afraid.'

The words ripped through me like a winter westerly across the Barellan wheatfields. I buried my head in the broad expanse of Mrs Edwards' chest and cried like a baby. When I could speak I said, 'Take me home, please.'

I meant take me home to Barellan circa 1958, but they took me back to the hotel in Houston. The events are a blur to me now, but I remember looking out the car window at the freeway traffic and seeing only images of Kenny: Kenny weaving home from the pub, singing his song, Barbara and me keeping him upright; Kenny crank-starting our old bombs; Kenny proudly showing me his shearing technique; Kenny winking at me curled up in the back seat, as he stole off down to the river at Darlington Point to smoke and fish all night.

Barbara was working as a nursing aide at Guildford in Sydney's western suburbs. She had come off a late shift and was half asleep on the lounge when a neighbour knocked on the door with a message to phone Mr Edwards. She walked up the street to a phone booth and dialled the number.

'Barbara, can you come over here, sweet?'

'It's very late and I'm on again in the morning. What is it?'

'I think it would be better if you came over.'

Barbara started to feel rising panic in her bones. 'What is it?' she shouted. 'Tell me now!'

'It's your father, pet. Ken's been killed in a road accident.'

Barbara told me she fainted on the concrete floor of the phone booth. In time, however, she rallied and packed a small bag and drove through the night to be with Mum. They were together when I phoned from Houston. Mum couldn't speak. She wailed into the phone and I wailed back. I told her I loved her, then Barb came on the line. Through the tears we tried to make arrangements. Of course I would come home immediately. Barb said, 'That's what Mum wants, but think about it first. We're all here to support her, and you can't do much to help Dad now. Think it through before you jump on a plane.'

Mr Edwards phoned with his condolences and the tears flowed again. When I had composed myself he said, 'I don't think there's much you can do for your family in Barellan. Frankly, I think if you go back there now, that's where you'll stay. And that's not what Kenny Goolagong would want for you.'

I spent much of the day crying into the phone, and by the end of it I had made my decision. It was a decision I have had to live with now for almost 20 years, and it hasn't always been easy. There have been times when I've wished I could roll back time and rewrite a couple of scenes differently. But I had a vision of my father sitting proudly in the stand at White City, his race tout's fedora at a jaunty angle, a 'rollie' in the corner of his mouth punctuating that cheeky grin. He was proud of his little Eve, and I would make him prouder yet.

I phoned Mrs Edwards in the next room. 'Yes, I'll be okay. Pack your bag, let's go to Phoenix.'

Chapter 20

THE SLIMS TOURNAMENT in Phoenix was a disaster. Afterwards Mrs Edwards said, 'Come on! Now you pack your bag. We're getting out of here.' We played tourists, the girl from Barellan and the girl from Angledool. We drove out to a dude ranch, then to the Grand Canyon, where I dropped tears into the black abyss and felt the spirit of that place humble me. I was a very small tennis player in a very big universe. The insignificance of the individual is never more apparent than when you look into the timeless face of a rock which has seen the coming and going of a dozen civilisations.

Finally we went to Aspen where a photographer-friend John Russell made a home for us and we relaxed and rejuvenated our spirits in the cool, clear air of the Rockies.

Despite the disaster in Phoenix, I had qualified for the play-offs of the Virginia Slims Championships in Los Angeles. We flew down into the smog to prepare, and found mounting speculation in the media and amongst the players that my grief would affect my game. It did, but perhaps not the way my rivals had expected. There was a burning passion within me to win this one for Kenny.

It took a tough three-setter to get past the Old Lady in the semifinals. Some days before the match Billie Jean had taken me aside and asked if I was okay. It was an act of genuine concern for a fellow player that was typical of the woman, despite her bad press, and it touched me deeply.

Chris Evert had also talked to me about my grief. She said, 'I'm so sorry about your father. I don't know how you can keep on playing.' Chris's remark made me realise that I was numb, perhaps still in shock.

In October I met Chris in the final. In our career clashes we were at seven-all, but the only time she had beaten me on that tour was because of my forfeit in Houston. In front of 7000 screaming fans in Los Angeles, I went into the lead against Chris in my personal battle, and pocketed $US 32,000 for my troubles. It would have bought Kenny a nice new car. I felt pangs of guilt then, and for a long time afterwards, thinking that things may have been different if I'd bought him his car straight away.

Love and best wishes — to two great ladies — John

Mum No. 2 by John Russell

I knew I had played almost as well as I could to take the Slims, but my opponents were exceptionally generous in their comments to *Sports Illustrated*. 'She was like a panther compared to me,' said Billie Jean. 'She had more mobility and she played beautifully. I started watching her, and then I'd remember all of a sudden that I had to hit the ball.'

'There was nothing I could do,' said Chris. 'She just hit winner after winner. Against Evonne good wasn't good enough. You had to hit the lines.'

Soon after the Slims championships I returned to Sydney for the start of the Australian season and received a letter from Roger, outlining his feelings again and expressing great regret that he had apparently frightened me off by speaking frankly. I responded, and this time I actually sent the letter. 'Well, I don't know what to write now, and you must think I'm a real bitch … I really didn't want to hurt you by … letting you know I didn't feel the same way. Maybe some day when I'm feeling more free from tennis and the people concerned, I can begin to really love someone the way that you loved me. At the moment I really don't care if I don't find anyone because I miss someone I loved very much, my father ... To be honest, I do love you, but in a good friend kind of way ... Well, Roger, I will not take up any more of your time ... I'm truly sorry...'

I was one mixed-up kid, I can tell you. I had just won the richest prize in women's tennis and lost my Dad in the same month. I had no idea how to deal with my see-sawing emotions. The next day I wrote to Roger again. '... I suddenly thought I'll probably regret it for the rest of my life if I lose you ... You must have felt lonely and sort of panicky when you didn't hear from me. Right now I feel panicky because I have a horrible feeling I've lost you ...' I played in Perth and Adelaide and came back to Sydney desperate for a letter from Roger. Nothing. At the Edwards' house, where I was now the only 'child', I wrote again. And again. 'Well, I've decided I'm going to keep writing just as I feel like it until I hear from you ...'

The Australian tour seemed endless. The months on the road, my grief for Kenny, my guilt about not coming home for his funeral, and the confusion I felt in my heart were all beginning to take their toll. I didn't realise it at the time, but I must have been very close to a breakdown. I wrote to Roger: 'At the moment I'm playing the Australian tour and I'm getting so tired of travelling and playing ... I wish I could just put away my racquets for about two weeks or so, just to relax and forget tennis. It seems so hard at the moment to get interested in what I'm doing ... The last two tournaments I was beaten by Olga Morozova, and each time I tried to push myself but I just haven't got my heart in it.'

Just before Christmas I finally got a letter and card from Roger. Oh, the relief! There was still a chance for us.

It was now January 1975 and I went to Melbourne to defend my Australian Open title with a lighter heart, but I was still an emotional basket case. After I'd beaten Martina Navratilova in the final I stood on the Kooyong Centre Court watched by a packed house and a national television audience. I thanked Mr Edwards and for his benefit said that he'd been like a second father to me. The word 'father' stuck in my throat and my mouth was suddenly parched. And then I broke down and wept.

It was all too much. Within 48 hours I was in New Zealand, on the road again. I can't even remember what happened, other than the fact that I had developed a ligament problem with my wrist, so now I was physically as well as emotionally drained. I pulled out of an exhibition and flew home to Sydney. Mrs Edwards picked me up at the airport. She said, 'You poor child, you look terrible.' I slept all the way home.

At dinner that night Mr Edwards produced my playing schedule for 1975. I looked at the 40 or so weeks of tennis which lay stretched ahead and cradled my head in my hands and howled. Mr Edwards was shocked. For the first time he realised how close I was to cracking. He came around the table and put his arm around me. He said, 'It's okay, pet. You need some time off.'

For some time we had discussed the possibility of me stealing a week and taking a complete break from tennis (I hadn't had one for over a year). Mr Edwards had agreed that I could just take off by myself and go anywhere in the world. Now that possibility had become a necessity. I told him I wanted to go to London to see Roger. There was nothing more than a pause to draw breath. 'Fine,' he said. We pulled out the diaries and found a week in February, wedged in between tournaments in Detroit and Philadelphia.

A day or two after my return from New Zealand Mr Edwards asked me to sign 'some paperwork'. I signed without thinking, as I so often had. A couple of years later I would discover that I had signed a most curious agreement. Since 1970 there had been a contractual agreement between me and Mr Edwards for him to act as my coach and manager for fees and expenses, but this piece of paper appeared to have been hurriedly drafted as a fail-safe, in case something went wrong between us. Although I was the only one to sign it in front of a witness, it purported to be a three-year contract retrospective to 1 July 1973.

I went to Barellan and spent a few days with Linda and the kids. Mum had coped with her loss as well as might be expected, and spent her days immersed in housework. I hired a car and drove them all over the district, visiting friends and relations and hearing again and again the stories of the tragic loss and the fine farewell Barellan had given my father. Although she said little about it, I realised that Linda had been deeply hurt when I didn't come home for the funeral. She forgave me, of course, and I think she even understood that if I had come home then I might have stayed home forever. But she was hurt nonetheless.

Before Mr Edwards and I returned to America, Jenifer Edwards married her bus-driving boyfriend, and I was bridesmaid again. But never the bride? I phoned Roger and we talked forever about my forthcoming visit. He sounded genuinely excited about it. I started marking off the days in my diary.

Gere Kitch was at the airport to meet us, which seemed strange to me, since World Team Tennis was still some weeks away. 'Oh,' said Mr Edwards, 'Didn't I tell you, pet? Gere's going to be travelling with us. We both need an assistant.' I needed assistance from Gere Kitch like I needed a hole in the head. We could barely even speak to each other.

Bud Stanner came to Detroit to watch me beat Margaret Court in the final of the Detroit Slims tournament. Afterwards the four of us had dinner together. I told Bud I was flying to London in the morning to see Roger. He said, 'That's a very, very good idea.'

Something about Bud's emphasis on the virtues of my getting away from Mr Edwards and Gere disturbed me. Not for the first time I considered this strange relationship between Mr Edwards and our personal assistant. Surely they couldn't be having an affair! It was too ridiculous for words. I dismissed the notion.

In the morning I flew to London. Roger met me at the airport and produced our schedule for the week. Schedule! I laughed and ripped it up. We had a lot of feelings to work out, and he had decided the best way to do that was to show me as much as he could of his life — who he was — so even without a schedule we moved between restaurants and pubs and homes of friends, down to see his parents, even a sightseeing journey to the white cliffs of Dover.

We planned a romantic dinner at Scott's, a seafood restaurant in the West End. Roger made a booking but first we went to Trader Vic's for a drink. We sat in a corner and gazed into each other's eyes as dinner time came and went. They say lucky in love, and it was never truer than that night in London. While we sipped on a cocktail down the road, an IRA bomb ripped a hole in Scott's, dissecting our reserved table.

By the end of the week we both knew this was real love, and I found the realisation fulfilling and relaxing. One night I said to Roger, 'Tell me why you think we should marry.' He had barely begun a 20-minute dissertation on the subject when I was fast asleep.

We phoned Mum in Barellan. She was delighted. 'About time!' she said. 'I had four kids when I was your age!'

I flew back to America in a dreamy daze. Yes, I would be Mrs Roger Cawley. It was right, it was time. We had set no date, no deadlines. All we knew was that we were going to be husband and wife.

A tournament official picked me up at the airport and took me to the hotel. I phoned Mr Edwards' room, eager to tell him my news. He'd just returned from dinner and I could tell he'd been drinking. Nevertheless I went straight to see him.

'Roger and I are in love and we're going to get married.'

He nodded his head a little unsteadily and spent long moments studiously stubbing out a cigarette. When he looked up at me again he had a strange smile on his face. He said, 'That's lovely, sweet. Of course, you know Gere and I are in love too.'

I excused myself, went to my room and phoned Roger. 'Do you know what he just told me?' I guess this was the final straw. Up to that moment part of me had subconsciously rejected the affair that had been going on under my nose. I told Roger I doubted I could continue in the company of Gere and Mr Edwards. 'In fact I think I just want to give the whole thing away. Let's forget about tennis and just be a happily married couple.' Roger calmed me down but we decided that night we would marry in Australia at the end of the year.

In the morning Mr Edwards was ashen-faced and businesslike as we prepared for another tournament. He took me aside and said, 'Pet, forget all about what I said last night. I'd had a few, I was just being silly.' I felt quite ill.

Relations between Gere, Mr Edwards and me became very frosty indeed over the next couple of weeks as we moved from tournament to tournament, hotel to hotel on the Slims tour. I seldom spoke to either of them, and Mr Edwards preferred to pass messages through Gere. ('He thinks you ought to look at the way Martina is playing. Guts all the way.') But it was clear he was speaking to other players and officials, because word filtered back to me that Mr Edwards was accusing Roger of all kinds of things. The whole situation was becoming quite absurd. Not only did I have a coach who didn't talk to me and a personal assistant who did nothing to assist me, but half the tennis world was laughing at our pathetic little triangle.

'What's going on with them?' Billie Jean King asked me in the locker room. 'Is it what it looks like?'

On 10 March Mr Edwards handed me a letter and asked me to read it carefully. The letter outlined the reasons why he believed I should abandon my plans to marry Roger. It implied that Roger had neither the credentials nor experience to take over his role as my manager, a job which at the time was the furthest thing from Roger's mind. He merely wanted to be my husband. I was incensed by it and phoned Roger immediately and read him every word. Roger responded by writing Mr Edwards a letter in which he sought to allay his fears about his future as my coach, and about his — Roger's — intentions. He added a detailed résumé of his business career and his current assets.

It was an entirely reasonable, rational response to a father-figure who clearly disapproved of his 'daughter's' choice. I doubt Roger would have been so amenable had we not agreed that I would give up tennis at the end of the year anyway. When there was no response from Mr Edwards, Roger phoned him.

He said, 'Evonne tells me you seem to be unhappy about our plans. I'm very sorry you feel that way, and I really can't understand why.' Mr Edwards grunted. Roger continued, 'Perhaps I should come to America and spend some time with you, get to know you a little and allow you to make your own informed judgment of me.' Mr Edwards actually spoke. He said yes, the trip wasn't a bad idea.

Roger flew to New York at the beginning of April and stayed overnight with his old friend John Paish and his wife, the former Australian tennis player Wendy Gilchrist. The following morning he flew to Savannah, Georgia, where I picked him up and we drove to Hilton Head Island. He had come to Hilton Head specifically to sit down and talk about our future with Mr Edwards, and I found it rather difficult to explain that Mr Edwards wasn't there. He and Gere simply hadn't shown up. He had, however, taken the trouble, for propriety's sake, to book Roger into the hotel, despite the fact that there were more than enough bedrooms in the Evonne Goolagong Villa. Roger said, 'Forget the hotel, I'll stay with you at the condo.'

After four wonderful, but totally Vic-free days on Hilton Head we were back at Savannah en route to the next tournament at Amelia Island in Florida. Roger's frustration over Mr Edwards was countered, I suppose, by his happiness at seeing me, but as the days had gone by, frustration and resentment had been getting the upper hand. We flew to Jacksonville and Mr Edwards and Gere were waiting with a rented car to drive us to Amelia Island. He kissed me lightly and nodded gravely at Roger. There was not one word of apology to Roger, no attempt to explain his non-appearance. Whenever Roger tried to engage him in conversation he busied himself in talking to Gere. This was my future husband he was treating like dirt, and I became silently enraged.

As we arrived at Amelia Mr Edwards explained to me the set-up. He, Gere and I were in a three-bedroom apartment, Roger was booked into a hotel. Roger accepted this with as much good grace as he could muster, but then the cat-and-mouse game began. Whenever Roger appeared, Mr Edwards disappeared. Finally, we trapped him in the apartment during a Virginia Slims meeting. When the meeting finished Roger confronted him. It got pretty heated and graduated to white-hot when Gere joined in an attack on Roger's suitability as a husband.

I don't anger quickly, but on this occasion I exploded. 'What the hell does this have to do with you? You're nobody in this conversation, Gere, so kindly stay out of it!'

Mr Edwards then turned on me. 'Don't you dare speak to Gere that way!' I couldn't go on with it. I stormed out of the room, my eyes filled with tears. Furious now, Roger let Mr Edwards have it.

'Okay Vic, I've had enough of this. I've come thousands of miles to try and make peace with you and you don't even have the courtesy to show up at Hilton Head, and now you're hiding from me. You're treating me like a piece of furniture. You tell me you're too busy to see me — well, I'll stay here in the apartment and wait until you've got a free moment! Shouldn't be a problem. Evonne's got her room, you and Gere have yours, I'll take the other one!'

That did it. Roger realised then that there was no hope that he and Vic Edwards would ever achieve any kind of cordiality. Mr Edwards had closed the door on that possibility. Roger knew that every day I spent with him from this day on would be one day closer to the end of the road, but Mr Edwards didn't seem to register much reaction at all. Gere did the talking, and abused Roger for interfering in their lives. Roger ignored her and told Mr Edwards there was no point now in discussing anything with him, that he and I would get on with our lives, and that he would stay with me, as planned, for the next couple of weeks. Mr Edwards didn't look up as Roger left the apartment.

The next stop on the tour was Austin, Texas, for the L'Eggs World Series, an IMG-run four-woman invitational worth $US 100,000. What a bizarre group we must have seemed at the airport and on the plane, clearly together but not on speaking terms. Mr Edwards communicated with me now only through notes delivered by Gere. 'Press conference scheduled 1600 hours. VAE.' At the Lakeway World of Tennis resort in Austin the four of us would maintain appearances by sitting down to breakfast together, but not speak a word across the table. Bud Stanner, who had flown down for the event, joined us one morning and found the palpable tension extremely amusing. He shook his head and laughed long and hard while Gere stared at him and no doubt prayed he would have a seizure. While I found the situation almost intolerable, I was glad that at least one person had seen it for the laughable soap opera it had become.

During the tournament Roger and Bud had a long, private conversation, in which Roger explained the impasse with Mr Edwards and his attempts to end it. 'As you can see, this situation is ridiculous,' Roger said, 'but as long as she plays tennis she will stay with him as coach, just as she wants to stay with you as manager.' Bud summed up the situation pretty well, and thereafter IMG dealt directly with me on most matters.

The World Team Tennis season was due to begin so we flew back to Pittsburgh for team practice and the launch of the second big year for the Pittsburgh Triangles. Roger booked a London flight out of Pittsburgh and came to Monroeville to spend his last day with me.

There was considerable interest in our first press conference, for during the off-season franchise owner Frank Fuhrer had never stopped bleating about where the team had failed and how he was going to fix it. There were personnel changes: Ken Rosewall had gone and Victor Alan Edwards had taken over as head coach; in the absence of Muscles, I was the lone star player, the one expected to win each set so convincingly that it would counter our losses. There was also a great deal of speculation about the future of team tennis, with five clubs pulling out of the league after its first season. Pittsburgh had one of the biggest payrolls in the league and one of the most volatile managements, so it was hardly surprising that the conference room at the Monroeville Racquet Club was crowded with pressmen when we walked in that Tuesday afternoon.

What was surprising was that Roger and I were the centre of attention. Lights flashed, cameras clicked and players and press offered their congratulations. Moments before, Mr Edwards had apparently confirmed reports of our engagement which had appeared in the London newspapers that morning. Unbeknownst to us, the *Daily Mail* had tricked a confirmation out of Roger's father, who had known for some weeks of our intention to marry. Acting on a tip from we knew not where, the *Daily Mail* had played the oldest trick in the newspaper world. They had phoned Donald Cawley, told him that we had announced our engagement and asked him to comment. Now life was imitating the media.

The *Daily Mail* also managed to stir up a minor controversy in the Triangles camp by inaccurately quoting Mr Cawley as saying that Roger would be 'possibly involved in managing Evonne's business affairs'. How this must have grated with Mr Edwards.

An extraordinary official announcement went out to the media of the world and stated: 'The Pittsburgh Triangles tennis team confirmed today that tennis star Evonne Goolagong was engaged to Roger Cawley of Canterbury, England.'

We didn't need Mr Edwards as manager of the Pittsburgh Triangles to announce our engagement, but there was no point denying it, and sadly, there was no point in confronting Mr Edwards about his increasingly irrational behaviour. Trapped in an engagement party not of our making, we held hands and fielded the questions.

The next morning's Pittsburgh *Post-Gazette* carried a major article on the engagement. It began: 'Tennis is the only game in the world where love meant absolutely nothing — until yesterday, when Evonne Goolagong and Roger Cawley met the press to confirm they will indeed marry … One of the reasons Cawley showed up, in fact, was to debunk earlier reports out of London that

'Gong, is my tie straight?' L'Eggs Tournament, Texas, 1975

he was about to assume Edwards' role in arranging Evonne's affairs. Cawley … wanted it made perfectly clear that the only thing he has usurped is Goolagong's heart.'

Elsewhere in the report there was a quote from Mr Edwards which shed some light on his pre-emptive — and presumptuous because he knew nothing of our plans — announcement: ' "It's sad," said Edwards, [not within our earshot!] "to see a tennis player go out. I'm not frowning on the wedding or taking out after love, but it appears now that Evonne will leave the game after 1976. Evonne gives her entirety to everything she does and it will be impossible for her to play tennis and be married at the same time for any length of time." '

In other words, Mr Edwards could see a split looming and wanted to cover himself. When the press left the conference room we found ourselves gazing at Mr Edwards with not much to say. Instead, we had a celebratory drink with him. Roger and I stared at each other in disbelief as he laughed and joked at the bar, and toasted our health and future prosperity. Later, things got even more weird when he invited Roger to his apartment for a farewell drink.

Roger remembers that: 'He sat me down and poured us both hefty scotches. He didn't apologise for any of his actions or even try to explain them. He simply told me that his only thought was for Evonne's future happiness and that he now realised that we would be happy together. He wished me well, told me he'd phone me with details about Wimbledon, and we shook hands, I think for the only time in our lives.'

Roger was more puzzled than delighted by this turn of events, but we nevertheless felt a great sense of relief that this stupid game appeared to be over. We were wrong, of course. Within a couple of days Mr Edwards had reverted to his belief that Roger was an unfit suitor. He resumed his tactic of denigrating Roger at every opportunity, while I grappled with the difficulty of discussing our wedding plans with Mrs Edwards in Sydney without divulging anything about her husband's adulterous affair, which was hanging like an ominous black cloud over both our lives. I loved Mrs Edwards dearly and after almost every conversation I put down the phone and wept for her. But I just couldn't be the one to tell her.

The problems underlying our phone conversations probably accounted for the misunderstandings that developed over that most prickly of family businesses, the planning of the wedding. My initial wish was for a big church wedding, surrounded by bridesmaids and family and friends, probably in Sydney. I even fantasised with Mrs Edwards about having it in St Mary's Cathedral, that beautiful and holy place where both Patricia and Jenifer Edwards had been married. Of course this was out of the question since neither Roger nor I was Roman Catholic, and I never thought another thing about it until I was contacted for comment on a report that the Catholic Archbishop of Sydney, Cardinal Freeman, was deliberating on whether the church could facilitate my request. A Catholic spokesman, Dr W. E. Murray had said that my request had created 'a most unusual situation'. Within a few days, however, the Sydney Roman Catholic Archdiocese had granted permission for us to be married in St Mary's Cathedral.

The only problem was that by now the very thought of such a high profile wedding filled me with dread. Who would such a wedding really be for? We weren't big party-goers, and I couldn't see Linda Goolagong relishing her day in the limelight. Increasingly, as Roger and I talked on the phone, it seemed to make more sense to marry in Barellan after the Australian tour, just a quiet country wedding with a bring-a-plate reception in the church hall.

As the weeks went by, however, I began to realise that my situation as part of the Triangles' eternal triangle — me, Gere and Mr Edwards — was simply untenable. I couldn't pick up the phone and tell my second Mum what was going on, so like it or not, I was an accomplice in his duplicity. And I couldn't stand it. I wanted out and I wanted out now, but we had a schedule.

Every time I lost an important match he told the press it was because I was in love and couldn't concentrate on two things at the same time. When I was beaten soundly by Martina Navratilova in Aix-en-Provence in France and we lost the Federation Cup to Czechoslovakia, he said, 'Evonne is not the player she was. She is the sort of girl who finds it difficult to do two things at once.'

At the time I found this vaguely insulting, but looking at it now with the benefit of hindsight, I can see that it would have been difficult for Mr Edwards to announce to the press, 'Evonne is playing below her best because I am having an affair with my personal assistant who is 40 years younger than me, and she is concerned about my wife's feelings.'

At the end of May I phoned Roger and asked him what he thought of a registry office wedding as soon as possible — like in a fortnight's time when we were due in London for Wimbledon. He was a little taken aback. Up to now we had never been specific about dates, let alone dates the week after next! But he said if that made me happy, that was what we would do. He would go to Canterbury and make the arrangements.

I then phoned Linda in Barellan. I hoped against hope that she would not be too disappointed. 'Oh, that's lovely,' she said. 'If it makes you happy, I'm happy.' I promised faithfully that we would renew our vows in a church ceremony in Barellan as soon as practicable.

So it seemed that if I was happy, everybody was happy. It was time to tell Mr Edwards. I chose my moment carefully, after he'd had a couple of loosening drinks but not enough to distort his judgment, such as it had become. I told him that Roger and I had decided that an immediate Registry Office wedding in England was in everyone's best interests, that my mother was really not interested in a big church wedding in Sydney and nor were we, and that as both he and Mrs Edwards would be in London at the time, it seemed appropriate.

There was very little reaction. He had said his piece often enough, and seemed prepared to accept our decision. I asked, 'You and Mrs Edwards will come, won't you?' He nodded.

The wedding was planned for the Canterbury Registry Office on 19 June, the week of the Eastbourne tournament. I had commitments with the Pittsburgh Triangles that prevented me leaving America until 16 June, but Roger made arrangements so that I would go straight to Canterbury from the airport, we would post the bans and I would then go straight to the Eastbourne tournament. He made hotel bookings for Mr and Mrs Edwards, Gere Kitch and Mr Edwards' secretary from Sydney, Mrs Barbara Worthington. There were no wedding invitations and we told no one except family and a few close friends of the intended date of the wedding. Our intention was to be married privately, in the company of the people we loved. In the case of Mr Edwards, the history of our relationship meant more than its current parlous state, and of course it would have been unthinkable for me to be married without Mrs Edwards in attendance.

If Roger and I are guilty of anything concerning the Edwards family and our wedding in Canterbury, it is this: we took for granted that Mr Edwards was coming; we took for granted also that Mr Edwards had told Mrs Edwards — we couldn't do that ourselves because she and Mrs Worthington were touring in Asia and Europe en route to London. Mr Edwards did not receive a written invitation, but nor did any of the other people who attended. They were all family, or near enough. Our verbal invitation was enough.

Most of the Pittsburgh Triangles were playing at Wimbledon, so it was a rowdy crew that boarded the aircraft for London. Our good humour seemed contagious and the cabin crew joined in the party. Somewhere over the Atlantic, however, my own good mood came crashing to the floor when Mr Edwards walked along the aisle and silently handed me a letter. I hated the formality of this approach he had, it seemed such a cowardly way to make a statement. But I hated even more the contents of this letter. He would not be coming to the wedding, he wrote, because he did not approve of what I was doing with my life, did not approve of my choice of husband. I carefully folded it, wiped a tear or two from it and put it in my bag for safekeeping. I have it to this day, and in the light of what was to come, I have had reasons to be glad that I didn't screw it up and throw it away. In 1975 that note became my own private reassurance that I was right and others were wrong — that this odd and famous relationship between a tennis player and her coach had truly reached rock bottom.

Chapter 21

$\mathcal{T}$HE TWA FLIGHT BEARING the Pittsburgh Triangles arrived at Heathrow shortly after 8 a.m. on 16 June. Roger was waiting in the terminal to tell Mr Edwards of the arrangements he had made for the Edwards party, and to whisk me up to Canterbury to post the bans before midday.

But when I walked into the gate lounge he realised immediately that something was wrong. I told him straight away, 'Mr Edwards isn't coming to the wedding.' I had barely got this information out when Mr Edwards and Gere Kitch strode out of the plane and past Roger without speaking. Roger looked at me and shrugged. I think we both felt: enough of the melodrama! This is our life together — let's start it!

The Triangles' baggage was all in together, but we had no time to waste with formalities. Roger hauled my suitcase off the carousel and we escaped for Canterbury without a word to Mr Edwards or anyone else. We dispensed with the necessary formalities and drove straight back to Eastbourne in time for me to play the American Pam Teeguarden in the opening round.

Pam was a tall, friendly girl who had a splendid serve and volley game on her day. She had knocked me out of the US Open in the first round and, like Betty Stove, Kerry Melville Reid and a few others, was quite capable of upsetting the applecart of promoters' expectations when the mood took her. I don't think I do a disservice to Pam, however, when I say that in the first round at Eastbourne that year, she was presented with me on a platter. I was frazzled, exhausted and thinking about becoming Mrs Roger Cawley when she bundled me out in two snappy sets.

Over the next two days Roger made several attempts to contact Mr Edwards to tell him of the hotel arrangements he had made in Canterbury, believing that once Mrs Edwards had flown in from Sydney he would reconsider and they would come to the wedding. Eventually, we both decided to leave it in the lap of the gods. We had done what we could.

The wedding at the Registry Office in Canterbury was performed by the superintendent registrar, Mr Geoffrey Skinner, and witnessed by Roger's parents, Donald and Olga, his brother Nigel, John and Wendy Paish, Peggy Michel

Canterbury, 1975. Signing a contract that is still going strong

and Roger's best man, Roger Mackenzie, a long-haired musician who later became a professor. When we walked up the corridor past the office of the registrar of births and deaths and emerged on the pavement as husband and wife, the first of the Fleet Street photographers was there to meet us. We fobbed him off and got in the cars and drove to Roger's parents' home in St Augustine's Road, where the photographers lay in wait already.

We had a small, impromptu press conference in the garden of the Cawley house and, inevitably, I was asked why Mr Edwards wasn't present. I explained that he had been invited but had chosen not to come, then thought nothing more of it as we went indoors for a simple and lovely wedding breakfast. In fact the wedding breakfast went longer than intended, and as I sipped my third champagne I suggested to Peggy Michel that perhaps we had better think twice about playing doubles that afternoon. On Roger's suggestion I phoned the tournament referee Bea Walters and asked for the match to be rescheduled.

She said, 'Oh, I don't think we can do that.'

'But I've just been married.'

'Oooh, Evonne! Have you really? How exciting. I'm sure we can organise something.'

With matron of honour Peggy Michel and best man Roger (Murgatroyd) Mackenzie

By late afternoon the press contingent had grown outside the house and the nature of the enquiries at the front door had changed. They no longer wanted to know if Evonne Goolagong had been married; they wanted to know if Vic Edwards had been slighted. The story was a nonsense and we said as much, little realising the newspaper headlines which were at that moment being set in metal on Fleet Street.

Roger, who obviously had no intention of letting me play doubles that afternoon, had made a booking at a hotel in Canterbury, but with the press hot on our tail, we decided against going there. My new in-laws made a couple of calls and it was arranged that we would be billeted for the night at the home of Roger's aunt and uncle in a village in Sussex on the way to Eastbourne. Evading the press, we drove to the village and watched ourselves on the television news before sharing a quiet dinner with Aunt Nina and Uncle Alec. It had been a long day and we were exhausted, but Uncle Alec was a gracious and enthusiastic host and kept refilling the wine glasses while he told interminable stories. Amusing as they were, we were so tired that we started to feel a bit desperate. Luckily, Aunt Nina rescued us, saying, 'Oh do shut up, you silly old fart!'

The next morning the postponed doubles match was scheduled for early afternoon, so we got up and set off for Eastbourne, but we had barely gone a block when a newspaper poster drew our attention. It said: 'EVONNE WEDDING ROW: I'm shocked and hurt says manager'.

Wimbledon was a few days away, and any controversy Fleet Street could beat up about a tennis player was good value, but this was a deep and hurtful shock. We stopped to buy the papers and pored over them as we sipped coffee in the car. The reports were so wrong, so unfair. Said the *Daily Mail*:

> To the Wimbledon set, it was the surprise of the year — for the couple had said they planned to wed in Sydney next January. For Vic Edwards, the man who has moulded the 23-year-old aboriginal girl into a star, it was the shock of his life. An hour after hearing of the registry office ceremony, he spoke in a faltering voice at his luxury rented flat in Victoria: 'I'm shocked and hurt. The last time I saw Evonne was when we flew into London from New York on Tuesday morning. Roger Cawley was waiting for her at the airport. My wife will be flabbergasted. Only two weeks ago Evonne told us she would marry in January, and we were planning a big wedding at St Mary's Cathedral in Sydney … I wasn't invited to the wedding. My wife and I tried desperately all yesterday to contact Evonne, without success …'

Mr Edwards had told a somewhat different story to the *Mirror*, which reported, 'Mr Edwards had opposed her wedding plans and turned down an invitation last week. Then on Wednesday he changed his mind. Mr Edwards, 65, said, "I didn't know where the wedding was going to be. I tried hard to find out. Evonne should have phoned me. I feel very hurt." '

We sat in the car for a long time, considering our next move. For me, it was a very delicate situation. I had in my bag the evidence to refute Mr Edwards' claim, which was in essence that I was an ungrateful ward, an Eliza Doolittle who had turned on her Henry Higgins in his dotage. But whose ends would I serve by drawing out the manufactured controversy which now surrounded my happy day?

'EVONNE WEDDING ROW: NEW EVIDENCE! Coach lied, says tennis star.'

The Fleet Street tabloids would be beside themselves, Mr Edwards would bluster his way through, but what of Mrs Edwards? She was the one whose feelings I kept returning to as I played through the consequences of my next step. Mr Edwards would have to live with his conscience, but Mrs Edwards

— what must she think of me? Would continuing the public row do anything to help overcome the enormous rift that her husband's deceit about the wedding invitation had created between us? I thought not, and yet I also knew that I could not confront her with the truth behind her husband's actions. My one hope, perhaps forlorn, was that Mr Edwards had told her the truth himself, and that in time she would come to me.

In the meantime, however, we resolved to stop feeding the scavengers. If asked, we would simply say that Mr Edwards had been invited and had chosen not to attend. The strategy was to make it so boring that the press would move on. We didn't want to be this year's Chris-and-Jimmy story and become constant fodder for the tabloids.

When Peggy and I came on to the court for our postponed doubles match, there was a wonderful round of applause from the crowd. 'Good luck, Evonne!' some people cried out. It was reassuring to know that the entire British public didn't see me as an ungrateful upstart.

As the wedding invitation story began to grow whiskers, the press turned its unflagging attention to another aspect of my marriage — would it affect my Wimbledon form? The answer was, of course, yes, no and maybe, and everyone from tennis experts to marriage guidance counsellors came out of the woodwork to comment. Typical of the informed comments was that of Henry Raven in the *Daily Telegraph*, 'And the just-married Evonne Cawley could do anything or nothing.' Or Ken Montgomery in the *Sunday Mirror*: 'Honeymooners don't win Wimbledon.'

I suppose there was some truth in this, in that my mind was far from the job, and traditionally this was when I had played my worst tennis. But the fact was that, inexplicably, I was suddenly playing at my very best. Pam Teeguarden had dispatched me from the Eastbourne singles, but in the doubles there Peggy and I were on fire until Olga Morozova and Julie Anthony got the better of us in the final.

There was no direct contact between the Cawleys and the Edwards as the Wimbledon tournament began, although our mutual friend Bob Howe from Dunlop relayed a few messages regarding tickets and other playing arrangements. It was a curious situation for the fourth-seeded player and her coach, and evidently Mr Edwards felt the strangeness so intensely that he felt compelled to invent some more fiction. After I'd beaten Helen Gourlay in the first round he told the press that I had phoned him and asked him to be at courtside. He was quoted as saying, 'When she rang me at last I said if she wanted me there, I would be there.' I made no such call, but now the 'reconciliation' story was up and running. The *Sunday Telegraph* even had me waving and calling out from the Centre Court balcony as Mr Edwards passed below. 'Edwards caught her eye and there wasn't a dry eye in the house.' This didn't happen either.

As I progressed through the rounds media interest in me intensified. We tried hiding out in the IMG tent, but that did not last long as a safe house. From the quarter finals on, we sat in our rented car in the car park across the road, listening to the tennis on the radio until it was time to go and play. I changed into my tennis clothes at the flat, and returned there straight after my matches.

It was a very odd Wimbledon, but nothing much mattered to Roger and me. We sat at home laughing about the whole ridiculous business, and by day I went out and won. Every victory was a bonus to me, because I really didn't expect to do well. Nor did anyone else, so my performances intensified the focus on the women's singles. Chris Evert was considered hot favourite, but she was under pressure from Billie Jean who was back in top form after a long lean spell, Virginia Wade, the home girl who was excelling herself, and the exciting young Martina Navratilova. Margaret Court and I were 'roughies' (at seven to one and nine to one respectively).

The complexion of the tournament changed, however, after Virginia and I fought out a two-hour quarter final which I eventually won despite being two points from defeat on two occasions. Within those two hours I probably played some of my best and worst tennis, and it suddenly became apparent to the tennis watchers that, if luck stayed with me, I might just win this Wimbledon. The quarter final also provided photographers with an irresistible opportunity to pass further comment on the Edwards/Cawley soap opera. They seized on the fact that Roger was sitting alone at one end of the players' box while Mr and Mrs Edwards sat at the other. I suppose the photo had its funny side, but the fact was that Roger sat alone because we gave five of my six tickets to Bob Howe to pass on to the Edwards party.

So now we were down to the big four — Chris or me into the final against the Old Lady or the other Old Lady, Billie Jean or Margaret. It is always easy to predict with hindsight, of course, but a serious analyst of the game, the players and our temperaments should have been able to predict the winner from that foursome. Billie Jean had the most to win and the least to lose in the twilight of her career. The rest of us were carrying burdens — mine was the emotional baggage of my wedding and the feud with Mr Edwards; Margaret's was recent injury and, as a 33-year-old mother, indecision about her future; and Chris was carrying the albatross each member of that quartet knew well enough — the Wimbledon title.

Margaret and I played a fast, hard-fought semifinal in which motherhood and the 10-year age difference paid a toll. And after a disastrous first set Billie Jean gathered herself to beat Chris and make it into what she swore would be her last Wimbledon final. In fact neither of us could believe our luck to be playing the final. Billie Jean said, 'I can't believe I'm still in the tournament. I still feel like I lost. I can't believe I went to the edge of the ledge and didn't go over.'

I told the press, 'This is a great honeymoon, and I'm enjoying it more every minute.'

But not for much longer. The Wimbledon women's final of 1975 was over in just 39 minutes. Billie Jean whipped me 6–0, 6–1 in the most comprehensive final victory since Doris Hart had the same scoreline over Shirley Fry in 1951. It was 4–0 in the second set before I even got on the board! You could almost hear the crowd groaning; in fact, it would have eased the tension of that eerie silence if I had heard a low moan or two. It was disappointing, almost embarrassing, but I didn't waste any tears over it. I had given the crowd plenty of value during the fortnight of the tournament and I had a bad day and finished second. Why feel bad about that?

Well, the press wanted an answer to the Evonne mystery. They demanded to know what happened 'the day the bride dropped dead'.

Of course Mr Edwards had the answer. 'I put this defeat down entirely to lack of proper preparation. This is the first important final she has played where we have not got together to thrash out a plan beforehand. She has said since her marriage a couple of weeks ago that she wanted to stand on her own feet and go it alone, but it should not have been like this.' But my preparation had seemed to be in order when I beat Virginia, and then Margaret, and as for pre-match planning, the only time we had ever discussed tactics was when we devised a plan to attack Chris Evert's backhand on grass. But Roger and I had had enough of his public slanging and kept our own counsel.

Before we left Wimbledon we met briefly with Bud Stanner in the IMG tent. Roger told him: 'We've come to the end of the road with Vic. Will you come to Pittsburgh and help us work it out?' Bud said he would fly straight there from London. The Edwards and the Cawleys went to Heathrow independently, checked in on the same flight, then cooled our heels at different ends of the terminal for more than an hour because of a bomb scare. Eventually we boarded the aircraft and sat two rows apart without speaking a word or even sharing a glance. It was an absurd state of affairs, and a sad one for Mrs Edwards, who still had no inkling of what was going on, other than my 'betrayal' of her love and affection.

Quite apart from the ongoing drama of my impending split with Mr Edwards, we had other problems to resolve, now that the rosy glow of the 'honeymoon' was beginning to fade. For one thing, since we had decided to marry in February, Roger had poured all his savings and available cash into purchasing a larger share of the fledgling business enterprise which he and his partners had built on copper contracts, but which now also embraced a number of lucrative investments. Our intention then had been that we would marry in Sydney and settle there, and that I would give up tennis, after my Pittsburgh Triangles contract was up in 1976, to stay home and raise babies. Now I wasn't so sure. I felt I had played near my best at Wimbledon and had plenty of tournament victories left in me. I suppose I also had something to prove to myself — that my early round wins at Wimbledon hadn't been flukes, that I didn't need Mr Edwards propping me up anymore.

We now weren't sure what our long-term plan would be, but in the meantime we had to be together, and that meant Pittsburgh, so Roger hurriedly organised leave of absence from his company.

Back in Pittsburgh on Monday, 7 July we met with Bud Stanner and Mr Edwards at the Racquet Club Apartments in Monroeville. The purpose of the meeting was to end our association with Mr Edwards as painlessly as possible. This was not as easy as one might imagine. We were both contracted to the Pittsburgh Triangles, he was contracted to me until 30 June 1976 (although I was not fully aware of the ramifications of this rather suspect retrospective arrangement), I was contracted to Bud Stanner's IMG; and Roger and I were contracted to each other through marriage.

We met one floor below my apartment in the unit Mr Edwards kept as his office. Bud Stanner was already there and the mood in the room was decidedly sombre, which was unusual from Bud's point of view. Roger and I had made up our minds at Wimbledon so there was no need for debate. Roger briefly outlined our objections to Mr Edwards' behaviour in London and then put our case for terminating the relationship, while Bud nodded and said nothing. When Mr Edwards finally spoke he simply said, 'Yes, that's what I want, too.' Then he looked to me. 'Is this what you want, Evonne?'

I said, 'Yes, I think it's time we went our separate ways.'

Mr Edwards lit a cigarette and blew a cloud of smoke towards the window. He said, 'You don't owe me anything, pet.' Perhaps if we'd parted a few months earlier, this would have been the signal for a tearful embrace, but there had been too much bitterness for that now.

There was a long silence before Bud Stanner said, 'Well, Vic, I guess we better put some paperwork together on this.'

Mr Edwards nodded; then, as we made ready to leave, he said to me, 'Would you go and talk to Mrs Edwards?' I said I would.

Back in Apartment 411 Bud Stanner drafted a letter for me:

Dear Mr Edwards

The purpose of this letter is to confirm the discussions we had in Pittsburgh on July 7 regarding the cessation of your services as my personal manager and coach. I wish to be totally on my own and I will work directly with International Merchandising Corporation (a division of IMG) on the handling of my professional affairs.

I trust that you will hand over all books, records, accounts, memoranda, letters and other documents to me or my authorised representative in an expeditious manner and that I can count on your usual good organisation to accomplish this.

Finally, I wish to express my sincere thanks for all the help both you and your family have given me over the years.

Very truly yours

Evonne Goolagong Cawley

It seemed such a cold way to end not only one of the great partnerships of sport, but a chapter of my life which had transformed everything about me, for better or worse. I was not the same person who had first come to Mr Edwards' house — 'We don't have to pay to go over our bridge at Barellan' — all those years before, and it was not just the passage of time that had made the difference. Because of the Edwards family I spoke differently, I dressed differently, I thought differently and I felt differently. There was now no alternative to the action I was taking, but that didn't make it any easier.

During his time with the Pittsburgh Triangles Mr Edwards kept up his regular monthly newsletters for VAETS staff and friends around the globe. The edition he sent out at the end of July made no mention of the fact that we had parted company, although he did concede, 'There have been many ups and downs, arguments, misunderstandings and upsets over the period of this Bulletin ... although I'm quite sure I am becoming a mental case, I am quite well physically and enjoy the challenge of WTT ...' In the August newsletter, however, he reported, 'In spite of success, it has been a very sad year for me in so many ways, but mainly in the fact that the person I raised from obscurity to world fame over a period of 14 years has now given me notice in writing of my cessation of services as her personal manager and coach, and therefore of course as her foster father and a complete break from the Edwards family and the staff of VAETS. We, the Edwards family bear no animosity towards her and wish her success and trust her decision to break from us will not bring her any unhappiness.'

I had seen Mrs Edwards at close quarters only once since our return to Pittsburgh, in the apartment lift. Other players and Mrs Barbara Worthington (Mr Edwards' secretary at VAETS) had been present, and the embarrassment had been acute. We each studiously avoided the other for the long, long seconds it took to reach the ground floor.

Now Roger and I set off to talk to her, a conversation we both knew was going to be hurtful. Mrs Worthington let us into the apartment and we sat down in the lounge room with Mrs Edwards, who'd obviously been crying. She said, 'Oh, Roger, how on earth can this have happened?' The fact that she addressed the question to Roger indicated that she believed she already knew who the culprit was.

A man alone. Mr Edwards in Pittsburgh

Roger replied, 'It didn't happen. I don't know what Mr Edwards has been telling you, but the fact is you were both invited to the wedding and he chose not to go. Evonne would like you to read this.' He handed her the letter Mr Edwards had given me on the plane. She read it carefully, folded it and handed it back to Roger. I could see she was struggling to retain her composure, but when the words came they were strong and quite forceful.

She said, 'I don't care. No matter what happens I will stand behind my husband.'

It struck me then that perhaps Mrs Edwards knew a lot more about her husband than we had given her credit for. Perhaps Gere Kitch was not the first woman to come between them, and perhaps she had developed a mechanism for dealing with his adultery. For years to come it was as if she had never seen that letter, unmistakably written in Mr Edwards' hand, unmistakably proving him to be a liar. She simply blotted it out and never even mentioned it to her daughters, my sisters, who for years were to loathe me for my supposed betrayal. During Wimbledon, in fact, I had received a long letter from Jenifer, formally ending our friendship and explaining why she believed me to be ungrateful and uncaring towards her family. This hurt me terribly, but I knew there was now nothing I could do to make things right between me and the Edwards. That initiative would have to come from their side.

Chapter 22

ALTHOUGH HE WAS NO LONGER my personal manager or coach, Mr Edwards remained part of my life as coach of the Pittsburgh Triangles. It was an extremely difficult situation for both of us, but we were under contract and had no alternative but to learn to live with it, not just for our sakes but for the sake of the team.

Mrs Edwards flew back to Australia and Mr Edwards and Gere Kitch resumed their affair, one which was by now common knowledge and the source of considerable mirth not just to the Triangles but to all of World Team Tennis. The question, 'Are they really on together?' was one I was asked wherever we played. I usually answered with a shrug.

Gere Kitch's role at the Triangles had become an increasingly controversial one, with almost all of the players in conflict with her. I had as little to do with her as possible. One August night in Boston we played the Lobsters during a heatwave. I managed to play the match in appalling heat, but I had an uneasy night at our hotel in Hartford, Connecticut, and woke up with severe stomach cramps. I was in agony so my room-mate Peggy Michel phoned Mr Edwards. He decided I should go to hospital and sent Gere in the ambulance with me. Gere's company did little to help my condition and I was greatly relieved to reach the hospital where we were parted. My cramps had been brought on by exhaustion and lack of fluids, so I sat out the evening's match against the Indiana Loves, but not with Gere.

Sometimes during our WTT matches Gere would sit behind Mr Edwards at courtside and refill his cup with scotch from a coffee flask. The team could laugh about this, but they were not so amused by the notes that Gere would leave under their doors almost every day, reminding them of promotional obligations.

One day Vitas Gerulaitis told Gere he would not be available for a practice session because he had a prior arrangement to conduct a clinic with his street kids, the 'G-Men'. Time off for such community duties had been negotiated in his contract with Frank Fuhrer. When he returned that evening he learned that he had been fined for his non-attendance. He stormed into Mr Edwards' office and accused Gere of not passing the message along. Fired up, he added, 'I'm not even gonna talk to you any more, Vic. I'll deal direct with Fuhrer if you can't keep your broad under control!'

He turned to walk out and felt Vic's ever-present scotch glass whizz past his ear. He guessed Mr Edwards hadn't thrown it.

Other players were also feeling the tensions. Kim Warwick, playing his first season with the Triangles, was constantly at loggerheads with Mr Edwards. After one particularly unhappy match Mr Edwards wrote in the VAETS Bulletin, '... When I told Kim that I wanted every game he was belligerent ... I spoke to him strongly and told him it was an order from me to win every game ...'

Mr Edwards completely ignored Roger's presence through all of this, even though Roger had actually started to train with the team in order to fight off his boredom and to get fit for practice sessions with me. Roger and Vitas would run together and occasionally hit balls. On the rare occasions he travelled to away games with me, he booked his own flights. As far as Mr Edwards and Gere were concerned, Roger simply didn't exist, although clearly his infrequent attendances at our practice sessions really irritated Mr Edwards. He wrote in the Bulletin, 'The worst part of the practice was the number of people around the court area ... some staff of Triangles, some hangers-on ... Players and myself were working our insides out for two hours in preparation for the match whilst others are sitting around doing nothing, laughing and talking loudly ...'

Fortunately for the Triangles management, team morale actually improved because of this united front against the coach and his assistant, and we finished the season as league champions. But it was obvious to all that Mr Edwards would not be reappointed for the 1976 season. In September Frank Fuhrer announced that Mr Edwards was leaving the Triangles. He said, 'It's impossible to bring him back and retain harmony in the team ... Many things happened during the season, both with the players and myself, that I just don't want to happen again.' Mr Edwards told the press he had accepted an offer to coach with the New Zealand Lawn Tennis Association and would be leaving America as soon as possible. But in fact he did not sever connections with America or Pittsburgh. He entered into an arrangement with the help of Gere Kitch's father to start a series of VAETS-style coaching schools in Pennsylvania.

Roger and I moved on in September to New York for the US Open with a great deal of relief and filled with optimism for the future. We were finally free of the constrictions which had plagued our relationship for five years. And it was becoming clear to us both that I wanted my future, at least for a while, to continue in tennis. This meant we had to redefine Roger's role. We had not married in order to be apart, so Roger would travel with me, putting his own business interests temporarily in the hands of his partner. He felt he could readily adapt to the tennis world, given his love for me, the sport and his interest in business. As he knew instinctively that my love of tennis would return, he wanted me to have the opportunity to be a champion, to be the best again — but this time on my own terms. We decided that my business interests were best served by maintaining my relationship with IMG, who were growing ever more powerful within pro tennis, and I no longer needed a coach. As my three-year contract with IMG was up for renewal, he met with Bud Stanner in New York and thrashed out a loose partnership arrangement through which they would bring deals to us, and us to them. Following my successful association with the Ginori clothing company, I had done a deal with a company called Tennis Love, but our real interest was in bringing out a specific 'Goolagong' signature line, and to that end Bud Stanner had opened negotiations with Cole of California.

On the other front, Roger set about getting fit and bringing his tennis back up to a level where he could test me out on the court. Soon Roger was fighting fit, and our practice sessions started to really work. For us, working together as a practice team was largely a matter of convenience, but it started a trend. When your practice partner can hit the ball back at you with more power than any woman on the tour, you gain in confidence. When your practice partner doesn't need the practice himself, all the benefit from the session is yours. Soon other women were practising with men, and today there are very few of the top women who don't have male practice partners.

The US Open was played that year for the first time on clay, which made Chris Evert and Jimmy Connors the firm favourites. In Chris's case the favouritism was justified — she beat me in three tough sets to retain the title — but Jimmy was knocked off his perch by the Spanish clay-court specialist Manuel Orantes.

In keeping with the topsy-turvy nature of our wedding plans, we honeymooned briefly in Honolulu and Fiji on the way to Australia for our second wedding. We were determined to fulfil all of the playing engagements on Mr Edwards' 1975 schedule, which meant there would be no time after the wedding, but doing things in the reverse order turned out to be advantageous anyway. We arrived in Sydney unannounced in October and managed to give the media the slip. Barellan was waiting to start the festivities, but first we had a little business to attend to.

Mrs Edwards had bundled up all my belongings when she returned from

Perfect Match

America and sent them to my Hilton Head Island address, but there was still the matter of all the papers relating to my business affairs. As IMG at this stage had no Australian office, Roger had to find a reputable solicitor to act for us. He found Paul Gregory, of Abbott Tout, who has guided us through the minefields of Australian business ever since. Paul arranged for an IMG accountant to fly in from Cleveland and together they sat in the office of VAETS in Roseville and sorted out my business life.

I had some business of my own to attend to. We rented a station wagon and bought the fanciest electric cooking range we could find in Sydney and began the drive to Barellan for what promised to be the biggest party since I brought the Wimbledon trophy home in 1971. The 'wedding' ceremony was to be a church blessing, followed by an open-house party which had been

'You're not flash are you?' Mum meets my husband, 1975

announced over the radio for days. In fact as we drove through one of the towns on the way, the local station announcer mentioned that the wedding was on, that everyone was invited and that we were on our way. Furthermore, if we had left Sydney on time we would now be in their town, he said, with frightening accuracy. A driver in the next lane looked over and waved excitedly. We couldn't believe it. We were home!

I'd never seen Mum so excited. The entire family had gathered to meet Roger and as the week wore on the house in Yarran Street would be ready to burst as the relations came in from all over Wiradjuri country. Linda hugged Roger and looked him up and down. He'd developed a deep tan in Fiji and Hawaii and this threw her a bit. She said, 'You're not as pale as I thought you'd be, for an English feller.' Then she studied the cut of his trendy flaired trousers. 'You're not flash, are you?'

Roger said he was definitely not flash, and there was a sigh of relief throughout the camp. We showed Mum the new range. 'A stove! Oh, Evie, my love! Aren't you wonderful. But there's nothing wrong with the old one!' This was true, but you didn't have to load up the new one with wood, so Mum accepted it with good grace.

The next rituals to be observed were the male drinking rites. Larry and Kevin took Roger to the Commercial Hotel to see if he was all right. They ordered middies (10-ounce/284 millilitre glasses) of beer. Roger said, 'That's a funny little glass. I usually drink pints.' Larry and Kevin exchanged knowing glances. They had a live one here! Several middies later the boys conceded that Roger could drink, even if he did talk strangely. Yes, he was all right.

Mully became Roger's shadow, trailing him everywhere he went. But he was a mischievous shadow. The boys had quickly worked out that Roger was not a country boy, even though he'd spent much of his boyhood in a village in Wales. Bugs and spiders horrified him, whereas they fascinated Mully and Ian. Roger had to check his shoes, his sheets, even the pockets of his trousers. He pretended (pretended?) to be terrified, which made Mully's day.

Underlying these normal family rites of acceptance was something that Roger had never really stopped to consider in relation to his love for me. Although he knew I was an Aborigine he didn't really know what an Aborigine was. In those early days I was frequently described as 'part-Aboriginal', just as an Englishman might be described as 'part-Irish'. Roger recalls now that it added a little touch of the exotic, but that he never really stopped to think about any racial or cultural difference between us. In one of their heated exchanges Mr Edwards had told Roger it would take a lifetime to understand the Aboriginal way of looking at life. It was not until the extended family gathered in Barellan for the wedding, that Roger began to realise what it was to be Aboriginal. Roger now says, 'I found it heartwarming and quite moving. These people had a greater sense of family than any I had known. They gave of themselves entirely, and expected no less in return. I thought of what the reaction might be in my family if some distant cousins arrived and set up camp for a week in the living room, and I realised I had much to learn from Evonne's people.'

Saturday, 11 October was the big day and by Friday night there were more than 30 people camped on the floor in our place. There was no privacy and you couldn't hear yourself think. The atmosphere was electric all over town, despite the persistent showers. We had no idea how many people would actually turn up for the wedding reception in the School of Arts and were worried about the catering, but the women of the town told us they'd organise everything. We couldn't pay for drinks either. Both the War Memorial Club and the Commercial Hotel put on kegs of beer. We were allowed to pay for the band, who came over from Griffith and got to play a few songs before Larry and our Uncle Georgie took over their instruments to belt out country rockers all night.

The crowd filled all the pews in the little St Clements Anglican Church and overflowed out onto the lawns, where people waited patiently in the light drizzle. Fortunately the rain stopped before we arrived from our changing rooms at the Commercial Hotel. There were photographers everywhere, and a bevy of reporters wanted us to stop and talk. We answered their questions and posed for photos with Linda, who looked absolutely beautiful in blue. Then the press, who seemed happy to join in the spirit of the occasion, left us alone while the Reverend Donald Hoore blessed our marriage vows.

'I do' again. Barellan, October 1975

The Rev. Hoore had a loud and tuneless singing voice, and I began laughing during one hymn. Seeing my head and shoulders shaking involuntarily, Mum began to cry with me (she thought), and could not be placated until the groom had kissed the bride.

The reception was a typical Barellan affair, a wonderfully joyous and chaotic occasion. The townspeople presented us with a silver service and Clarrie Irvin made an emotional speech. My one great regret was that Kenny Goolagong could not be there. When I allowed myself to think of him — and that was every time I looked at Uncle Lylie, his image — I saw him smartly dressed and beaming with pride, and had to fight back the tears.

The singing and dancing went on until dawn, but we crept away somewhat sooner, emotionally drained. There was little chance of sleep, however. The relations were partying on in every other room in the house. At one point Roger was jolted out of his half-sleep when the twanging of guitars gave way to a more tribal vocal drone, as the men, a little worse for wear, embarked on a mock coroboree to amuse me and impress the Englishman.

'That's wonderful!' he cried. 'Is that your Aboriginal language? Do they know the words they're singing?'

'They wouldn't have a clue,' I told him.

From Sydney we flew to Hilton Head Island for the World Invitational Tennis Classic in October, then on to Europe for a round of indoor tournaments that had been scheduled by Mr Edwards earlier in the year. The tournaments themselves were not important, but the tour presented an opportunity for Roger and me to work out our husband and wife act on the road. Basically this involved creating a routine and sticking to it. We ate steak and salad every day — maybe mixed with a little pasta in Europe — trained hard, and, still on our honeymoon, stayed away from other tennis players.

By the time we returned to Australia in early December for the summer season, we had become a lean, mean tennis machine. We were now about to embark upon a schedule of our making, not Mr Edwards'. And that made all the difference. I felt renewed, free at last.

But it had to be fun, and that was the beauty of working with Roger. There was no pressure to perform, no lectures if I lost. Tennis had become a game to me again, and the high standard of my playing showed that I was enjoying my work.

For his part, Roger was enjoying the freedom of the touring lifestyle and the fun of making up the rules as we went along. By now women's tennis was lucrative enough to enable the top players to pick and choose both tournaments and business offers, and there were plenty of both.

Promotion trip on Sydney Harbour, December 1975

I successfully defended my NSW Open title at White City in January, then took my third Australian Open title in a row, defeating Czech player Renata Tomonova in the final in a scorching Melbourne heatwave. It was a good way to start 1976, and we celebrated by taking Mum and the family — who had come down from Barellan to watch — out to dinner. But I didn't get out of finals day without at least one press attempt to rekindle the Vic Edwards story. Mr Edwards was at Kooyong and he did come over and congratulate me after the final. I thanked him and moved on. The encounter was brief and as cordial as either of us would have expected under the circumstances. I wouldn't have called it a reconciliation, but some of the papers did. Sydney's *Daily Telegraph* even went as far as to dig out a photo of Mr

Roger and his shadow (Mully) at the Australian Open, January 1976

Edwards cuddling me after my victory over Chris Evert in the Bonne Bell Cup in 1974. They published this under the headline, 'Tennis dad ends feud'.

Of course the feud wasn't over, but my anger had passed, even if Roger's hadn't. I felt sad for Mr Edwards, and even more sad for poor Mrs Edwards, but life is too short to dwell on such things, and every day I was Mrs Cawley I felt stronger, happier and determined to play the best tennis of my career.

For the past couple of years I had been ranked by the London *Daily Telegraph* number three in the world behind Chris and Billie Jean. In 1976 Billie Jean was off the tour because of injury, and that left just Chris and Martina Navratilova, who was becoming more dangerous every day. I felt confident I could get the better of them both and regain the top position I had last held in 1971. At the L'Eggs World Series in Austin in March, however, it was Chris who got the upper hand again, and it would be Chris again who would continually challenge me throughout the Virginia Slims tour.

We took a week off and visited our photographer friend John Russell in Aspen, Colorado, before the start of the Slims tour. The insurance people wouldn't let me actually ski, but I got to play in the snow and meet Jean Claude Killy. And the mountain air must have done me some good, because I went on to win in Chicago, Akron, Dallas, Boston and Philadelphia, finished second to Chris in San Francisco and Dallas, and continued through to the play-offs in Los Angeles at the top of the Slims prize money board.

I was on the hottest streak of my career and I had never felt better about my tennis. In 15 consecutive victories on the Slims tour I did not drop a set. Consistency, once my greatest enemy, was now my greatest ally. The other players on the tour couldn't believe it. 'I just can't believe how anyone can win as easily as Evonne has been winning,' Chris Evert told the *New York Times*. I couldn't believe it! But Roger could. He could see that marriage had given my life a pattern and a purpose, and that the simple truth was that I played my best tennis when I was happy.

In Los Angeles most of the Slims players checked into the Beverly Hills Hotel. Roger and I gave the hotel and its notorious Polo Lounge a wide berth and instead rented an apartment close to the airport at Marina Del Rey. Here we could practise in peace and spend the rest of the time relaxing, walking along the beach or sightseeing. Steaks and salads, a movie or two, plenty of early nights; our approach was to keep active, rather than sitting around sweating on the richest event in women's tennis.

When the tournament began at the LA Sports Arena I had only one near-hiccup in the early rounds when American Marita Redondo, a tough player who had upset promoters before in Dallas by taking me out ahead of time, almost did it again, taking the first set in 19 Slims matches from me. After that scare I had no real problems in getting past Frankie Durr and Martina Navratilova (coming back from injury and with a weight problem) to reach the final against Chris.

But Chris had a couple of problems going into this final. Her on-off relationship with Jimmy Connors was in 'off' mode, she was number two seed for the first time in ages, which wasn't doing much for her confidence ... and, hell, it was my turn!

The final was one of the best matches Chris and I ever played, each of us keeping to our own strategy to unsettle the other and making a bare minimum of errors. I had to get to the net, Chris had to pin me to the baseline. The atmosphere in the packed arena was tense and excited as I took the first set, and then Chris came back at me and grabbed the second in a tie breaker. In the decider Chris had me staggering at 3–2, but I came back with four straight games to win the title and $40,000.

The recently introduced computer rankings placed me at number one in the world, almost five years since the last time I had worn that mantle. This time I felt ready for it.

After a wonderful night celebrating — on dacquiris — we flew home to Hilton Head and Roger went straight to bed, but no sooner had I seen him safely horizontal than he let out a piercing scream. His body had seized up and he couldn't move a muscle. Terrified, I phoned Ted Robison of the Hilton Head Company, who called an ambulance immediately. Roger spent three days in hospital where the doctors conducted every test possible and fed him with numerous drips. We never did get to the bottom of his seizure, but it was sufficient deterrent to any further liquid celebrations.

While Roger was in hospital I was moved from condominium to condominium to cater for the requirements of paying guests at the resort. As flattering as it was to have a villa named after you, I realised I was not really cut out for this kind of lifestyle.

During the World Invitational series we had instructed an estate agent named Spain Kelley to look out for a home by the water for us. Now he had short-listed three homes in Port Royal Plantation, a development on which there were only private homes. We picked up Roger from the hospital and went house-hunting. I fell in love with the house in Wagener Place at first sight. It was roomy and private and looked out over a beautiful expanse of private beach. We didn't mess around. We told Spain we'd take it.

Then we flew out for Pittsburgh and World Team Tennis the next morning.

During the Slims tour we had talked to the Pittsburgh Triangles management about our dissatisfaction with some parts of the arrangement. Most of our dissatisfaction centred around Frank Fuhrer's insistence on using me for promotional work (some of it only vaguely related to the team) to the detriment of my tennis. A few new clauses were added to my 1976 contract (to release me from unnecessary promotional work) and both sides were satisfied. In addition, Roger had been offered a job as tour manager for the team for the duration of the hectic four-month season.

Yet when we got off the plane in Pittsburgh there was a car waiting to take us to a radio station for a talkback session while the rest of the team went to dinner. If this was the start of our new relationship with team management, it wasn't very promising. Things got worse over the coming weeks as I was sidelined with tendonitis and the Triangles lost five matches back to back.

Fearing for the future of his franchise, Frank Fuhrer panicked. He threw all his efforts into a disjointed campaign to attract full houses to home games and get some momentum going. The strategy made matters worse. The WTT schedule was so tight that players simply didn't have time to do Fuhrer's bidding and team morale slumped. Unable to divide his loyalties between Fuhrer and me, Roger resigned as tour manager. Soon Fuhrer was also feuding with Triangles player-coach Mark Cox and the bad blood spread right through the team.

I suppose the bottom line was that we were losing, and in WTT you had to win or the whole show collapsed. 'It's just not that much fun any more,' said Vitas Gerulaitis after another loss. 'Every time we lose we have a team meeting.'

Roger became so frustrated with the Triangles that he punched the wall in our apartment one night and put a hole in it.

Through all the dramas of the Triangles, however, I continued to enjoy my most successful year, and flew off for the Wimbledon break with season figures of 26 sets to two against, which must have given Frank Fuhrer some joy, although he was good at disguising it.

On our first appearance at Wimbledon we were taken aback by the presence of the 'Cawley Clan', a group of young tennis fans from all over Britain. The fan club and the fancy champagne flight across the Atlantic (on Concorde for the first time) underlined the significant change in my lifestyle which had occurred over the year since our marriage. We hadn't become extravagant, but we had come to realise that the touring life could be made more comfortable than that which I'd known for years. Roger was shocked that I washed my tennis clothes in the hotel bathroom after every match. 'We can afford to send those out,' he said. I supposed we could, but I'd never thought of it. I continued to do much of my own washing but we did rethink our travel arrangements. The Edwards entourage, which often stretched to four people, always flew at the back of the plane on the cheapest flights available, despite the fact that we usually had a tight itinerary. We decided that this touring tennis pro would in future stretch out to the limit of tax-deductible luxury.

The fact of the matter was that women's tennis had become highly lucrative, and now that Margaret Court and Billie Jean King were basically in retirement, Chris Evert and I were the major beneficiaries. We won the most tournaments, we had the biggest endorsement contracts, and we were the players who pulled the crowds. The Virginia Slims tour had been one of the major reasons for the explosion of interest in the women's game, but it really dated from Billie Jean's exhibition match with the veteran player Bobby Riggs at Houston Astrodome in 1973. That bizarre 'battle of the sexes' had drawn some 30,000 people — the biggest crowd ever for a tennis match — and Billie's convincing win over America's hottest player of 1939 had put women's tennis well and truly in the spotlight for the first time.

The Slims slogan, 'you've come a long way, baby', was very true by 1976, but perhaps there was still a long way to go. As the Wimbledon fortnight began, the number one seed, Chris Evert, in her capacity as president of the Women's Tennis Association, presented the Wimbledon committee with a demand for equal prize money with the men, or 40 of the top women would boycott the tournament from 1977. Seven of the top seeds, including me, joined in the boycott threat.

Chris was certainly talking tough, but the committee was not about to be bullied. Women didn't deserve equal pay, said chairman Sir Brian Burnett, because they didn't play as many sets as the men, their early round matches weren't as popular and the competition at the top level wasn't intense enough. Those of us who had battled to reach tournament finals over the years found that particular logic hard to follow, but unfortunately Sir Brian was proven correct by what happened over the next week or so.

Without Margaret or Billie Jean, there was a lack of depth at the top end of women's tennis for the first time in years. Martina Navratilova got herself into a flap over bad line calls and virtually put herself out of the championship, while Virginia Wade, coached for a win by her New York Sets team-mate Billie Jean King, received the kind of treatment from me that her coach had dished out in the 1975 final — 6–1, 6–2 in 48 minutes, and I was into the final against Chris.

Although I was favoured to beat the defending champion in heatwave conditions on Centre Court, I never once felt in the two hours of the match that I would win. All I could do in the torrid three-setter was hang on, while the partisan crowd willed me to get up and teach the Ice Maiden a lesson. (They didn't dislike Chris any less since equal pay had become an issue.) In the end Chris took the decider 8–6 and my long winning streak was over.

Back in Pittsburgh, Frank Fuhrer and the Triangles made one last noisy attempt to rescue the 1976 season. Fuhrer offered free tickets to the next home game to all those who had paid to see Pittsburgh lose. 'The Triangles are the winningest team in Pittsburgh sports history,' he bellowed, 'and I don't believe people should have to pay to see us lose.' Fuhrer dragged out local politicians, wrestling bears and even Bobby Riggs, and slowly the crowds came. At the same time, despite incredible staff turnover at management level, the Triangles started to play well again, launching the most remarkable comeback in the three-year history of the league — a comeback which almost brought us the league championship for the second year in a row, until the New York Sets beat us in the play-off.

The 'Cawley Clan' at Wimbledon, 1976

As our comeback gathered steam, Vitas Gerulaitis and I threw a huge pyjama party at the Monroeville Sheraton to celebrate his 22nd and my 25th birthday. The entire team — the entire town, for that matter — showed up and the party lasted two days, but Roger and I didn't see much past the first few hours before the exhaustion of a touring Triangle overtook me.

In September Roger and I rented an apartment at Forest Hills in New York and settled in for the US Open, with Paul Denny along as my personal physiotherapist, a role which had become increasingly necessary through the gruelling second half of the WTT season. At Forest Hills, however, the aches and pains and muscle strains were joined by a new and very different ailment. I'd been feeling a little off-colour in the mornings but put it down to nerves, then on finals day I walked on to the court feeling very strange indeed.

How I was feeling wasn't helped much by an approach as I walked from the clubhouse from a gentleman in a suit, who asked, 'Are you Evonne Goolagong Cawley?' I said I was, and made ready, not altogether happily, to sign an autograph. But he produced an envelope and handed it to me, saying, 'I am here to present you with this subpoena. Oh, and good luck!'

Roger opened it and discovered it had something to do with someone called Mott, who was suing me. I didn't understand and I had a game to play. Roger read on a bit further, then he cried, 'Unbelievable! Vic Edwards is suing us for $30,000 in unpaid fees!' He was furious, but I simply couldn't deal with it at that moment. I was feeling weird enough already.

I walked on to the court for my final against Chris and played well enough to take the first three games from her. Then something most peculiar happened. I completely lost my timing and started to see the ball as a distant blur. I remembered something that Margaret Court had once told me about a final she played against me, and the pieces suddenly fell into place.

Chris won a dozen games straight to keep the title, and I walked off the court in a daze to confront the prospect of a law suit from my old mentor, and to tell Roger we were going to have a baby.

PART 6

Supermum!

Second course, 1980

Chapter 23

_M_Y PREGNANCY HAD YET to be confirmed, of course, but from the moment I walked off the court at Forest Hills after one of the worst thrashings of my career — a defeat which would determine the top two world rankings — I was preoccupied by it, although I did not tell Roger just yet.

Firstly we had to deal with the considerable shock of being sued by Mr Edwards. Roger was furious. He had not been able to forgive Mr Edwards for his behaviour during our wedding, and for him this merely confirmed my former coach's bitter hatred of our marriage. How else, he reasoned, could you explain his action in having me served with a subpoena as I went on to play the most important match of the year? Surely a person who really still cared about me would have exercised better timing than this.

The thrust of Mr Edwards' case was that I owed him $30,000 fees for the final year of his contract — that contract he had written retrospectively in early 1975 when our relationship began to look a little shaky. He had performed no work for me during the final year and we were under the impression that he had verbally released me from the contract at our Pittsburgh meeting in July 1975. Furthermore, there was a side issue of to whom I had been contracted. The January 1975 agreement had been with Victor Allan Edwards Pty Ltd, a company partly owned by Mrs Eva Edwards. But now she and Mr Edwards had separated and he was living in America with Gere Kitch.

I said to Roger, 'If we owe it, let's pay it. But I'd rather see it go to Mrs Edwards than Gere Kitch.' We handed the matter to our lawyers and finally flew home to our new house at Hilton Head. (It stayed in the hands of the lawyers for almost two years before we were advised through his New York law firm that Mr Edwards was quietly withdrawing his action.)

The opening day of the World Invitational in October 1976 coincided with an appointment I had made at the Hilton Head Hospital to see Dr James Dickensheets for a pregnancy test. I had told Roger I suspected I was pregnant and he was absolutely delighted. We decided, however, that if the results were positive we would keep the news quiet until after the tournament.

Dr Dickensheets completed his tests, walked out of the room and came back in a few minutes later holding a pickle. He said nothing, but handed me the fetish food with a big grin on his face.

Elated, I drove to Sea Pines Racquet Club at the other end of the island to play my first round match against the young British girl, Sue Barker. Hilton Head Island is just 20 kilometres (12½ miles) from one end to the other, and you can cover that distance fairly quickly. Not as quickly, however, as the bush telegraph. When we got to Sea Pines I went to the locker room to prepare for the match while Roger walked into the clubhouse where ABC Television had set up a closed circuit television coverage. He was amazed to hear the network commentator discussing with Pancho Gonzales the possible effect my pregnancy might have on the match!

When the Invitational finished we held a brief press conference and confirmed the island's worst-kept secret. Yes, I was expecting our first child in May. Yes, we were thrilled. In fact we were more than thrilled — we were ecstatic!

Other than morning sickness my pregnancy didn't bother me in the least, and we decided to fulfil our playing commitments in Australia during the summer. We flew to Sydney in mid-November to prepare for the first tournament of the season, the Colgate International. Predictably, I suppose, the media lay in wait with a million questions about the baby. Were we hoping for a boy or a girl? Where would the baby be born? And what about a name? Roger and I had to do some snappy choosing on this one. From out of the blue I chose Coco for a boy. Roger said Corinthian. Coco Corinthian Cawley. They must have thought we were quite mad!

The Colgate was a fairly uneventful tournament in which I was bundled out of the quarter finals by my old rival, Holland's Betty Stove, which gave me pause for thought about continuing to play competitively further into my pregnancy. The heat of the noonday sun wasn't conducive to my condition and I couldn't expect to be scheduled to play in the cooler hours all the time.

It was the events off the court that made that time in Sydney memorable. On the evening before my second-round match I received a phone call at our hotel from Trisha Edwards, with whom I had not spoken since before my wedding in England in June 1975. She sounded distant and a little awkward but she managed to say, 'I thought I might come out to White City tomorrow. Maybe we could have a talk.' I told Trisha I welcomed that.

I ran into her as I went to buy coffee. She hugged and kissed me with an emotional intensity I wasn't expecting. Neither of us could speak for a while, and I remember thinking it strange that it should be Trisha — the one I felt I knew least — who should be the one to welcome me back to the bosom of the Edwards family.

Eventually she asked, 'What do you know about this Gere Kitch?' I said, 'Well, there's your main problem.' Trisha and I went back to the hotel, made ourselves coffees and talked the whole thing through. Mrs Edwards had never been able to tell Trisha and Jenifer the truth about the wedding invitation, but as their father's behaviour became more and more erratic, Trisha had begun to sense that I had perfectly good reasons for leaving Mr Edwards. Now his affair with Gere Kitch was out in the open and he was divorcing Mrs Edwards after 37 years of marriage. There had been tears and bitterness in the Edwards family about this, but the emotionalism had now subsided and they were engaged in a kind of cleansing process which involved unravelling everything about Mr Edwards' behaviour. Well, almost everything.

We were reunited with Mrs Edwards at Trisha and her husband Errol's house in Manly a couple of days later. There was generally great relief that this sad chapter in our lives was over. Now Mrs Edwards wanted to hear every minute detail of our relationship with her husband. There was no point trying to sugarcoat it. Mrs Edwards was facing a bitter property settlement debate in the courts, and needed to be fully armed.

We fled Sydney for the peace and quiet of Barellan and the joys of Linda's home-cooking, but we had only been in town for a few days when the press tracked us down. The Pittsburgh Triangles had folded after three seasons, and owner Frank Fuhrer had cited my pregnancy as one of the main reasons. It seemed a little unfair to blame the poor baby for the demise of his club and the loss of $1.4 million, but Fuhrer also had a farewell spray for Roger and Vitas Gerulaitis, both of whom had given him 'a lot of aggravation' he said. We didn't have a lot to say in reply. We had already decided my World Team Tennis days were over, and we had practically written off the $66,000 Fuhrer still owed us. Life was too short to dwell on the past, and we had a future full of nappies and bottles to get on with.

When we returned to Hilton Head early in 1977 I started to become serious about this pregnancy business. I was beginning to show a little bit, but thus far the baby was about the size and consistency of a baseball, and didn't bother me at all as I trained, rode my bike and did my regulation sit-ups and stretches. I was as fit as I'd ever been in my career and found it difficult to pace myself on the tennis court. It was my nature to run down every ball. To let the ball bounce twice was unthinkable. So, despite advice to the contrary from all quarters, I continued to play at full steam on the practice court, even though I had temporarily abandoned the tour.

We had become close friends with my obstetrician, Dr Neil Love (who operated in partnership with the equally aptly named Dr Cradle) and one day on a routine visit he said, 'Evonne, I know you're frighteningly fit, but you're overdoing it. You're dilating! Do you want to have the baby on the court? If you can't slow down, don't play tennis.' I stopped playing that day.

Since I was out of commission for a few months anyway, I decided to have my teeth capped and straightened at the same time. I must have looked a sight, padding around the house in my carpet slippers with my belly and my braces!

We had become great friends with another Hilton Head couple, Dick and Opal Duke, who were both members of the Hilton Head Racquet Club. Dick was looking for a business opportunity on the island and we decided to form a partnership to buy the Racquet Club. It was an exciting prospect and we tossed around plans for expanding and improving the place, which we would rename 'Goolagongs'.

On the day the purchase was approved, however, Roger had other things on his mind. Because the baby was upside down in the womb, Dr Love had decided to deliver it by Caesarian section on 12 May, and we had managed to talk Linda into coming to Hilton Head to be with us at the birth. As this was her first trip outside Australia and she was bringing my youngest brother Mully with her, Roger decided to fly to Australia to escort them. He worked out that it was theoretically possible to do the entire round trip in just over 48 hours, and this was his intention. But he obviously didn't know my mum.

Linda was in a total flap. Not only had she never flown before and was terrified at the prospect, but she'd had incredible difficulties obtaining her passport because, like so many Aboriginal people of her age group, she'd been delivered by an Aboriginal midwife and thus had no birth certificate.

Although she had pills from her doctor to calm her down, Roger decided against flying her back to Sydney in the small plane from Narrandera in inclement weather. He rented a car and drove non-stop to Sydney Airport, Mully wide-eyed and silent in the back. There they boarded a plane for the United States. By the time she arrived at Hilton Head, Linda was a veteran flier. 'Do you know,' she said, 'we saw the sun come up three times.' Mully just grinned — at everybody and everything.

America was far beyond Linda's comprehension. There were things here that she didn't know and didn't trust. Like all the press-button gadgets on our Cadillac, for example. Or Roger's remote-control garage-door opener. The first time he used it in her company, Linda said, 'Isn't that nice! Someone saw us coming.' I had been conditioned to the world beyond Barellan since

I was 11 years old, and sometimes it still even amazed me. But Mum, at 47, knew virtually nothing of the outside world. Cocooned by her illiteracy, she responded to the simplest things with awe and wonder, and in those last weeks of my pregnancy, nothing gave me more pleasure than having her with me, bringing my two worlds together.

One of the strangest aspects of those final weeks — and Linda was dumbfounded by this! — was the heated competition for rights to the first baby picture. It had never occurred to us that the birth of our first child might create a media circus, but as 12 May loomed, several major news organisations became involved in a bidding war. When a local Hilton Head photographer was offered $10,000 by an Australian magazine group to burst into our property and take a shot of the baby, we decided to head them off at the pass. Roger phoned John Russell in Aspen and asked him to fly down to take the photos and sell them to whomever he chose.

Hilton Head was a great place to have a heart attack, but not such a great place to have a baby. Because of the numbers and influence of the wealthy retirees, the Hilton Head hospital was brilliantly equipped to handle any sort of treatment required by people over 50, but its obstetrics facilities were non-existent. So for our first child we had to travel 45 minutes to Beaufort on the mainland. This old Southern town seemed a funny place for an Aboriginal woman to give birth to a child who would become an Australian citizen, but the staff at Memorial Hospital made me feel at home, clearing a space in the public ward and curtaining it off for my privacy.

Just before 9 a.m. on 12 May 1977 Neil Love performed a 25-minute Caesarian and Kelly Inala Cawley came peacefully into the world, weighing 3.3 kilograms (seven pounds five ounces) and dark-haired and beautiful. Kelly had been Mrs Edwards' choice for a girl's name and we were happy to oblige. Inala was our choice, an Aboriginal word meaning 'peace' or 'peaceful place'.

Soon after I had taken Kelly home to Port Royal Plantation, Mrs Edwards flew in from Sydney to be with us and we began to make plans for a holiday trip to Wimbledon. This was to be a real holiday, a couple of weeks of rambling through England with all the people who had been near and dear to us, culminating in the Wimbledon centenary celebrations at which all the previous winners still living were to be presented to the Queen. We planned to take my two Mums, Mully and Kelly, Keren Fergus, a young New Zealand girl we had employed as a nanny, and our friends from the Racquet Club, Ted and Kathy Robison. In England we planned to join up with Trisha and her husband Errol, who were flying in from Sydney, and Roger's parents. In all there would be 12 or 14 for dinner each night.

Proud parents with Kelly, Hilton Head, 1977

Grandma. Linda on Hilton Head, 1977

For this big 'thank you' trip, we used London as our home base and every day we went out sightseeing or shopping. Mrs Edwards and Linda found energy they never knew they had.

I went with them one day to buy Mum a handbag. We found ourselves in the designer shops of Beauchamp Place and Linda was approached by a shop assistant in tails as she examined yet another bag and put it back. 'May I help madam?' he said.

'Yeah,' said Linda, 'Where are your cheap bags?'

'Madam,' he replied, 'we don't *have* any cheap bags.'

Mum and I fell out of the shop giggling.

One day we took everyone to Paris, flying over on the morning shuttle and racing around the city on the Metro like true Parisians. There wasn't a famous landmark we didn't see, and in the late afternoon we visited Montparnasse, where Linda insisted on having her portrait done by a street artist. She cherished that picture as long as she lived. Exhausted, we caught the last plane back to London. On our return we discovered we'd missed the Borg–Gerulaitis semifinal, held by many to be one of the best tennis matches of the 1970s. But there were no regrets in our camp. I think we'd had the better day.

At Wimbledon for the Centenary parade of winners, Linda sat next to Roger. As the Queen made the presentations Mum whispered, 'This is much more exciting than the tennis.'

During my pregnancy Roger and I had often discussed my return to tennis after I had had the baby. It wasn't just a question of 'how soon?'. It was a question of 'if?'. I wasn't at all sure how I would feel, once the baby was in my arms. Perhaps I'd be so daunted by motherhood that I would have to devote myself entirely to it, as Mr Edwards had predicted years before. And I wasn't too sure about bringing up a child on the tennis tour either. Kelly was not a good sleeper, but our wonderful nanny took some of the pressure off my night-duty, and soon I felt able to resume training.

Although Roger was dubious, I started to exercise cautiously a few days after we came home from hospital. I waddled along the beach in front of our house, tentatively at first but with more authority each day. Roger would sit on the balcony and watch me beat a path between the two breakwaters, back and forth, back and forth, frightened that I would wind myself or break my stitches. By the time we came back from London I felt I'd walked myself into match fitness. So in late July I returned to the practice court.

The purchase of the Hilton Head Racquet Club had faltered over a list of preconditions on the sale which made it difficult for us to do what we'd hoped to, but Roger and Dick Duke now looked at land parcels on the island with a view to building 'Goolagongs' from scratch. So when we decided to play the Canadian Open in Toronto in August as a tryout for the US Open at Forest Hills, Dick offered to fly us up in his company plane. At the last minute, however, he phoned to say that his franchise operators had a prior booking on the plane. He was terribly sorry, he said, but he and Opal would fly up in time for the final.

Toronto was cold, wet and miserable. The four of us — Roger, Kelly, Keren Fergus and I — checked into a hotel near the courts at York University and sat by the television and shivered. My first-round match with the German Katja Ebbinghaus was postponed because of the rain, so we shivered for another 24 hours. When I finally got on the court with her, I knew I was in trouble almost immediately. I put enough shots together to take the second set, but in the third I was just holding on. I wasn't particularly upset. It was just a miscalculation. I wasn't ready. Back to the old drawing board. I went back to the apartment and slept for 15 hours.

Needing the match practice, I played on in the doubles partnering Rosie Casals. In the middle of the week Opal Duke rang to say that she and Dick would still come up at the weekend for the doubles final. But the Dukes didn't make it for the doubles, which Rosie and I lost. Soon after I came off court Opal rang again. Dick had died of a heart attack at just 48. Shattered, we flew straight back to Hilton Head to be with her.

I withdrew from the US Open and stayed at home practising with Roger, planning to test the waters again in late September at the World Invitational Tennis Classic. This tournament was at home at Sea Pines, where I was known and loved, and I felt the relaxed atmosphere at Hilton Head might help me to get my game in tune.

In the meantime, however, we had plenty of business to attend to. While Dick Duke's death had put our tennis club plans on hold, we had entered into several new business deals, including a triangular deal with the American department store, Sears, and the shoe company, Bata. This was not to be just a simple endorsement of a tennis shoe. Bata was to manufacture a whole range of shoes under the name 'Goolagong' and market them exclusively through Sears, the retail giant with stores right across America. This was the start of a long and fruitful relationship with Sears, and also the beginning of our plans for a career after tennis. But I felt there were still a few games left in the old girl yet!

The 1977 World Invitational was rain-interrupted for the first time in its history, but it turned out to be a blessing in disguise. When play was called

With some vocal friends in Los Angeles, 1977

off early on the first day I had plenty of time to get Kelly ready for her christening party. We had arranged for a minister from the Episcopal Church to come to the house and christen her in front of godparents Opal Duke and Bud Stanner, guests Bjorn Borg, John Newcombe, Sue Barker, Di Fromholtz and Vitas Gerulaitis, and a few Hilton Head friends.

With the arrival of the rain, I started to wonder if I was going to repeat my Toronto performance. But as soon as I started playing I realised how unfit I had been for the Canadian Open. Kerry Reid and I played well in the doubles, and I pushed Virginia Wade all the way in the singles final, going down in a tight three-setter. I felt a spring in my heel and a determination in my bones. Nine months since I'd bowed out in the Colgate International in Sydney, and not quite five months since I'd given birth to Kelly, I was seriously back in the game.

Chapter 24

I HATED PLAYING EXHIBITIONS. Always had, with the possible exception of those matches I played with Margaret Court while sightseeing in South Africa in 1971. But prior to heading to Australia for the 1977–78 season, I committed myself to a series of them to ensure that I really was as match fit as I thought.

I played in Cincinnati with Rosie Casals, Vitas Gerulaitis and Jimmy Connors, then somewhere else against Virginia Wade. It really didn't matter where or who I played ... it was all about hitting balls in front of a crowd. And the match practice paid off, for it exposed some weaknesses that had developed in my game and some physiological changes for which I needed to compensate. For one thing, I found that my heavy wooden racquet — one of the heaviest used by any top player, woman or man — was starting to hurt my shoulder. When I served or smashed I almost winced in pain.

On our way to Australia, we stopped off in Fiji for a final training session in the heat before starting the Australian season, but in spite of reaching peak fitness, I could not rid myself of the nagging shoulder complaint. Perhaps it was time to look at my equipment. As soon as we arrived in Sydney I went to Dunlop-Slazengers and traded my wooden racquet for a light metal one.

The start of the Australian season was considered by most of the so-called experts as the real test of my comeback, and there was considerable negativity about my chances.

Writer Alan Trengove, who had written me off when I went to South Africa the first time, was still writing me off. 'The chances are her retirement from the game is not far off ... The problems in travelling the world with a small baby are considerable. When a woman also has to practice tennis constantly and try to maintain perfect fitness and concentration, the life is likely to be a great strain.'

Of course, there was a great deal of truth in this, not to mention the merest hint of sexism. Dear old Teddy Tinling was more confident that I would succeed, citing history as his reason. 'It has been quite obvious with some of the past world's champions that the advent of a happy marriage has provided the ingredient which previously precluded them from scaling the Everests of tennis on their own ...'

A big question mark hung over me as I prepared for the Colgate International, and it was one the promoters played up for all they were worth. Although I was the number eight seed, I was the number one drawcard for that very reason. But my return to big time tennis in Australia was almost over before it began. I was towelling myself off after a shower at our hotel in Kings Cross, thinking about driving down the hill to White City, when I suddenly remembered that Sue Barker, who was supposed to have been playing on Centre Court before me, had forfeited with a back strain and my first-round match was about to start. I dragged Roger out of the shower and finished dressing while he drove. Fortunately we had green lights all the way.

On my way to my first final in 16 months, American player Terry Holladay caught me napping in the quarter finals when she took the only set I was to lose all week. Then, at 3–all in the decider fading light forced us off the court and I had to come back the next morning and start all over again. The final against Kerry Reid was a lot less taxing. After 48 minutes I was back in the winners' circle with a $24,000 pay cheque.

I went on to the Toyota Classic at Kooyong feeling like I owned the summer. I can't explain the feeling adequately, but it was similar to the way I felt during my Virginia Slims winning streak in early 1976. Unstoppable is too strong, but let me put it this way — anyone who stopped me in this kind of mood was going to have to be damned good. The new racquet had all but cured my shoulder problem, I was gaining in strength with every match, Kelly was travelling like a trouper ... and on top of all this, I was back home. Real home.

Mind you, I was no longer the 19-year-old who had won Wimbledon. Motherhood had changed my body and my tennis. After Kelly's birth I'd had to have post-operative pain-killing injections for some time, and on one occasion the needle had gone into my sciatic nerve, causing periodic numbness right down my leg. I found I could no longer hit my backhand the same way. It became a short-swing slice, which worked just fine on grass. Another change was that I needed a long massage after every match or I couldn't go on the next day. But none of this mattered if I could maintain the right mental approach.

After playing all week in blistering Melbourne heat, I beat Wendy Turnbull in the Toyota final in bleak, chilly weather, having made sure that Kelly's nanny Keren Fergus had her rugged up against the unseasonal weather. I was playing close to the best tennis of my career and there were no doubters now.

We had given Keren, our nanny, the week off to visit her family in New Zealand, and Kelly started teething on the plane-ride back to Sydney. We got no sleep at all and arrived exhausted. The only nurse we could hire on short notice had to drive from Newcastle, some two hours away. Since there was no prospect of any sleep before then, we put Kelly in a stroller and took her for a long walk through the streets of Sydney. I was so tired I kept tripping over the wheels, and eventually I stopped, slumped in Roger's arms and howled, 'I'm so tired!'

Restored to sanity, a few days later I won the NSW Open, then followed it with the Australian Open to make a clean sweep of the Australian tour. In the final the umpire had to break with tradition and address the players by their Christian names, there being two Mrs Cawleys. Helen Gourlay, whom I had last beaten in a major final in Paris in 1971, had married an Englishman named Richard Cawley. The coincidence created a great deal of mirth in the commentary booths.

Roger, Kelly and I returned to Barellan triumphant and spent a happy time in the Riverina heat introducing Kelly to the extended Goolagong clan. Relaxed and supremely confident, we headed back to America in January to begin the 1978 Virginia Slims tour.

Our plan for 1978 was to play the Slims tour and then see how things looked. We had said no to World Team Tennis (new commissioner Butch Bucholtz had organised an off-season draft of Pittsburgh players and I had been offered a large amount of money to play for the San Francisco Golden Gators) in order to spend more time at home with Kelly and to prepare for the big tournaments. But — and there was always this proviso on our plans now — if it didn't feel right, we would walk away from tennis and go play mum and dad.

And it didn't feel quite right, initially at least, in the season opener in Hollywood, Florida in mid-January. It had been a while since I'd played on 'carpet' (a synthetic court surface) and having come directly from grass play, I found it difficult to adjust to being unable to slide into my shots. Fortunately, I got used to it again after the early rounds and lost service only once in taking the final from Australian Wendy Turnbull.

In order to reach the final, Wendy had to get past the formidable figure of Renee Richards, a 43-year-old player of power and authority who had begun life as Richard Raskin. As a male, Richards had been a passable player who had made the quarter finals at Forest Hills a couple of times. As a female, following a sex-change operation, she was of major concern to some of the tour players. The Women's Tennis Association accepted the membership of

Tennis mum

the tall, dignified transsexual in 1977, after a fight in the Supreme Court, but it wasn't until the 1978 tour began that the players realised what a threat she could be.

Kerry Reid's husband, Raz, who had played against Richards when he was a man, was particularly incensed when Renee's power serves got the better of Kerry in Phoenix. Kerry stormed off the court and Raz hurled a towel at her opponent. Kerry hoped her walk-off would spark a major player protest which would see Richards boycotted. It never eventuated, but Renee Richards never got much further than the first round.

The court at Hollywood had been laid over concrete, and was thus harsher on my feet than anything I'd played on in a long time. The surface took its toll on me during the week, and at times during the final I had severe pain in the ball of my foot extending into my ankle. I saw a doctor immediately after the tournament and he diagnosed planter faciatis, a condition in which the muscles in the ball of the foot basically seize up, placing increased pressure on other parts of the foot and lower leg. I was not particularly worried. I had suffered similar minor, but nagging injuries in the past and figured that my body would look after itself. I was wrong.

A couple of weeks later, in Dallas, the pain was so intense I had to have a novocaine injection in the sole of my foot before I could play. The doctor had to jab the syringe into my tough skin several times before it penetrated. He confided in me later that there was no more painful place to receive an injection, and I am inclined to take his word for it.

The Maureen Connolly Brinker tournament had been absorbed into the Slims tour but its high profile, social nature was a very different style of event, one I had always enjoyed playing. This year it was memorable for the professional debut of 15-year-old American Tracy Austin, a powerful girl with braces on her teeth who had sent shock waves through women's tennis — particularly through Chris Evert — at Forest Hills the previous September. America hadn't seen anything like Tracy since … well, since Chris! But the general concensus was that Tracy was a much better player than Chris had been at 15. There was no doubt she had the ability, but did she have the temperament? Becoming a media sensation at 15 was not the best start to a tennis career, but Tracy seemed oblivious to the hype at Dallas, spending a lot of off-court time playing with Kelly.

Tracy upset Martina Navratilova in a brilliant quarter final, then made it into the final against me. This was our first meeting on court and the Texans filled Moody Coliseum to see it. Putting everything she had into it, tiny Tracey won the first set and had the crowd on her side. But what she didn't have was big-match experience, and I didn't give her much of a chance to acquire it at my expense in the next two sets.

The tour rolled on to Boston, and I hobbled after it. We had taken great pains to conceal the extent of my foot problem, but both Roger and I realised that something had to be done about it. We resolved to take a fortnight off and seek treatment for it.

Boston saw the re-emergence of Chris Evert, who had been in self-imposed exile since November. There had been a lot of speculation about Chris's 'holiday', and it was not something she would talk about. I suspected there had been a combination of factors — general (and understandable) tour burnout, her on–off relationship with Jimmy Connors, and the sudden rise of Tracy Austin. I think perhaps Chris looked over her shoulder and saw the young 'Chris Evert' coming after her. It was enough to make her want to go away and regroup.

Anyway, she was back now, and anyone who had doubts about her determination to win simply didn't know Chris. We were both on the comeback trail but I was over the first hurdles and Chris wasn't, and that was probably the difference in our gritty, three-set final at Boston. I was in pain in several places (despite another hit of novocaine), but Chris lost her timing after taking the first set. I beat her but I knew the next time we met it would be just as tough.

Two weeks later I lost the final of the Slims championship to Martina in Oakland, California, and limped off to cross-check my wounds list. In addition to the faciatis, I now had severe blood blisters, a damaged arch and a calcaneal bursitis at the base of my left Achilles tendon. Put simply, my feet were a mess, but I had the better part of two months to fix them up, and our plan for the summer was to play only on the relative comfort of English grass.

Nevertheless, pain had become part of my daily routine and I had to consider for the first time in my career whether continual tennis may have permanently damaged my body and my health. Roger had recently read Margaret Court's autobiography, and the injuries she described after the birth of her first child were very similar to mine, starting in her feet and legs but later spreading to other parts. We got in touch with Margaret, who recommended a Harley Street (England) specialist named Dr Guy Beauchamp.

In order to work around my visits to Dr Beauchamp, we planned a light preparation for Wimbledon centred on the minor grass court tournaments at Surbiton and Beckenham and the revamped, Colgate-sponsored Chichester tournament.

We flew to London in late May and I went straight to Dr Beauchamp, who immediately put me on a daily regimen of stretching and massage, and began regular ultra-sound treatment. But he also said, 'It's not going to just go away. There'll be quite a lot of pain. Are you sure you want to continue playing?' I told him I did.

I strapped my ankle heavily before playing at Surbiton but it was such a wonderful relief to feel the give of grass beneath my feet that I soon forgot my injuries. Not for long. I broke down in practice before the fourth round and had to seek a postponement while Dr Beauchamp adjusted my troubled foot. I came back the next day and eventually won the tournament, and the two that followed it, but my Wimbledon campaign was still very much in doubt.

With Bjorn Borg and Vitas Gerulaitis, we hired courts at the Cumberland Club in North London so we could conduct our final practice sessions away from prying eyes and spend as much time on court as we pleased.

It was a strange Wimbledon. I met the Rumanian Virginia Ruzici in the quarter final on Court 3 and was in trouble almost immediately. At the end of the seventh game I could take the pain in my left ankle no longer, and broke down and wept as I approached the umpire. Roger leapt to his feet and rushed on to the court to assist me, breaking the rules of the tournament by his presence. He said, 'Come on, call it a day. It doesn't matter.' But I decided to try to play on and won the match as quickly as I could.

Later, tournament referee Fred Hoyles said that Virginia could have claimed the match on a default. I felt sorry for her, but love knows no bounds, nor Wimbledon rules, and I did beat her on her merits.

Further practice was out of the question and Dr Beauchamp advised me not to play on. My ankle was sore and swollen. I was a wreck. On the day of the semifinal I couldn't even get up the stairs to the ladies dressing-rooms. But pull out? In those days Australians didn't pull out of Wimbledon, and if I could get past Martina I was into the final against Chris. Just two matches from the crown. Pull out? Never.

Before the semifinal Dr Beauchamp left Harley Street and came to Wimbledon to give me painkilling Zylocaine injections but warned that because of the anaesthetic I was running a real risk of not being aware of the pressure I was putting on other parts of my foot and lower leg. Serious injury was a strong possibility.

As I left the IMG tent to play the semifinal I walked past a large gin and tonic which Roger was about to drink to calm his pre-match nerves. My need was greater. Although I hadn't taken alcohol before a match since that hilarious night in South Africa with Margaret Court, I drained the glass and went out to face the music. The combination of alcohol and Zylocaine obviously had an effect.

My match plan was to avoid running whenever I could — I would go for winners no matter what. And it worked. We were a set each and were 3–all, break point to me, in the tight decider when I saw Martina coming to the net, and so I attempted a lob.

Roger, providing colour commentary in the BBC booth, says he heard as clear as a bell the piano-wire snap of my tendon as I came down clutching my leg in agony. Roger left the BBC booth and came to courtside, this time resisting the temptation to come to my aid. But as I limped back to the baseline to resume play I saw him grimly shake his head and mouth the words, 'Please, that's enough.'

I would not retire but I could not play tennis either, and Martina won the three games she needed against a passive opponent. It was not the way either of us liked to win, and she said as much. Martina went on to win the championship and begin her long reign as the world's best player. I went home to Hilton Head, as uncertain as I had ever been about my tennis future.

Roger and I had always taken the view that the best cure for the tennis blues was a complete break from the game, so we took a long one. We decided to have a holiday in Las Vegas, taking in the shows. Since our second wedding in Barellan we'd had a standing joke that our marriage was now legal in Roger's homeland and in mine, but not in the country in which we had chosen to live. This was something we said so often that it never occurred to me Roger might be seriously contemplating a third wedding. As it turned out he did have plans for a wedding, but they were anything but serious.

On our second night in Vegas he confessed that he'd booked the tackiest 24-hour wedding chapel in town for an instant wedding the following afternoon, after which we would celebrate appropriately. It sounded like fun, but that evening we went to see the singer Glenn Campbell perform and, since I'd played exhibition tennis with him in the past, we were invited to join him and girlfriend Tanya Tucker after the show.

At some point in the evening I mentioned that Roger and I were getting married again. Glenn got down on bended knee and proposed to Tanya. A friend of Glen's piped up: 'It will be a double wedding and we'll have it at my place!'

In the morning we dressed appropriately in suits and gowns and waited in the foyer. A limousine arrived and took us to the friend's house where there were a number of guests waiting and two huge wedding cakes — the second just in case Glenn and Tanya decided to go through with it. The chief

On tour with baby

justice of Nevada read a specially-chosen Navajo wedding ceremony. It was strange but quite beautiful.

I barely picked up a racquet during the rest of 1978, a pre-Christmas charity event at Hilton Head to raise money for a new obstetrics wing at the hospital being one of my only competitive outings. But I had not given up on tennis; rather I was narrowing my goals in keeping with my physical limitations. Hard courts were out. In future I would play only on grass and clay.

I began to see Dr John Marshall, a New York sports doctor and orthopaedic surgeon who had successfully treated Billie Jean King and footballer Joe Namath. He felt that my problems could be corrected without surgery and put me on a rigorous exercise program involving stationary cycling, swimming and the application of hot and cold compresses. The treatment seemed to work, although much of my improved condition could be put down to the fact that I simply wasn't doing what caused the problem.

Nevertheless, I tentatively returned to tennis in the American spring of 1979, playing tournaments in Washington DC and at home on Hilton Head before we flew off to Europe again, this time playing in the Italian, German and French Opens on clay, before starting the English season on grass.

The lead-up to Wimbledon was as successful as it had been the previous year, but without the pain. Taking it easy seemed to have paid off, and I breezed through Beckenham and Chichester with the only hiccup being not of my own making, and not on the tennis court. The Chichester tournament was being sponsored by Crossley Carpets and had been put together by IMG, so it had a touch of commercialism about it as never before. Someone thought it would be a good idea if I competed as Evonne Goolagong, the name used most commonly in America. That was fine by me but a BBC interviewer suggested on air that people might get the idea my marriage was on the rocks. I denied this, of course, but the British tabloids know a story when they hear a denial, and they were away with 'Eve Of Wimbledon Drama For The Cawleys'. I rang my mum, Roger rang his, and we got on with our lives.

When Wimbledon began, I gathered strength with each round and when I beat Virginia Wade to make the final four, the newspapers forgot all about our impending marriage break-up and labelled me 'Supermum'. Not quite super enough to beat newly-wed Chris Evert-Lloyd in my semifinal, however, in what was a below-par match. In fact, let's be honest — it was one of the lousiest semifinals ever played at Wimbledon, but only two of the spectators knew why. In an extraordinarily bad piece of biological timekeeping, both Chris and I had the worst day of our period. The commentators were speechless. We were inept, but she less so than me, and the new Mrs Lloyd (she had married British player John Lloyd just a few weeks before) advanced to the final.

It was an appalling exit from the most prestigious court in the world, but strangely enough, I felt buoyed by my overall performance in England and quite confident that I could indeed become 'Supermum', emulating the feat of Dorothy Lambert Chambers who became the first mother to win Wimbledon in 1914. I had weathered a whole season without breaking down. Anything was possible.

Chapter 25

*L*ATE IN 1979 I WON THE American Indoor Championships in Minnesota, playing the best tennis I had since 1976. When I followed this two weeks later by thrashing Tracy Austin and Virginia Wade in the Florida Open, I began to feel that my time was coming.

We flew out to Australia for the four-tournament season and to make a television commercial for the Australian Open sponsor, Toyota. We planned a great summer, with plenty of time between engagements to spend with the family. Kelly was a two-year-old terror now, and Linda had seen so little of her that I wanted to be sure they got to know each other again.

No sooner had we arrived in Australia, however, than I came down with a flu virus that wouldn't go away. I was forced to withdraw from the Toyota Classic and the NSW Building Society Classic while I underwent a series of tests at Royal North Shore Hospital. There was a great deal of speculation in the media, but the fact was that doctors in Sydney could not find anything wrong with me.

Roger had his own theory, claiming that my constant battle against injury over two years had simply left me mentally and physically drained. There may have been some truth in this, and part of me was ready to give up the battle and go home and make another baby. However, another part of me wanted desperately to go back and win Wimbledon one more time. This is what my ambition in tennis had become stripped down to. Since 1971, on so many occasions I had been so close.

Then something happened in Sydney that propelled me down the road to the All-England Club for another shot at the title, faster than any amount of prize money or lofty ambition.

When he called me in to tell me the good news that there was seemingly little wrong with me, the doctor I had been seeing looked me up and down and said, 'Mrs Cawley, why are you doing this to yourself? Surely you don't need the money!'

I turned on him angrily and told him that my tennis had nothing to do with money — it had to do with achieving. When I had calmed down a little I said, 'I want to win Wimbledon again, and I intend to.' And I walked out of that surgery more determined than I had ever been in my life.

We went home to Hilton Head for Christmas, and in the New Year I got straight back into tennis, playing the Colgate Series in Washington DC, then joining the Avon tour in Oakland, Detroit, Dallas, Boston and New York. While I didn't register any wins, I finished in the top four or eight in all these tournaments and was relatively happy with my form. But the momentum was not building. I was not on a roll and felt that perhaps I never would be again. After an energetic two sets I was tired beyond belief. After a three-setter, like the marathon I played against Tracy Austin in the Avon Championships in New York, I was a basket case. The tiredness fed on itself and with it came a deep depression, which was not normally in my nature.

Something was wrong and both Roger and I knew it, but I forced myself to play on. I could see that Roger was becoming increasingly worried, but I prevailed upon him to make our arrangements for Wimbledon. He said, 'I don't think you're well enough, Gong.' But I responded, 'If I don't feel well I won't play, but right now I think I can do it.'

Roger went ahead and rented a house for us, but no sooner he had done so than I bombed out of the Family Circle Classic at Hilton Head in April in the first round, barely able to finish my match against Regina Marsikova. Why didn't I simply stop? I don't know. I suspect I was driven by an ambition which, for perhaps the only time in my career, overrode common sense.

Exhausted before I started, I went to the next tournament at Amelia Island in Florida and collapsed during my first set against South African Yvonne Vermaak. I was dizzy and highly emotional. For the first time in my life I was unable to continue. I had to quit. Roger took me home and checked me into the Hilton Head hospital under the care of our friend, Dr Neil Love. More tests, and more tests.

Neil was strangely sombre when he came to see me with the results. He said, 'Look, it's probably nothing to worry about ... I'm betting you have an iron deficiency and that a course of pills will sort it all out. But we can't be too careful with things in the blood, so I'm going to arrange for some more tests to be carried out, just to be sure.'

'To be sure of what?'

'Well, leukaemia is a possibility, but in my opinion not at all likely ...'

Neil's bedside manner was impeccable, but there is no way to drop the name of a life-threatening disease into a conversation lightly. Of course I didn't have leukaemia, but what if ... what if? I sat by myself and considered the possibility for a long, long time before dismissing it from my mind entirely.

We didn't speak of it, we never entertained the thought that what I had was anything more sinister than fatigue. In the meantime, Neil arranged further tests and put me on a course of drugs to correct my iron deficiency.

I asked Roger, 'We're still going to Wimbledon, aren't we?'

He smiled. 'Of course, we are. I'm not going to lose the deposit I've put down on the house.'

As the English grass court season approached, I attempted to keep up my level of fitness by cycling and walking, but I kept away from the tennis court for fear of tiring myself and aggravating my condition. A couple of weeks before our departure for London Neil Love phoned with good news. I had been given the all clear. I had a little-known blood disorder whose symptoms were very similar to leukaemia, but which had previously only been known to occur in long-distance runners. Once recognised, it was easily cured. I had never allowed myself to believe there was anything seriously wrong with me anyway, but now my spirits soared.

Unlike previous years, in 1980 we left our Wimbledon run late and entered only one warm-up tournament, Chichester. Even then, Roger was so uncertain about my match readiness that he warned the promoters — our agents, IMG — that I may not be fit to play. But I felt fitter by the day, and, mindful of my embarrassing semifinal performance in 1979, I asked Neil Love to prescribe a pill to alter my menstrual cycle and ensure that all would be right for Wimbledon fortnight.

Although I hadn't played any tennis in two months, I quickly found my timing on the Chichester grass and lost the final in a tight match with Chris Lloyd, who was also coming back after a lay-off. Chris's form at Chichester, and the following week at Eastbourne, where she beat Martina Navratilova, prompted the pundits to reassess the women's field. Martina, the defending champion, was red-hot favourite with Tracy Austin a couple of points behind her, and Chris a few points behind that. My odds weren't as long as Billie Jean's, but they were long enough. I had been given my big chance as 'Supermum' in 1979, and I'd blown it. The press are an unforgiving mob, and in 1980 they didn't rate me with a real chance.

That was perfect as far as I was concerned. There is no animal more dangerous than the Wimbledon underdog.

We hired the Cumberland Club courts again to practise in private and I found myself reluctant to go home. I was almost 29 and I had been playing competitive tennis for two-thirds of my life. For the first time since I could remember the game was my life.

Not that we didn't make time for other things. I spent an hour or so on

The portfolio pic, 1980

the masseur's table as often as I could to keep my back and shoulder in good condition, and we fed my spirits by leaving Kelly with her nanny and going out occasionally. At Tramps we drank champagne on our wedding anniversary. I woke up the next morning still feeling light-headed, and played as though charmed on the practice court.

When the Wimbledon tournament began I was still largely ignored by the media, but the players — particularly those who had been at Chichester — cast an interested eye over the proceedings. After I beat American Sharon Walsh in my first match on an outer court, Roger bumped into Martina Navratilova in the crowd. 'Evonne's playing really well,' she said, shaking her head and grinning. But if Martina sensed that I had the fire in my belly, few others had noticed. David Lloyd, John's brother and himself a British Davis Cup player, commented on BBC radio that I was 'not a factor' in the tournament and would be hard pressed to progress beyond my next round match against Betty Stove. Roger was sitting in another BBC booth providing colour comments at the time, and seized on the delicious irony of the situation.

'Well,' he began thoughtfully, 'I, too, have studied the draw and David is probably right. But if by some fluke Evonne manages to scrape home against Betty Stove, she'll play Hana Mandlikova, where anything could happen. And if she gets past Hana, she plays Wendy Turnbull, who has never beaten Evonne. That would put her into a semi with Tracy Austin …' The path to the final was by no means easy — it never was at Wimbledon — but if I'd done the draw myself I wouldn't have changed much.

Away from the All-England Club I sensed a warmth about London I hadn't felt for years. The weather was awful (although the rain seemed to hold off for most of my scheduled playing time) but there was a real sense of summer in the people on the streets and in the pubs. I don't know why, but Londoners had struck a festive chord. When we came to and from our rented house in Knightsbridge the drinkers hung out of the doors in the little corner pub and said hello. Roger was apt to wander up there for an evening pint and the locals became very friendly with us. Parking in the area was by residential permit only, and we didn't have one, but the lads in the pub looked after us. They kept a constant lookout and if a parking policeman approached our car with ticket book in hand, they were there like a shot, explaining that I was a very busy lady and wouldn't be parked there very long. It worked — we didn't get a ticket during our stay.

As the excitement of Wimbledon built during the latter stages of the first week, I suddenly became aware of how much this tournament had changed, how tennis had changed, how I had changed in the decade since I had first come here. Walking from the dressing-room for my match against Betty Stove, my first on Centre Court, I recalled the words of Bob Howe when we had stood on the balcony above Centre Court in 1970. 'This is the Holy Court of the Holy Grounds. To play here will be one of the great experiences of your life. There is nothing quite like it.'

I received $3600 when I first won in 1971. In 1980 first-prize money was almost $40,000. The number 40 female player in the world — who happened to be Renee Richards — had already made more money in 1980 than I did in my entire year as Wimbledon champion. At the top of the tree Martina Navratilova had won $446,000 since New Year's Day, and 17-year-old Tracy Austin was about to become the sixth player in women's tennis to win more than a million dollars, accumulated in just 21 months as a professional.

Winning Wimbledon now was a ticket to easy street, creating a flow of riches that female tennis players could only have dreamed of at the start of the 1970s. I felt honoured to be still playing with the women who had worked so hard to make this all happen — troupers like Billie Jean King and Rosie Casals. But in the context of the annual proceedings at the All-England Lawn Tennis and Croquet Club, none of this meant a thing. Here at the home of tennis, no player with true feelings for the game played for the money. It was an honour to play on the Holy Court of the Holy Grounds, and, as I had said years before, much to the chagrin of the Libbers, I would do it for nothing.

Betty Stove, an often-underrated player who had been in the top ten for many years, took the first set of the tournament from me, but I steadied my game and came back to win comfortably. In the next round Czech player Hana Mandlikova really gave me pause for thought, winning the first set in a tie breaker and serving at 4–1 in the second. But again I took control and directed proceedings from then on.

I was starting to feel wonderful, better than I'd felt about my tennis in a long, long time. The two three-setters had tested my endurance, and it seemed that the viral complaints that had been sapping my energy for the first half of the year had finally disappeared. There was also the possibility that no virus could survive a London summer like this one — on the first day of July a chilly wind whistled across the courts and the temperature struggled not far above freezing.

We had booked a court at Queens Club to practise in the mornings during the tournament, but I was so keyed up all I wanted to do was hit against the practise wall, much to the amusement of the other players. It was all I needed, just to get the rhythm going in my arms and legs. The rest was second nature by now.

In the quarter finals I met Wendy Turnbull who'd been whingeing incessantly about appearance fees I was supposed to have received in Australia. So I gave her something else to think about. Now I was only two matches away from the championship. Finally the press had started to notice that I was playing at Wimbledon, although few of the experts gave me any chance at all of getting past the pig-tailed player from Rolling Hills, California.

Tracy Austin had won at Eastbourne, while Betty Stove had eliminated Martina in an early round. Thus she was barking at Navratilova's heels for the number one computer ranking and Martina had to finish better than Tracy or forfeit her premier ranking. So, with Martina playing Chris in the other semifinal, there was more riding on the outcome of these two matches than a Wimbledon crown — at least as far as some people were concerned. In my book, however, there was only one prize, and that was the gold plate to be handed out by the Duchess of Kent.

Before meeting Tracy in the semifinal, I had a close look at her form when John Newcombe and I played Tracy and her brother John in the mixed doubles. When she aced Newk I suppose I should have been worried, but then I looked at the shape my partner was in and realised the problem was with the receiver rather than the server. The Austins walked all over us, but I didn't feel as bad about it as Newk did, who apologised for his hangover.

There was a break in the clouds for my semifinal with Tracy, and some of the braver spectators even took off their overcoats. I thought Tracy looked a little nervous, so I tested her from the baseline, using drop shots and lobs to keep her moving. I broke her serve twice to take the set comfortably. But in the second she came back renewed. She peppered me with a superlative range of ground strokes and ran me ragged chasing them down. I didn't take a game, and, for the first time in the tournament, I was out of steam and staring defeat in the face. I had to change my tactics completely. There was only one way to go — forward. I would win or lose this match at the net.

My serve became stronger as the match went on, but the third set was close, with first Tracy then me taking the lead. At 4–all I became aware of a strange delayed reaction cheer after every point. I later found out that the entire concourse outside the Centre Court seating was blocked with people following the progress of the match on the electronic scoreboard, which registered the scores about 10 seconds after the point had been won.

I broke Tracy's serve to lead 5–4, but again she came back fighting to break point. I threw the ball badly on my second serve and should have started over, but something made me hit it anyway. It landed perfectly, spinning right down the middle, causing Tracy to miss. Lucky? It was for me. Two points later I was into my sixth Wimbledon final, and my second against Chris, who had downed Martina in the other semifinal.

On the morning of the final Roger seemed extremely agitated and his behaviour quite odd. I soon found out why. He had arranged a surprise visit from some friends from Hilton Head. Company on the day of a final was usually something I shunned, but this time it seemed absolutely right. We caught up with our friends over a leisurely breakfast, then they came with us to Queens Club and watched while I hit against the wall.

I'd never felt so eager before a final, and this, after all, was the thirty-fifth chapter of one of the great rivalries of modern tennis. The lifetime scoreline was 22–12 in Chris's favour, but no one had her tagged as outright favourite for the championship. In fact we had both been somewhat overlooked as contenders in favour of Tracy and Martina who had been expected to fight out the final. And as for who would be the favourite of the packed gallery — not even that was as cut and dried as it once was. I was still well loved by the Poms, but Chris had come a long way from her Ice Maiden days and

With Chris Evert before the 1980 Wimbledon final

Plate No. 2, 1980

her on-court demeanour had won her many fans. My God, she had even followed my lead and married one of them!

In the dressing-room I stopped and chatted to Andrea Jaeger, the talented 14-year-old who had become the new Tracy Austin even before the old Tracy Austin had stopped being the new Chris Evert. Andrea and her sister were gorging on lollies, as kids will. I helped them out with a couple of handfuls, reflected on the rapid passage of time in this sport, then showered to refresh myself for the final.

The sky was black above Centre Court, but I wasn't thinking about the weather. I was thinking about the title, how close it was after all these years. Closer than those other heartbreaking finals? I thought so, even if Chris was my toughest opponent. It had sometimes been said that I had the game to beat Chris, but rarely used it. On this bleak Friday afternoon I used it from the start. The first set was a 6–1 rout. Chris didn't play particularly badly, but I was in near-perfect touch.

I was one game up in the second set when the cloud which had been threatening all afternoon, burst above us. We were off the court for 63 nerve-wracking minutes, a break I didn't need. When we came back Chris had changed her attitude as well as her clothes.

I reached 3–0 before she came at me like a tiger, winning four games in a row. At 6–5 Chris served for the set. I could not let it go to a third set. The longer the match went on, the more likely it was that Chris's consistency would beat my dash ...

I broke back and we played the tie breaker. (This meant that the winner would be the first to reach seven points with a two-point margin over their opponent.) The crucial point came at 3–all with a sizzling rally of 31 shots. But for once it was Chris who made the error. I got to 6–3 and therefore had three championship points up my sleeve. I blew the first, but it was all over on the second.

This was the first time in history that a singles championship at Wimbledon had been decided on a tie breaker. More importantly, it was the first time in 66 years that a mother had won. *Now* they could call me 'Supermum' if they wished. And they did.

Tennis matches are nothing to cry about. Win or lose, they have seldom reduced me to tears. But on 4 July 1980, I cried. At the post-match press conference I managed to fight back the sobs and say a few more things than I'd been able to in 1971.

This win was so much more important, so much more of a triumph for me than the last one. I just floated through that win in 1971, not aware at all of what was going on or what I had achieved. This time it meant everything to me. When you work hard for something and you plan for it, and overcome pain for it and achieve it when people say you can't do it, it really means a lot. So often in the past two years I just wanted to give the game away, but I knew in the back of my mind that I'd be sorry later if I didn't try everything to get back into it.

Roger has always given me confidence, encouraged me when things were tough and pushed me when I was getting lazy. He was always right. He always knew what he was doing. He made it possible for me to keep playing tennis after I had Kelly. I wasn't sure that having a family and playing the tour would really go well together, and if it didn't, then I knew I would have to give up tennis. But Roger made it easy and I thank him for that. Without his support I wouldn't have a second Wimbledon crown.

In the back of the car heading back to Knightsbridge to get changed for the celebration — Kelly on my knee, Roger by my side — I was still teary, but underneath the torrent of emotion was a deep and abiding happiness, the kind of happiness that comes when you know that you have truly, sincerely, given of your best, and your best has been THE best.

I closed my eyes just for a moment as the rain lashed the windscreen, and I saw the faces of the people — now all dead or gone — who had helped me get to this day, this triumph. I saw dear old Mr Kurtzman, hunched over the wheel, driving along some backroad through the wheatfields to get me to a tournament, occasionally looking sideways at me to see if I was asleep and almost driving off the narrow, unsealed road.

I saw Kenny Goolagong, loudly bragging about me in the pub, then clutching me to his chest and breathing beer into my ear as he whispered softly, 'Go get 'em, Eve. Show 'em what you can do.'

And I saw Mr Edwards, so old and angry now and out of my life, and I hoped that he would be proud of me in spite of everything.

PART 7

Home

Back home in Barellan, 1993, with some
mementoes from Mum's house

Chapter 26

*T*HERE WAS NO TICKER-TAPE parade when I came home with my second Wimbledon trophy, but the reception I got from the residents of my adopted home, Hilton Head Island, was no less enthusiastic.

I was given the keys to the city at a huge public ceremony and was feted wherever I went on the island, which was quite extraordinary in a place where the residents rubbed shoulders with sporting celebrities every day. It seemed that my neighbours had taken a special pride in my achievement in winning Wimbledon as a mother, and they made me feel as though I had lived in South Carolina all my life.

When I got back to Barellan later in the year it all happened again. Our old friend Clarrie Irvin chaired the Welcome Home Committee and organised a splendid day of celebration and sporting events. (Roger starred in the footie-kicking contest, miscuing the ball in his shiny city shoes and finishing a dismal last!)

But I was not about to rest on my laurels. I felt I had played so well at Wimbledon that I could now go on with it at the top level, and began to prepare myself for the US Open. My body had other ideas. The injuries which had held off earlier seized me again in August, and, after an early exit from the Canadian Open I flew home from Toronto, tired, sore and monumentally depressed, and pulled out of the US Open.

I moped around the house until Roger decided to snap me out of it by taking me on a motor yacht cruise in the Caribbean with some friends. The idyllic location must have brought out the romance in us, for it was while sailing in the Bahamas that our second child was conceived.

We had only just returned to Hilton Head, full of the joys of life once again, when my sister Barbara phoned from Sydney. I could tell immediately she was upset. 'Barb, what is it?'

'There's something about you in the press here … you're not going to like it.'

Barbara had been called in by the head nurse at the hospital where she was working and shown the cover of the *Bulletin*, an Australian news magazine,

Left: At home on Hilton Head Island with Roger, 1980 *Right:* At home with Kelly; Morgan is on the way. Hilton Head, 1981

which had been published that day. The sister had been worried that other sections of the media might contact Barbara for a response on my behalf, and thought she should be forewarned.

'Oh, Evonne, it's so unfair, so hurtful,' she said. I told Barbara not to be concerned, that it would soon blow over, but I put down the phone and cried tears of rage.

I should have known something was looming, for, inexplicably, the prominent Aboriginal spokesman and leading civil servant Charles Perkins had relaunched an attack on me within days of my second Wimbledon win, saying he 'couldn't care less' about my achievements because I didn't care about my race. I had known Charlie slightly since my days at the Foundation for Aboriginal Affairs in Sydney in the late 1960s, so his acerbic nonsense came as no surprise. He had said much the same things after I reached the Wimbledon semifinals in 1979. In fact it seemed that whenever Charlie Perkins needed to buy himself a headline I was the currency he used. He was, of course, entitled to his view of me, even if it was based on total ignorance of my involvement with my Aboriginal family throughout my playing career, and even if it was somewhat ungenerous coming from a fellow sportsman. Charlie Perkins made me angry and a little sad, but what appeared in the *Bulletin* of 30 September 1980 totally enraged me.

Alongside a cover picture of me playing tennis, Australia's leading news weekly ran the lines: 'To my cousin, Evonne Cawley. Poetry by Kevin Gilbert. A plea for her to use her influence to draw world attention to the plight of the Aborigines.'

Inside the magazine Kevin Gilbert wrote in a preamble to his poem: 'If an Afghan won Wimbledon, his countrymen would expect him to draw attention to the invasion, the usurpation of authority, the land theft, the murders, denial of human rights and the accelerating mortality rate under the heels of the Russians. Evonne Cawley has been asked to do no more than that on behalf of her people, suffering similar circumstances under the heel of white Australia.'

The poem that followed made me angrier than anything I had ever read.

I wonder, Evonne, when you're playing straight sets
And you 'haste' your opponent so well
Do you ever look back at your grandmother, black,
And catch glimpses of her in her hell?
Do you ever see past the net on the court
To the horrors that make you scream 'Fault'?
Do you open your eyes when the whites victimise
Your family? You never scream 'Halt'.
Remember, Evonne, the song of the swan
I sang you in Griffith's heat haze,
Wheeling your pram through the dust past the dam
To the tent shanties we lived in so long
Remember old tin, broken flagons, the din
The people so poor and oppressed
Scratching for crusts of damper and meat
Day after day without rest.
Remember my aunt, your grandmother 'Doll',
Our cousins, our blood kept in chains?
Remember the hate, the mortality rate,
The tumble-down shacks, the rains.
Win your games, Love, may they all be straight sets
But 'I accuse' for our people again.
Go on and win with your calm easy grin

And when sycophants raise wines to 'toast',
Say a few words so the truth can be heard
About victims with no chance to win.

According to the *Bulletin*, Kevin Gilbert was 'perhaps the most talented of our Aboriginal writers', but I had never heard of this 'cousin' who claimed to have pushed me in my pram. I phoned my mother, playing down the ferocity of the words I could at least be thankful she would never read.

'Oh yes, Kevin. That's Junie's young brother. He's had a troubled life, that one. Wheeled your pram? Never. He may have seen you once when he visited Three Ways. That's all I can remember.'

Gilbert's words offended me deeply. For one thing, a convicted murderer whose first 40 years had brought only shame to his race was in no position to throw stones. For another thing, he was so hopelessly, cruelly, stupidly wrong in his assumptions about my feelings for my own people, about the memories of the tin shanties which for me had never dimmed. And I honestly believe that every time I played the greats of the game I was doing more for the 'victims with no chance to win' than I might have achieved with a hundred soapbox speeches about the defeatist attitude amongst some Aborigines, which has been described as 'poor bugger me'. Fortunately, for every Kevin Gilbert, there have been a dozen Aboriginal achievers like Pastor Doug Nicholls, Lionel Rose, Lynch Cooper, and now Cathy Freeman, Manduwuy Yunupingu and Maroochy Berambra, with their hands out not for pity but for the prize — the prize of achievement, which is just as attainable for our people as it is for white Australians.

I had just written the above words when I learnt that Kevin Gilbert had died of emphysema at the age of 60. I tried to phone his sister, Auntie Junie Mason with my sympathies but got no response from her phone. Kevin Gilbert's passing does not change my opinion of what he wrote. But I was saddened, nonetheless, that I had never been able to confront him face to face. We might have met at my grandmother Dolly's graveside in Condobolin in 1989, when Junie Mason placed her old mate's fishing line on the grave as a mark of love and respect, but Kevin Gilbert wasn't there.

Roger and I felt so strongly about the injustices which the *Bulletin* had published that we instigated legal action against the publishers, Kerry Packer's Australian Consolidated Press, seeking a public apology. The case dragged on interminably until Mr Packer finally offered us an out-of-court settlement, which we accepted. A full apology was subsequently published in the *Bulletin* and in all the newspapers which had carried advertisements for that particular issue of the *Bulletin*. It was a significant concession from a magazine which had once championed the cause of 'Australia for the white man' and printed all manner of racial slurs under the banner of 'Aboriginalities'.

As my belly began to swell again I suffered dreadful morning sickness. I was in daily contact with my mother who not only wanted a full report on my symptoms, but used the information to establish a database which told her the gender of the child long before ultrasound could. Linda would ask: 'Now, what do you feel like eating? Oh, yeah. And you feel crook even after you've eaten them? Oh, yeah. It's a boy. Definitely a boy.'

Mum was right, of course. Neil Love delivered our second child by Caesarian section on 28 May 1981 in the little hospital in Beaufort — Stan Smith and I still hadn't won the battle for a maternity wing at Hilton Head. Morgan Kyeema Cawley was everything Kelly wasn't — wrinkled, jaundiced, scratched and decidedly motley. When Roger first saw him he said: 'Ooh, what an ugly baby!' (He was joking, of course, and within a month our son was as beautiful as Kelly had been.) We named him Morgan because I had read the name somewhere and Roger liked it because he had loved the movie, *Morgan: A Suitable Case For Treatment*. Kyeema came from the same Aboriginal phrase book as Inala (Kelly's middle name), and meant 'the dawn', or 'new beginning'.

When Roger phoned Mum to let her know that mother and son were doing fine, Linda picked up the phone in Barellan and said, 'How's my grandson?' She had never doubted the accuracy of her prediction.

During my pregnancy we had once again faced the prospect of life after tennis. This time it seemed that there would be no way back. I was not yet 30 but my body was trying hard to tell me that the rigours of competing at the top level were not meant for a mother of two. The hormonal changes to my body brought about by motherhood had made me more susceptible to injury, particularly in the legs. I didn't completely accept this as an inevitable consequence of raising a family — Margaret Court had played on after her second child, overcoming similar injuries — but we nevertheless began to look at our business options after tennis. The most exciting project we undertook, in partnership with a couple of Hilton Head friends, was to design and build a pub and nightclub complex. Roger became totally involved in the minute details of construction and interior design, while Kelly and I played our part by going down to the site and helping the construction workers clean up each afternoon.

We called the club 'Evonne's' and the pub 'LTFG' — looks terrible, feels great, which it did. For the first few months Roger was the owner-operator, arriving early in the morning to do the book work and the ordering, and leaving the club after midnight each night. He thrived on the long hours and helped make the venture a great success, but we never saw him any more. Roger was as aware of this as we were, and once the business was up and running smoothly, he slowly extricated himself from its day-to-day affairs.

In the area of product endorsement my new 'Supermum' image again catapulted me into the frontline in corporate America. Bud Stanner in Cleveland sifted through the dozens of offers to represent everything from Kentucky Fried Chicken and the aptly-named Brown 'n' Serv Sausages to King Coil Mattresses, and presented us with some very attractive options. Among these was an interesting extension of my existing arrangement with Sears.

For some time we had had a triangular deal with the shoe manufacturer, Bata, and Sears to market 'Goolagong' leisure shoes. Now Sears wanted to go further and introduce an extensive range of 'active-wear' under my name. 'Go Goolagong' active-wear was to include skirts, shorts, socks, warm-ups, even sunglasses, with all these products being sold in Goolagong boutiques in every Sears store throughout America. It was an exciting and lucrative deal which involved me not only lending my name to the stores but featuring in the extensive Sears catalogues (my first real modelling assignments) and making in-store appearances.

Another interesting deal came to us through my bout of illness in 1980. When the makers of the iron supplement Geritol read of my iron deficiency problem and leukemia scare, they approached us to spearhead a campaign to reposition their product in a changing market place. Geritol had long been known as the product that 'fortifies the over 40s', but its manufacturers were now watching the baby boomers spend a fortune on vitamin supplements at a much earlier age, and they wanted a piece of the action. It sounded like a job for Supermum!

Geritol's repositioning was quite simple really. They just added some other vitamins to the mix and offered a pill that would fortify the yuppies as well as their parents. To sell it, they used me and my family. We featured in a series of print advertisements and television commercials around the country, the most memorable of these being the one in which 'Mommy beats Daddy'. Poor Roger had to grin and bear it as Supermum, Geritolled to the eyeballs and fortified beyond belief, ran him all over the court. Since Billie Jean had thrashed old Bobby Riggs in Houston in 1973, it had been quite acceptable for a woman to beat a man at tennis, but the spectre was no less fascinating. Until our departure from America years later, Roger had to endure the legacy of those commercials wherever he went. 'Did she really thrash you?'

After Morgan's birth I went back into training almost immediately, not because I had a schedule of tournaments in mind but because I really felt that I could keep going — and wanted to — provided I did not let my fitness level deteriorate. Indeed, I did play and in 1982 I was ranked number 17 in the world after some middling performances. But I was up against it from the start. I constantly nursed an injury. As one healed, another would flare up. Moreover, I found that one of my greatest assets — my speed around the court — had diminished. Without the freedom of movement I felt lost, and soon became incredibly frustrated with my game.

I began to feel that my performances on the court were unfair to myself and to the people who came to watch, who paid their money in expectation of seeing me playing at my best. While no one in tennis actually retired any more — there were always charity events, senior tours, corporate outings and so on — I realised that my tour days were over. I played a few tournaments in 1983, then called it a day.

When I abandoned my comeback I went back to Hilton Head and felt quite good about my decision, but it didn't last. Within days it hit me like a ton of bricks. I woke up one morning and felt shockingly depressed for no particular reason. It was a bit like the baby blues, but it would not go away and it began to affect our family life. I was an emotional wreck. I felt like crying all the time and would burst into tears at any time — in a restaurant, in the car, anywhere.

Roger's parents came to visit and that made matters worse. Although they never expected it, I felt I had to play the entertainer and try to suppress my feelings. Roger had no idea what was going on in my head and I had no way of explaining it adequately to him. It was something I just had to play out. I had been through brief periods of post-euphoric depression after both my Wimbledon wins — a natural reaction for anyone who has achieved the success of dreams — but this was something more, and I slowly came to realise that I had to re-evaluate my entire purpose in life. It is an over-simplification, but there is some truth in the notion that when old people retire from their jobs, they get ready to die. When sports people retire, they still have their lives ahead of them. To do what? Since the age of 11 I had given myself completely to tennis. Now, in my early thirties I had to replace it with something.

In writing this book I have reflected at some length on that period of my life, and have come to believe that my reaction to the fundamental change in it was a very Aboriginal one. When the Europeans came to Australia the pattern of Aboriginal life was irrevocably altered, and many Aborigines simply could not cope with the change. They just withered and died, unable to accept or understand the new ways that had been forced upon them. Of course, the trauma of change is not solely the property of Aborigines, but I believe that recent history has demonstrated that our Stone Age culture had greater difficulties than most in adapting to the 'shock of the new'.

I did not allow myself to wither and die, but I did have to reach deep into myself to find the spirit to accept the change in my life and deal with it. What began as brooding turned into an affirmation of what I had been and what I could become. I thought long and hard about how fortunate my life had been, and the opportunities that lay ahead, and, with the loving support of my family, I slowly began to redirect myself.

Much of this energy was focused towards our house extensions. The charming three-bedroom home we had bought in 1976 simply wasn't big enough half a dozen years later for a family of four, plus nannies and constant house guests. We extended it to six bedrooms! Apart from the nannies (we had about 15 over the years, usually two at any one time and many of them from New Zealand, which, for reasons we've never fathomed, seems to breed a superior nanny to anywhere else) we had decided to take on the awesome responsibility of looking after two teenage 'sons'.

The youngest Goolagongs, Ian and Mully, were in their late teens at the end of the 1970s and showing great promise in tennis and golf respectively. We were prepared to help launch them into professional sporting careers, but at the same time we believed it was important that they realised such careers did not come without great personal sacrifice and discipline. We promised to match their savings if they both got jobs and began to put away money for the trip to America.

Ian arrived in 1978, Mully a year later. Ian won a tennis scholarship to study at South West Texas State University, an institution conveniently situated near Newk's Tennis Ranch in San Antonio, where he was able to take on a coaching job to help support his business studies. After college he played the satellite tours in America and Europe for two years and showed considerable promise. The highlight of his tennis career — and one many pros would envy — was his Centre Court appearance at Wimbledon in 1982.

I was back on the tour and playing in the singles, so we thought it would be fun to emulate Tracey and John Austin and enter the mixed doubles as a brother and sister team. Indeed it was fun, and we soon developed into a formidable package. Much to Ian's amazement, our first round clash with Tony Roche and 15-year-old Jenny Byrne from Perth was scheduled for Centre Court. The Holy of the Holies! How many players go through an entire career

Playing in the US Open, 1982

Still pregnant, with Kelly and our 'sons' Ian and Mully at Disneyland, 1981

without receiving such an honour, and here was Ian playing on Centre in his first and only Wimbledon appearance! He started strongly but soon succumbed to nerves. Roger and John Paish, watching from the players' gallery, nearly split their sides when Ian nervously started to tap the sole of his shoes with his racket, removing the non-existent clay from the grooves, a familiar sight on the clay courts of Barellan, but a little strange on the hallowed turf of Centre Court. We lost an entertaining three-setter but Ian has his Centre Court memories forever.

In the end he gave up the tour for love, and went home to Melbourne, where he had finished his schooling while living with Uncle Fred Briggs, and married Lynn, his childhood sweetheart. Ian has since carved out a career in Australia as a teaching pro, and on 12 May 1993 (Kelly's birthday) he and Lynn had their first child, Rodney Kenneth.

Mully, who had matured into a good-natured but painfully shy young man — much the way I had been until I went to Sydney — had his eye on the golf tour. He had the strokes but we weren't sure about his aptitude; however when Roger organised the use of the Port Royal Plantation facilities for him in return for some work around the clubhouse, he got down to business and quickly reduced his handicap. Within a year he was competing in tournament golf.

Mully developed as an individual during the time he was with us at Hilton Head but he found the golf tour a hard nut to crack. He never became disconsolate, however, and kept plugging away at his game with considerable optimism. During this period he became very close to us, an adored 'big brother' to our children and a soul mate and 'son' to Roger. Eventually he returned to Australia and took up with a girl who had a child from a previous relationship. In 1989 there was a tragic accident while the child was in Mully's care. The little girl, Rhiannon, fell on her head and died.

Mully was distraught with grief, and he and the child's mother, Mandy, fell into each other's arms, there to seek comfort from a world too cruel to be true. It was not a firm foundation on which to build a lasting relationship, but they came together to our home in America to try. Roger and I watched in helpless pity as these two tortured souls tore each other apart. Inevitably, the relationship came to a merciful end, but for Mully the pain of that poor child's death continues.

When Mully first tried out for the golf tour in America, one of the people who gave him assistance was Australian golf champion Jack Newton. In the 1960s, when we were both teenagers, Jack and I often featured together in newspaper and magazine articles as prospective champions, but we never actually met until he played the professional tournament on Hilton Head. He and his family became friends and welcome house guests.

In 1983 Jack himself was in need of assistance. He had suffered horrendous injuries after walking into the propeller of a plane at Sydney Airport and faced huge medical bills. His friend and golfing colleague Bob Shearer asked Roger and me to help. We flew to Myrtle Beach, South Carolina, and played tennis against all comers in a curtain raiser to a pro-am golf tournament the next day. Dozens of Jack's friends rallied to the cause and helped solve his financial problem — a testament to the popularity of this courageous sportsman.

One night in Hilton Head in 1984, I had a call from Patricia Edwards, who told me that her father was gravely ill in hospital and wanted to make his peace with all his daughters, including me. I asked Trisha if all the other girls were going to see him. She said she thought they would, despite their differences.

I said, 'Then I suppose I will too.' I told her I would clear my diary and phone back with my flight details. But before I could do anything Trisha phoned back the next day to tell me that Mr Edwards had passed away. It is difficult for me to recall exactly my reaction to this news, but I know I spent a lot of time rewinding the events of the 1970s which had so soured our relationship. Would things have worked out differently if I had understood him a little better? Or if he had made the effort to come to terms with me as a woman of independent spirit? Or were our separate fates sealed long before our conflict? I had not seen Mr Edwards for several years now, and unfortunately when I closed my eyes and thought of him I saw not the upright figure of the coach putting his star pupil through The Drill, but the pitiful figure of a man who had forsaken his family — my second family — for a love they could not understand nor accept. In his final years Mr Edwards had married Gere Kitch and had two children with her, but I found my sympathies at this time lay with the Edwards family I knew.

I decided against returning to Australia for the funeral. Under the circumstances I didn't think it fair to the memory of my own father that I should miss his, yet return for the man who had been a kind of foster father to me. The Edwards family understood and respected my decision, and on the day of the funeral I shed a tear or two for all of them in their loss, and I suppose I shed a tear for myself too, because for all that had happened, I had some fond memories of Mr Edwards too, and I sincerely regret that he did not go to his rest with my forgiveness.

In the southern winter of 1985 I was invited to Australia to help launch a new women's tournament for the sponsor, Johnson & Johnson. I explained that I was no longer playing on the tour but the promoter prevailed upon me to come out and publicise the event. (Getting out of tennis can be as hard as getting into it!)

We decided to bring the whole family out for a short holiday, during which I spent a busy week in Sydney doing media calls. The day before the event I played a practice match with a young Aboriginal girl and chipped a bone in my toe. Having gone this far already, I played in the tournament anyway, and was unceremoniously bundled out in the first round by the Australian girl, Amanda Tobin.

This was the end of my mainstream tennis career. Not the way I would have scripted it, I suppose, but definitely, indisputably the end.

The 'fat ones' play the 'skinny ones'. Madison Square Garden, 1988

Kelly was eight when I played that tournament, Morgan only four. My daughter thus had only vague memories of her mother as a tennis player, my son none at all. I was therefore delighted when two years later, in 1987, I was invited to play in an exhibition doubles match at Madison Square Garden in New York with the whole family in attendance. When that famed doubles team of years gone by, Billie Jean King and Rosie Casals, took to the court to play the middle-aged but well-preserved Maria Bueno and me, the hushed audience heard Morgan declare: 'Look Dad, the fat ones are going to play the skinny ones!'

I was equally delighted in 1988 when the children were present again for my induction into the International Tennis Hall of Fame at Newport, Rhode Island. At last the long and sometimes painful process of leaving tennis was completed.

As tennis receded into the background of my life in the mid-80s another sport came to the fore. As a child I had always loved to go fishing with my father — not that Kenny Goolagong was always keen to take me on his midnight forays down to the river bank at Darlington Point. Now that I had time on my hands I rekindled my interest in angling. After I had dropped the kids at school, several times a week I would steal off to a peaceful lagoon

Induction into the Tennis Hall of Fame, Newport, Rhode Island, 1988

Left: At Wimbledon's over 35's event *Right:* Deep-sea fishing off Naples, Florida, 1989

not far from our home and fish for hours. The lagoon was swept by sea water almost every high tide and it generally held a wide variety of fish species. I became expert at guessing what I had on my line before I got it to the surface. I loved this solitary time, and found that I enjoyed the cleaning and gutting as much as I enjoyed catching the fish. I liked the idea of going empty-handed to the lagoon and returning with dinner for the family. It must have been the hunter-gatherer in me.

Eventually I became so obsessed with my fishing that we had to have a boat. We called it *True Blue* and we became serious bluewater anglers, trolling along the coast for mackerel and other sportfish whenever we could.

Fishing also played a part in our decision in 1986 to move to a warmer climate. Hilton Head had changed in the years since we settled there. It had grown beyond belief and become a major tourist centre. Where once there had been no traffic lights, now there were many, not to mention daily traffic jams. Furthermore, until I stopped playing tennis I had never spent a northern winter at home. I had never realised how cold it got in South Carolina. The summers on Hilton Head were glorious but the winters, for sun lovers like us, were sheer hell. When it actually started to snow Roger and I looked at each other and shook our heads. We jumped into the car and drove south to find somewhere in the sun.

Our travels led us to Naples on the Gulf Coast of Florida. Here the air and water were warm, the streets were clean, the people were friendly and the pace was slow. Even more importantly, the fishing was great! We made our decision almost instantly, although I worried about Kelly, who had made her first real friend in the little girl next door at Hilton Head. As it turned out it took her about two years to fully adjust and make new friends.

We sold our house and business interests on Hilton Head, threw out our old furniture and accumulated junk and moved to Florida, where we soon made new friends and became involved in a hotel development company called Shelter Can-American Corporation. Roger sold shares in the resort while I handled the public relations duties. I became particularly friendly with Deborah Morris, the boss's assistant, and we soon found that we shared the fishing obsession. Over the next few years Deborah and I were to dangle a line in many fine fishing holes, not the least of which was our girls-only expedition to the salmon-infested streams of Canada.

During our years in Naples I started to do 'corporate outings' — American jargon for functions at which sports stars fraternise with company executives. It was well paid, quite good fun and a great way to meet business contacts. And I don't mind a bit of hit and giggle on the tennis court now and then, although I much preferred the slightly more serious play of the over-35 tournaments, which I had begun to play after reaching the eligible age in 1986. There was much less pressure attached to these events but the competitive edge of the former champions was still very much in evidence.

I played in the US Open and at Wimbledon with Kerry Reid and slowly got the cobwebs out of my game. I found that I really enjoyed the company of the ageing legends of tennis — people like Ken Rosewall, Bob Lutz, Ilie Nastase, Stan Smith, Neale Fraser, Owen Davidson, Rod Laver and particularly Roy Emerson. These players had been my heroes throughout my playing career, and to me they represented the generation of players who were true gentlemen of the court. It might seem strange to bracket 'Nasty' Nastase that way, but Ilie was one of the players I would pay money to watch. So was John McEnroe. Of today's players I would only pay to watch Pete Sampras, a wonderful player who combines power with finesse in the style of the greats I have mentioned above. Unlike Ilie or McEnroe, Sampras also has the temperament of the gentlemen of the court, and I hope to enjoy his tennis for many years to come.

Another player I have admired greatly for other reasons is the late Arthur Ashe, who did so much for the game and for his race. I remember when I was a junior at White City all those years ago, and the word filtered down that Arthur wanted to meet me. What an honour! Arthur and another American player took me to lunch and quizzed me about my life and my Aboriginal heritage. They did their best to make me feel at ease but I doubt I was able to tell them much of interest. It saddens me that Arthur did not live long enough for me to send him a copy of this book. As a gift from one proud black tennis player to another, I know he would have appreciated it.

My other great interest in the Naples years was supporting a charity called WINGS, which was an organisation which financed and built shelters for battered women and children. I became involved as a patron along with the actor Robert Wagner. The WINGS administration became like an extended family to us, and together Robert and I helped raise hundreds of thousands of dollars to save women from their dangerous situations. We organised celebrity golf and tennis days and dinners and auctions. The WINGS events were held annually over a few days at the Claremont Club east of Los Angeles, but whenever I was on the West Coast I would spend some time cajoling sponsorship deals or organising celebrities for the events.

Charity fund-raising had been a part of my life for many years, but through my involvement in WINGS I began to use a 'reciprocal' approach — I would appear at, say Chris Evert's charity event in Boca Raton, in return for her appearance at Claremont for WINGS.

Despite my love of charity work, somewhere, somehow, during this period of my life I realised that this could not be the pattern of my remaining years. In Naples I had everything I could possibly want, except a sense of place. I had always said that I would return to Australia when the time was right, and as the years went by it became increasingly evident to me that that was where I belonged. Sooner or later, we would have to go. Roger knew it and the children knew it, but when?

Since 1985 we had been talking to Australian writers and producers about my possible involvement in a book and documentary series about Aboriginal culture, and that had triggered my longtime interest in Aboriginal themes again. I yearned to know more about my people, and never came back from a trip to Australia without cases filled with books and tapes and art. On one trip I flew to Adelaide for the first Aboriginal Sports Awards. At that function I saw my first corroboree and was spellbound by it. I felt I could sit and watch and listen all night. Just the sound of Aboriginal voices speaking in tribal tongues was magical to me, and I came away feeling that my return would be sooner rather than later.

One afternoon in March 1991 I had a strange waking dream as I went for my regular walk. My mind wandered to an interview in which a reporter asked me what influences my mother and father had on me during my career. 'But my mother's not dead,' I responded stupidly, rather missing the point of his question.

Roger joined me and we walked back home together. When we reached the house Kelly was in the doorway in tears. 'Oh Mum,' she wailed, 'I'm sorry but Gran has died.'

At first I wondered whose Gran she was referring to. Then it struck me. Linda was dead. My dear sweet mother was gone. She had been in hospital earlier in the week with a chest complaint thought to be pleurisy, but she had discharged herself and gone home. It was only later that I discovered she had also suffered a minor heart attack. When I phoned her she had sounded tired but she was eagerly awaiting the delivery of a new car I had bought for her. I said, 'Don't you go running around everywhere in it until you've fully recovered.' Linda just laughed. She suffered another heart attack in her sleep and did not wake up on the morning the new car was to be delivered.

My grief overcame me and with it came a dreadful guilt. Mum had not seen the children for five years. Morgan was now a soccer-playing 10-year-old and Kelly a curvaceous teenager. We had planned to go back to Barellan in July and let the children spend time with her, but now all Morgan had was distant memories and some tapes of Aboriginal music she had made for him on a trip to the West Australian desert. It was not enough, and it filled me with sadness. My father's death had taught me a valuable lesson in giving voice to your feelings. Dad had rarely been able to do that and we, his children, were a little reticent to speak openly too. I remember sitting Ian and Mully down in Hilton Head and pleading with them to tell each other and all of our family how much we loved one another because you could never tell what was around the corner. My lecture worked and Linda well knew the love of her children in the last years of her life.

About a month after the funeral I was suddenly overcome by a feeling of great peace and serenity. I knew then that Mum was all right. I also knew that I owed it to her, and to Kenny, to learn everything I could about them, about their ways and their families and their histories. For their sakes, as well as my own, I had to immerse myself in the study of what it is to be a Wiradjuri Aborigine. For the first time my yearning to understand my Aboriginal self had a clear focus. I had answered my Aboriginal critics repeatedly with the explanation that I had served my people best by becoming a great tennis player, a symbol of achievement. But I had done that by 1980 and by 1985 I had retired from mainstream tennis completely. For six years after that, what had I done?

The answer, when I was brutally honest with myself, was not enough. I had allowed my own needs and desires to be subjugated by those of my children, a natural enough response of a mother. We had stayed on in Naples for the sake of the children's schooling, but had that become an excuse for inertia? Roger had always thought out our lives together in terms of 'five-year-plans', the latest of which had Kelly about to enter college before we moved back to Australia, while Morgan, four years younger, would have been beginning high school. All of this made a great deal of common sense, but suddenly emotions seemed more important than practicalities.

With Linda's passing, the slender threads of my Aboriginal identity rested only with my brothers and sisters, whose lives in some cases were no more connected with Aboriginality than was mine. This was my personal mission, not theirs, and I could not rely on them to fly the family flag until circumstances enabled me to return. I had to go home and I had to go home now!

From the moment I made that decision, my body may have been in America but my spirit was home again.

Chapter 27

*T*HE SEARCH FOR MY Aboriginal identity had to start with the children. Born in Beaufort, South Carolina, raised in the resort communities of Hilton Head Island and Naples, Florida, they had no real comprehension of what it was to be Aboriginal. If I was going to devote myself almost entirely to this search, I felt that it was fair and just that the children should at least begin to understand something of this alien culture, in part their own heritage.

Having severed our business ties in Naples, put our house on the market and resettled in Noosa Heads, Queensland, by the start of the 1992 school year, we began to plan the practical elements of this grand journey of self discovery. Noosa was a good base for a number of reasons, not least of which was that it was very like the previous places the children had lived. It was a relaxed, sunny place by the sea with a relatively small population and yet access to all the services we needed, including a good school for the children.

We enrolled them at Matthew Flinders Anglican College, Buderim, where they became acquainted with school uniforms for the first time. ('Do you mean I have to wear that costume?' Morgan protested.) Despite these 'cultural' differences, both children soon adapted to the change and came to love their new environment, particularly Morgan, who had to have a surfboard so that he could take his place in the surf at First Point.

We decided as soon as it was practical to take the children to Far North Queensland first, because in some ways it was like an Aboriginal theme park, whereas the cultural differences were much more subtle in Wiradjuri country, where traditional life had long ceased to exist. In the region stretching north from Cairns into the lower part of Cape York Peninsula, we could experience life in relatively remote Aboriginal communities, the realities of black/white relations in small country towns, and a range of significant cultural sites, such as the Quinkan rock art galleries and the Battlecamp massacre site. Add to this some of the best views in Australia, reef, rainforest, crocodiles and a four-wheel driving adventure over rough roads and river fords, and you had a package that would seem palatable to even the most jaded and world-weary of kids.

But Kelly and Morgan were neither jaded nor world-weary. They had been

The Cawleys, Florida, USA, 1989

fortunate to see many parts of the world at an early age and to experience things many of their peers had not, but they understood that these things were privileges, not rights. Roger and I had instilled in them the values our parents gave to us, and to a large extent we had sheltered them from the glare of the spotlight of fame, that curious and mixed blessing.

So they were excited. No, they were more than excited; they were beside themselves. 'Will we see lots of alligators, Mom?' Morgan wanted to know.

'Crocodiles, Morgs, and in Australia it's Mum not Mom.'

During the southern winter of 1991 we had motor-toured along the Australian east coast, getting a feel for the country again. As that vacation neared its end in Cairns, we had taken the children to see the marvellous Tjapukai Aboriginal dance troupe at their theatre in Kuranda. A year later as we began our first pilgrimage into Aboriginal Australia this seemed an appropriate place to start. If Far North Queensland was an Aboriginal Disneyland, then the Tjapukai mob were the 'It's A Small World' ride.

At the end of the performance the dancers called us up onto the stage and we joined them in singing 'Proud To Be An Aborigine', which I am — and we are. But for an 11-year-old soccer star it was a bit much. Morgan sulked for a bit, but he soon forgot the indignity of his stage performance as we crossed the Daintree River and drove deep into crocodile country.

There were many valid reasons for allowing our sojourn to become a minor media event — among them the opportunity to gauge the children's reaction to travelling in the bush in the company of a camera crew in preparation for their involvement in a future film — but there was also a downside. Since we had resettled in Australia the 'Sixty Minutes' program had been after me to do a story. Now we had agreed to allow a crew to accompany us on the trip north. 'Sixty Minutes' seemed intrigued by the prospect of a couple of wide-eyed, gum-chewing American kids having their romantic illusions shattered. Their reporter Richard Carleton interviewed Morgan and Kelly on the beach near Cape Tribulation and asked them about their expectations. He asked: 'Do you know that some Aboriginal communities have serious problems with drinking and violence? Are you frightened of what you might find?'

I was incensed by the question, not because I wished to hide from my children anything about the realities of Aboriginal life, but because it was such a blatant attempt to plant preconceived notions and fears in their minds. I made my feelings known to both Carleton and his producer, and that part of the interview did not make it to air, although I was later asked questions of similar ilk. This was fine; indeed it was the program's prerogative to seek an 'angle' on the story of my journey of rediscovery.

But what annoyed me then, and continues to annoy me despite the fact that the 'Sixty Minutes' piece was generally well received, is that there existed a presumption that I wanted to see and show my children a homogenised version of Aboriginal life, and that the reality would come as some kind of shock — that perhaps we would all cry and thus create a 'great television moment'.

This presumption overlooked the fact that for five years prior to my mother's death I had studied Aboriginal lore and culture in preparation for my eventual pilgrimage, and that for my entire life I had remained in touch not just with my immediate family but with the families which made up our clan group. What I had not done, and so badly needed to do, was to pick up all the pieces of this grand jigsaw puzzle and attempt to make some sense of the picture they formed. It was never going to be easy, and much of it, I knew, would be spent tracking down my past in gloomy rooms full of cobwebs and dust in dilapidated houses in country towns that had seen better days. It would take time and patience, and my children had neither.

So we took them to Aboriginal world in miniature — a place where, in the space of a couple of weeks, we hoped they might begin to understand this singular obsession of their Mum's.

Beyond the Bloomfield River — forded proudly by Roger, using a four-wheel-drive vehicle for the first time in the manner for which God intended it — we made our first bush base in the tiny community of Ayton, between the mouth of the river and the Wujul Wujul Aboriginal community a few crocodile swims upstream. Bounded by the rainforest mountains of the Greater Daintree on one side, and the blue waters of the Coral Sea on the other, this was hardly the plains country of the Wiradjuri, the terrain of my bloodstock. But for all its natural beauty the Bloomfield Valley offered a raw and unadorned view of Aboriginal life. At one end of the valley the Wujul community — still known here, as in other parts of Australia where memories die hard, as the 'mission' — had been one of the places which attracted mention in the Royal Commission into deaths in custody, that investigation into the most tragic symptom of the Aboriginal malaise. In 1992, under the guidance of Wujul chairman George Kulka, the community was fighting back. Work and cultural programs had begun to replace idleness and despair. The people were returning to their traditional skills. It was now a place of hope.

At the other end of the valley in Ayton, a town founded by Danish sawmillers and kept alive for half a century by tin miners, there was now an interesting mix of blacks and whites, perhaps best illustrated by the cattleman and bush bard, Bob Harlow and his wife, Viv. I had an introduction to the Harlows and we made our first call at the little roadside stall known as 'Viv's Place'.

Viv Harlow, a middle-aged Aboriginal woman whose strong and pleasant features were adorned by an ever-present slouch hat and Hawaiian shirt, sat outside her shop deeply immersed in a game of Scrabble. There were pies and pasties in the warmer, she said, cold drinks in the fridge. But I was soon to discover that Viv's offhand manner concealed a heart of gold — black gold, the kind of matter-of-fact maternalism I had seen so often in Aboriginal women. Over the days to come Viv and I were to share some wonderful times together, fishing for whiting in Plantation Creek, talking stories and laughing. (Viv did a lot of laughing.) A teenager in Cooktown in the 1950s, she had married a Cape York drover and settled above the Bloomfield on a cattle run called the Ten Mile. In her rough-hewn kitchen Viv showed me a faded photograph of Bob on horseback, her first-born son Alan bouncing around in a fruit crate tied to the saddle as his parents negotiated the jump-up (an incline) to get him home from the Cooktown hospital.

What harsh but happy lives these people had led, concerned with little more than the imperative of survival, and yet somehow developing through the simplicity of their own existence an understanding of the complexities of

Kelly and Morgan interviewed by a 'Sixty Minutes' reporter. Far North Queensland, 1992

Above: Fishing at Plantation Creek with the late Viv Harlow, 1992 *Right:* The daring Cawley clan fords the Bloomfield River, 1992

The Cawleys join teacher Norman Tayley in a 'Kuku Yalanji' language class at Bloomfield State School, 1992

others. We immediately loved the Harlows, a feeling obviously shared by the rest of the population of Ayton, who joined us under the shade trees for an after-work barbecue.

Early in 1993 as this book neared completion we learned of Viv Harlow's tragic death from heart failure at the age of only 51. On a miserable wet season afternoon in Mossman, black and white folk from all over the North packed the tiny church to bid her farewell. I wished I had known her better, for when Viv died even the skies cried.

Many of the people we met at the Harlows' barbecue were teachers or helpers at the Bloomfield State School, and we were given the run of the place when we visited. Bloomfield was one of a handful of Queensland schools where Aboriginal language and lore had been introduced as a subject for both black and white students, and the results were impressive. We sat in on a class given by Norman Tayley in the local tongue 'kuku yalanji'. Our kids joined the mixed race class in reciting the Aboriginal words for parts of the anatomy. There seemed to be a genuine interest shown by all the kids, even our own! My optimism was further buoyed when, after class, we all joined in an impromptu football game. It was quite wonderful to hear little white boys calling to their Aboriginal mates in the kuku yalanji tongue, and the mates responding in English.

At the Wujul Wujul community we asked George Kulka to explain life in a remote Aboriginal station in the 1990s. George, a shy, smiling man who carries a pannikin which rivals in size the monster which is never far from my brother Larry, filled the vessel with tea and led us around his well-ordered domain. This was the first of many tours of communities, and Wujul still stands out in my memory as one of the best. Its social and economic problems are many — while it is a 'dry' community, some members are still given to binge drinking, the roads are bad, the water supply erratic — but in its freewheeling approach to all manner of industry — from maritime to cattle to tourism (the Wujuls pull tourists' cars out of the river for $100 a toss) — the community shows a spirit which I admire. That spirit was exemplified by Molly Spider and Mabel Webb, two old women we met one day at the Old People's lodgings.

At four in the afternoon the two frail old ladies were gumming away at a dinner of canned spaghetti, their favourite tucker. When they had finished they would make their way on walking frames into the garden, from which vantage point they could watch the light fade over the dusty town square. Molly was 106 years old, according to her grand-nephew George Kulka the oldest living Aborigine. If this was so she had been a young girl in the North when the explorers, the Jardine brothers were still in the habit of shooting any Cape York clansman who stood between their herds and a good feed, and she would have been born in the year when the feared Native Police finally stopped patrolling the far parts from Birdsville to Bamaga, 'dispersing' Aborigines with that most persuasive tool of negotiation, the gun. Now Molly Spider said little with her toothless mouth, but much with her wise old eyes, which sparkled and then clouded over as she surveyed me and my family. Who was this young woman? Was she a Murri? She looked a bit that way. And what was all the fuss about? Had she caught a big goanna?

Mabel Webb was a relative youngster in her mid-80s. George interpreted for her, but Mabel had been around and she soon took over the conversation in her own English. 'I bin habin' two husbands,' she said proudly. She giggled a bit, like a shy schoolgirl. 'Oh, there bin some happy time.'

They were like the ancient shade trees in the square, these old ladies. You looked into their eyes and saw the history you yearned to rediscover. How much had they seen, I wondered? And how many stories could they tell me if I sat with them for a week or two?

From the Bloomfield we drove on into Cape York Peninsula, avoiding the wide and dusty development road by sticking to the coast, then skirting Lakefield National Park to arrive in Laura through the back door. Alerted to our impending arrival, the seven pupils (black and white) of Laura State School had painted a large welcoming banner which they had draped opposite the hub of activity in Laura, the Quinkan Hotel.

We had come to Laura for a special reason. Since Morgan was a baby I had read to him from books I had gathered on various trips back to Australia. Whenever possible I sought out books with Aboriginal themes. He loved to hear the stories of the Dreaming, and his eyes would grow wide as he absorbed the images of bird-women and snake-men. Morgan's favourite Dreamtime characters were the Quinkans, the 'good blokes and bad blokes' whose legends form the spiritual backbone of the Kuku clans of Cape York. These goblin-like creatures are said to be responsible for the shaping of the terrain from the Bloomfield out to the source of the Palmer River, and on up towards Coen, as well as for the complex tapestry of human relationships between the clans. According to whose legends you listen to, the Quinkans are the source of all good or all evil, and in some cases, both. They were powerful characters, these Quinkans, and we wanted to feel their presence.

At Laura we found Tommy George, an Aboriginal elder and protector of the sacred rock art galleries close to town. With Tommy we drove out to Mushroom Rock in the late afternoon for our first glimpse of the world's oldest surviving art gallery, the ochre symbols under the protective ledges of granite and sandstone, where Aboriginal clans sought shelter from wind, sun and rain 40,000 and more years ago. First contact with these fragments of living ancient history, these insights into the life of my ancestors, was awesome. And in the days that followed, that tingling feeling of absolute awe was never to leave me. Roger, whose interest in Aboriginal themes is usually more academic than sensual, felt it too, and the children knew instinctively that this was a special event in all our lives.

The author of the Quinkan books that Morgan so loved was a former airline pilot named Percy Trezise who had spent much of the past 40 years exploring the rock galleries of the region and researching the legends, transmitted orally through the generations, that gave the symbols life. Percy had spent hundreds of nights sitting by campfires with the Old People, and knew as much as any white person about their Dreaming. I found the descriptions of his travels, his work with Aboriginal painter Dick Roughsey and his interpretation of the stories he had heard, all published in his 1969 book *Quinkan Country*, fascinating. One story I appreciated, concerned the belief of the Kuku clans that a dead person's spirit left its earthly body on the third day, which was the appropriate time for wailing farewells and rituals.

Why the third day and not the second or fourth, asked Percy? These Kuku beliefs predated Christianity and yet both had arrived at the same time frame

Morgan and I explore Mushroom Rock

With tribal elder Tommy George at Mushroom Rock, near Laura, Cape York Peninsula, 1992

for resurrection. Percy surmised that the belief must have its origin in some common feature of the universe. Lying in his swag under the big night sky, it occurred to him that 'the last of the old moon is seen early in the morning, low in the eastern sky paling with the coming dawn. It appears as a thin disc standing on end, and looks like an old man humped over with age. For the next two days and nights it cannot be seen at all, but on the third it appears again, this time just after sunset and low in the western sky, symbolically lying on its back like a baby cradle.'

My own belief, like my mother's before me, is that there is one God for all people, and whether he or she appears to you as a bearded person in flowing robes and sandals or one of a hundred totems of the Dreaming, matters not. What matters is that there is something, someone, larger than ourselves.

Percy Trezise's son Stephen was our guide to the more remote rock art galleries of the Jowalbinna Valley. We drove out to the bush camp that Stephen has established not far from the Trezise family homestead on a flat by the creek, framed by the sandstone cliffs that were once the seasonal homes of the Cape York clans. Steve is a down-to-earth, no-nonsense kind of fellow, and his camp is much the same. I thought the canvas tent/cabins spread around the central mess area were quaint, and the whole camp quite lovely in the last, soft light of the day. My city-bred family thought otherwise.

'No way!' said Kelly. 'There isn't even a door. Snakes could just slither right in! I'm sleeping in the car.' Her father tended to agree, but after a hearty camp-cooked meal, they both began to come to terms with the bush.

There are few more delightful places to greet the dawn of a crisp spring morning than the Jowalbinna Valley. We sat by the embers of the campfire and watched the sun put colour into the sandstone walls. For how many thousands of years, I wondered, had Aborigines crouched over campfires in this very spot, before seeking shelter from the intense heat of the summer sun in their shady cave retreats, there to stake tenancy claims through a representation in ochres of their clan totems around the walls of the shelter.

We hiked deep into the valley with Steve before beginning the climb up into the galleries. There, so far away from everything in that beautiful place, I felt very close to my forebears. I later wrote in my notebook, 'Just squatting here and seeing these things in their natural surroundings — it's so beautiful, so simple and pure. The feelings, the vibrations from the Old People, going back so many thousands of years … It's so strange and strong. I can feel the links. I would never have believed you can feel so close to your ancestors.'

Every Aborigine who can manage it should see the rock art galleries of our forebears; those who can't manage it should be given a travel grant instead of some sit-down money (welfare payments). And they should see this amazing art the way the original artists would have seen it as they crouched in their caves and admired their work — no fences, no boardwalks, no car parks or pie stands. There is a body of opinion that preservation of these sites should rank way above public access, but I tend to agree with Stephen Trezise's view, 'Of course the galleries have to be looked after and treated with the respect they deserve, but some of the art has lasted upwards of 30,000 years with people bashing sticks and stones on it and lighting fires under it. Letting a few people at a time see it at close quarters and actually feel its power will do more good than harm.'

If seeing the Quinkan galleries put me in touch with the lifestyles of the ancient Aborigines, Battlecamp brought me closer to the tragedy of more recent Aboriginal history. Since my return to Australia I had read widely for the first time about the inhumane treatment of Aborigines by settlers and soldiers. The revelations about massacres and rape had a profound effect on me. I was angry that I — like so many Aborigines — had not been made aware of this darker side of our history, that it had not even been part of the school curriculum, and I felt the hurt so personally that I began to have nightmares about it. I read about children being stolen from their mothers and woke up screaming for Morgan. History, which since schooldays had been an abstraction to me, suddenly became a living thing.

We were driving the rough road across the Battlecamp Range, heading back towards Cooktown when on a sudden impulse I tugged on Roger's arm and asked him to pull up. Roger detected a sudden note of urgency in my voice, which he thought totally out of character. He thought I must have seen a rare animal or something, but I just got out of the car and wandered off into the scrub.

I had read a little about the Battlecamp massacre of 1873 and knew we were in the vicinity, but I cannot explain why, at a certain point on the escarpment, I felt this sudden and quite irresistible urge to get out of the car and feel the spirit of that land.

When James Mulligan found gold on the Palmer River in early 1873 the port of Cooktown sprang up almost overnight, and daily the miners trudged or rode in bullock carts from the riverbed over the range and down to the bustling, hustling shanty town at the mouth of the Endeavour River. The gold rush attracted ne'er-do-wells from all over the colonies, and there was a steady stream of prostitutes steamered in from the south to help relieve the prospectors of their new-found fortunes. But supply was soon outstripped by demand and the Cooktown pimps, aided and abetted by the scurrilous Native Police, began raids on the outlying Aboriginal camps to 'kill the bucks and take the gins', as the songwriter Ted Egan put it so forcefully a century later.

By November 1873 the clans had had enough. More than 500 warriors from all over the hill country gathered at a camp and prepared themselves for battle, painting their faces and bodies and singing the songs of war. The returning miners passed word of this impending attack, and a heavily armed force of Native Police, miners and Chinese shopkeepers rode out to meet them. They caught the warriors still in preparation for battle, and their Snyder rifles made short work of the 500. Australian history still records this as a 'battle' rather than a 'massacre'. As an Aborigine, I see it differently.

As far as I am aware, nothing marks the exact site of the Battlecamp massacre, and I may not have even been on it that day. But the pull of the spirits of the dead was strong. I wandered around, touching the earth and the stunted trees, and I felt a great sense of belonging. I think, too, I felt proud of my people for standing up against the barbaric behaviour of the invaders, however little hope they had with spears against guns. I felt the white man's bullets ripping through the flesh of my ancestors, and was aware of the strange metallic taste of death in my mouth. For a moment my mind wandered back to Willoughby Girls High when all those years ago, I had written so innocently and routinely about the white settlers clearing the Aborigines from their lands with a gun. I thought that perhaps I had never been less of an Aborigine than I was then, nor more of one than I felt that day at Battlecamp.

I spent a long, long time in that place which at first appeared forbidding, but became, in time, a forgiving place. I sat alone on that hillside and felt my eyes fill with tears. Then I composed myself and walked back down to the car and my family.

'Mom,' said Morgan, breaking the silence of the ages, 'I'm hungry. Is there like a candy store around here someplace?'

'It's Mum, Morgs. M-U-M. Mum.'

During our time in North Queensland Kelly spent her spare moments reading a book called *I Dreamed Of Africa* by Kuki Gallmann. In it she found a quotation from Marcel Proust's *A la Recherche du Temps Perdu (Remembrance of Things Past)*: 'The real voyage of discovery does not consist in seeking new landscapes, but in having new eyes.' When she later wrote about her own voyage of discovery for a school project, she included the quote on the cover, under the heading 'A New Foundation'.

I was moved and quite relieved when I saw that the trip had made such

At the Battlecamp Massacre site, 1992

an impact on her, because I well knew that Aboriginal children of my own generation rarely had the opportunity to come to terms with their own history, much of it kept from them by well-meaning parents who did not wish to burden them with the 'shame' of their heritage. I was moved even more — to tears in fact — when I read on to Kelly's conclusion. She wrote:

> Our exciting trip is something I'll be thinking of for the rest of my life. This may seem strange, but when I was there, my instinct told me this is where I belong. Coming to Australia was probably the best thing my family has ever done. From having my first taste of Aboriginal life, I've become more excited about my heritage ... Learning about my people is one of the greatest feelings.

Chapter 28

*W*HEN MY GENERAL INTEREST in Aboriginal culture and my specific interest in my family and Wiradjuri history became known — through television and magazine interviews — I was inundated with letters and telephone calls from people who had known one distant branch of the Goolagongs, Ingrams, Briggs or another.

All were well meaning and many were genuinely helpful. For example, an Aboriginal historian named Alick Jackomas (he was of Greek heritage but had married into the Cummeragunga mob) sent me the Hamilton and Briggs' family trees. A regional historian named Robert Ellis sent me vital information about the Goolagong line. And most importantly, I was put in touch with an organisation called Link-Up, which was established in 1980 to help reunite 'the stolen generation' with their Aboriginal families. The pain of discovering who you are can be as intense as the joy, as so many people of Aboriginal extraction are finding out. Carol Kendall from this worthy group helped me piece together the fragments of my own heritage. During the writing of this book I was contacted by a prison welfare worker regarding a young prisoner who was Aboriginal but had no knowledge of his mother. I put him in touch with Link-Up and within days I received the wonderful news that the young man's mother had been traced. Of course, that was not the end of the problem, but it may have been the start of the solution.

It soon became obvious to me that what I wanted to know about my family could not be gleaned solely from distant phone conversations, nor from the huge pile of faxes gathering dust in the research office we had set up in Noosa Heads.

The hip-bone-connected-to-the-thigh-bone family tree information was, of course, fascinating and necessary. It revealed to me that all, in our complex family, was not always as it seemed. Indeed, I was almost a year into the research for this book before I realised that I was not descended from the Briggs line, that my mother was in fact an Ingram adopted by Eric Briggs. However, it was becoming apparent that genealogy was not the main game in all of this. I needed not just to know the names of my people but to see and feel the places they came from, to hold in the palm of my hand the remaining fragments of their presence here. Just as it is an Aboriginal custom in parts of the country to decorate the graves of loved ones with the material possessions they held most dear in life, so I needed to decorate my research with real pieces of the lives of my forebears.

I had to go back to Wiradjuri country.

During the winter of 1992 I had received a disturbing letter from Auntie Junie Mason, whose name crops up at several points in this book, but whom I had never met — or at least had no recollection of meeting — despite the fact that we had both been at my grandmother Dolly's funeral. I knew she was blood, however, because my mother had explained the connection after Junie's brother, Kevin Gilbert, had published his poem about me in the *Bulletin*.

Now Junie wrote to me,

> This letter will no doubt come as a shock to you as I have ... information that I hold within ... entrusted to me by the Old People as we fished the Lachlan and 'Bidgee Rivers ... I have had to think long and hard on this, but if you contact me I will help you where I refused others, only if you convince me it will not be exploited by relatives — some have tried. Do I know you, your parents, grandparents (both sides) who have all passed on? Yes to all questions, very close ... how proud all above were of you in their quiet, lovable and dignified ways. I loved them all very much, and even now the memories and pain of their going still remain, but I think of them often ... I always assumed your mother or grandmother may have given you the answers. Did you ever ask them? I knew your father all his life, your maternal grandmother all my life and your mother since our early teens ... I will help, but don't wait too long, Evonne, if you seek the truth.

Junie's letter gave her address as the Lakeview Caravan Park, Wangi Wangi, on Lake Macquarie near Newcastle, New South Wales, but after a series of phone calls I found that Junie had moved already. Had I waited too long? It was only a matter of days. And what were these mysterious truths that others wished to exploit? Was there a dark secret in the Goolagong closet? Junie claimed to have the answers but I didn't even know the questions!

Nevertheless, I had to seek out someone who had been so close to the Old People of Condobolin, and I eventually got a new address for her at a block of council flats in the western suburbs of Newcastle. I flew to Sydney, rented a car and drove the couple of hours north. I found Junie, frail and breathless in her mid-60s, sitting on a solitary chair in a tiny flat littered with cardboard boxes containing the material sum of her existence. She seemed to have smoked too many cigarettes in her time and was now paying the price, but she had laughing eyes, a quick wit and a splendid spirit.

We talked for a long time without touching on the big secrets, and I began to feel she was ill at ease in the unadorned flat.

'What is it, Junie?'

'Oh, I just moved in this morning, there's no electricity on yet and I don't know where to start with my unpacking. To tell you the truth, it's all a bit much for me.'

I helped drape some makeshift curtains over the windows to protect her belongings from prying eyes, fished out some clothes for her and took her to a nearby hotel, where we checked into a suite and sat up half the night talking — but still not about any 'secrets'. In the morning it was decided that Junie would come with me to Condobolin. 'There's so much that's going to hurt you, Evonne,' she said, 'but I'll be there to help you.'

On the long trip out west Junie talked the legs off a chair for an hour or so at a time, summoning up names I had never heard and events that still seemed unrelated to what little I knew of my family history. Then she would fall so silent that I had to watch out of the corner of my eye to make sure she was still breathing. As she dozed I wondered what all this was about. She was a sweet old thing, but we were getting no closer to the secrets of the Old People. Had she considered me unworthy of the knowledge, I wondered, or was it simply that I had yet to ask the right questions? What were the right questions?

Towards the end of the journey I began to realise that there were no right questions. My return to Wiradjuri country had begun as a wild goose chase, but if I had any ill feelings towards Junie as a result, these were balanced by the great sense of relief that there seemed to be no horrific event in my past. And anyway, Junie was family, too. The demons of the past receded and, as we drove into familiar country, we began to enjoy the present.

In Condobolin I dropped Junie at the Gundy Wightons' where she had arranged to stay, and ventured alone down Bathurst Street to reacquaint myself with the place. It was good to be back in Condo, that lovely old town and Wiradjuri 'safe place' where I had spent too little time in recent years. Hoping to find some literature about the Aboriginal history of the town, I popped into the newsagency and came out with the only two books available on Condobolin. In one of them, a slim volume called *Condobolin And District — Australia As It Really Is*, reprinted from 1915, I found some interesting reminiscences about the Wiradjuri in the district, penned by a pioneer settler.

Mr E. H. Moulder recalled the good old days of the 1860s when Condo's racecourse crossed the main street and on race days 'the black denizens of the bush were very much in evidence and had a right gay old time'. He also had some second-hand information about a trip by waggon from Bathurst to Euabalong Station at about the same time, with the squatter in the box seat and a stockman named Barney Doyle as outrider. At a race-track near Forbes 'there were hundreds of blacks from far up and down the river'. They exchanged greetings with the squatter, then noticing the cloud of dust on the road, in the midst of which was to be seen Barney leading a spare horse, they asked, 'What name white fellow come up?' They were told it was Barney Doyle. 'At this there was an absolute bolt on the part of the darkies; and next morning when the travelers went to the camp to make some inquiries of old Cranky, the King of the Cargelligo Blacks, lo, not a black was to be seen. They had gone, bag and baggage, leaving spears, woomeras and other belongings in their haste to get away from Barney. The reason for this was that Barney waged a war of extermination on all blacks for disturbing the stock on the station, and it is said, not without reason, that he carried a cavalry sabre and horse pistols, and used them indiscriminately on the blacks of both sexes, if he found that, by the taint in the air from their bodies, cattle had been driven from their feeding ground.'

I read this in a milk bar over a coffee, and as I sat in a booth trying to work out which part of Mr Moulder's essay offended me most deeply, Uncle Lylie Goolagong snuck up on me. It was always both a delight and a shock to see Uncle Lylie. He was now some 15 years older than Kenny had been at the time of his death, and of course he had made do with one arm for some years now, but he was Kenny to a tee. The resemblance was uncanny still, even with Lylie in his sixties. He stayed fit, he told me, by tending his rose garden and walking each day to the TAB to place his two dollar bets, then on across town to the hospital to see his older brother, my Uncle Gordon. Gordon Goolagong, once the life of every party, was now blind and suffering from diabetes, the scourge of the Aboriginal population.

'Would you like to see Gordon?' Lylie asked.

'Oh, of course I would.'

We drove over to the hospital. I said to Lylie, 'You don't want to run along behind to keep your fitness level up?'

'She'll be right, my gel,' he laughed.

Uncle Gordon was sitting on the verandah of the small hospital in pyjamas and dressing gown, next to a wizened little man with darting eyes and a perpetual grin. This was Tony Rose, the walking Condobolin encyclopaedia who helped me so much in preparing the historical information on the

Condobolin Goolagongs that appears in the first section of this book. Tony, a white man, was almost family to Lylie and Gordon. He did most of the talking, while Uncle Gordon clutched my arm and smiled into the void. 'Oh, this is nice,' he said in his slow, distinctive voice. 'This is more than nice.'

Lylie and I drove around, revisiting the old haunts. At Willow Bend most of the corrugated iron shacks of the old mission had gone, replaced by neat new brick homes, and at The Murie, the old settlement where the Goolagongs and their Wiradjuri relations lived out the middle years of this century, there was nothing but a few scraps of wire and the rocky remains of a hundred campfires. Lylie picked up a stick in his remaining hand and dug around the ashes of an old fire. 'We still come down here sometimes,' he said. 'We caught a goanna and cooked him up right here just a month or so ago.' The recollection obviously pleased him. He wanted me to know that the old ways had not completely disappeared.

We walked along the bank of the Lachlan for a while and I asked Lylie about the Old People. He spoke openly and told me as much as he knew about the family history, which was not a great deal. He seemed a little confused when it came to Grandmother Dolly's two husbands, Roy and Jimmy Goolagong, but then everyone in Condo was. Was this the secret of the Old People mentioned by Junie that had to be so jealously guarded, that my grandmother married two cousins? Surely not. This was not exactly a rare thing in the Aboriginal community, where blood lines crossed back and forth to the very borders of genetic acceptability, where instinctively the elders knew when it was time to take a trip along the river or across the plains in order to encounter new clans.

My circuitous path around the Goolagongs of Condo led me ultimately to Auntie Rosie, Dolly's younger sister and the last of the Old People. She had a shock of white hair and was said — by Junie — to have become very shy, almost reclusive, but I found her nothing of the sort. As a child I had known her only vaguely, but after a short time in her company I felt comfortable enough to ask her directly about the dark secrets of the Old People.

Rosie laughed. 'You bin talkin' to Junie! It's your history, your knowledge. There's nothing you shouldn't know, gel.'

Relieved to have my suspicions confirmed that there were no skeletons about to fall out of our family closet and that I had the approval of the oldest living Goolagong, I got on with my research. On my last day in Condo I arranged to have a family photograph taken on the lawns of the hospital. Enough Goolagongs showed up to field a Boomerangs football team with a well-stocked reserve bench, although I don't think it would have been of the

Left: Walking with Uncle Lylie at The Murie, 1992 *Right:* The oldest and youngest of the Condobolin Goolagongs. Auntie Rosie with a great-grandchild. Condobolin, 1992

The Condobolin Goolagongs, 1992

With Tony Rose, Condobolin's walking encyclopaedia, in 1992

same calibre as the premiership-winning Boomerangs of the 1930s. Tony Rose, who had at his nicotine-stained fingertips the scorelines and team compositions of each of the Boomerangs' grand finals, agreed with me.

'There'll never be another football team like them Boomerangs, not without Jimmy Goolagong,' he said, watching from a wheelchair under the trees as the family assembled. I caught the old man's eye a couple of times as the various generations posed for photographs around Uncle Gordon and Auntie Rosie, and I felt so sad for him, orphaned as a child and denied the comfort of real family all his adult life. I wished I could wave a magic wand and make him a Wiradjuri Koori.

'Come on, Tony. Come and get in the picture. You're not very black, but you'll do!'

Tony Rose sprang out of his wheelchair and bolted happily for the centre of frame.

The search for Linda Goolagong's family proved to be more difficult, despite the fact that her family tree had been researched several times over. The problem lay with the fact that her father turned out to be Lindsay Lawrence 'Sousie' Ingram and not Eric Briggs, whose line is tantamount to Aboriginal aristocracy and can be traced back to the first unwilling union of a black girl and a white sealer. But the Ingrams were also a solid Wiradjuri family and I have learnt much about them since locating Aunt Zillah Williams (née Ingram) in Griffith.

At Linda's funeral I had been given an early photo of Mum and Dad. Through the tears of the moment I paid little attention to where it came from, but the more I looked at it the more its source interested me. Through my sister Barbara I discovered it had come from Zillah Williams, Sousie Ingram's daughter, my mother's half-sister. I visited her in Griffith and she provided me with a wealth of information about this line of the family, including the first picture I had seen of my real maternal grandfather.

I also discovered that the Briggs and Ingram families had come together long before Grandmother Agnes Hamilton moved from Sousie Ingram to Eric Briggs, taking my mother along with her. In fact, in her fascinating autobiography *If Everyone Cared*, that important Aboriginal figure, Margaret Tucker MBE, reveals that she is directly related to both the Briggs and Ingram families.

Margaret Tucker's story, dramatised in the television series *Women Of The Sun* and documented in the program *Lousy Little Sixpence*, so closely parallels the experiences of my mother's life and her mother's life that I can barely read a page of her work without feeling she is telling my story too.

But as I said earlier, in my story feelings were as important as facts. I knew precious little about either — indeed, I could count on the fingers of both my hands the members of my extended family I really knew well, and where they fitted and how they lived their lives were complete unknowns. I had to know how my parents felt, what went through their heads as they passed their early days in shanties and missions and riverside camps. I had to go to these places and let the trees and the mudbrick walls and the hard-baked earth tell me how it was.

Although there was no real 'plan' to my research, I came home to Noosa from each trip away and sifted through the old pictures I had been given and the notes I had made, trying to make some sense of it all. This was a long and arduous process, and often the sheer enormity of the task would threaten to engulf me. Never in my life had I been a 'scholar', and I found that I had to escape the confines of a desk and get back in touch with people as often as possible. So, instead of one or two trips to Wiradjuri country I made a dozen, often tying them in with other work.

On one trip to Griffith to go through some old photographs at the Three Ways with Clancy Charles, and to speak to the Aboriginal schoolchildren about truancy — I constantly receive invitations to speak at schools and cannot accept them all, but Kooris get special attention — I was contacted by a man who had some links with my mother's side which I still do not fully understand. However, he had in his possession an old piece of film footage which he thought might interest me. It showed me in my mother's arms at an Aboriginal mission 40 years ago, he said.

Excited, I had the film transferred to video and watched it time and time again. The baby was not me and nor was it my mother holding it, but the footage was remarkable nonetheless. Shot at the Darlington Point mission known as 'The Sandhills' in 1950, the brief, flickering black and white film documented the weekly visit of Miss Campbell, the regional head of the Australian Inland Mission, for which occasion a large group of residents had put on their finery and stood in line for the camera, which slowly panned across them. I could not identify the woman holding the baby, but the pretty and bashful girl next to her was unmistakably Melinda Goolagong, not yet 21, married three years and the mother of Barbara and Larry. Although there was no sign of it in the trim figure, she may have also been carrying me.

The excitement of seeing my 'first' mother come alive on the screen had barely dimmed when I received news that my second mother, Mrs Edwards was critically ill and had called for her daughters. Without hesitation this time, I flew to Sydney and took a cab to the Royal North Shore Hospital.

In the taxi my mind drifted back to my first visit to the hospital some months before. Although I'd phoned, I hadn't actually seen Mrs Edwards since our return to Australia a year earlier, and I felt a little guilty at not having made the effort to see some one who had meant so much to me. For a couple of years Mrs Edwards had been battling cancer, but she was a tough old bird, and by all reports cancer was coming off second-best. Vicki Edwards, the third daughter who had left home at about the time of my arrival in 1965, met me at the airport with her daughter, Danielle — my godchild. I immediately felt comfortable with them despite the passage of the years and the fact that I was a little apprehensive about the reception I was going to get from Mrs Edwards after so long.

As if to prepare me, Vicki explained that her mother had been irritable with everyone, and that they had put it down to the effects of chemotherapy. But when I walked into the room I saw she was past the reprimands she would occasionally dish out when we were children. Now she was a very old lady, frail in body and in spirit, and I could see that she was nervous about our meeting. To compensate she talked endlessly about my life, her illness, the children, the doctors and nurses. At one point she mentioned the research into my Aboriginal history, which she had read about in a magazine. Her brow furrowed. 'Lot of silly rubbish,' she said. 'Don't you let these people push you into anything. It just doesn't sound like you.'

I don't suppose it did. In her eyes I was still that little girl who needed protection from all that might hurt her in the world. I smiled weakly and tried to hide my disappointment. Oh, Mrs Edwards, I wanted to say, come with me in spirit on this journey! Share my joy! This is what Linda would want. Give me your approval, too.

When we were alone Mrs Edwards moved closer to the edge of the bed and grabbed my hand. 'Oh, Evonne, I've missed you so much.' I squeezed her hand and tried to hold back my tears. I thought of old Mrs Kurtzman at the nursing home in Griffith, unable to see or remember much any more, and of all the white Old People, who were just as special to me in their own ways, just as much a part of my story.

'I've missed you too,' I said softly.

And now her hour had come. All the Edwards girls were there, chatting furiously to mask the great sadness of this time. Mrs Edwards drifted in and out in a haze of medication, but when she was conscious she recognised us all, and we each had time to say our farewells. She was ready now, but her tough old body had never known how to quit, and it was too late to learn now. She clung tenaciously to life for longer than she needed or wanted to, and when it was over I am sure she was as relieved as were those who had kept the vigil by her bed of pain.

The last of my parents was gone.

Chapter 29

*O*VER THE EASTER BREAK in 1993 Barellan Central School held the first full-scale reunion in its 75-year history. I had managed to catch up with several of my schoolmates in Barellan and elsewhere, but this was too good an opportunity to miss. Despite the frantic rush of preparing this book by the publisher's deadline, I decided I had to go.

I drove all day and half the next, playing the songs of my youth in my head as I passed through the flat country of the Western Plains, so much like home. I could hear the voices, see the faces of the playground, and I hoped that the reality would live up to the fantasy. Would the old mates be the same? And the funny Tubb brothers? And would Mr Hammond, the policeman, come? His children went to our school.

Barellan was as neat as a pin, with about 20 more cars than usual parked in front of the pub. But for their more recent vintage, it might have been a harvest party back in the good old days when wheat was king.

'Evonne! It's Judy!' Cries from passing cars on Yapunyah Street, more and more people on the usually-deserted main street footpath as the out-of-towners carted their swags up the rickety stairs of the Commercial Hotel.

I made my own camp with my little sister Janelle and her husband Grant, in Mum's rambling old home on the edge of town, where plastic fruit and flowers and pictures from my tennis career still dominated the interior and big, black, delicious yabbies still ruled the dam. We were soon joined by Gail, over from Narrandera, Barbara, down from Sydney, and Mully from his home on the New South Wales Central Coast. Finally Larry and his wife Loris came over from their fishing and camping spot on the Murrumbidgee.

Kevin was visiting his children and Ian was at a tennis tournament in Mildura, but we had a quorum of Goolagongs so I put Mum's film on the video player. It was wonderful to watch their reactions in the darkened room as Linda flickered onto the screen with her shy smile and tilt of her pretty head.

That weekend I talked myself hoarse and made the rash promises to keep in touch that we all hoped to keep. I had cups of tea with old Lucy Smith and Clarrie and Dot Irvin, and had a few laughs with Jean Gladman and

The practice wall

the Tubb brothers. I hit tennis balls against the old practice wall again as Colin Bandy, my first boyfriend, led his Clydesdale horses down Mulga Street in front of a waggon-load of laughing children. And I made up the fourth for a set of doubles with the Hammonds, and found the former Constable Hammond just as handy around the court as he had been 30 years before.

It was comfortable to be in the old town with so many old friends. It was comfortable, and, like so many children raised in country towns, I was fortunate to have that firm foundation, that sense of belonging that just isn't the same in the cities. But it wasn't home. Home was a state of mind that I had not yet quite attained.

'Where to now?' asked Barb, chewing on a blade of grass beside Mum's dam on a glorious Easter Sunday morning.

'Remember when we first got Mum a car?' I said. 'And she took off for weeks and weeks at a time, and we never knew where she'd been?'

Barbara nodded and smiled. It had been the bane of her existence for years, putting grey hairs in her head. I mused, 'Where do you suppose she used to go?'

'I bet she followed the families and the rivers. She would never have been far from a friendly face or a good fishing hole.'

Barellan reunion, Easter 1993. With my old tennis partner, Mr Hammond

I resolved then and there to follow the 'Linda lines', those sacred tracks that would take me into parts of the country, and parts of myself, that I had never seen. The logical starting point was Cummeragunga, the famous old mission where so much of my story began, but between Cummera and me lay Larry's camp at Gogeldrie Weir, and if I was seriously going to 'go bush', there was no better way to ease back into the campfire life than with big brother at my side. In fact, with the exception of the odd night at civilised camps like the Trezises' at Jowalbinna, I had never actually been camping. When I was a kid we may have 'camped' at the river or by the side of the road, but 'camping' was not the point, nor what we called it. It was just how we travelled. When Kenny got too tired to drive on, we pulled up and slept, kids in the car, parents on a blanket outside.

Now, however, I had a deluxe swag, its heavy canvas cover still crisp and green. Inside it I had a favourite pillow and an all-weather sleeping bag. I had a small tent too, and a camp oven and some basic food supplies. I was prepared for any challenge of a physical nature. I wasn't sure about the rest.

'Come on, Barb, let's go and camp at the river with Larry.' And we did, arriving at his pretty campsite below the weir as the last light of the day turned the Murrumbidgee silver. Barbara and I were thrilled to hear the birds,

Left: With Larry and Barbara at Larry's Gogeldrie Weir camp. Easter 1993 *Right:* Preparing yellowbelly for the camp oven

the ones whose names and sounds ran together — the mopokes and curlews, and the ones we knew as 'galooches' and 'come-out-tonights'.

When the darkness took over I sat before the fire and watched the menacing shadows of the trees out over the water, and the memories came flooding back. How we had feared the shadows of the bush night as children, but how tantalising was that fear!

While the yellowbelly cooked slowly in the camp oven, Larry told the bunyip stories Mum used to tell, and the ones about the bugeen — a Wiradjuri word for the avenging witch doctors of the Murray Valley. Then he laughed and grabbed his guitar and strummed a few chords of a gospel song. Just as Dad passed on to Larry his love of tinkering with car engines, Mum passed on her love of music. She taught Larry the basic chords at a very early age and soon he could play 'Dolly Dimple' from start to finish. In his very early teens he got a job selling guitars door-to-door, and made enough to buy his first electric guitar and amplifier. Later on, when I had gone to Sydney, he formed a band called 'The Red Velvets'. They wore black pants, white shirts, cowboy string ties and red vests embroidered with 'RV', and they played all the bush dances. Unfortunately, the band's career came to an abrupt halt when their manager ran off with all their equipment.

But Larry never lost his love of the guitar, and it is never far from him, particularly since he has taken it up as an instrument of God. He sang and played beautifully at Mum's funeral.

'I'll see if I can sing the fish onto the hooks,' he grinned as he began to sing His praises. Late in the evening Larry said, 'Well, Eve, I hope you find what you're looking for.'

I knew he meant it because Larry's own search had been long and arduous, but ultimately fulfilling. The man I left packing up his camp at Gogeldrie

At Mum's mud-hut birthplace near Darlington Point, 1993

Weir on a sparkling morning was 9 kilograms (20 pounds) overweight and diabetic, but he was at peace with himself. Larry Goolagong knows exactly who he is, and where he fits into the universe.

From the weir I drove downstream through Darlington Point, and stopped off to pay my respects at the remains of the mud hut next to the Warangesda ruins, where Mum was born. I bet she'd done the same thing often enough, heading south to the Murray.

Cummeragunga. I'd always loved the lyrical sound of the name, like Goolagong it evoked a certain Aboriginal feeling. It actually meant 'my country'. This mission on the New South Wales side of the Murray, not far from the river port of Echuca, was the birthplace of Aboriginal rights, the home of the Yota Yota clans of the Goulburn and Murray Valleys, but a spiritual home in many ways to all our people. William Cooper, who married my great-grandmother's sister, was expelled from Cummeragunga for exposing conditions there, but in 1938 he had been one of the organisers of the Australia Day 'day of mourning' in which Aborigines gathered in Sydney to protest the denial of their rights. The following year, back on Cummeragunga, he led a march across the Barmah Bridge into Victoria, saying that Cummera Aborigines would no longer accept the administration of the New South Wales government. In this he was 30 years ahead of his time — it would take the 1967 referendum to hand back responsibility for Aborigines to the Crown.

In addition to its reputation for political volatility, Cummeragunga was considered to be the cradle of Aboriginal sportsmanship, with such fine athletes as Doug Nicholls and Lynch Cooper learning their skills on the playing fields adjacent to the river. This Easter Monday, however, the playing fields, long ago returned to the burrs carried on the wind, were deserted. Cummera is still a strong community, but it is no longer the centre of the universe.

I sought out Elizabeth Hoffman, the Yota Yota chairman and a woman who knew both my mother and my grandmother. Aunt Lizzie, as she insisted I call her, was busily researching a land claim on the beautiful Barmah Forest, but she made time to show me the collection of old photographs at the Yota Yota offices. Some I had seen before but many were new to me. Lizzie was particularly proud of the pictures of her grandfather, Bagot Morgan, a man with the face of a warrior.

When we had climbed every limb of the family tree, Lizzie said, 'Would you like to go and see the Old People?'

We drove out past the community's vegetable plantation to the cemetery, where a couple of families were tending the graves of their loved ones. We moved through the family groups, from the Hamiltons to the Walkers to the Morgans and the Charleses. Many of them were now unmarked and it sent a momentary chill through my bones to think that I was walking on my past.

'Your mother used to come here often,' Lizzie said. I could understand why Linda would have found comfort at Cummeragunga. It seemed a spiritual place.

With Lizzie's permission I made camp along the river bank on Yota Yota land and cooked a fine dinner under a starry sky. But then I had the strangest feeling that I was being watched. I climbed into my swag inside my tent but couldn't sleep. When the rains came I was wide awake, huddled in the dark with my heart pounding. I suppose it was fear that I felt, but it was the fear of the bunyip stories I had felt as a child — fear with a soft and comforting edge.

In the morning I called at Aunt Lizzie's house and told her of my restless night.

'That'll be the Old People,' she nodded matter-of-factly.

I had a loose plan after Cummeragunga, but it was more loose than it was a plan. Trying to find a waterhole campsite each night, I would describe a large arc across outback New South Wales, moving through territory foreign to the Wiradjuri, but to places where I guessed Linda might have roamed.

With Auntie Lizzie Hoffman at Cummeragunga, 1993

Barbara had been right — Mum would have followed the rivers, especially in the parched western country. There were reference points on the map where I knew she had been often — Swan Hill, Moulamein, Darlington Point — but something instinctively drew me towards the Darling River. Larry was planning a fishing trip to Menindee, and he spoke the name of this place — a legendary fishing spot — with something approaching reverence. It rang a bell with me. Maybe I had heard Mum talk about it. I added it to the marks on the map.

First stop was the small town of Moulamein, where Linda and Kenny were married in 1947, my mother too heavy with Barbara to allow a wedding photo to be taken. Slap bang on the way to nowhere, between Deniliquin, Echuca, Swan Hill and Balranald, Moulamein appeared to have fallen into a deep slumber while the river towns had prospered. It wasn't difficult to find St Martin's Anglican Church Hall, a shabby barn of a building with patterned curtains on the windows as though a family were living in it. It wasn't much of a shrine, but it was another piece of the visual jigsaw put in place.

Beyond Balranald I left the main highways behind and struck off into what I had heard bushmen describe as 'mongrel country'. It was thoroughbred to me, the most starkly Australian landscape I had seen. There was something compelling about the more forbidding parts of the country, and I always related my imaginings of such places back to my Aboriginal studies. What would it

Left: The hall where Mum and Dad were married in 1947 *Right:* Lake Mungo, 1993

have been like for Aboriginals living here? Would water have been easy to find? Would they have needed to wear animal skins as protection against the chill of the desert night?

I reached Lake Mungo, its dry bed skirted by sandhills on which stone artefacts that predate the last Ice Age have been found. In recent years this extraordinary place, ringed by the so-called 'Walls of China', has drawn Aborigines from all over Australia, eager to feel the power of this seat of 'civilisation'. I felt the power, too, as I wandered in the sandhills, but I also saw Lake Mungo as important in the context of the familial map — what I had begun to call the 'Linda Lines'.

According to the Dreaming, the clans of the Cargelligo area on the Lachlan River wandered west on hunting trips to the vicinity of what is now Hillston. On one occasion a hunting party chased a giant serpent too far west into the lakes country, where it finally succumbed to the spears of the warriors and died in a crescent, forming what is now known as the Walls of China. My father was born in the country of those warriors and he died where they chased the serpent, at the edge of the dry lakes. Long after his death my mother might have followed the trail of the serpent, en route to the fishing holes at Menindee. Was it coincidence, or were we all following the trail of a serpent?

The sky closed in and it began to rain as I explored the China Walls, so I drove on across the scrub to Pooncarie, then followed the bank of the Darling River in search of a camp. A good friend who spends a lot of time in the bush had told me the golden rules of camping rough, 'Keep your water bottles full, give yourself half an hour of light to set up your camp, and don't take the track nearest the homestead.'

Night crept up on me a bit in the gloom, and I found myself peering at the treeline, looking for an appropriate place to turn off and find a spot on the river. Nothing seemed to be right so I took a rough station track in desperation and bumped through giant mud-holes for what seemed like kilometres. A light rain began to fall again, but I ploughed on and found a camp by a billabong. It was a little rough but it would have to do. I quickly lit a fire in case the rain got heavier, and by its light I erected my tent. The drizzle stopped and I busied myself over another camp oven cook-up, chopping clove after clove of garlic into the mix with the great satisfaction of the solitary. At home I am not allowed a heavy hand with the garlic, but here too much was never enough.

In the night a fierce wind blew up and threatened my tent, but the strong pegs did their job and in the morning the air was crisp and the skies were perfectly clear. I heated a billy over the fire and made myself a warm bird-bath, which I delighted in as the birds came down to the billabong and began their morning song. I scraped the remains of last night's hotpot onto some toast and washed it down with good strong tea. ('Two fistfuls of Bushells, two-and-a-half swings of the billy, let it brew for a minute then bash it with a stick. No gum leaves.')

In the little township of Menindee — the last cold beer stop for the Burke and Wills expedition — I stopped at the general store for bait before trying my luck for yellowbelly at Weir 32.

'I know you,' said the lady behind the counter. 'Your mum used to come here all the time.' It was the same all over town. Linda Goolagong had been a big hit in Menindee. I had been right!

At Weir 32, about 12 kilometres (7½ miles) out of town, it was immediately evident that the carp were biting, if nothing else, for they were also on the nose. The custom on the inland rivers is to unhook this loathed European species (introduced to Australia to reduce river weed in an act of folly almost as great as the introduction of the cane toad in Queensland) and hurl the fish

Boiling the billy near Menindee, 1993

over your shoulder into the bush where it will die an agonising death. Every dead carp helps reduce the plague, but its rotting carcass doesn't do much for the general ambience of the popular fishing holes. At Weir 32 it was positively revolting, but I pressed on and unloaded my fishing gear when I noticed one of the Aboriginal women hauling in a good-sized yellowbelly.

I fished all morning (with some minor success) in the company of the Aboriginal women and their large band of children, but it was lunch time before we struck up a conversation. They were from Karuah, near Newcastle, and the children were fostered out from Aboriginal families all over the city area. Every school holidays the women filled their mini-bus with kids and headed west to fish and camp by a peaceful river. There was no heavy-handed instruction in the old ways, more a gentle appreciation of the simplicity of traditional Aboriginal life.

'Where will you camp tonight?' I asked as they cooked johnny cake (damper or bush bread) over an economical fire. (I rather hoped I might camp with them.)

Fishing with new friends at Weir 32. Menindee, 1993

'We sleep where night catches us,' one of the women said. And it didn't catch them on the Darling at Menindee that night.

I pushed along the Darling to Wilcannia, taking the station road on the eastern bank, rather than the busier road on the western side. The difference might have been three or four cars in a morning, but it was important to me. I wanted to lose myself, to immerse myself totally in the spirit of the land. And it worked. The further on I went, the more I felt that what I was doing was right. It is difficult to explain, but in my searching thus far, one element had been missing. Terra Australis. The wide brown land. I needed to touch it, feel it, let the soil run through my hands.

Wilcannia broke the spell. It was a wild west town where every building looked as though it had been a pub at some time in its life, and wished it still was. Some of the colonial architecture was quite lovely, but what struck me most was the colour of the population. With the possible exception of Johannesburg, I had never seen a town so black!

I fished with some Aboriginal boys just upstream from the town bridge, but again the river was dominated by carp, so I wandered through town and, intrigued by its blackened windows, went into a pub for a lemon squash. Half a dozen Aboriginal men sat at bar stools in the pokey bar. One was very drunk, the others working towards it. I ordered my soft drink and one of the men said, 'You look a bit like Evonne Goolagong.'

'That's because I am.'

The very drunk man took great exception to this. No one was going to walk into his bar in his town and say they were Evonne Goolagong.

'Bullshit!' he said in a voice so loud the effort made him gasp. 'You don't look anything bloody like her!'

Awakened by the fuss, the publican came over and said he had owned the garage opposite White City (an interesting contrast to his current job) and had seen me as a little girl. The identity crisis passed and the drunk calmed down. When I got up to leave a few minutes later, he took my hand and started to weep. 'We're so proud of what you done,' he cried.

The incident in the pub at Wilcannia made me realise that there were some limitations that came with who I was. Wherever I went in the towns someone would recognise me, and a denial would create more fuss than an admission. I wanted to do the things ordinary Aborigines did, to talk to them about their lives and perhaps share small parts. But it was difficult in the towns, and for a time after Wilcannia I stuck to the bush. I was getting better at camping, and my camps were pictures of well-ordered domesticity on the run. As my confidence in the bush grew, I even dispensed with the tent and lay under the canopy of stars at night, content in my weather-proof swag. I began to identify the constellations I had known as a child — the saucepan, the Southern Cross, and so on.

One night as I washed up my dinner things I saw the most extraordinary light in the sky — a blue-white blaze in the east that momentarily lit up my camp. I learnt on the radio news the next morning it had been a meteorite falling to earth.

As I passed through Bourke I remembered that Professor Fred Hollows, who had done so much for Aborigines and their congenital eye problems, had recently been buried there. I turned into the large cemetery, wanting to pay my respects, and began walking the rows of headstones, looking for a new one. That I was looking for a sizeable monument is perhaps evidence that I didn't know Fred Hollows. A young couple saw me searching and approached.

'Can we help?'

'I was looking for Professor Hollows' grave.'

'That's it over there, under the trees. It took us a while to find it, too.'

They pointed to a nondescript mound of red earth under the shade of some scrubby trees, marked only by a white wooden cross. When I inspected it at closer range I found that the great man's name had been spelt out in twigs on the side of the mound. I knelt by the grave and adjusted the unreadable 'R'. Then I stuck a bush flower in the soil and said a silent prayer to the Old People for the soul of this humble hero.

I camped on the Barwon River at Brewarrina and rock-hopped the ancient Aboriginal fish traps in the orange glow of the dusk. This was another sacred place for me, a place where, despite the intrusions of town noises like cars and cats and pub brawls, one could feel the spirit of the Old People, the fishermen who gathered in their thousands in this camp of plenty; where Charlie Perkins brought his Freedom Riders in 1965. But the stench of racism has lingered over another generation.

Now, however, I felt in Brewarrina a rising tide of tolerance and optimism. The underground museum of Aboriginal art and artefacts is a start, and I hope in time that 'Bre', the 'camp of plenty', will be a place in which all Aborigines can take great pride.

I left the rivers and pushed on into the arid border country where New South Wales and Queensland meet; the land of opals and drought. There was nothing to see at Weilmoringle and even less at Goodooga, but in this second town I was looking for someone, so I dropped in at the pub — a one-room affair which was the only commercial premises open in the middle of a hot, dusty Saturday.

At Mrs Edwards' wake a few weeks earlier, a member of her family, hearing I was going bush, had offered me the names of some Aboriginal people who lived in the vicinity of the Prentice family seat of Angledool. Amongst the names scrawled on a paper party plate was that of a lady named Tiny Skuthorpe. I had no idea why this person thought Tiny might be able to help me, but I decided to look her up anyway.

'Anyone know where Tiny lives?'

A girl playing the poker machine said she did. She directed me to the old mission at the edge of town, saying, 'Almost everyone's moved into town now, but Tiny and Ernie are still out there. They'll never move.'

The corrugated iron shacks by the dry creek bed were easy to find and they made my spirits soar. These were the constructions I remembered at Three Ways and The Murie, the earthen floors swept twice daily with a leafy branch. Tiny had gone to the Brewarrina Show, but, a small boy told me, Ernie would be out in a minute.

It was a long minute but when Ernie emerged from the shack he was

Paying my respects to Fred Hollows, Bourke, 1993

immaculate in a rodeo shirt, pressed pants secured with a cowboy belt and new gum boots. Ernie Skuthorpe was a man I imagined to be around 70, whip-thin, and so shy that he hid his eyes beneath his hat. After a while he seemed to warm to me. I told him I wasn't sure what I wanted, that somehow I'd followed my mother's spirit to this place, and that now I had carved a full arc and found myself in another mother's country. Mrs Edwards had been raised as Eva Prentice at Angledool, just an hour away.

Ernie laughed. 'I know what you mean. I come from Charleville myself, come here a long time ago. A man gets to travellin' he can get himself mixed up. You go down to Angledool and find young Rex, my boy. Ask him to show you the snake and the turtle.'

Ernie said finding Rex Skuthorpe in Angledool would be no problem. There were only a dozen houses and Rex, being a supporter of the St George rugby league team, had painted his entire house in the team colours of red and white. I drove to Angledool and had to put my sunglasses on as I approached Rex's monument to St George. But there was no answer when I knocked on the door.

At the other end of the town I heard a man's voice inside a house and, seeing me, he called out. 'Just a minute, on the phone.'

Opal miner Bob Barrett eventually emerged. I had no idea who this man

Rex Skuthorpe shows me the snake totem. Angledool, 1993

was but he said, 'Oh, you must be Evonne. I'm Eva Edwards' nephew. In fact that's the Prentice family house right across there.'

I looked across the street at the home of 'Angledool Gran', an almost legendary figure in the Edwards household. It seemed so strange that in this one-street town of a handful of people, this parched and scrubby place of dry uncomfortable heat and dry unbearable cold, the threads of my life should all come together.

I knew Linda Goolagong had followed the river as I had done, and I knew in my heart that she had been to Brewarrina. But she would not have gone that extra mile to Eva Prentice country. A gap in my map of about two thumb-lengths separated the union of the two women who had made me what I am.

It was a strange feeling. In my life to this point I felt I had bridged the gap not just between these two good women of different races, but between a great many people, black and white. Now, in some way, I could take the Linda Lines to their natural conclusion. In Angledool I could bring my two mothers, my two cultures, together forever.

Bob Barrett took me down the road to Rex and Dixie Skuthorpe's place and bashed on the door. Rex was in all right, he was having a nap. Rex, the Aboriginal ranger for the district, agreed to take me to the ruins of the old mission on the edge of town to see the snake and the turtle. We found the piles of stones known by these names, fashioned so long ago (presumably as Dreaming totems), even before the establishment of the Angledool mission and its subsequent dismemberment in the 1930s.

'They took 'em all off to Brewarrina,' said Rex, 'but the old folks, they didn't want to go. They turned around and walked straight back!'

It was hard to imagine such an attachment to this harsh country, but I had learnt early in my wanderings that a sense of place is often more important than a place that makes sense in the eyes of outsiders.

And there is much about Aborigines — particularly old ones! — that the western world finds difficult to comprehend, but one thing I have learned in writing this book is that the Old People (alive and dead) have no legacy of hate. There is no lasting place for bitterness in our culture, the core of which is acceptance of people, things, even fate. Mum used to tell us that the worst word in the language — any language — was 'hate'. This word, she said, was worse than any swear word. 'People who use it are just igorant,' Linda would say, and we kids would laugh behind her back. But Linda had the sentiment right, if not the pronunciation.

The Old People had entered my consciousness at Cummeragunga that sleepless night and they wouldn't leave me alone. I sat upright in my swag one night with a clear vision of them. They were naked tribal warriors calling to me: 'Go back, go back, you cannot go forward until you understand the past.' The dream didn't unsettle me, as it had at Cummeragunga. I understood perfectly what it meant. The job was not over.

I stopped to pick up a stone as a souvenir of Angledool.

Rex asked, 'You like stones?'

'I collect them everywhere I go.'

'I've got a stone I want you to have.'

Back at the red and white house he presented me with a grindstone and a muller, used through the millenium in the preparation of grass seeds, a staple of the dry parts. I knew they were things that he treasured, and that he gave them to me as a gesture of faith in my search. I thanked him as best I could, which was totally inadequate.

Those stones are in my free hand now as I write these final words, the cycle complete, this journey over.

I have come home, but I do not yet know it as well as I want to. This, then, is not the end, but the end of the beginning.

Acknowledgements

Literally hundreds of people from several continents and many walks of life assisted in the research and writing of this book. The authors apologise in advance for all those whose contributions are not recognised here, due to constraints of space and memory, but which were appreciated nonetheless. In particular, we would like to acknowledge the support of so many Aboriginal people, from ATSIC's Mrs Lois O'Donoghue through to those members of communities and out-stations who made us welcome in various parts of Australia.

For assistance in research into Aboriginal (particularly Wiradjuri) history, we thank: Dr Peter Reid, Elizabeth Hoffman, Darren Williams, Aggie Williams, Patty Undie, Robert Ellis, Alick Jackomos and Elaine Lomas. Family history: Carol Kendall of Link-Up (and emotional support), Fred and Lorna Briggs, Clancy Charles, Michael Wighton, Les Kubank, Zillah Williams, Barbara Goolagong Robson, Janelle Goolagong and Ian Goolagong. Personal memories: Isabelle Tarrago, Patricia Edwards Hill, Clarrie and Dot Irvin, Frank and Jean Gladman, Lucy Smith, Faith Martin, Jean Summerville, Junie Mason, Bob Morgan and Michael Anderson.

For making available scrap books and photo albums: Mrs Priscilla Kurtzman and the Pioneer Park Museum, Griffith; Grace Grant; White City Tennis Museum; Sue Finlay-Stone; the Goolagong family.

For their splendid photographic contributions: Paul Wright, Doug Drummond, Alan Jones, John Russell and Jackie Jarratt. For inspiration along the way: Kerry Orton, Ernie Dingo and the poets Don Mattera and Bill Neidjie. We would also like to thank Bill Neidjie and Magabala Books of Broome for permission to reproduce verse from *Kakadu Man*. For help along the track: Murray Chapman and Kerry Swain (contacts and directions); Archie Roach (soundtrack).

Simon & Schuster Australia have been model publishers — quick with encouragement and assistance, slow to anger when deadlines had to be redrawn. Special thanks to publisher Kirsty Melville and our sympathetic editor, Susan Morris-Yates. Thanks, too, to Deborah Brash, the book's designer.

Finally, the authors would like to thank their other halves, Roger Cawley and Jackie Jarratt, who lived through this, too, and provided support, encouragement and much hard work along the way.

Evonne Goolagong Cawley and Phil Jarratt
Noosa Heads
May 1993

Photographic Credits

The authors and publishers would like to thank the following photographers, organisations and agencies for their kind permission to reproduce the photographs listed on the following pages:

Russ Adams, 250, 285; Australian Consolidated Press, 177, 178; Australian News and Information Bureau, 113, 249; Australian Photographic Agency, 80, 81; Michael Baz, 349 (top); Bild-Zeitung, 163; *Border Morning Mail*, 104; Central Press, 148, 212, 227, 230; Clancy Charles, 37, 39, 48, 87, 88; W. R. del Veldhuyo, 301; Doug Drummond, 3, 358, 359, 362, 366; Fairfax Newspapers, 122, 295; Frank and Jean Gladman, 53, 55, 88; Herald & Weekly Times, 136, 172; George W. Hourd, 190; Jackie Jarratt, 51, 55, 372, 373; *The Leicagraph*, 75, 90; Le-Roye Productions, 150, 194–5; Fred Mullane, 337 (right); *Narrandera Argus*, 207, 209 (left); News Limited, 139 (right), 150 (right); Carol L. Newson, 348; Press Association, 199 (left); John Russell, 1, 257, 263, 309, 337, 344; Art Seitz, 247; Shepherd Baker Sullivan, 169 (right); Stephenson Newspapers, 146; *Toowoomba Chronicle*, 169 (left); Gundy Wighton, 26, 27 (right), 31 (right); Zillah Williams, 31 (left); Paul Wright, front jacket, 6–7, 10, 15 (right), 335, 378, 379, 380, 381, 383, 384, 386, 387, 390, 391.

The authors and publishers have made every effort to trace the copyright holders of all the photographs used. They will be pleased to hear from anyone who has not been acknowledged. Many of the photographs reproduced without acknowledgement are the property of Evonne and Roger Cawley and the Goolagong family.

$\mathscr{I}\, n\, d\, e\, x$